Applying Shari'a in the West

LUCIS SERIES 'DEBATES ON ISLAM AND SOCIETY'

Leiden University Press

At present important debates about Islam and society take place both in the West and in the Muslim world itself. Academics have considerable expertise on many of the key issues in these debates, which they would like to make available to a larger audience. In its turn, current scholarly research on Islam and Muslim societies is to a certain extent influenced by debates in society. Leiden University has a long tradition in the study of Islam and Muslim societies, past and present, both from a philological and historical perspective and from a social science approach. Its scholars work in an international context, maintaining close ties with colleagues worldwide. The peer reviewed LUCIS series aims at disseminating knowledge on Islam and Muslim societies produced by scholars working at or invited by Leiden University as a contribution to contemporary debates in society.

LUCIS LECTURES AND OCCASIONAL PAPERS

LEIDEN Publications

Additional to the LUCIS series the series 'Islam & Society' of smaller publications, lectures, and reports intends to contribute to current debates about Islam and society aimed at a larger audience.

Applying Shari'a in the West

Facts, Fears and the Future of Islamic Rules on Family Relations in the West

Edited by Maurits S. Berger

Leiden University Press

The publication of this book is made possible by a grant from LUCIS, the Leiden University Centre for the Study of Islam & Society.

Leiden University Press English-language titles are distributed in the United States and Canada by the University of Chicago Press.

Cover design: Tarek Atrissi Design
Lay-out: Hanneke Kossen, Amsterdam

ISBN 978 90 8728 170 0
e-ISBN 978 94 0060 105 5 (pdf)
e-ISBN 978 94 0060 106 2 (ePub)
NUR 759

Contents

Introduction
Applying Shari'a in the West

Maurits S. Berger

How can we make sense of the new phenomenon of shari'a in the West? In 2003, a respectable institution such as the European Court of Human Rights ruled that 'sharia clearly diverges from [the European] Convention [of Human Rights] values'.[1] But equally respectable authorities, such as the Archbishop of Canterbury and the Lord Chief Justice of England and Wales, argued in 2008 that shari'a does not necessarily have to contradict Western legal and political values.[2] Clearly, the presence of shari'a in Western societies is of increasing concern among Europeans, North Americans and Australians. Crucial questions remain unanswered, however: what *is* shari'a, especially in a Western context, and what are these Western values it is diverging from, and why is that so? Is shari'a indeed applied in the West, and by whom? And if so, is shari'a a static notion or does it adapt to Western values or structures?

A body of literature on the issue of shari'a in the West is gradually emerging, focusing primarily on the ways private international law deals with shari'a and on the compatibility (or lack of compatibility) between shari'a and Western legal concepts.[3] This volume will contribute to this academic discussion by taking the *practice* of shari'a by Muslims in the Western legal context as the basis for analysis. Two assumptions underlie this approach. First, it is futile to study shari'a in the West as an autonomous and holistic notion, because this overlooks the realities of its practice on the ground. The fact is that while shari'a as a concept of divine rules has developed over centuries of scholarship into an autonomous 'Islamic' legal system, the practice of this system has become fragmented in the Western context, and perhaps even distorted, because it has had to accommodate the dominant Western legal system. Second, we can only understand the interaction between these two legal systems if the notion of a Western 'legal system' is seen in the much wider context of the social, political and cultural values upheld by Western societies. These values, together with preconceived Western notions of shari'a (the 'fears' mentioned in the subtitle of this volume) have an impact on the practice of shari'a.

Based on these premises, the discussion in this volume is divided into three sections. The first section contains descriptions and analyses of, on the one hand, the practice of shariʿa and in particular that of Islamic family law within the legal frameworks of a selection of Western countries; and, on the other hand, national responses to these particular forms of shariʿa. In the second section, a number of thematic issues that recur in the country studies will be addressed. The third section contains contributions on the need and modalities for adaptation by either Western or Muslim legal systems, so as to accommodate each other.

Before we discuss these sections in more detail, however, we must first address a fundamental question: what do we mean by shariʿa?

What do Western Muslims Mean by Shariʿa?

Rather than defining shariʿa as a legal discipline of Islam,[4] or as a set of practices and laws applied in foreign countries,[5] our interest is primarily in what Muslims in the West mean and want in terms of rules prescribed by Islam. This starting point warrants two remarks. First, it explains why we prefer to use the term 'shariʿa', not 'Islamic law', in this volume: while the latter is confined to the domain of 'law' in the legal sense, which concerns certain relationships between people or between people and the state, 'shariʿa' denotes the much wider domain of rules pertaining to *all* relationships between people (including those of a social and moral nature), as well as the rules governing the relationship between man and God (such as prayer, burial, slaughter, and so forth). As we will see below, only by taking this wider perspective on 'shariʿa' can we obtain a clear view of what Muslims in the West do and want in terms of religious rules.

The second remark concerns the approach taken to assessing the nature and scope of shariʿa in the West. By posing the question, 'What do Muslims *do* in terms of shariʿa?' rather than 'What *is* shariʿa?', we adopt a legal-anthropological approach that takes Muslims as its reference point, rather than an abstract notion of shariʿa.[6] Such an approach is necessary if we want to develop a proper understanding of shariʿa in the West. To reflect upon whether shariʿa is a violation of European Convention principles or might be in compliance with English law may lead us into an empty academic discussion if the specific rules of shariʿa that are being discussed are not actually adhered to by Muslims in the West. It is clear that shariʿa punishments are contrary to Western values, as is the notion of a theocracy, but what is the use of discussing these legal notions if they deviate from what Muslims in the

West are striving for? We must therefore move away from shari'a as a form of theological-legal scholarship, and first determine what rules are adhered to by, or otherwise relevant for, Muslims in the West.

From this perspective, it is striking that so little is known about what Muslims in the West mean by shari'a. To my knowledge, only three surveys have been conducted among Muslims in European countries, and one among Muslims worldwide, in which Muslims were asked for their opinion on 'shari'a'. The latter survey was a 2008 Gallup poll representing 90 per cent of Muslims worldwide, in which 'shari'a' ranked highest – together with 'democracy', one should add – on the list of what Muslims wanted.[7] Of the other two surveys, one was conducted in 2004 in the Netherlands, and found that 51 per cent of the Dutch Muslims interviewed favoured a Muslim political party, and 29.5 per cent thought that its political programme should be based on shari'a.[8] (The subsequent newspaper headlines that 'one third of Dutch Muslims favour sharia' were therefore entirely wrong). A British poll of 2006 found that 40 per cent of British Muslims support shari'a law being introduced in pre-dominantly Muslim areas in Britain,[9] while a British study of 2007 found that 28 per cent of British Muslims would prefer to live under shari'a law.[10] What is of interest to us here is that none of these surveys defined shari'a, nor asked their respondents to do so, therefore leaving us ignorant of what Western Muslims mean by shari'a. However, based on what we know from existing studies and from the following chapters, we can deduce three possible answers to this question, each leading us in a different direction:

Shari'a: a virtuous abstraction

The first answer to what Muslims might mean by 'shari'a' in a Western context is shari'a as a slogan or an abstraction with a virtuous connotation. Shari'a stands for 'the law of God', or 'all that Muslims need', and, effectively, for everything that is 'good' for Muslims. We might compare the use of this abstraction with that of 'justice': it is perceived as virtuous and necessary, but few people will be able to provide a full definition of the concept, particularly when it comes to putting it into practice. We can observe a similar attitude among devout Muslims towards shari'a: it is something virtuous and they want it to be applied in their lives, even though they do not know exactly what shari'a means in practice. Although this notion of shari'a is thus of little use to those who want to define it as a set of rules, it is precisely this notion that makes shari'a such a powerful force in the minds of many Western Muslims. Indeed, it might explain the high percentages in the abovementioned surveys:

when asked about shari'a, what devout Muslim would give a negative response?

Shari'a: foreign national laws

Muslims living in the West who are also nationals of their country of origin sometimes have the national family law of this latter country applied to them as a matter of private international law: a Pakistani couple in England might be divorced in accordance with Pakistani (Muslim) family law, a divorce pronounced in Iran in accordance with Iranian (Muslim) family law might be recognized in Germany, and a polygamous marriage that is legally concluded in Morocco might be recognized (but not enforced) in the Netherlands. While national Western courts are less and less inclined to apply foreign national laws to residents with a foreign nationality, these residents continue to navigate their way through a legal labyrinth for the practical reason that they often retain strong ties with their countries of origin.

Therefore, the Western Muslims who maintain that Western courts should apply 'shari'a' or 'Islamic law' in their case are in fact referring to the Islamic nature of their national law, rather than to the complex system of Islamic scholarly jurisprudence. Strictly speaking, this is not 'shari'a' as described in the vast corpus of Islamic legal jurisprudence, but national laws that have drawn upon that corpus and modelled the selected rules into a format – a legal code – that is unknown in shari'a. Several of the following chapters will touch upon this particular application of shari'a. However, our interest in this volume is not in shari'a as foreign national law being applied in Western courts by virtue of private international law. Our focus is on indigenous practices of shari'a in the West: what is it that Western Muslims do and want in terms of shari'a? And that is the third notion of shari'a, as we will see below.

Shari'a: the practices and desires of Western Muslims

Only limited research has been undertaken into manifestations of shari'a in the West, and that research which does exist mostly follows the conventions of the respective academic discipline: social scientists tend to look at social factors, including radicalization and religious ritual; lawyers tend to examine family law;[11] and Islamic finance has been the domain of practising lawyers and bankers, rather than scholars.[12] The study of *fatwas* and the '*fiqh* for minorities' (*fiqh al-'aqalliyat*) might yield novel insights into changing concepts in Islamic jurisprudence,[13] but research has hitherto failed to indicate the extent to which these changes are actually embraced by Muslims in the West. The overall picture of shariʿa in the West is therefore fragmented in qualitative terms (the interpretation and manifestations of shariʿa) and almost non-existent in quantitative terms (the actual practice of shariʿa and how many Muslims adhere to this).

However, based on the research that has been done so far, and as is confirmed in the following chapters, we may build up a general picture of shariʿa as practised in the West. Devout Muslims in the West are indeed committed to living in accordance with shariʿa, but this is limited to the following domains:

- religious rules, such as those pertaining to prayer, fasting, burial, and dress code;
- rules relating to family law, in particular those pertaining to marriage and divorce;
- rules relating to financial transactions, in particular the ban on interest or usury;
- social relations, in particular gender relations and relations with the non-Islamic environment.

Three observations can be made with regard to these four domains of shariʿa rules. First, this collection of rules appears quite haphazard, both in scope and in content. From an Islamic legal-theological perspective, however, this set of rules has an internal logic, because all of these rules share a high ranking in the hierarchy of Islamic rules prescribed by classical orthodoxy: they are explicitly mentioned in the Qur'an, by the Prophet, or by scholarly consensus, and are therefore the first to be followed by any devout Muslim.

The second observation is that of the abovementioned rules, only those related to family law and the prohibition of usury or interest can be considered 'law' or 'legal rules', according to modern standards. The other rules pertain to religious rituals or social conduct and, as such, are mostly outside the scope of legislation in Western countries (except, for instance, when national burial or slaughter laws seek to accommodate religious practices).

Finally, these domains of shariʿa pertain to Muslims' daily lives, and appear to have little to do with political views on the need for an Islamic restructuring of Western societies. Of course, such views do exist among some radical Muslims, just as there are Muslim extremists who interpret shariʿa as a call for militant action against alleged Western injustices. We must emphasize, however, that our goal here is to gain a general impression of what the majority of devout Muslims in the West desires and practises in terms of shariʿa.

Shari'a Practices in a Western Legal Framework

We now come to the next step in our discussion, which is how Western legal systems respond to these shari'a practices. This is the starting point of this volume. In the first chapter, Mathias Rohe provides the scope of the discussion by presenting a comprehensive overview of all the reasons that give rise to a need or obligation to apply rules of shari'a. He distinguishes between the 'external reasons' produced by Western legal systems, such as private international law or the English legal accommodation of Islamic finance, and the 'internal reasons' produced by Muslims themselves, such as a religious, legal or cultural need to have shari'a applied. We will see this dual perspective recurring in the subsequent country studies.

The next six chapters are country studies that give an impression of the scope and modalities of the religious legal needs of Muslims in the West, and Western legal possibilities and responses to these needs. The six studies demonstrate that we may, for a variety of reasons, divide what we have so far called 'the West' in three regions, namely America and Australia, North Western Europe, and South Eastern Europe. Each of these regions has a different historical, social-economical and legal relation with Islam and Muslims.

Three Western regions

Among the Western legal systems, those of America and Australia perhaps allow Muslims the most freedom to apply forms of shari'a, particularly in family law. This can be partly attributed to the fact that the Muslim communities in these countries are often middle or upper class, and are therefore more prone to taking an intellectual and activist position regarding shari'a. The responses, however, are quite different. In their chapter on America, Bryan S. Turner and James T. Richardson conclude that regardless of 'liberal' problems with religion and public concern vis-à-vis potential radicalism among Muslims in America, the vast majority of Muslims in America are finding ways to adjust to American secularism, while also expressing their religious identity in various ways. In the chapter on Australia, on the other hand, Jamila Hussain and Adam Possamai reflect on 'the new Australian conservative modernity,' which is a combination of resurgent social values of Christian conservatism, active government priorities of disengagement and a rapidly expanding culture of surveillance and obedience. In this new phase of modernity, the authors argue, a process of de-legitimization of diversity is occurring, especially with regard to Muslims.

The chapters on the North Western European countries of the Netherlands and the United Kingdom illustrate how different the circumstances of the Muslim communities in these countries are from those in America and Australia. While they all are migrants or of migrant origin, the Muslim communities in the Netherlands and the United Kingdom are mostly lower-class, and lack political or religious unity and leadership. In his chapter on the United Kingdom, Jørgen Nielsen describes how in their need for unified regulation of family law, Muslim communities in the United Kingdom have been hindered by internal divisions and disagreements on the interpretation of that law, resulting in the emergence of various 'Sharia councils.' Nielsen argues that these tensions among Muslims living in Europe can be attributed to Europe's imperial past, and that the arguments about the place of shariʿa in Europe therefore have a deep symbolic meaning that is associated with minority identity, and which can only be overcome after a long period of negotiation and trial and error. While this process has been going on in the United Kingdom for at least three decades, the development of any form of unified Islamic family law or of councils that might provide guidance or rulings on shariʿa is still in its infancy in the Netherlands, as becomes clear in Susan Rutten's chapter. Moreover, the Dutch political climate has become such in the past decade that any initiative is met with hostility and political, as well as legal, objections. Insofar as Dutch Muslims want to undertake initiatives in this direction, they will therefore do so mostly within the context of the Dutch legal system, which, according to Rutten, may be well equipped to cope with legal and religious pluralism and consequently with shariʿa, although some human rights issues remain to be resolved.

The chapters on the South East European countries of Albania, Kosovo and Greece bring us into an entirely different context. First and foremost, the Muslim communities in these countries have been living there for more than five centuries and have a long history of institutionalization. This history was cut short with the implementation of communist rule after 1945, but it has gradually re-emerged since the fall of communism and the Yugoslav wars of the 1990s. Remarkable in this respect are the cases of Albania and Kosovo, the only countries in the West with Muslim majority populations. Besnik Senani describes how these countries are struggling to accommodate secularism to Islamic identity, with the clear aim of being as 'European' as possible. In doing so, some political leaders in Kosovo and Albania have gone so far as to distance their national culture from Islam, sometimes even claiming more proximity to Christianity than to Islam. Angeliki Ziaki describes a very different situation in Greece, even though this country shares a historical Ottoman legacy with Albania and Kosovo. The Muslim minority lives in the most eastern part of Greece, where, as enshrined in the 1923 Lausanne Treaty, it has historically been allowed a high degree of religious autonomy. This includes having its own muftis, who preside over shari'a courts that have exclusive jurisdiction in family law matters. Although some observers criticize this situation as 'neo-milletism', alluding to the *millet* system under Ottoman rule, Ziaki argues that it is possible to achieve a symbiosis between Greek secular and Islamic law.

Shari'a in the West

When surveying these studies, one of the most noticeable findings is that practices of shari'a are adapted to the legal, social, political and historical contexts of each Western country, creating a diverse picture of 'shari'a in the West.' For example, the strict distinction between a civil and religious marriage, as is legally prescribed in most Western countries, can create a legal social and political grey zone where choices between the two are made: are the two marriages to be conducted separately and if so, in what order, and what is the status of a civil or religious marriage if only one has been concluded and not the other? These questions are not pertinent to Muslims, but to people of all faiths who want to marry religiously. In countries like the United States, Australia, United Kingdom, Spain or Sweden the conflict has been resolved by allowing the two ceremonies to converge. In countries like the Netherlands, France and Germany, on the other hand, the distinction between religious and civil marriage is strictly adhered to as a principal matter of separation of state and religion.

Another example where national context and history make a difference in the reception of shari'a is that of the Islamic institutions where decisions regarding shari'a are taken, in particular regarding family law matters. These institutions, known as Sharia boards, courts, councils or tribunals, may be integrated into the formal judiciary system (as is the case in Greece), or may operate in an informal manner (as is already the case in many Western countries with regard to Jewish and Catholic 'courts'), or may operate between formal and informal domains by means of arbitration (as in the United Kingdom and, until 2007, in Ontario, Canada).

And, as a final example, we might mention the allowances made for social conduct, in particular the use of religious dress. Here we see an interesting difference between the United States and Western European countries: while both regions adhere to similar notions of secularism and liberty, the manifestation of religion – including that of Islam – in the public and political domain is much more accepted in American society than in European society. This particular form of secularism is clearly much stronger in Western Europe and consequently has its effects on the public manifestations of Islam. We will return to this subject below.

When we turn our view to the Muslims in the West, perhaps the most conspicuous commonality that emerges from the six chapters is that there is no enforcing agency with respect to shariʿa other than Muslims themselves. Applying and enforcing shariʿa is mostly a matter of voluntary willingness to submit to these rules, whereby social actors – one's peers, family, or the Muslim community – may add a degree of pressure or coercion. Enforcement of shariʿa may also result from Muslim communities having organized themselves, either to coordinate certain services for their community or to act as intermediates with the government. In the case of America and Australia, Muslims have established organizations that act as lobby groups, scholarly councils or advisory boards. Efforts to create similar unified initiatives have failed in the United Kingdom, resulting in a large number of councils that act primarily as tribunals aimed at solving marital and other disputes among Muslims. If we move to the European continent, the Netherlands serves as an example of a Western European country where such councils do not exist (and are considered undesirable from a political perspective), but where the government has been active in coaxing the Muslim community to organize itself as a representative community. This governmental engagement is representative for most North Western European countries where Muslim communities, until now, are still divided and therefore relatively powerless and without much of a representative constituency. In South East Europe, we see yet another form of organization: here, the Muslim community has historically been granted specific autonomous privileges by the state to regulate certain affairs internally, such as religious education, mosque construction, and family law, and often receives financial support by the state to do so. If we juxtapose all these Western practices of shariʿa in the West we may conclude that shariʿa mainly manifests itself within the boundaries set by the freedom of religion, and the state's involvement is therefore limited accordingly.

This brief overview might prompt the conclusion that there are many different forms of shariʿa in the West, due to the differences in Western legal systems. This is not entirely correct. In the first place, there are no different 'forms of shariʿa'; instead, within a single concept of shariʿa, we have identified four domains of rules practised by devout Muslims, and within each of these domains we observe modalities in the ways they are practised. These modalities may be the result of internal differences regarding interpretations of shariʿa, or the consequence of what a national legal system allows or disallows with respect to a particular Islamic practice. In the latter case, there may be differences between Western legal systems, but these differences lie in the details. In terms of legal principles, Western countries' legal systems hold a majority of their principles in common. The overriding principle is that of the freedom of religion, even though Western states may differ as to how they regulate their involvement with these institutions. Therefore it is not necessarily the principles of legal systems that have created the diversity of shariʿa in Western countries, but the cultural and social context in which these principles are embedded. This is the subject of the second section of this volume.

Western Responses: Law Versus Culture

The country studies clearly show that the conflicts arising vis-à-vis practices of shariʿa in the West are not only legal in nature. On the contrary, very few shariʿa practices are a violation of the law; they are more often a violation of what we suggest to call 'culture', which we define as all norms relating to political, cultural, social or other normativity shared by the majority of society. While the legal response to shariʿa practices is simply 'this is (not) allowed under law', the cultural response can be summarized with the maxim, 'this is (not) the way we do things here'.

Most cultural contestation occurs in the domain of religious behaviour, particularly in Western European countries. Examples include the headscarf, the face veil (*burqa* or *niqab*), religious dress, and the refusal to shake hands with the opposite sex. Sometimes such responses are brought to court or to the legislature and may, when accepted, then become part of the legal response: a behaviour that is considered 'not the way we do things here' is then turned into 'this is not allowed under law.' In the particular case of Islamic rules, however, the prohibition of a certain dress or behaviour that is culturally deemed undesirable may contradict fundamental legal freedoms. The French law of 2011 banning the face veil illustrates this dilemma: on the one hand, the State Council, adhering to the legal response, advised against such a ban on the basis of the principle of personal autonomy, which allows a woman to freely wear what she wishes;[14] and, on the other hand, the legislature, adhering to the cultural response, deemed open-faced encounters in public a matter of 'social contract' that warranted legislation.[15]

Another issue that gives rise to public indignation is that of Islamic family law. In her chapter on Islamic marriage in the Netherlands, Annelies Moors provides an interesting insight into how religious marriage – which is allowed in Western legal systems as a matter of personal freedom – has come under scrutiny for political and security reasons, because it has become associated with a deliberate attempt on the part of Muslims not to participate in Dutch society. On the other hand, in chapter 9, Nadjma Yassari demonstrates how and why German courts have been quite willing to hear cases on the issue of the bridal gift (*mahr*), which is one of the conditional elements of Islamic marriage.

All of the country studies provide additional examples of this dichotomy between 'bad shariʿa' and 'good shariʿa.' While Islamic dress, the building of mosques and the use of Islamic family law tend to give rise to controversy, Muslim initiatives to construct Islam-compliant financial instruments (banks, mortgages and insurance) are often applauded. The United Kingdom has been a European frontrunner in adapting national fiscal and financial laws to facilitate these new developments, partly to meet the needs of British Muslims, but also to remain compatible with the expanding international market of Islamic finance. To refer again to the ruling by the European Court of Human Rights: clearly not all 'shariʿa' conflicts with European human rights values, just as not all 'shariʿa' is considered undesirable in a Western context.

It is clear that a large part of the discussion on shariʿa is fuelled by pre-conceived notions about its nature and what Muslims might (secretly) want. The cultural bias vis-à-vis Muslim practices is highlighted in the contribution by Fournier and Reyes on honour crimes in Canada. Although honour crimes are not specifically 'Islamic' – a point frequently made by Muslim scholars – it is a practice that tends to take place among certain ethnic communities from Muslim countries and as such presents an interesting case study. Just like shariʿa, honour crimes are branded in the West as foreign and therefore different. While this may indeed be the case in quite some aspects, the authors point at the *a priori* rejection of these institutions as alien practices. The authors argue that the rulings by Canadian courts in honour crime cases focus on the cultural "Other" but fail – or refuse – to see the similarities, not only between these crimes and those committed in Canada with similar honour intentions, but also in the legal origins of these crimes in the national laws of both Western and Muslim countries.

The legal – cultural dichotomy perhaps provides the key to understanding the conflicting reactions to 'shariʿa': the West has produced legal systems that may allow for certain practices, Islamic practices included, but at the same time, the West has preserved a cultural heritage that may conflict strongly with these very same practices. This explains much of the confusion arising in discussions on shariʿa. For instance, the law may explicitly allow the building of mosques, even though there is nationwide opposition. Similarly, the law may protect people's freedom to meet and greet each other how they wish, but not joining mixed-gender social gatherings or refusing to shake hands may be considered an insult by local custom. On the other hand, legal and cultural responses may also concur: Western laws allow interest-free finance, and its Islamic version is accepted in most Western countries. No wonder that Muslims in the West are often bewildered about what they are allowed to do, and what not. Which brings us to the third section of this volume: do Muslims adapt their interpretations of shariʿa to the many Western legal and cultural responses, or is perhaps adaptation needed from the part of the Western legal systems?

Adaptation in Western or Muslim Legal Systems?

Some of the country studies in this volume touch upon the issue of Muslims adapting their Islamic rules to Western legal requirements, or the necessity of adapting Western legal systems to the needs of Muslims. In this third section of the volume, Marie-Claire Foblets explores the need for and potential of Western legal systems to accommodate Islamic rules: *should* Western legal systems do so and, if so, *can* they do so? She answers both questions with a cautious affirmative (compare Mathias Rohe in chapter 1, who holds the opposite view). Given the fact that religious demands are an emerging societal phenomenon in the West, Foblets argues, it is the state's duty to offer adequate responses. These responses should preferably embrace diversity from the perspective of freedom of religion or of thought, guaranteed as a fundamental right of individuals. Moreover, since these religious demands are very often visibly connected to those of identity, they must therefore be handled sympathetically and with respect for their significance to those concerned. In order for a Western legal system to make the necessary accommodation to religious diversity, the principle of the autonomy of the will should be taken as the starting point. This will allow for the incorporation of religious rules in civil law, more freedom of choice in private international law, and religious arbitration.

The two other contributions to the third section discuss the reverse situation, that is, the need for and potential of Islamic legal practices to adapt to the Western legal systems in which they operate. The two contributions take different positions. Zainab Alwani and Celene Ayat

Lizzio argue against providing a singular, comprehensive model for the integration of Islamic values within largely secular systems, but instead advocate the need to look for similarities in the aims of both (Islamic) religious and (Western) civil law. According to these authors, it is entirely counterproductive to advocate norms drawn directly from pre-modern Muslim legal discourses without a full consideration of their outcomes and effects in specific European contexts.

Abdullah Saeed continues this latter argument with his discussion of the novel development of shariʿa rules that are adapted to their Western context, the so-called '*fiqh* for minorities'. This new discipline of Islamic legal scholarship is based on the argument that living in accordance with shariʿa should improve a Muslim's life. If the strict application of shariʿa rules makes his life harder – for example, if the Muslim had to fast for a disproportionally long time somewhere in the far North of Europe, or was prevented from rising up the social ladder due to the prohibition of a mortgage, preventing him from buying a house – then, according to minority *fiqh*, shariʿa itself demands that its rules be adapted. Saeed argues that this new scholarship must be repositioned within the broader debate on the reform of classical Islamic law that applies to all Muslims, not only those in the West. According to Saeed, such repositioning requires that temporary and ad hoc solutions be replaced with a more principled discourse of reform, leading to real change and new understandings of how Muslims should practise Islam in today's world, regardless of where they are located.

Conclusion

This volume does not only provide new insights in the concept of shariʿa in the West, but also provides a framework of how shariʿa in the West can be studied. The premise of this volume is that one needs to focus on the question 'What do Muslims *do* in terms of shariʿa?' rather than 'What *is* shariʿa?' Taking this perspective provides us with two insights: first, the practice of shariʿa is limited to a limited set of rules (mainly related to religious rituals, family law and social interaction) and, second, most of these rules do not pertain to the Western definition of 'law.' The framework of this volume then continues to explore two more interactions: the Western responses to these practices of shariʿa and, in turn, the Muslim legal reaction to these responses.

On the Western side we see that there is unity on matters of legal principle but quite some diversity on the interpretation of these principles. This interpretation can be partly attributed to historical, social-economical and legal differences among Western countries, whereby we might observe a general division into three Western regions: America and Australia, North Western Europe and South Western Europe. The diversity of Western responses to shariʿa can be further explained by distinguishing between legal responses, on the one hand, and what we suggest to call the 'cultural response': while Western laws might provide general (religious) freedoms that allow Muslims to practise their shariʿa rules, Western public and political discourse may oppose these practices because they allegedly contravene with cultural identity.

Muslims, in turn, react to the Western responses to the Muslim practices of shariʿa rules. Some may stubbornly adhere to these rules as a matter of religious freedom, others may abandon them to avoid too much confrontation, and yet others may seek to find common ground between their religious rules and the rules of the Western societies where they live.

The framework and rich material provided in this volume will contribute to our understanding of shariʿa in the West. It is a phenomenon that is relatively new and therefore still in flux. Developments succeed each other in rapid order, often highlighted by shrill debates in the public and political domain, whereby action and reaction are often hard to separate. In this respect it is important to note that much is still to be known about the actual practices and intentions of Muslims in the West with regard to shariʿa before we can make final judgements about the (in)admissibility of shariʿa in the West.

Notes

1 ECHR, Refah vs Turkey, 13 February 2003, Nos. 41340/98, 41342/98, 41343/98 and 41344/98. See for commentaries: D. McGoldrick, 'Accommodating Muslims in Europe: From Adopting shariʿa Law to Religiously Based Opt Outs from Generally Applicable Laws', *Human Rights Law Review*, 2009 (Vol. 9, No. 4).

2 'Islam in Civil and Religious Law in England', lecture by the Archbishop of Canterbury, Dr Rowan Williams, Lambeth Palace, 7 February 2008; 'Equality before the Law', speech by Lord Chief Justice of England and Wales, East London Muslim Centre, 3 July 2008. See for commentaries: Rex Ahdar and Nicholas Aroney (eds.), *Shari'a in the West*, Oxford: Oxford University Press, 2011.

3 Ahdar and Aroney (eds.), *Shari'a in the West*; Andrea Büchler, *Islamic Law in Europe? Legal Pluralism and its Limits in European Family Laws*, Burlington: Ashgate, 2011; Samia Bano, *Islamic Dispute Resolution and Family Law*, London: Palgrave, 2011; Robin Griffith-Jones (ed.), *Islam and English Law: Rights, Responsibilities and the Place of Shari'a*, Cambridge: Cambridge University Press, 2013; Mark E. Hanshaw, *The Unfamiliar Abode: Islamic Law in the United*

States and Britain, Oxford: Oxford University Press, 2010; Julie MacFarlane, *Islamic Divorce in North America: A Sharia Path in a Secular Society*, Oxford: Oxford University Press, 2012; Jørgen Nielsen and Lisbet Christiffersen (eds.), *Shari'a as a Discourse: Legal Traditions and the Encounter with Europe*, Burlington: Ashgate, 2010; Matthias Rohe, *Muslim Minorities and the Law in Europe: Chances and Challenges*, Global Media Publications, 2007.

4 See for recent publications, e.g. Wael B. Hallaq, *Shari'a: Theory, Practice, Transformations*, Cambridge: Cambridge University Press, 2009; Muhammad Hashim Kamali, *Shari'ah Law: An Introduction*, Oxford: Oneworld Publications, 2008.

5 See, e.g. the twelve country studies in Jan-Michiel Otto, *Sharia Incorporated. A Comparative Overview of the Legal Systems of Twelve Muslim Countries in Past and Present*, Amsterdam: Amsterdam University Press, 2011.

6 This legal-anthropological approach has been advocated by a few scholars, and mostly when discussing shari'a in Muslim-majority countries – see, e.g., Baudouin Dupret, 1996 'La *sharî'a* comme référent legislative. Du droit positif à l'anthropologie du droit,' *Egypte Monde Arabe* (25), pp. 121-175.

7 John L. Esposito and Dalia Mogahed, *Who speaks for Islam? What a Billion Muslims Really Think*, New York: Gallup Press, 2008.

8 To be more exact: to the question 'should the programme of this [Muslim] party be based on shari'a?', 10.2% answered 'Yes, entirely' and 19.3% 'Yes, to some extent' (Foquz Etnomarketing, *Onderzoeksresultaten 'Politieke Voorkeuren Moslims' t.b.v. Redactie Nova*, Nieuwegein: Foquz Etnomarketing, December 2004, pp. 10-12).

9 ICM Research, 'Muslim Poll – February 2006', prepared for the *Sunday Telegraph*, available on www.icmresearch.com.

10 There was a difference in age: 37% of 16-24 year olds preferred shari'a compared to 17% of 55+ year olds. See Munira Mirza *et al.*, *Living Apart Together. British Muslims and the Paradox of Multiculturalism*, London: Policy Exchange, 2007.

11 E.g., Natasha Bakht, 'Family Arbitration Using shari'a Law: Examining Ontario's Arbitration Act and its Impact on Women,' in *Muslim World Journal of Human Rights*, 2004 (Vol. 1, Issue 1); Samia Bano, 'Cultural Translations and Legal Conflict: Muslim Women and the shari'ah Councils in Britain' in A. Hellum, S. Ali and A. Griffiths (eds.), *Transnational Law and Transnational Relations*, Ashgate Publishing, 2011; Maurits S. Berger, 'Sharia in Canada. An example for the Netherlands?' in: *Crossing Borders*, The Hague: Kluwer Rechtswetenschappelijke Publicaties, 2005; John R. Bowen, 'How Could English Courts Recognize shari'ah?' *University of St. Thomas Law Journal*, 2010 (Vol. 7, No. 3), pp. 411-435.

12 E.g., Kilian Bälz, 'Islamic Finance for European Muslims: The Diversity Management of Shari'ah-Compliant Transactions', *Chicago Journal of International Law*, 2006 (Vol. 7).

13 E.g. Alexandre Caeiro, *Fatwas for European Muslims: The Minority Fiqh Project and the Integration of Islam in Europe* (PhD thesis), Utrecht: Utrecht University Press, 2011; Dilwar Hussain, 'Muslim Political Participation in Britain and the "Europeanisation" of Fiqh,' *Die Welt des Islams* 2004 (Vol. 44, No. 3), pp. 376-

40; Fiqh Council of the Muslim World League, 'A message from Muslim scholars to Muslim Minorities in the West', *Daawah*, 2002, (No. 4); Shammai Fishman, 'Fiqh al-Aqalliyyat: A Legal Theory for Muslim Minorities', Center on Islam, Democracy, and the Future of the Muslim World, Research Monograph, 2006 (No. 2).

14 Conseil d'Etat, *Etude relative aux possibilités juridiques d'interdiction du port du voile intégral*, 25 March 2010 (available online at: www.conseil-etat.fr/cde/media/document/avis/etude_vi_30032010.pdf.).

15 See the explanations of their respective law proposals by the Cabinet (*Projet de loi interdisant la dissimulation du visage dans l'espace public* (No. 2520, 19 May 2010)) and by the Socialist Party (*Proposition de loi visant à fixer le champ des interdictions de dissimuler son visage liées aux exigences des services publics, à la prévention des atteintes à l'ordre public* (No. 2544, 20 May 2010)).

SECTION I

COUNTRY STUDIES

1 Reasons for the Application of Shari'a in the West[1]

Mathias Rohe

Introduction

Shari'a – or 'Islamic law',[2] in the narrow understanding – is broadly perceived to be the opposite of a secular legal order. The heated debate that took place in the aftermath of the Archbishop of Canterbury's famous speech about the possible introduction of some parts of shari'a law into the English legal system is but one example of this.[3] On the other hand, some of the small extremist groups that promote shari'a in the West, which bluntly reject the ruling secular legal order, such as 'shari'a4Belgium' and 'shari'a4Holland', seem to justify such prejudice against shari'a. Very often, the fact that there is little information about the meaning of shari'a and about the scope and limits of its application in the West leads to simplistic debates on all sides. The public climate has become unfavourable even for an academic debate on these issues. I myself was repeatedly denounced for promoting the replacement of the German legal order by shari'a, simply because I wanted to inform the public about the *existing* German legal order with respect to the treatment of Islamic norms.[4] This has convinced me all the more that it is necessary to address such issues, since they are real phenomena concerning a considerable number of people living in Western countries.

This chapter is confined to the legal provisions of shari'a, which only constitute a part of shari'a. While religious provisions, such as those on ritual prayer, fasting, and so forth, fall under the freedom of religion according to international and Western constitutional law, the application of foreign legal rules is an exception in legal orders all over the world. This is due to the now ruling principle of territoriality of legal orders, which replaced personal law systems in Western states centuries ago. The system of territoriality creates unified legal orders that grant internal plurality, thus retaining the right to make a final decision on whether foreign laws can apply or not.

With regard to the application of shari'a in Western secular states, the reasons for this are twofold. They are 'external' insofar as the law of the land simply prescribes the application of such norms in a given case, more or less irrespective of the intention of the parties involved. 'Internal' reasons are those rooted in the desires of the parties themselves. The latter can be sub-divided into technical/institutional, cultural and religious reasons. In some cases, external and internal reasons may meet where the law of the land creates spaces for the optional application of such norms, should the parties choose to do so. In addition, there is a difference between formal and informal application of these rules: whereas formal application requires recognition by the law of the land and enforcement by its institutions, informal application only depends on the free will and consent of the persons involved. We will discuss those categories in which shariʿa may be applied below.

External Reasons for the Formal or Informal Application of Shariʿa in the West

There are *four fields* of law where Islamic norms may be applicable or recognized for mainly external reasons. First, private international law may lead to the application of shariʿa within the limits of public policy; second, in some states Islamic norms have been integrated into the existing law of the land; third, given legal facts created under shariʿa may be recognized under Western laws for social reasons; and lastly, there are cases of maintaining personal law systems, including shariʿa for Muslims, for historical reasons. We will elaborate on these reasons below. The possibilities for applying shariʿa in the West are clearly restricted to the field of private law. Public law, and penal law in particular, are necessarily homogeneous in every country according to common international standards; thus, in these fields, the law of the land alone can and has to be applied.[5]

Private international law

Private international law (the rules regulating the conflict of laws in matters concerning civil law[6]) is a possible level of direct application of shariʿa legal rules. To be precise, shariʿa as such cannot be applied here, but only state laws based on shariʿa rules. In the area of civil law, the welfare of autonomously acting private persons is of prime importance. If someone has organized his or her life in accordance with a certain legal system, this deserves protection when the person crosses the border. However, it is also within the interest of the legal community that in certain matters, the same law should be applicable to everyone who is resident in a particular country. This is especially the case in matters touching the roots of legal and societal common sense, like the legal relations between the sexes or between adherents of different religions.

When it comes to the areas of family law and the law of succession, the application of legal norms in European countries is often determined on the basis of the nationality of the persons involved, rather than by their domicile.[7] Other than in Canada, the United States,[8] or Switzerland, many European courts, such as those in Germany, France and Austria, are therefore often obliged to apply Islamic legal rules when these are the national law of the persons involved. In this respect it may generally be stated that until now, shariʿa has had a particular strong position in family law and the law of succession. This can be explained by the fact that shariʿa in these areas has a multiplicity of regulations derived from authoritative sources (Qur'an and *sunna*). Furthermore, a powerful lobby is obviously trying to preserve this area as a stronghold due to religious convictions, as well as for reasons of income and the exercise of power (which is very similar to the situation in Christian Europe in the past). The Tunisian lawyer Ali Mezghani states that '[i]n Islamic countries, it is difficult to deny that family law is the site of conservation.'[9] This is true despite the fact that reforms have taken place in several Islamic countries, and still are in progress.[10]

However, the application of such provisions must comply with the rules of public policy. If the application of legislation influenced by shariʿa leads to a result that is obviously incompatible with, for example, the main principles of German law, including constitutional civil rights, the provisions in question cannot be applied. In family law, the main conflicts between 'Islamic' and European legal thinking concern the constitutional (and human) rights such as equality of the sexes and of religious beliefs and the freedom of religion, including the right not to believe. Conflicts mainly arise from provisions reflecting classical shariʿa, which preserve a strict separation between the sexes with respect to their social roles and tasks (for example, in marriage and divorce laws, and in matters of guardianship, custody and inheritance), as well as the far-reaching legal segregation of religions under the supremacy of Islam.[11]

Introduction of Islamic legal provisions

In addition to general rules of private international law, a few European states have introduced legal provisions concerning family and succession matters to be applied in general, or to the Muslim population in particular, allowing a *de facto* application of shariʿa rules.

In the United Kingdom, Muslims may apply to have their marriage registered. Furthermore, according to the Divorce (Religious marriages) Act 2002, courts are enabled to require the dissolution of a religious marriage before granting a civil divorce.[12] The Adoption and Children Act 2002 amended the Children Act 1989 by provisions (Sect. 14 A) introducing 'special guardianship' as a legal means of parental responsibility besides adoption, which is forbidden by shari'a.[13] This institution may have been aimed at accommodating Muslims in particular, but it is open to everyone, thus bridging the borders between separate legal systems.

In Spain, it has been possible to apply Islamic rules regulating the contracting of marriages to Muslims since 1992.[14] In order to ensure the necessary legal security, there are compulsory provisions for the registration of these marriages.[15] This kind of legal segregation is very limited, concerning mere formal regulations without any relevant material quality. Interestingly, the legislator in Spain has also amended Article 107 of the Código Civil regulating the right to divorce. The amendment enables women resident in Spain to get divorced even if the law of origin or of their matrimonial home prevents them from doing so. The legislator stated expressly that this amendment was intended to solve problems in this respect, especially regarding Muslim women.[16]

Recognition of legal facts created under foreign shari'a laws

The third legal reason for the applicability of shari'a is the legal recognition of facts created under shari'a, such as polygamous marriages. This must be distinguished from the aforementioned implementation of foreign norms under international private law. German social security laws treat polygamous marriages as legally valid, provided that the marriage contracts are valid under laws applicable to them at the place of their formation.[17] (Of course, polygamy fundamentally contradicts German and other European legal standards; therefore it cannot be contracted legally in Europe and is even punishable under German law, Par. 172 Penal Code.) The legal reasoning behind the recognition of these polygamous marriages is to avoid depriving these women of their marital rights, including maintenance. Thus, according to German social security law,[18] widow pensions are divided among widows who were living in polygamous marriages. However, German law differentiates between mainly private aspects of marriage and predominantly public ones, especially those relating to immigration law. Law governing the latter aspects provides only the first wife in polygamous marriages with marital privileges within its scope of application, such as residence permits.[19] The treatment of polygamous marriages in Germany differs from that in other European countries. In the United Kingdom, the courts rejected the claim to a widow's pension by a woman who was engaged in a polygamous marriage, resulting in none of the wives in the marriage receiving a payment.[20]

Personal law systems

The fourth reason why shariʿa can be applicable is in the case of a system of personal law that has remained in existence due to historical reasons. Thus, in Greece, the Treaty of Lausanne (1923) contained rules, which are still in force, leading to the application of traditional shariʿa law on Muslims of Turkish origin (see chapter 7 in this volume),[21] while the Turkish Republic has continuously reformed its civil laws and introduced legal equality of the sexes in family law in 2002. This can hardly serve as a model for Western secular states. Despite widespread efforts in the Islamic world to improve women's rights, many legal orders in this region are still far from the legal standard of equality of the sexes achieved in the West. It would simply be unacceptable to implement such rules in the existing systems, and – apart from the United Kingdom (see chapter 4 in this volume) – it is highly unlikely that any European public or legal order would be ready to concede legal pluralism in family matters at the expense of current public policy.

In Britain, the Union of Muslim Organisations of the United Kingdom and Eire has formulated a resolution demanding the establishment of a separate Muslim family and inheritance law that is automatically applicable to all Muslims in Britain,[22] without any effect so far. Some developments in recent years suggest that a considerable number of Muslims in the United Kingdom do indeed desire the application of shariʿa rules in these fields. According to a poll taken of 500 British Muslims in 2006, 40 per cent supported the introduction of shariʿa law in predominantly Muslim areas of Britain.[23] The underlying idea might be found in the legal situation on the Indian subcontinent – being the prevailing region of origin of Muslims in Britain – which was and still is ruled by a system of religious separation in matters of family law.[24] The same is true for most Muslim states in the past and present. But introducing religiously or ethnically-orientated multiple legal systems in Europe does not represent a realistic or even desirable option.[25] Such systems may have been helpful and even exemplary in the past, when they granted rights and freedoms to minorities that would otherwise have been disregarded. However, this will always result in problems in the form of inter-religious conflict over laws, as can be seen in Egypt, for example.[26] Besides that, freedom of religion contains the freedom to change one's religion or not to belong to any religion. This freedom would be unduly constrained by forcing people into a legal regime defined by religion. Furthermore, there is no uniform Islamic legal system of substantial rules to be identified. In addition to that, the former Ottoman territories in the Balkans, as well as the Turkish Republic, abolished shariʿa law a long time ago. Most of the Muslims who are natives of these states – constituting the vast majority of Muslims in a considerable number of European states, such as Austria, Germany and Switzerland – would reject the re-introduction of such rules in European countries. In France, such issues are not even debated publicly.

Instead of such institutionalized forms of religious-based family law systems, Muslims are entitled to create legal relations according to their religious intentions within the framework of optional civil law (see further below). This system reflects the emergence of relatively strong states claiming to regulate or at least supervise family matters according to legally consented principles.

Internal Reasons for the Formal or Informal Application of Shariʿa in the West

In addition to the external reasons that may lead to the application of shariʿa in the West, there are also internal reasons. These fall into four categories:

Technical/Institutional reasons

In cases of intermarriage and the conduct of 'international' lives, the persons involved may have a mere 'technical' interest in creating legal relations that are recognized in all of the countries involved, irrespective of the specific content or the religious connotation of the law. Problems arise when some religiously-founded foreign state laws refuse to recognize decisions by secular states (administrations or courts) in matters of family law, while they would recognize informal acts by religious personnel or alternative dispute resolution (ADR) decisions on the basis of their religiously-orientated laws. This is the case not only with respect to some Muslim states, but also to the state of Israel regarding Jews.[27] In these cases, the resort to such informal bodies is likely to be based on the technical aspect of recognition rather than on personal affiliation to religious law. In this regard, international efforts to improve mutual recognition of state decisions are urgently needed if state institutions want to preserve their prerogative. As long as recognition is in doubt, improvised solutions can be found even in state courts or administrations. For example, in cases of divorce, courts might mention that the husband has agreed to the procedures followed in Western law, which could be then recognized as a *talaq* (repudiation) under shariʿa law. In addition, Muslim witnesses could be invited to document this.[28]

In other cases, mere formal reasons such as the lack of documents required for marriages under the law of the land might draw immigrants to enter into informal religious marriages in order to create a socially accepted fundament for living together. Iraqi refugees in Germany who were willing to marry under German law are currently facing this problem with regard to documents proving their capability to marry under Iraqi law (which in this case is applicable according to German private international law: Art. 13 EGBGB). So far as these marriages are not recognized by state law – as is usually the case – conflicts including 'divorces' can only be resolved under the informal mechanisms provided, such as through mosques or Muslim organizations by applying shariʿa, often in hybrid forms rather than according to a particular Islamic state law.

Cultural reasons

When it comes to Muslim immigrants, various research projects in Europe in recent years have clearly demonstrated that considerable numbers of them maintain the structures of family life that they had in their countries of origin.[29] Some of them are reluctant to use the legal remedies provided by the law of the state of their new domicile, because they believe that they are bound to legal orders other than the law of the land. Others are simply unaware of the fact that in certain matters, including family law (for example, with respect to contracting marriages and divorce), the formal legal rules of the state of domicile have to be observed; otherwise, the intentions and acts of the parties involved are not legally enforceable.

Thus, a marriage that is contracted solely according to traditional Islamic rules may be socially accepted within a community, but it deprives the spouses of legally enforceable rights in the state of domicile with respect to the maintenance or inheritance usually connected to marriages. On the other hand, these women cannot obtain a divorce in state courts because they are not regarded as married according to the law of the land. Therefore they seek 'internal' solutions within their community.[30] Here, accessible information about the rules of the law of the land for immigrants is needed.

Furthermore, the socio-legal orders in many of the persons' countries of origin tend to perceive family matters as private matters, except for extreme cases of violence or other conflicts. This can lead to the avoidance of 'intervention' or conflict resolution on the part of the state, and for groups of immigrants to opt for merely informal, socially-accepted solutions. Again, there is a need for information about the protective function of state law for weaker parts of the family.

In addition, a lack of cultural sensitivity in some state institutions, including courts, may lead to distrust and reluctance. Evidence such as that from Canada[31] supports this view. To this respect, courses or other means of information for state officials should become more established. The aim is certainly not to change the applicable law. Nevertheless, in my experience as a judge for several years, the feeling of being personally understood is in many cases crucial for sustainable conflict resolution, particularly in matters open to settlement.

Last but not least, new forms of socio-legal navigating are emerging, in particular among younger Muslim couples. They deliberately use the lack of legal validity of mere 'religious' marriages. By this, they can combine social acceptance of their relationship within the family and the community with avoiding the legal consequences of a valid civil marriage. Evidence from Denmark,[32] for example, shows that such couples marry validly under the law of the land when children are born or when they decide to purchase real property. Apart from the religious legitimization aiming at the social environment, this behaviour very much reflects common usage in contemporary Western societies. Chapter 8 of this volume elaborates these cultural strategies in detail with respect to the Netherlands.

Religious reasons

With regard to religious reasons, we have to make a fundamental distinction between the case of using the law of the land under religious auspices on the one hand, and the rejection of that law by consequently applying shari'a in an informal way on the other.

Islamic norms may be applied *within the existing framework of the law of the land* as far as this law is dispositive for the parties involved. This is the case, for instance, in vast parts of contract law. As an example we may note the fact that various methods of investment are offered, which do not violate the Islamic prohibition of usury (*riba*, which according to traditional views means the general prohibition of accepting and paying interest).[33] Concerning project finance, Islamic legal institutions such as the *murabaha* or the *mudaraba* can be used.[34]

These are certain forms of partnership intending to attract capital owners to participate instead of merely granting credit, the latter bearing the risk of contradicting the *riba*-rules. Commerce and trade have already responded to the economic and legal needs of traditional Muslims. German and Swiss banks, for instance, have issued 'Islamic' shares for investment purposes; that is to say, share packages that avoid companies whose business involves gambling, alcohol, tobacco, interest-yielding credit, insurance or the sex industry, all of which are illegitimate in shariʿa.[35]

In the United Kingdom, a special concept of 'Islamic' mortgages has been developed, which allows Muslims willing to purchase real estate to avoid conflicts with provisions concerning *riba* (when paying interest on 'normal' mortgages).[36] An Islamic mortgage consists of two separate transactions aiming at one single result. Until recently, each transaction was subject to taxation. Now the double 'stamp duty' has effectively been abolished, because it had been preventing Muslims from successfully engaging in the real property market due to the formal system of taxation without sufficient reason. Even the German state of Saxony-Anhalt placed an Islamic bond (*ṣukuk*,[37] 100 million euros as a start) based on a Dutch foundation a few years ago.[38] For traditional Muslims, the availability of such forms of investment in Europe is of considerable importance. To my knowledge, many of them lost huge sums of money in the past to doubtful organizations from the Islamic world bearing a 'religious' veil, or to similar organizations based in Europe.[39]

In the field of matrimonial law, the tendency of implementing Islamic norms in optional law can also be identified in Germany in connection with matrimonial contracts.[40] Thus, in Germany contractual conditions regulating the payment of the 'Islamic' dower (*mahr* or *sadaq*) are possible and generally accepted by the courts (see chapter 9 in this volume).[41] Other contractual regulations, especially those discriminating against women, could be void according to Paragraph 138 of the German Civil Code on the protection of good morals.[42] So far there have been no court decisions on such issues, published or known. However, to my knowledge some German notaries refuse to assist in formulating wills[43] containing the classical Islamic regulation on half-shares for female heirs.

The second case – fundamentally different from the one above – is the informal application of Islamic norms for reasons of religiously driven *rejection of 'worldly' laws* given by 'infidels'.[44] 'Eternal god-given law' is then (wrongly[45]) opposed to 'weak man made law'.[46] In Germany, one of the few voices publicly demanding the introduction of shariʿa and Muslim arbitration to avoid any application of 'infidel' laws is the extremist founder of an Islamic centre in Berlin. In a book on 'The Rules of Personal Status of Muslims in the West',[47] he repeatedly declares non-Muslims to be infidels and rejects German legal rules and judgments as 'rules of the infidel'.[48] Consequently, he urges Muslims in Germany to maintain the rules of traditional Islamic family law. Incredibly, he even argues that the traditional punishment for adultery – flogging or stoning to death – should be applied to Muslim women in Germany who are married to non-Muslims, even if they are unaware of the 'applicability' of these rules in their cases.[49] He denounces the German system of social security as evil, because it grants wives independence from their husbands' maintenance payments and thus enables them to 'disobey' their husbands.[50]

Some other religious extremists and traditionalists also argue that Muslims should not accept the legal norms and judgments of 'infidels'. They should instead establish their own bodies of dispute resolution and elect their own judges.[51] But would extra-judicial dispute resolution then create a viable solution for weighing up the relevant interests of the parties involved in a manner consistent with the community's standards, as well as with the indispensable principles of the law of the land (see the next section below)?

These two different situations illustrate the possible conflicts between the law of the land and a parallel normative order: it is up to the law of the land – representing the community of citizens and inhabitants of a country – to decide on the space and limits of optional law. Liberal legal orders tend to open up a broad space for individual choice for good reason. Nevertheless, there are sensitive areas of legal relations where typically parties with different kinds of bargaining power meet. The family and its legal interrelations is such a case in many respects. Here, the need for state protection for the weaker parties is obvious. In general, compulsory norms in all spheres of law are justified by this protective goal. In addition to this, they grant necessary common standards defined by legislation and thus peace in society. These standards are obviously subjected to changing social convictions and lifestyles; legislation will react to such changes sooner or later, legally protected same-sex relations being only one striking example of this. In any case, it is up to the law of the land given by the sovereign to define the limits of normative plurality. Thus, the establishment of informal structures opposing the principles of the law of the land is certainly a threat to the latter – and to the individuals protected by it.

Alternative Dispute Resolution (ADR) and Shari'a

Within the scope of private autonomy, the parties concerned are free to create legal relations within the limits of public policy and to agree on the ways and results of non-judicial dispute resolution. In matters of family law, relatives will often be consulted first. Should that fail, informal or existing formal dispute resolution bodies might be involved, as well as state courts. Certain decisions, such as officially recognized divorces, are restricted to state courts in Europe. Others might be open to ADR mechanisms. Some of the reasons for choosing ADR may particularly apply to family disputes: confidentiality and the choice of arbitrators on the basis of personal trust can be even more attractive than in other ADR cases, such as those concerning economic claims. Besides that, the specific reasons for preferring ADR are threefold: institutional, cultural and religious, as suggested above.

With regard to ADR in family matters, we can discern both a major advantage and a disadvantage. The advantage is that the official acceptance of ADR, which allows for freedom in choosing the rules applicable to the case at hand, might create a feeling of religio-cultural acceptance among those interested in preserving religiously based laws and conflict resolution mechanisms. On the other hand, there is a danger that the institutional homogenization of conflict resolution within a community such as the Muslim community may neglect existing internal diversity within that community, and may even increase internal pressure on 'weak' members of the community ('the paradox of multicultural vulnerability' according to Ayalet Shachar[52]) to make use of the ADR mechanisms against their interest and will. This danger is real, since religiously based family laws tend to treat the sexes and religions unequally according to the patriarchal structures underlying these laws. Thus, in opting for ADR, one has to decide which interests are to prevail: those of religious communities as a whole (which means mainly the interests of their leaders) or the interests of individuals.

When it comes to the present situation in Europe, we find an extraordinary example of law and ADR influenced by Islam in the United Kingdom, where an 'angrezi shariat' (English shari'a) appears to be developing.[53] This seems to be due to the fact that many Muslims in Britain still have strong family ties to their respective native countries on the Indian subcontinent, governed by religiously orientated laws in matters of personal status.[54] In some cases, mainly those concerning family relations, they seek socially acceptable solutions for legal problems within the Muslim community through the aid of accepted mediators. The Islamic Sharia Councils in England, which were established in 1980-82, seem to be examples of such a kind of mediation.[55] The Councils do not have an official function, but they focus in particular on mediation in the area of the law of personal status. There are frequently cases in which a Muslim wife has obtained an English divorce that she subsequently wants confirmed according to shari'a by the pronouncement of *talaq* (divorce) by the husband, so that the divorce will be accepted in the social environment within or outside the country. Similarly, it is very often the case that a husband refuses to divorce, and that while the wife wishes to do so, she is reluctant to start divorce proceedings in the civil courts.[56] Even if the matter does not go to the civil court, the Council's decision may become important; it is not legally enforceable in England, but it seems to be recognized in the state of origin as well as within the religious community.[57] Convincing the husband to pay the *mahr* (dower) constitutes a further possible task for the Council.

While the decisions of the Sharia Councils appear to be based on a relatively reform-oriented approach to the legal sources, they maintain the traditional framework of shari'a, including unequal treatment of the sexes and religions in general. Thus, the English legal system does not remain untouched by such proceedings, since they differ considerably from basic decisions in English family law. For example, the councils use the instruments given in some Islamic states for wives to obtain a divorce in court on the basis of the so-called *khul'*, which is a contractual or statutory right.[58] The wife, however, must then pay back the dower, which will very often have been intended to serve as an old-age pension. This somehow rewards the husband's persistence in refusing a divorce, which is not acceptable according to the standard of the law of the land. Certainly, an individual's personal status is a 'private matter', thus leaving scope for individual preferences, including those based on religious or cultural convictions in general. Nevertheless, the institutions of the law regarding personal status and, in particular, the balance of rights and duties among the persons involved not only affect society as a whole, but also reflect this society's basic common convictions concerning what is probably the most important part of social life. Therefore it is up to the national legislator to establish a legal personal status order that grants protection to everyone living in the country.

Thus, on the one hand, ADR can serve as an instrument to achieve socially accepted solutions within a community living at a certain distance from society as a whole. It might give access to groups that would otherwise refrain from any kind of formal (non-violent) conflict resolution. On the other hand, members of that community who refuse to use the community's special bodies for conflict resolution may well be accused of undermining the community's position, and of being a 'bad' member. This could press individuals into using a religiously-driven system of conflict resolution against their will or interests, as the Canadian example concerning the debate on introducing shari'a boards in the Province of Ontario clearly demonstrates.[59] As a consequence, unconditionally accepting communitarian bodies such as these could lead to ongoing cultural segregation and to a 'culturalization' of individuals seeking their individual ways within a broader society. Introducing parallel power structures may endanger socio-legal cohesion: where common legal standards, such as those regarding equal rights of the sexes, religions and convictions, are considered to be fundamental for society as a whole, solutions that deviate from these will certainly cause massive tensions. At the same time, individual religious choices are endangered if these individuals are unable to avoid the application of religiously-based laws containing provisions that promote unequal treatment.[60] This is why most European legal orders do not allow family status disputes to be formally decided by ADR mechanisms.

Even in cases where ADR is formally accepted by state laws (for example, with respect to religious arbitration bodies such as the Beth Din and the Muslim Arbitration Tribunals in the United Kingdom[61]), the question remains as to whether the mere existence of an ADR agreement is sufficient. Certainly, within the scope of private autonomy, agreements between adult and mentally healthy persons are supposed to be valid and fair unless there is any specific evidence to the contrary. However, in the context of migration and societal segregation, formal freedom to agree or not to agree can be factually restricted to just one option, if the relevant party has to expect substantial disadvantages in social life in the case that they choose the 'wrong' option. Thus, if factual pressure on the weaker party is not a merely theoretical threat, the official recognition of communitarian bodies for ADR and their decisions could prevent the weaker party from obtaining the protection granted by the law of the land and enforced by official courts. As suggested above, despite various reforms in several Muslim states, shari'a of personal status does not grant equal rights to females and non-Muslims.

We should certainly reject the simplistic picture of Muslim women generally being oppressed, powerless victims. The German Supreme Court[62] has stated that there is no room for the presumption that Turkish wives living in 'typical Muslim marriages' are deprived of autonomous decision-making in their daily lives. Nevertheless, the problems that do arise, which are often caused by cultural motivation, are obvious and openly discussed among Muslims themselves. The commissioner for women's affairs at the Central Council of Muslims in Germany has stated in an interview that, 'Islam is not in need of a commissioner for women's affairs. It is not Islam that suppresses women, but men. And therefore Muslim women are indeed in need of a commissioner for women's affairs.'[63] It should be mentioned in this context that the Central Council of Muslims in Germany declared in its charter on Muslim life in German society on 20 February 2002 (the 'Islamic Charta'[64]) that Muslims are content with the harmonious system of secularity and religious freedom provided by the Constitution. According to Article 13 of the charter, 'The command of shari'a to observe the local legal order includes the acceptance of the German statutes governing marriage and inheritance, and civil as well as criminal procedure.' In the Swiss canton of Zurich, the Union of Islamic Organizations in Zurich[65] has expressly stated in its Basic Declaration that the Union does not intend to create an Islamic state in Switzerland, nor does it place shari'a above Swiss legislation (Section 1). The Union also expressly appreciates Swiss law concerning marriage and inheritance (Section 5). Similarly, the renowned French *imam* Larbi Kechat has stated that 'Nous sommes en harmonie avec le cadre des lois, nous n'imposons pas une loi parallèle.'[66] According to Belgian experience, the vast majority of Muslim women living in between the rules of Muslim family law and women's rights also claim the protection of Belgian substantive law.[67] Thus, initiatives aiming at the promotion of shari'a by ADR mechanisms should not be overestimated regarding their importance for Muslims living in the West.

Finally, advantages and disadvantages concerning the reliability of mediators and arbitrators have to be weighed up against each other. The idea of promoting officially-recognized ADR mechanisms for Muslims in Canada was to grant the arbitrators the necessary personal and technical skills, including legal knowledge, by creating a system of education and recognition for them. Indeed, one should be aware that refusing to recognize 'official' ADR bodies would not prevent people from using unofficial mechanisms involving persons of unclear background and skills. Two solutions are possible here: either to implement a system of official ADR or – the preferable approach in the author's opinion, for the reasons given above – to heighten the cultural sensitivity of the state court system and implement information programmes focusing on the advantages of the existing legal system.

The situation is entirely different when the ADR deals with conflicts other than those relating to marriage and divorce. Recently, a book appeared in Germany on how 'shari'a judges' settle criminal disputes among Muslims in the country.[68] While forms of mediation between perpetrators and victims are established in penal cases – usually under the supervision of the state (for example, according to Article 46a of the German Penal Law Code), the limits should be clear: the exercise of pressure on victims or witnesses cannot be tolerated by the state. Nevertheless, the relatively small number of cases reported does not indicate the establishment of a parallel 'shariʿa' system. Rather, it seems to be restricted to parts of the population originating from huge Middle Eastern family clans that are used to 'settling' conflicts according to their *cultural* traditions. In addition, special motifs relating to an immigration background may be well involved: official criminal prosecution in major cases would often lead to the loss of the perpetrator's residence permit, thus possibly affecting his whole family living within the country or family members in the country of origin dependent on his financial support. In such cases, there might be a tendency not to involve state bodies, so as to avoid such effects. Another case involving Salafis was reported in Spain in 2009. According to these reports, a group of seven persons originating from North Africa allegedly 'sentenced' a woman who had committed adultery to death in a 'shariʿa court' condoned by the victim's family.[69] They were later set free because the woman had disappeared and thus could not identify the accused before the court. Until now, little research has been done in this field.

Preliminary Conclusions

In general, legal plurality does not usually endanger socio-legal cohesion in mere 'international' cases. If persons only stay temporarily, developing few links to the state of residence, far-reaching legal diversity can be seen as a natural phenomenon in a globalized world. But 'internal' cases involving considerable normative differences and citizens or long-time residents do have such potential. Thus, they require greater homogeneity in basic legal decisions. How, then, to properly differentiate between 'international' and 'internal'? In this regard, I would favour the choice of forms of residence as the most significant connecting factor in family law issues, as immigration countries usually do for good reason. Concerning internal law, it is necessary to undertake thorough studies of the scope and limits of dispositive law and ADR. In the field of family relations, state protection seems to be indispensable; thus, most Western legal orders are restricting the options available, especially with respect to basic legal institutions and ADR.

To overcome mere technical or institutional problems by applying the law of the land, international efforts to improve the mutual recognition of state decisions are needed. In those cases where documents are lacking, administrations and courts should be ready to find creative solutions or make more use of hardship rules.

Besides that, immigrants from countries maintaining a personal law system and their descendants should be reasonably informed about the legal situation of their new home country. Research in the United Kingdom in particular has shown that to a considerable extent, religious marriages have been concluded under the misguided impression that they are valid under the law of the land. This includes information about the role of state law and institutions in family-related issues: in the West, the state and its legal system have achieved a strong position in recent last centuries. Economic solidarity within extended families has been largely replaced by more or less state-run systems of social security. At the same time, the state has assumed the role of the main protector of weaker family members, particularly children and wives in patriarchal cultural environments.

Problems remain in cases where parties are reluctant to bring their cases to state courts for various reasons. If they refrain from doing so, without any alternative available, the conflicts will continue and might even escalate. Thus, if state court solutions are to be maintained, it is absolutely necessary to respond to people's reasons for rejecting these courts; something that can be achieved without touching the content of the law, for example, by increasing cultural sensitivity among judges and in administrations. In Germany, for instance, the Academies for Judges (*Richterakademien*), which serve as institutions for the training of judges and other legal personnel already in office, provide a number of short courses (up until now mainly taught by myself). Much more could be done in this field.

Practical experience proves that non-lawyers tend not to be interested in the law as such, but in the outcome of its application as far as they are personally concerned. Thus, in cases of differing options, the choice of the respective norms is often driven much more by personal worldly interest than by more abstract convictions about how the law should be in general. Therefore, the demand for shariʿa should not necessarily be seen as a general refusal to accept the ruling law of the land. Nevertheless, the latter attitude does exist and is highly problematic in terms of social cohesion. In any case, it is mandatory to carry out a sound analysis of the considerably varying aspects – technical/institutional, cultural and religious – in order to provide acceptable solutions from the perspective of the legal order, as well as those affected by the law.

It is essential that the basic rules of secular legal orders in liberal societies are accepted by society as a whole. But can such legal orders not only be obeyed, but also accepted by devout Muslims, and seen as 'theirs' as well? The overwhelming majority of Muslims living in the West seem to answer in favour of that. They recognize that these legal orders are also engaged in a search for justice. Understanding the 'maqasid al-shari'a', the deeper reasons for Islamic rules, in the search for an overlapping consensus between the latter and the rules of secular states, could be a viable solution at a contemporary intellectual level (see also chapters 12 and 13 in this volume).

Examples of public discourse by Muslims in recent European fora express aspects of the thinking behind this approach. At a conference held in Sarajevo in 2007, the prominent Bosnian Muslim lawyer Enes Karić, who teaches at the Islamic Faculty there, explicitly stated that the caliphate is not part of the religion of Islam. He considers shari'a to be a set of rules with moral goals, and secular states to be products of their actions. Therefore, in his view, 'A state which is willing to provide a sufficient social structure, e.g. funds for students or pensions, which intends to establish economic and social justice, which respects and promotes human rights, is an Islamic state in this sense.' (He also cited the Islamic maxim *adl al-dawla iman-ha, zulm al-dawla kufr-ha* – justice is the belief of a state, injustice is its unbelief – and said that the concept of citizenship is a major European achievement.) Finally, he said that the European secular democratic state under the rule of law fulfils the conditions for justice, and concluded: 'Therefore, we don't need a double system.'[70]

It would thus be highly advisable to support a Muslim research and educational system driven by such thinking, dealing with the conditions of life in secular societies and their basic values. Muslims should play their fair part in the debate about the future of our common laws.

Notes

1 This article is based on research that took place in the context of RELIGARE (see www.religareproject.eu), a three-year project funded under the Socio-economic Sciences & Humanities programme of DG Research, under the European Commission's Seventh Framework Research Programme.

2 There are two fundamentally different understandings of shari'a. In a narrow sense, which is common among non-Muslims but also to be found among Muslims, shari'a stands for draconic penal sanctions, such as stoning to death or cutting off hands, and for unequal treatment of the sexes and religions. In a broader sense, shari'a means the totality of Islamic normativity, including religious commands and the set of methods for discerning and interpreting norms (*usul al-fiqh*). See Mathias Rohe, 'Application of Shari'a Rules in Europe', *Die Welt des Islams* special issue, 2004 (Vol. 44, No. 38), p. 323.

3 See Rowan Williams, 'Civil and Religious Law in England, a religious perspective' (lecture delivered on 7 February 2008), available at http://www.archbishopofcanterbury.org/articles.php/1137/archbishops-lecture-civil-and-religious-law-in-england-a-religious-perspective.

4 E.g. by the equally fanatic and poorly informed German feminist Alice Schwarzer, see Patrick Bahners, *Die Panikmacher, Die deutsche Angst vor dem Islam,* München: C.H. Beck, 2011, pp. 233-251, and the statement by the author, available at http://www.zr2.jura.uni-erlangen.de/aktuelles/kanal.shtml.

5 See Mathias Rohe, 'Islamic Norms in Germany and Europe,' in: Ala Al-Hamarneh and Jörn Thielmann (eds.), *Islam and Muslims in Germany*, Leiden/Boston: Brill, 2008, pp. 49, 62.

6 Of course, in the sphere of public law and especially of penal law, foreign law is not applicable. Public law regulates the activities of the sovereign himself, and penal law has to define rules that are necessary to grant a minimum consensus of common behaviour in the relevant society.

7 For further details see Mathias Rohe, 'Islamic Law in German Courts,' *Hawwa* 2003 (No. 1) p. 46.

8 See Marie-Claire Foblets and Adriaan Overbeeke, 'Islam in Belgium,' in: Richard Potz and Wolfgang Wieshaider (eds.), *Islam and the European Union*, Leuven: Peeters, 2004, p. 25; Edwige Rude-Antoine, 'La coexistence des systèmes juridiques différents en France: l'exemple du droit familial,' in: Philippe Kahn (ed.), *L'étranger et le droit de la famille,* Paris: La Documentation française (Mission 'Droit et Justice'), 2001, pp. 147, 161.

9 Ali Mezghani, 'Le juge français et les institutions du droit musulman,' *Journal de Droit International* 2003, pp. 721-722.

10 See Mathias Rohe, *Das islamische Recht. Geschichte und Gegenwart*, 3rd ed., Munich: C.H. Beck, 2011, pp. 171-181; 207-234.

11 For details see Mathias Rohe, 'Islamic Law in German Courts,' *Hawwa,* 2003 (No. 1), pp. 46.

12 See Lord Nazir Ahmad, 'Notes on the Judicial Situation of Muslims in the United Kingdom,' in: Thorsten Schneiders and Lamya Kaddor (eds.), *Muslime im Rechtsstaat,* Münster: LIT Verlag Münster, 2005, pp. 71-72; Urfan Khaliq, 'Islam and the European Union: Report on the United Kingdom,' in: Potz and Wieshaider (eds.), *Islam and the European Union*, 2004, pp. 219, 246.

13 This prohibition is based on Qur'an surah 33: 4; for present legal orders in the Islamic world see D. Pearl and W. Menski, *Muslim Family Law*, 3rd ed. London: Sweet&Maxwell, 1998, chapters 10-25.

14 See Joaquín Mantecón, 'L'Islam en Espagne,' in: Potz and Wieshaider (eds.), *Islam and the European Union*, 2004, pp. 109, 130-132.

15 See Article 59 Código Civil in conjunction with the administrative provision of the general directorate of the Civil Registry and the Notary of 10 February 1993.

16 BOE 30-09-2003, Ley Orgánica 11/2003, de 29 de septiembre, de medidas concretas en materia de seguridad ciudadana, violencia doméstica e integración social de los extranjeros, 4.

17 See LG Frankfurt a.M. FamRZ 1976, p. 217; LG Osnabrück NJW-RR 1998, p. 582; AG Bremen StAZ 1991, pp. 232, 233; BFHE 152, 537; Staatsanwaltschaft bei dem LG Muenchen I IPRspr. 1996 No. 62; VGH Kassel NVwZ-RR 1999, pp. 274, 275.

18 See Para. 34, Sect. 2 Social Code I.

19 See OVG Koblenz 12.03.2004 (10 A 11717/03), unpublished.

20 Court of Appeal in Bibi v. Chief Adjudication Officer [1998] 1 FLR 375. None of the women were accepted legally as widows. See the critical remarks by David S. Pearl, *Islamic Family Law and Its Reception by the Courts in England*, Harvard Law School Islamic Legal Studies program, Occasional Publications, May 2000, p. 14.

21 See Konstantinos Tsitselikis, 'The Legal Status of Islam in Greece,' in: Mathias Rohe (guest ed.), *Shari'a in Europe, Die Welt des Islams – International Journal for the Study of Modern Islam*, 2004 (Vol. 44 No. 3), pp. 402; Konstantinos Tsitselikis, in: Jorgen Nielsen *et al.* (eds.), *Yearbook of Muslims in Europe*, Leiden: Brill 2010 (Vol. 2), pp. 233-237, 242.

22 See Sebastian Poulter, 'The Claim to a Separate Islamic System of Personal Law for British Muslims,' in: Chibli Mallat and Jane Connors (eds.), *Islamic Family Law*, London: Graham&Trotman, reprint 1993, p. 147.

23 Available at http://www.icmresearch.co.uk/pdfs/2006_february_sunday_telegraph_muslims_poll.pdf (p. 14).

24 See Jacob Levy, *The Multiculturalism of Fear*, Oxford: Oxford University Press, 2000, p. 180; Sebastian Poulter, n. 22, p. 148; Lord Nazir Ahmad, n. 12, pp. 71 ss, 74 referring to the respective demands of the UMO and the Muslim Council of Britain.

25 See Mathias Rohe, 'Religiös gespaltenes Zivilrecht in Deutschland und Europa?,' in: Heinrich De Wall and Michael Germann (eds.), *Festschrift Link*, Tübingen: Duncker&Humblot, 2003, pp. 409.

26 Shariʿa applies there not only if Muslims are involved in inter-religious relations, but even in any other inter-religious cases, e.g. between Christians of different denominations; see Mathias Rohe, n. 11, pp. 208 s.; 379. Also: Maurits S. Berger, *Sharia and Public Policy in Contemporary Egyptian Family Law* (PhD thesis), Groningen: Hephaestus Press, 2006.

27 See for legal problems relating to the Jewish get (divorce), see Michael Freeman, 'The Jewish Get and the State,' in: Richard O'Dair and Andrew Lewis (eds.), *Law and Religions. Current legal issues* 2001 (Vol. 4), pp. 365, 377.

28 See e.g. the procedures in an unpublished Iranian divorce case in the local court of Siegburg/Germany in November 2011 (unpublished). Cf. the report 'Scheidung mit Richter und Mullah,' KStA 16.11.20122, available at http://www.ksta.de/region/amtsgericht-scheidung-mit-richter-und-mullah,15189102,12032204.html.

29 See Zaki Badawi, in: Michael King (ed.), *God's Law versus State Law*, London: Grey Seal, 1995, pp. 73, 75; Marion Simonet, 'L'étranger entre deux droits: les facteurs d'adhésion des populations étrangères aux systèmes judiciaire et juridique français,' in: Kahn (ed.), *L'étranger et le droit de la famille*, 2001, pp. 118, 139-141.

30 See S.N. Shah-Kazemi, *Untying the Knot. Muslim Women, Divorce and the Sharia*, London: Nuffield Foundation, 2001, p. 47.

31 See Anne Saris, Jean-Mathieu Potvin, Naïma Bendriss, Wendy Ayotte and Samia Amor, *Étude de cas auprès de Canadiennes musulmanes et d'intervenants civils et religieux en résolution de conflits familiaux*, Montréal, 2007, pp. 44.

32 Report given by Anika Liversage on a RELIGARE expert seminar on Unregistered Marriages and Alternative Dispute Resolution in European Legal Systems on 4 Sept. 2012 in London (papers to be published with Ashgate in 2013).

33 See Abdullah Saeed, *Islamic Banking and Interest. A Study of the Prohibition of Riba and its Contemporary Interpretation*, Leiden/New York/Köln: Brill, 1996; Munawar Iqbal, *Islamic Banking and Finance*, Leicester: Islamic Foundation, 2001; Mathias Rohe, 'Islamisches Wirtschaften aus rechtlicher Sicht', in: Harald Herrmann and Kai-Ingo Voigt (eds.), *Globalisierung und Ethik*, Heidelberg: Springer, 2005, pp. 103, 107.

34 See Reinhard Klarmann, Islamic Project Finance, Zurich/Bâle/Genève: Schulthess, 2003; Kilian Bälz, 'A Murabaha Transaction in an English Court', *ILAS*, 2004 (Vol. 11), p. 117.

35 See Angelo Venardos, *Islamic Banking and Finance*, New Jersey: World Scientific, 2005, p. 70.

36 See Iqbal Asaria, 'Islamic home finance arrives on UK's high streets', *Muslim News* 25 July 2003 (No. 171), p. 6.

37 It is based on a combination of leasing contracts concerning the state's real property; see 'Finanzmarkt: Islam-Anleihe aus Magdeburg', *Die Bank* 1 January 2004.

38 See 'Sachsen-Anhalt bereitet erste islamische Anleihe vor', *FAZ* 06.11.2003, p. 31; 'Anlegen mit Allahs Segen', *Handelsblatt* 14 July 2004, p. 29.

39 See the reports on dubious investments in Turkey supported by certain organizations in 'Neuer Markt auf Türkisch', *SPIEGEL ONLINE* 29 January 2004 (accessed on 29 November 2004 at http://www.spiegel.de/0,1518,283591,00.html); 'Der verlorene Schatz', *Die Zeit* 29.11.2006, available at www.zeit.de/2006/46/G-Holy-Holdings?page=4; BGH VI ZR 57/09 23.03.2010, available at http://beck-online.beck.de/?vpath=bibdata\zeits\dstr\2010\cont\dstr.2010.1040.1.htm&hlwords=#xhlhit

40 See Rohe, n. 10, pp. 366.

41 See BGH NJW 1999, p. 574; OLG Celle FamRZ 1998, p. 374.

42 § 138 Sect. 1: 'A legal transaction which offends good morals is void'; see Rohe, n. 11, p. 366.

43 The validity of wills does not depend on such assistance according to German law of succession.

44 See only the clear statement of the extremist criminal Faisal Shahzad ('We do not accept your democracy or your freedom, because we already have shari'a law and freedom', 'Bomb plotter receives life sentence', *Washington Post* 6 October 2010, p. 10), who had planned to blow up a car bomb in Times Square in New York in May 2010.

45 Legal norms always need human interpretation when they are applied, irrespective of the reason for their validity; secular law has immunized its core rights (human rights rules) against democratic majority decisions which could try to restrict or abolish them; see Rohe, 'Islam and the Democratic state under the Rule of Law – and Never the Twain Shall Meet?', in: Marie-Claire Foblets and Jean-Yves Carlier (eds.), *Crises are Challenges*, Leuven, 2010, pp. 215-236.

46 See e.g. the very superficial and incorrect juxtaposition of shariʿa and secular law in teaching materials written by Amir Zaidan (director of the IRPI – Islamisches Religionspädagogisches Institut – in Vienna). In his course 'Einführung in die Scharia – Kurs 1' (p. 16) he describes secular law as a matter in need of constant adjustment because of human incapability, as dependent on individual and particular group interests, as a mere reaction to social developments, as mostly confined in time and space and without giving any help with orientation. Obviously he has no conception of the very same challenges for shariʿa in the past and present.

47 Sālim Ibn ʿAbd al-Ghanī al-Rāfiʿī, *Ahkām al-ahwāl al-*šakhsīya *li-l-muslimīn fī al-gharb*, Riyadh 2001. See Rohe, 'Islamisten und Schari'a,' in: Berlin, Senatsverwaltung für Inneres, Islamismus, Berlin 2005, pp. 98, 109.

48 Rohe, 'Islamisten und Schariʿa', 2005, p. 618.

49 Rohe, 'Islamisten und Schariʿa', 2005, p. 394. See also the results of an essay competition among Muslims in Britain on issues concerning penal law (Abdullah Mohammed in: *The Federation of Students Islamic Societies, Essays on Islam, Essay Competition, Winning Entries 1995*, Leicester, 1995, pp. 14, 37). The winner quotes a Muslim author saying that Europeans are afraid of the application of Islamic penal norms (ordering harsh corporal punishments which are contradicting human rights) because they have a criminal nature and wish to commit unjustifiable crimes.

50 Rohe, 'Islamisten und Schariʿa', 2005, p. 79.

51 See Ibn Baz and Uthaymeen, *Muslim Minorities – Fatawa Regarding Muslims Living as Minorities*, Hounslow, 1998, esp. pp. 71; The Fiqh Council of the Muslim World League on its 16th session in Mecca, reported in 'A message from Muslim scholars to Muslim Minorities in the West', *Daawah* No. 4 1422 A.H./ Feb. 2002, pp. 8, 11.

52 Ayalet Shachar, 'The Puzzle of Interlocking Power Hierarchies,' *Harvard Civil Rights-Civil Liberties Law Review* 2000 (Vol. 35), pp. 385, 386, and also *Multicultural Jurisdictions. Cultural Differences and Women's Rights*, Cambridge: Cambridge University Press, 2001, p. 62.

53 See Pearl and Menski, 1998, pp. 3-81.

54 See Shah-Kazemi, 2001; Mathias Rohe, 'Religiös gespaltenes Zivilrecht in Deutschland und Europa?', in: De Wall and Germann (eds.), *Festschrift Link*, 2003, pp. 409, 415.

55 Pearl and Menski, 1998, pp. 3-81; Zaki Badawi, in: Michael King (ed.), *God's Law versus State Law*, London: Grey Seal, 1995, pp. 73, 75-80; Shah-Kazemi, n. 30.

56 See Ph. Lewis, *Religion, Politics and Identity among British Muslims: Bradford since the 1990s*, London: I.B. Tauris, 1994, p. 119 regarding the circumstances in Bradford; Shah-Kazemi, 2001.

57 See Pearl and Menski, 1998, pp. 3-100.
58 See Mathias Rohe, 2011, pp. 222-226; Pearl and Menski, 1998, pp. 3-100.
59 See Mathias Rohe, 2011, pp. 319.
60 See e.g. the decision in Re S 'Abduction: Intolerable Situation: Beth Din' [2000] 1 Family Law Report 454, 460; there, a Jewish lady was not allowed to bring her case under laws granting equal treatment, since it was her own religion that made Israeli Jewish courts competent to decide.
61 These should certainly be main issues of our research, if they are accessible.
62 BGH (Federal Supreme Court) NJW, 1999, 135.
63 "Verschleiert, aber selbstbewußt", *FAZ* 27.02.2001, p. 14.
64 An English version can be found at http://www.islam.de/?site=sonstiges/events/charta&di=en (accessed on 30.01.2004).
65 Vereinigung der Islamischen Organisationen in Zürich (VIOZ), Grundsatzerklärung 27 March 2005.
66 Larbi Kechat, 'Le coran a été relevé au VIIe siècle: dans le contexte socioculturel de l'époque, entretien réalisé par Guy Gauthier', in *Panoramiques* 1997 (Vol. 29), L'islam est-il soluble dans la République, pp. 183, 189.
67 See Marie-Claire Foblets and Adriaan Overbeeke, 'Islam in Belgium', in: Potz and Wieshaider (eds.), *Islam and the European Union*, 2004, p. 34.
68 Joachim Wagner, 'Richter ohne Gesetz. Islamische Paralleljustiz gefährdet unseren Rechtsstaat', Berlin, 2011.
69 See 'Juicio islàmico por adulterio a una mujer en Reus' (Salud Muñoz), Elmundo.es 06.12.09, available at http://www.elmundo.es/elmundo/2009/12/06/espana/1260084030.html.
70 Lecture held during a conference in Sarajevo organized by the German Friedrich Ebert-Stiftung on 19 November 2007. See also Enes Karić, 'Islam und Säkularismus', in: Hamideh Mohagheghi and Klaus van Stosch, *Moderne Zugänge zum Islam*, Paderborn: Schöningh, 2010, pp. 115, 121-124.

2 America

Islam and the Problems of Liberal Democracy

Bryan S. Turner and James T. Richardson

Introduction

The main theme running through our chapter is that, while liberal governments such as that of the United States claim to favour the separation of church and state, governments constantly intervene to regulate religions in multicultural societies, precisely because religious beliefs and practices create problems, real and perceived, of governance.[1] For instance, states often intervene in the domestic space to protect the interests of children in interfaith marriages or in unpopular religious communities.[2] In New York State in 2011, legislation was passed to recognize gay marriages, and yet state governments have regularly intervened to control the practice of polygamy, for example among the Fundamentalist Church of Jesus Christ of Latter-Day Saints.[3] The state intervenes to regulate the employment and practice of chaplains in prisons and in the military.[4] In France, the state has banned the wearing of the veil in public spaces. Therefore, in modern societies, there is widespread 'management of religions' by the state.[5]

One might ask why the management of religion is a problem for liberals. Surely the regulation of religion is a pragmatic and necessary response to religious diversity? However, the problem is not the intervention but rather *the absence of a level playing field*, which is an essential aspect of liberal tolerance. The law must treat individuals and social groups on the same basis, and the state must not be seen to treat certain groups with special favour. This principle is very important when it comes to the recognition of religious practices. Jews should not receive special advantages over those that Hindus enjoy, and vice versa. In America, the ideal of the separation of church and state makes this principle central to constitutional rights. In practice, however, things are very different. Some religious groups are allowed special privileges, but others are not. The issue of equality versus respect for difference has become very acute in the case of Islam, and no more so than over the shariʿa. In some American states, politicians are pressing to ban the shari'a, but both Judaism and Catholicism have religious courts. Is this freedom of religion equally applied and available?

Brian Barry, an important critic of multicultural celebration of difference, argues that in modern societies, our commitment to the importance of difference has undermined an equally important value: the principle of equal treatment.[6] He cites the exemptions and advantages enjoyed by the Amish community in the United States, which appear to have little relevance to the actual practice of their religion. Perhaps the most important absence of fair treatment in modern American society is that, while Jewish and Catholic tribunals are allowed to operate in certain areas of life, there is a widespread move to stop any institutionalization of Muslim tribunals applying aspects of the shari'a. The result is endless contradiction and confusion within cultural and legal practices.

Another example of such a contradiction occurs in the area of financial affairs. While there is widespread fear of the shari'a as applied to domestic disputes, there is growing acceptance of so-called shari'a-compliant mortgages, shari'a banking practices and institutions, and a growing commercial acceptance of shari'a insurance schemes in America and other Western nations.[7] While the public is fearful of the presence of the shari'a in American court systems, there appears to be more acceptance of shari'a finance, presumably because it is 'good for business'.

The liberal dilemma is intensified because we live in a world in which religious differences are deeper and much more complex than in the past. We should note that when early philosophers, such as Richard Hooker and John Locke and the colonial leader Thomas Jefferson, addressed the issue of religious tolerance, they were mainly concerned either with conflicts between Catholics and Protestants or between Protestant sects. Although opposition to the presence of Jews in Europe had often been the cause of violence, the seventeenth and eighteenth-century debates about tolerance were typically about tolerance *within* Christendom. By contrast, modern societies are multicultural and multi-faith. Extensive labour migration, as well as the acceptance of refugees from war-torn areas of the world, has transformed the West, including the United States, by creating significant diasporic communities that are often organized on the basis of religious identity. Arguably, the Westphalian model of tolerance based on a clear separation between the private (individual conscience) and the public (the state and the law) no longer holds in societies with substantial Hindu, Jewish, and Muslim minorities.[8]

Intolerance is not just about domestic political issues, because with globalization, the conflict between religions appears to be on the increase. In the Middle East, and especially after 9/11 and the invasion of Iraq, there is now ample evidence of conflicts in Islam between Shi'ite and Sunni communities, as well as conflicts between Christians and Muslims. In Iraq there have been serious attacks on Catholic churches; in Egypt there is mounting tension between Muslims and Copts; and in Syria there is widespread fear that if and when the Assad regime collapses, there will be reprisals against both Alawite and Christian communities. Beyond these Middle Eastern conflicts, there have been growing tensions between Muslims and Christians in Nigeria, where Muslims represent about 45 per cent of the population. Spreading peacefully to northern towns like Osogbo in the 1820s, Islam established its presence in Nigeria by more forceful means during the Fulani Jihadist invasion of the 1830s. In response to the spread of Pentacostalist evangelicals in Nigeria, various reform movements were created in the 1990s to attract young people to reformed Islam and to spread the religion across the country. As a result, Nigeria has become the focus of an often-violent religious confrontation.[9] Consequently, American foreign policy has to try to improve the image of America and reduce tensions between religions. For example, the United States government spent $70,000 on advertisements on six Pakistani television stations in September 2012, disavowing an amateur movie depicting the Prophet in a prejudicial and hateful manner.[10] The management of religion is therefore a strategy of both American domestic and foreign policy.

These modern difficulties within and between religions may be explained partially by the rise of fundamentalism in various world religions. However, we prefer to refer to this development as a *growth in piety*. The spread of veiling is one very obvious example of new forms of 'urban piety', and we can likewise regard demands for the implementation of some aspects of the shariʿa as yet another aspect of new piety movements. In much of North Africa and the Middle East, the Arab Spring was followed by demands for more traditional piety and the revival of the shariʿa.[11] The growth of 'urban piety' also creates additional problems within the public domain. Although the secularization thesis in the sociology of religion in the 1970s predicted the decline of religion in the West, there has in fact been significant religious revivalism across many societies. This revivalism is often associated with reformed Islam, but the manifestations of such piety are global.[12] Puritanical forms of religiosity are associated with the rapid urbanization of traditional communities and the growth of literacy among the urban lower and middle classes. This tendency can be seen in the development of urban piety in Southeast Asia among newly urbanized Muslim populations.[13]

These piety movements tend to create religious enclaves by sharpening the differences between the pious and the outside world.[14] Religious differences are often reinforced by in-group marriages, separate educational institutions, and various exemptions from public services and institutions (occasionally involving exemptions from taxation and military service). Such developments tend to create cultural and religious fissures in the public domain, in which religious groups become socially and geographically separate. The result is growing social fragmentation.

This argument can be challenged, of course. In the United States it is often claimed that inter-racial marriages have increased, suggesting that the racial divisions of American society in the past have been repaired, and hence sociologists such as Jeffrey Alexander have argued that the civil sphere in the United States is relatively successful and harmonious.[15] More recently, Robert Putnam and David Campbell, in their report on the 'Faith Matters' surveys in 2006 and 2007, noted that three religious groups in America – Buddhists, Mormons and Muslims – are viewed unfavourably, and that certain religious groups have strong feelings of mutual solidarity.[16] Nevertheless, between one-third and half of all Americans are in interfaith marriages, and the majority of Americans feel comfortable in a pluralistic religious world. For example, some 80 per cent of Americans believe that 'there are basic truths in many religions'.[17] They conclude their study with the observation that 'Geographic segregation by religion has largely ended, while social segregation along religious lines is also mostly a thing of the past'.[18]

Islam in America: A Historical Summary

Before examining the shariʿa in America in more detail, we offer a brief sketch of the situation regarding Islam in America. Muslims first came to America as African slaves.[19] Black American Islam developed into a radical political movement under the Nation of Islam, and various radical leaders emerged from this anti-white political protest, most notoriously Malcolm X.[20] While black African-American Islam is a significant social group, very little research has been undertaken on the role of shariʿa within this community. However, in this chapter we are concerned mainly with recent Muslim migrants. Unlike both Britain and France, Muslim migrants to America in the second half of the twentieth century were typically well educated, and they quickly assimilated into American society, at least in economic terms. By the late 1980s, Muslim intellectuals had come to the conclusion that America was no longer incompatible with Islamic belief and practice, but a 'place of order' or *dar-al-aman*, signifying that Muslims could comfortably live in the United States while also recognizing that it is a place of outreach. The majority of pious Muslims – like pious Christians – see America as a corrupt and immoral society in which Muslims have a responsibility to call people back to Islam, a practice known as *da'wa*. However, many Muslims from minority traditions such as Isma'ilis see America as democratic and pluralist, and therefore a society in which they can flourish and enjoy religious freedom. This argument about successful assimilation has received further support from a significant ethnographic study of Muslims in America by Mucahit Bilici (2012), entitled *Finding Mecca in America*. Despite discrimination and prejudice, Muslims are settling successfully in America, where they find freedom to practise their faith without draconian interference from the state.[21] In fact, for many Muslims, America has now become *Dar-al Islam* (the Abode or House of Islam). This phrase is often contrasted with *Dar al-Harb* or the House of War, but a better and less controversial translation might be the arena of struggle against those things that threaten the integrity of Islam.[22] Another term, as we have seen, is *dar-al-aman*, or a place of stability and proper order where people can peacefully practise their religion. Thus Bilici suggests that ironically, Muslims find they are better able to practise Islam in America than in many Muslim-majority societies with authoritarian governments.[23]

In this environment, a new leadership emerged from within the Muslim middle classes. Unlike the traditional *imams* of an earlier period, the new professional leadership was not trained in the traditional religious literature, and approached the shari'a from the perspective of Western training. This initially resulted in some tension and competition between the traditional leadership and the new professional class. Many of these legal professionals came to believe that shari'a from outside America did not satisfy the needs of educated Muslims living in a multicultural and secular environment. One example is Khaled Abou El Fadl, professor of Islamic Law at UCLA.[24] He complained, for example, that the shari'a Scholars Association of North America meeting in Detroit in November 1999 was composed of *fiqh* scholars (legal experts) who had typically never lived in America, knew nothing about actual conditions, and came from totalitarian and corrupt regimes in the Middle East.[25]

While this 'import' of foreign scholars and scholarship was an important problem, the American Muslim community was also faced by the uncontrolled and often badly informed on-line debate about *fatwas* where the discussants have no real legal training or legal sophistication. As one young American Muslim of Indian background exclaimed, 'The Internet has made everyone a mufti'.[26]

Several attempts were made early on to improve this situation. In the 1970s, a *fiqh* council was set up by the Muslim Students Association, but it was mainly concerned with narrow issues like the appropriate dates for fasting. In 1988 the Fiqh Council of North America was created, but its critics claim that it was dominated by 'naturalized Muslims' who knew little about American laws relating to the family, property and divorce. Because Islam is a devolved religion and consensus comes from the community, such organizations rarely have much authority. It is also very important to realize that the shariʿa is not state law and historically could not automatically depend on the state to enforce *qadi* justice (that is, judge-made law). The situation is also complicated by the diversity of legal traditions in Sunni Islam, of which there are four dominant schools. One outcome of these developments is that much of the richness of traditional teaching has been lost in the United States, where there remains a dearth of scholars trained in the full breadth of Islamic law.

As we have noted, one interesting development in the West concerns Islamic banking and finance. Many Muslim financiers argue that there is no serious incompatibility between Islamic norms relating to investment, banking and profit sharing, and American laws relating to finance.[27] To take one example: the American financial house LARIBA (the Los Angeles Reliable Investment Bankers Association) called itself a 'faith-based financing' business in response to President Bush's call for faith-based initiatives.[28]

Growing Fears Concerning Islam

By the beginning of this century, it would be reasonable to claim that second or third-generation American Muslims had become successful American citizens and were well integrated.[29] This positive situation was transformed by the terrorist attack on September 11, 2001. After the tragic event, Muslims were often identified as un-American outsiders who were fundamentalists and dangerous. While Muslims struggled in the majority of cases to re-affirm their loyalty and American identity, right-wing elements have attacked Muslim customs (such as veiling) and have more recently led a specific attack on what is seen as the significant advance of shariʿa in American courts, alongside the growth of halal-certified goods, even including Thanksgiving Day turkeys.[30]

Thus the positive picture of 'American Grace' presented by Putnam and Campbell and of Americanized Islam by Bilici appears to be contradicted by the response of the American public to the rise (alleged or otherwise) of religious radicalism, especially Islamic radicalism. Since 9/11, the possibilities for pluralism and tolerance have been severcly tested and constrained by a discourse focused on terrorism and security. In particular, Islam as a civilization has come to be defined as fundamentally incompatible with Western values. Muslim communities have thus been marginalized by a mixture of official processes of securitization and popular hostility.

Moreover, the argument that America now has a benign social environment of religious and racial tolerance is questionable given the widespread hostility to the proposal to build a Muslim cultural centre close to Ground Zero,[31] the religious standpoint of the Tea Party movement (demonstrated by reluctance to endorse Mitt Romney as the Republican candidate because he is a Mormon), and the persistent notion that President Obama is a Muslim, among other things. There also is growing opposition to the idea that the shariʿa could be referred to in American court proceedings.

While there is evidence that Muslims in America have been quite successful in terms of social mobility and their integration into American culture,[32] growing concern about the shariʿa is indicative of divisions in modern America that may not have been obvious in the Faith Matters surveys on which Putnam and Campbell based their argument. Various lobby groups opposed to the shariʿa, such as ACT for America and the Society of Americans for National Existence, now operate in the United States to warn people about the spread of shariʿa.[33] Many of these groups operate on the margins of mainstream politics, and it is possible that their animosity to Islam as a cultural threat will not have any long-term consequences. However there is a more fundamental issue being raised by the shariʿa, namely the growth of legal pluralism.

On 11 November 2011 (the Veterans Day holiday in America), nearly one thousand people attended a conference in Tennessee with the theme, 'The Constitution or shariʿa'. The conference, organized by the shariʿa Awareness Action Network, which is a coalition of religious liberty and national security groups, focused on the alleged perils of shariʿa and efforts to promote the 'Islamatization of America'.[34] The conference was held at a large fundamentalist Protestant church after the hotel that was to be the original venue cancelled due to 'security concerns.' The conference attracted participants from across America and several other countries, who were told about efforts of the Muslim Brotherhood to infiltrate the government, as well as the concept of 'lawfare,' by which was meant the use of the judicial system to fight the spread of shariʿa and its 'stealth *jihad*.'

The moral panic about Islam and the shari'a is being fostered by some prominent politicians in America, including several Republican presidential candidates. Congresswoman Michele Bachmann (Republican from Minnesota) has spoken of the 'threat' of Muslims bringing shari'a law into the United States and has claimed that Muslims want to 'usurp' the Constitution. Herman Cain has said he would not appoint a Muslim to his administration, and former Speaker of the House Newt Gingrich has also expressed concern about Muslims in the government.[35] Earlier in 2011, New York Congressman Peter King sponsored, despite vehement protests, a hearing of the Homeland Security Committee he chairs on the alleged threat of Muslim radicals in America. The hearing, held on 10 March 2011, attracted widespread attention both in the United States and overseas.[36]

Legal Plurality and the Spread of Shari'a

The idea of 'legal pluralism' was originally associated with anthropological research into the continuity of customary law in colonial societies, where it often existed alongside Anglo-Saxon common law. We may describe legal pluralism as a situation in which there are competing 'bodies of law' within a given sovereign territory. It is often thought to be a problem emerging in the modern state, where the unified sovereignty of the state is challenged by different competing, and occasionally overlapping, systems of law. Although legal pluralism is often associated with both globalization and post-colonialism, legal pluralism in fact existed in Europe throughout the medieval period in terms of *ius commune*, commercial law (*lex mercatoria*), and ecclesiastical or canon law.[37] Modern Muslims also like to imagine a time when the shari'a had dominant and exclusive authority, but this notion also turns out to be mythical.[38] We do not intend in this chapter to seriously engage with the technical literature surrounding the anthropological study of legal pluralism, and for our purposes it may be less problematic to use the term 'legal plurality' to describe modern societies grappling with diverse legal traditions.

While the ideas of state sovereignty and a unified legal code may be political fictions, they are useful fictions: any functional system of law would have to have some minimal agreement about a final umpire who could arbitrate between competing legal claims. The growth of legal pluralism becomes a problem in societies where a common citizenship is fragmenting under the impact of globalization and the decline of shared culture.

In some societies, such as the United Kingdom, there is evidence of the development of religious arbitration, but these 'courts' are confined to private disputes (typically around marriage, divorce, adoption and so forth).[39] If accepting religious law means in practice accepting third-party arbitration, then legal plurality might not in itself pose a direct threat to state sovereignty. However for some critics, such as the popular press in the United Kingdom, which expressed almost hysterical concern over a lecture in which the Archbishop of Canterbury seemed to endorse the shariʿa, arbitration is merely the 'thin end' of the legal wedge, raising the problem of whether an arbitration hearing is in fact a 'court'.

Many of these debates are concerned with the formal use of the shariʿa in the West, where judges may refer to marriage contracts made under shariʿa norms in disputes over inheritance or the care of children. However, there is also informal and unregulated use of shariʿa, for example, through the spread of 'online *fatwas*' providing informal legal judgements and opinions about matters relating to how Muslims should live in a secular society. With the global spread of the Internet, some degree of informal but popular opinion formation is taking place between individuals in ways that may be compatible with shariʿa as a consensus-seeking legal tradition. This development involves the informal growth of religious codes in everyday life.

The informal spread of shariʿa tribunals in America and elsewhere and appeals to online shariʿa judgements can be defined as 'the sharia-ization of the everyday world'.[40] From the perspective of religious orthodoxy, however, there are some important questions surrounding such online legal opinions. The first is that Internet religious opinions can no longer be controlled by traditional religious authorities, and there is therefore an erosion of religious authority.[41] The second related issue is what we might call '*fatwa* shopping', namely the search for a particular religious opinion that will satisfy an individual's specific requirements.

The prospect of shariʿa courts operating in formally secular societies has given rise to acrimonious public debate in America, as well as Britain, Australia, and Canada. Recent protests, as we have noted, against the Archbishop of Canterbury's public lecture on 'Civil and Religious Law in England',[42] and the public dispute over the introduction of shariʿa into arbitration courts in Ontario, Canada, are examples of the moral panic concerning shariʿa.[43] In both episodes, practical objections were raised about how women's rights could be protected and how arbitration could be enforced.

American Legal Exceptionalism and Shari'a

Having considered various examples of the spread of the shari'a, there is one simple objection to our argument, namely that the American Constitution in fact prohibits the spread of legal plurality by defending the central authority of the Supreme Court as the sole arbiter of law in the United States. However, a report from the Center for Security Policy (2011) claims that it has discovered fifty significant cases of the shari'a in American courts, and fifteen Trial Court Cases and twelve Appellate Court Cases where it was found to be applicable in the case of the bar.[44] The claims made in this report are, however, greatly overblown, as noted by University of Windsor law professor Julie McFarlane and by Wajahat Ali and Matthew Duss, writing for the Center for American Progress.[45] MacFarlane states that a closer examination of the cases cited in the CSP report shows that American judges usually reject any interpretation or ruling based on Islamic law. Most of the cases dealt with family matters (marriage contracts, divorce, child custody and inheritance), and judges assumed jurisdiction because of questions about basic fairness to the parties involved and other concerns, such as the 'best interests of the child' in custody disputes. MacFarlane concludes that American courts take an exacting approach to contracts that refer to Islamic law principles. Ali and Duss point out the many internal contradictions in the CSP report, and note that, since most Muslims oppose terrorism, the report alienates them from those trying to stop terrorism fostered by a small minority of Muslims.

There have been several efforts to preclude the use of the shari'a in legal proceedings in states in the United States, and more are being developed. In 2010 the State of Oklahoma passed a constitutional amendment with a 70 per cent voter approval precluding use of the shari'a in its court system. A suit was brought immediately by the Council on American-Islamic Relations (CAIR) on the grounds that the amendment was in violation of the Establishment Clause of the US Constitution, which precludes the favouring of one religion over another by the government. A federal judge in Oklahoma granted an injunction delaying implementation of the amendment, and that ruling was affirmed by the 10th Circuit court of Appeal in Denver.[46] Court documents filed in the appeal by the CAIR and the American Civil Liberties Union, as reported in a television newscast, state:[47]

> The measure tramples the free exercise rights of a disfavoured minority faith and constrains the ability of Muslims in Oklahoma to execute valid wills, assert religious liberty claims under the Oklahoma Religious Freedom Act, and enjoy equal access to the state judicial system.

Julie MacFarlane claims that following the Oklahoma example, two other states (Tennessee and Louisiana) passed similar constitutional amendments, and similar efforts were underway in nineteen other states as of March 2011.[48] These efforts demonstrate a high degree of concern about the shari'a in America that might be characterized as a 'moral panic', given how little reference to the shari'a is actually occurring in courts in the United States.[49] Furthermore, there is little evidence that the majority of Muslims want the full implementation of the shari'a as an alternative to secular common law, and certainly there is no evidence suggesting that Muslims want access to Islamic criminal law in the West. When the Western media discuss the shari'a, they often equate it with the *hudud* rules specifying what are often horrendous punishments, such as stoning and cutting off the hands of thieves. Such reports neglect the reform of criminal law in Pakistan, for example, where the conservative legacy of Syed Mawdudi has been challenged by younger scholars and political activists.[50]

Relevant Research on Muslims

Although there has been little recent systematic research directly focused on the shari'a as a comprehensive system of norms and laws in the West, an earlier study by Haddad and Lummis did survey Muslims in five sites in the United States on the basic values of Muslims in America.[51] They found that most Muslims were supportive of American values, and that they were finding ways to make their religious practices mesh with other aspects of their life. There have also been a few recent studies of specific issues that relate to aspects of the shari'a, particularly family matters such as marriage, divorce, and custody of children (see below). The Pew Foundation has also published considerable research on Muslim social status, views, and attitudes, but none to date dealing directly with the shari'a.[52] The aforementioned professor Julie MacFarlane has done perhaps the most relevant research for this chapter, with her four-year in-depth study of divorce within Islamic communities in the United States and Canada.[53] Her research, motivated by the controversy that erupted in Ontario, Canada, in 2003, involved interviews with over 100 highly-educated divorced Muslim women and men (80 per cent women), as well as over 110 others (about 40 *imams* and 70 others working with divorce issues) from Muslim communities in selected cities in the United States and Canada (75 per cent from the US). She pointed out that many Muslims desire a religiously sanctioned marriage, which is achieved through a contractual marriage agreement referred to as a *nikah*. This is easily accomplished and usually also accompanied by a formalized civil marriage. However, getting a divorce is much more complicated if the persons involved want it to be religiously sanctioned. This is the case because Islamic law and tradition allow the male much more power to end a marriage, and on terms that are more advantageous to him than to the female in the marriage. This imbalance of power and rights has been noticed by many commentators, and is the subject of considerable controversy.

MacFarlane's research reveals that informal processes of applying shari'a elements to marriage and divorce in the United States are occurring, even though there is no formal recognition via statute in any state. Such informal processes are occurring because they are desired by those involved in important family-oriented rituals. However, MacFarlane reports that none of those interviewed advocated establishing a formal legal status for Islamic family law, preferring to retain the use of the civil law system as well as informal shari'a-based processes when desired. She also says that there is little agreement among American and Canadian Muslims about what shari'a means in terms of its application, noting that there is much debate among Muslim scholars and leaders about its core principles. MacFarlane describes the concern over shari'a as a 'moral panic', and laments that so much misinformation is being promulgated by the mass media and some politicians regarding what Muslims are doing and what they want when they live in Canada and the United States.

Inger Furseth has done research on Muslim women's views concerning arranged marriages.[54] She interviewed a sample of Muslim women in Los Angeles, and found that they were divided on the value of arranged marriages. Some thought such marriages important as a way to have the young person remain in touch with his or her culture and family's country of origin. Others were much more flexible, and had accepted more Western norms about marriage, allowing the young person more choice, or at least the right to veto an arrangement for a marriage that they did not like. Her research demonstrates that American Muslim women are not of one mind on this issue, a finding that perhaps should not surprise anyone, but which has implications for applications of the shari'a when a marriage results in a divorce. As noted above, there is considerable controversy about the issue of divorce within Muslim communities, and the issue of religious versus civil divorce is quite contested.

Furseth also did interesting research on the clothing worn by some Muslim women in America, an issue that some assume is derived from the shari'a, and which has caused major controversies in some Western societies.[55] If controversy erupts in America about the garb of Muslim women, this research will be quite germane. Furseth studied Muslim women in Los Angeles (the same sample as for her work on Muslim women's views of marriage) on the issue of their dress code, and what it means to wear traditional Islamic clothing. She points out that there has been a growing emphasis on wearing a headscarf among Muslim women in recent decades, especially since the tragic events on 9/11. She attributes this to the women who wear the garb's efforts to emphasize their religious identity. Furseth's work emphasizes that Muslim women who cover themselves are exercising human agency, and disputes the idea that they are being coerced by Muslim males to do so. Indeed, she notes instances from her sample where the husband was opposed his wife's wearing of the headscarf. While the role played by social networks in the decisions to cover oneself is acknowledged, the important networks are female ones. In her conclusion, Furseth suggests that 'wearing the hijab has increasingly become a symbol of Muslim's women's courage to represent Islam in the public sphere and show solidarity with co-Muslims.'[56] One conclusion to be drawn from this research is that American Muslim women are beginning to challenge and modify the practice of Islam. For example, in many traditional Muslim societies, women do not attend the mosque, and when they do, women are typically segregated from men. However, in many American mosques, women are gradually undermining these norms by claiming a space within the mosque with or alongside men.[57]

Conclusion

Legal pluralism or plurality, while viewed positively by some, can contribute to the ongoing erosion of citizenship as a shared cultural, social and political framework. Legal pluralism and multiculturalism require a lively and effective framework of active citizenship if they are to be successful. The weakening of common ties, establishment of separate religious schools, growth of legal pluralism, wearing of distinctive religious dress in public spaces, ethnic segregation and development of symbolically segregated communities such as the proliferation of *eruv* in the Jewish world, and the consequent if unintended creation of parallel communities, can promote an acute differentiation of identity and have a divisive effect on society, leading to 'the enclave society'.[58]

Religious differences and identities are often championed in the name of human rights, namely freedom of conscience. The paradox of these individual rights is that *we need effective and viable states if rights are to be enforced*, and the enforcement of rights is a necessary condition of political life. Hence, despite much of the contemporary commentary on the decline of the state and the growth of porous political boundaries, we need to be concerned that any decline in the authority and coherence of the state – associated with neo-liberal globalization – will in fact undermine the political foundations that are necessary to sustain legal pluralism and multiculturalism, and lead to the decline of participatory citizenship.

Our argument is that the real political issue behind the possible growth of shariʿa arbitration is not (or not just) the conventional feminist anxiety about equal treatment, but a broader concern about the current state of citizenship in democracies such as in the United States. The notion that citizens have a right to choose the legal systems under which they are to be ruled in the name of cultural difference and multiculturalism makes questionable political sense, and could destroy the very institutions that protect our cultural diversity. In *Genealogies of Citizenship,* Margaret Somers provides a vigorous and passionate defence of citizenship as the necessary foundation of democracy and our best hope of sustaining social solidarity, equality and mutual trust. Her basic argument is that 'democratic citizenship regimes (including human rights) can thrive only to the extent that egalitarian and solidaristic principles, practices, and institutions of civil society and the public commons are able to act with equal force against the exclusionary threats of market-driven politics'.[59]

We find some solace in the empirical research reported above, based on studies of American (and Canadian) Muslim communities. The research reported by Pew and that reported by MacFarlane and by Furseth shows strong support among most Muslims for the values of American society, and little support for any extremist ideas or programmes. As Pew states in one of its recent reports, 'Muslim Americans have not become disillusioned with the country. They are overwhelmingly satisfied with the way things are going in their lives (82 per cent) and continue to rate their communities very positively as places to live (79 per cent excellent or good)'.[60] Indeed, Pew reports that Muslims are more satisfied with the situation in America than non-Muslim members of American society (56 per cent vs. 23 per cent). MacFarlane's finding that no one in her study was promoting or desired the establishment of formal shariʿa tribunals or courts is also of note. Furseth's research also demonstrates that, while the Muslim women she studied are seeking ways to identify with their faith, they are not trying to force Islamic values upon others. Indeed, her work shows that there is some tension *within* Muslim communities over such issues as dress and arranged marriages, suggesting that there is no monolithic Islamic set of cultural values that is invading American society and attempting to make others accept those values. Bilici also argues that debates are occurring about Muslim dress codes and the shariʿa within Muslim communities.

Obviously, more research is needed, but based on what is available so far, we would suggest that, while there are grounds for some concern about the implications for the potential development of legal pluralism and the spread of the shariʿa in America and elsewhere, those fears may be groundless, given the apparent fact that the vast majority of Muslims in America are finding ways to adjust to American secularism, while also expressing their religious identity in various ways.

Notes

1 See James T. Richardson (ed.), *Regulating Religion: Case Studies from around the Globe*, New York: Kluwer, 2004.

2 Stuart Wright and James T. Richardson (eds.), *Saints under Siege: The Texas State Raid on the Fundamentalist Latter Day Saints*, New York: New York University Press, 2011.

3 Cardell Jacobson and Lara Burton (eds.), *Modern Polygamy in the United States*, Oxford: Oxford University Press, 2011.

4 James A. Beckford and Sophie Gilliat, *Religion in Prison*, Cambridge: Cambridge University Press, 2008.

5 Jack Barbalet, Adam Possamai, and Bryan S. Turner (eds.), *Church and State. A Comparative Sociology*, London: Anthem Press, 2011.

6 Brian Barry, *Culture and Equality: An Egalitarian Critique of Multiculturalism*, Cambridge, Mass.: Harvard University Press, 2002.

7 Michael Nazir-Ali, 'Islamic law, fundamental freedoms, and social cohesion' in: Rex Ahdar and Nicholas Aroney (eds.), *Sharia in the West*, Oxford: Oxford University Press, 2011, pp. 71-89. And Jamila Hussain, *Islam: Its Law and Society*, 3rd edition, Sydney: Federation Press.

8 Jeff Spinner-Halevy, 'Hinduism, Christianity and liberal religious tolerance', *Political Theory*, 2005 (Vol. 33, No. 1), pp. 28-57.

9 David O. Ogungbile, 'Tradition and Response: Islam and Muslim Societies in a Nigerian City', in: Tugrul Keskin (ed.), *The Sociology of Islam. Secularism, Economy and Politics*, Reading, UK: Ithaca Press, 2011, pp. 319-342.

10 Farhan Bokhari and Borzou Daragahi, 'Protests across Pakistan over anti-Islam film claims 20 lives', *The Financial Times*, 2012 (September 22-23), p. 3.

11 Maaike Voorhoeve (ed.), *Family Law in Islam. Divorce, Marriage and Women in the Muslim World*, London: I.B. Taurus, 2012.

12 José Casanova, *Public Religions in the Modern World*, Chicago: University of Chicago Press, 1994.

13 Joy Kooi-Chin Tong and Bryan S. Turner, 'Women, piety, and practice: A study of women and religious practice in Malaya', *Contemporary Islam*, 2008 (Vol. 2), pp. 41-59.
14 Bryan S. Turner, 'The enclave society: Towards a sociology of immobility', *European Journal of Social Theory*, 2007 (Vol. 10, No. 2), pp. 287-303.
15 Jeffrey C. Alexander, *The Civil Sphere*. Oxford: Oxford University Press, 2006, p. 453.
16 Robert D. Putnam and David E. Campbell, *American Grace: How Religion Divides and Unites Us*, New York: Simon & Schuster, 2010.
17 Putnam and Campbell, *American Grace*, 2010, p. 543.
18 Putnam and Campbell, *American Grace*, 2010, p. 550.
19 Robert Dannin, *Black Pilgrimage to Islam*, Oxford: Oxford University Press, 2002.
20 Manning Marabel, *Malcolm X: A Life of Reinvention*, New York: Viking, 2012.
21 Mucahit Bilici, *Finding Mecca in America. How Islam is becoming an American Religion*, Chicago: University of Chicago Press, 2012.
22 Ian Richard Netton, *A Popular Dictionary of Islam*, London: Curzon Press, 1992, p. 67.
23 Bilici, *Finding Mecca in America*, 2012.
24 Khaled Abou El Fadl, *Islam and the Challenge of Democracy*, Princeton, NJ: Princeton University Press, 2004.
25 Also see Yvonne Haddad and Adair Loomis, *Islamic Values in the United States*, New York: Oxford University Press, 1987.
26 Karen Isaksen Leonard, *Muslims in United States: The State of Research*, New York: Russell Sage Foundation, 2003, p. 125; Emily Wax, 'The Mufti in the chat room: Islamic advisers are just a click away from ancient customs', *Washington Post*, July 13, 1999.
27 Nazir-Ali, 'Islamic law, fundamental freedom, and social cohesion', 2011.
28 Leonard, *Muslims in the United* States, 2003, p. 105.
29 Pew Research Center, 'Muslim Americas: Middle class and mostly mainstream', available at http://pewresearch.org/pubs/483/muslim-americans accessed 11/11/2011.
30 See Jillian Rayfield, 'This Thanksgiving beware the shari'a turkey', for a strange story about fear of eating halal turkey and 'stealth shari'a' food in America. http://www.readersupportednews.org/opinion2/277-75/8567-this-thanksgiving-beware-the-sharia-turkey, accessed Oct. 26, 2012.
31 See Voice of America,' Ground Zero mosque controversy puts many Muslims in defensive', August 31, 2010 for one discussion of the controversy and its aftermath. http://www.voanews.com/english/news/Ground-Zero-Mosque-Controversy-Puts-Many-US-Muslims-on-Defensive--101960113.html accessed Oct. 26, 2012.
32 Pew Research Center, 'Muslim Americas: Middle class and mostly mainstream', 2011.
33 See Ali Wajahat, Eli Clifton, Matthew Duss, Lee Fang, Scott Keyes, and Faiz Shakir, 'Fear Inc.: The roots of Islamaphobia network I America' August 26, 2011 for a discussion of the funding sources for organizations promoting Islam-

aphobia in American and elsewhere available at http://www.americanprogress.org/issues/2011/08/islamophobia.html accessed Oct. 24, 2012.

34 See Christian News Wire, 'Constitution or shari'a conference a huge success', Nov. 15, 2011. Available at http://www.christiannewswire.com/news/7318718270.html (accessed Oct. 26, 2012) for more details on this conference, and see http://shariafreeusa.com/available-now-the-constitution-or-sharia-preserving-freedom-dvd-set/ for a DVD of this conference.

35 See Policy Mic, 'GOP could sway Muslim vote if it weren't for hateful rhetoric', September, 2011 available at http://www.policymic.com/articles/2396/gop-could-sway-muslim-vote-if-it-weren-t-for-hateful-rhetoric (accessed Oct. 24, 2012) for details and for a lament that this rhetoric is driving Muslims away from the Republican party, where many might find a political home given their relatively high incomes and views on such issues as homosexuality.

36 See John Feffer, 'U.S. islamophobia: Chicken a la king', available at http://www.voltairenet.org/U-S-Islamophobia-Chicken-a-la-King (accessed Oct. 26, 2012) for a fuller discussion of the hearing and related events that have promoted the rise if Islamaphobia in America.

37 Brian Z. Tamanaha, 'Understanding legal pluralism: Past to present, local to global', *Sydney Law Review,* 2008 (Vol. 30), pp. 375-411.

38 An-Na'im, *Islam and the Secular State*, 2008.

39 Erich Kolig, 'To Shari'aticize or not to Shari'aticize: Islamic and secular law in liberal democratic society', in: Ahdar and Aroney (eds.), *Sharia in the West,* 2010, pp. 255-278. Also see chapters 1 and 4 in this volume.

40 Kolig, 'To Shari'aticize or not to Shari'aticize', 2010.

41 Frederick Volpi and Bryan S. Turner, 'Making Islamic authority matter,' *Theory Culture & Society*, 2007 (Vol. 33, No. 1), pp. 28-57.

42 Rowan Williams, 'Civil and religious law in England: A religious perspective', Foundation Lecture at the Royal Courts of Justice, available at Archbishop of Canterbury homepage, www.archbishopofcanterbury.org, 2008; also see volume focusing on this presentation by Ahdar and Aroney (eds.), *Shari'a in the West,* 2011.

43 Natasha Bakht, 'Were Muslim barbarians really knocking on the gates of Ontario? The religious arbitration controversy – another perspective', *Ottawa Law Review,* 2006 (Vol. 40), pp. 67-82.

44 Center for Security Policy, 'Shari'ah law and American state courts: An assessment of state appellate court cases. Occasional Paper Series, May 17, 2012. Available at http://www.centerforsecuritypolicy.org/search.xml?search-clause=shari'ah+law+and+American+state+courts&x=49&y=4 accessed Oct. 27, 2012.

45 Julie MacFarlane, 'Shari'a law: Coming to a courthouse near you? How Muslim Americans understand and use Shari'a in marriage and divorce', Washington, D.C.: Institute for Social Policy and Understanding. December 2011. Available at http://www.ispu.org/GetReports/35/2459/Publications.aspx accessed Oct. 27, 2012. Wajahat Ali and Matthew Duss, 'Understanding shari'a Law: Conservative's skewed interpretation needs debunking.' Center for American Progress. Accessed December 2, 2011 at http://www.americanprogress.org/issues/2011/03/sharia_law.html

46 See Andrew Cohen, 'In Oklahoma case another legal obstacle to banning Shari'a law', available at http://www.theatlantic.com/national/archive/2012/01/in-oklahoma-case-another-legal-obstacle-to-banning-sharia-law/251190/ accessed Oct. 27, 2012.

47 Quote obtained from: Ariane de Vogue, 'Federal appeal court considers Shari'a law', Sept. 12, 2011, available at http://abcnews.go.com/blogs/politics/2011/09/federal-appeals-court-considers-sharia-law/accessed on November 14, 2011.

48 Julie MacFarlane, *Islamic Divorce in North America: A Shari'a Path in a Secular Society*, Oxford: Oxford University Press, 2012.

49 US District Court Judge Vicki Miles-LaGrange blocked the measure in November 2010, ruling that any harm that would result from a delay in certifying the election results would be 'minimized' because the defendants were 'not aware of any situation where shariʿa Law has been applied in an Oklahoma court.' Obtained from Ariane de Vogue, 'Federal appeal court considers Shari'a law', 2011.

50 Javed A. Ghamidi, *Islam. From Revolution to Implementation*, Lahore: Al-Mawrid, 2006.

51 Haddad and Loomis, *Islamic Values in the United States*, 1987.

52 Pew Research Center, 'Muslim Americans: No signs of growth in alienation or support for extremism', Available at http://people-press.org/2011/08/30/muslim-americans-no-signs-of accessed 11/11/2011.

53 McFarlane, *Islamic Divorce in North America*, 2012.

54 Inger Furseth, 'Competing and changing ideals of motherhood: Views on arranged marriage among middle class immigrant Muslim women in the Los Angeles area.' Forthcoming in: Fariha Khan (ed.), *Global Islam in Everyday America*, 2012.

55 Inger Furseth, 'The hijab: Boundary work and identity negotiations among immigrant Muslim women in the Los Angeles area', *Review of Religious Research* 2011 (Vol. 52), pp. 365-385.

56 Furseth, 'The hijab: Boundary work and identity negotiations among immigrant Muslim women in the Los Angeles area', 2011, p. 382. For an in-depth discussion of Muslim women establishing their identity in the American context see Yvonne Y. Haddad, Jane Smith, and Kathleen Moore, *Muslim Women in America*, Oxford: Oxford University Press, 2006.

57 See Haddad, Smith, and Moore, *Muslim Women in America*, 2006.

58 Turner, 'The Enclave society', 2007.

59 Margaret Somers, *Genealogies of Citizenship. Markets, Statelessness and the Right to Have Rights*, Cambridge: Cambridge University Press, 2008, p. 8.

60 Pew Research Foundation, 'Muslim Americans: No signs of growth in alienation or support for extremism', 2011, p. 4.

3 Australia

The Down-Under Approach and Reaction to Shari'a: An Impasse in Post-Secularism?

Jamila Hussain and Adam Possamai

The Socio-Cultural Heterogeneity of Muslims and the Implication for Shari'a

A recent report[1] based on a research project on the Convention on the Elimination of All Forms of Discrimination against Women reviewed official documents from 44 countries with a Muslim majority. It discovered that among these countries, there were significant differences with regard to Muslim family law. The document concluded that there is no single functioning worldwide Islamic law. Islamic family law, wherever it is practised, is based on the laws and principles set out in the Qur'an and Sunna. However, because there are multiple schools of law and different family law provisions that are influenced by local cultures where Islamic law operates, no single tradition can claim ownership of it.

Through various migration patterns, Muslims in Australia have come from over seventy different nations. Thus they come from various local cultures that have different legal provisions. This makes Muslims the most ethnically diverse religious group in Australia. Some Muslims came from countries where Islam is the religion of the majority, and others from religiously diverse countries. And, of course, we now have a growing population of Muslims born in Australia. Ethnically speaking, this is a religious group that has a wide range of experiences of Australian society, and Muslims in Australia are divided along ethnic and ideological lines.[2]

The shari'a is a devolved law, sensitive to local traditions, and in this sense unlike so-called Roman continental law. Unsurprisingly therefore, the detail of provisions about marriage, marital property, alimony, divorce, inheritance, custody and guardianship of children differs among the different Islamic countries and ethnic groups. The understanding of the practice of shari'a, or parts of it, in a secular society such as Australia, must thus be nuanced, taking into account the multiethnic composition of its Muslim community.

While shariʿa is not officially recognized in Australia, it informs the ideas and conduct of Australian Muslims in various ways. The operation and regulation of shariʿa in Australia is essentially 'underground' for Black,[3] or what we prefer to call an unofficial parallel system. Although shariʿa has not been integrated into the legal system in Australia, it continues to be applied at a local level in Muslim communities and mosques[4] in certain ways and in areas of law that we will elaborate upon below. Sometimes, because of the lack of a formal mechanism of Islamic adjudication in Australia and because of the shortage of trained Muslim scholars, some women travel to their country of origin to apply to a shariʿa court.[5] Muslims may feel more comfortable combining shariʿa norms and Australian laws in their understanding of the law. Further, given the ethnic diversity of the Australian Muslim community, there is no dominant shariʿa authority that can act as an overarching system and no dominantly authoritative person.[6] As there is no hierarchy in Islam, and as there is a divergence of opinion as to whom should administer a shariʿa court,[7] each Muslim is free to seek guidance from any scholar of his or her choice, leading to what is called '*fatwa* or forum shopping'. This shopping-around has also extended to the Internet. In 2009, Black and Hosen pointed out that requests for *fatwas* from Australia on the 'Islam Q&A' website were so numerous that Australia ranked seventh out of 128 countries in terms of the number of these demands.[8]

As there is no formal process for Islamic adjudication in Australia, Muslims consult *imams* to settle issues relating to divorce and other private disputes. Islamic legal processes seek consensus rather than the adversarial environment typical of Western (common) law traditions. The overriding concern of most *imams* is to save the marriage and to avoid expensive and often bitter conflicts within a divorce court. However, when a marriage has broken down, many Muslims believe that an appropriate way must be found to divorce, which fits with their faith and cultural values. Some Australian Muslims report that they would not accept the authenticity of a divorce unless it was conducted according to their religious norms.[9] At the same time, other Muslims are satisfied to have divorce procedures conducted according to secular law. In the past, many Muslims were confronted by a range of difficulties, including their lack of familiarity with the legal systems of their adopted countries, the previously adversarial nature of the courts administering these systems, the unsympathetic nature of some judicial officials, and the differences of law relating to property, domestic violence and custody. Recent changes to the Family Law Act and the encouragement of greater cultural sensitivity have made the Australian family law system more 'user friendly' for all ethnic groups,[10] as we will discuss below.

Shari'a in Australia

Since 9/11, and the Bali bombings in 2002 which killed 202 people, including 88 Australians, the role of Islam in Australian society has been the subject of much discussion in the public and political domain. Central to the debate about Muslim identity has been the issue of women's rights under Islam, and the role of shari'a. The debate has also concentrated on issues such as permission to establish Islamic schools, controversy about 'gang' rapes,[11] and shari'a as regards family law matters. The debates were occasionally sparked by controversial remarks by Muslim clerics, often involving disparaging comments about women. All these factors have resulted in some Muslims becoming victims of discrimination, harassment and racial profiling.[12] Debates over national security have brought into focus issues of multiculturalism and acceptance of diversity,[13] and, as argued below, issues of post-secularism.

While the Archbishop of Canterbury's speech in the United Kingdom[14] was widely reported in Australia, a full national debate about shari'a never really developed. The notion of the adoption or assimilation of shari'a was rejected outright by government ministers and spokespersons, with no explanation or discussion as to its particular attributes or how it actually operated in practice. When the Coalition Government (comprising the Liberal and National Parties) was in office in Australia from 1996 to 2007, Prime Minister John Howard attempted to gain political support by publicly condemning shari'a.[15] In the post-9/11 atmosphere, Howard seemed to consider that it would be unwise to be associated with Islamic values and that, in any event, it would go against his strong political lines on 'law and order' and 'Islamic threat' to say anything positive about shari'a. On assuming office in 2007, the new Labor government of Kevin Rudd was likewise not prepared to engage in a public dialogue about recognizing shari'a, or parts of it.[16]

Black and Sadiq[17] have observed mixed responses to shari'a in Australia, predominantly by non-Muslims, and they have made reference to 'good and bad shari'a'. For instance, it could be noted that while there is a public outcry over family law (see recent case studies below), there has been support for legislative change in Australia to facilitate Islamic banking and financial services. It seems that Islamic banking and finance laws are 'good' shari'a worthy of adoption, whilst personal status laws (marriage, divorce, separation, custody of children and inheritance) are not.[18] In the following paragraphs we will investigate what could be seen as bad in these latter cases of 'bad' shariʿa.

The Relationship Between Shariʿa and Australian Law

Muslims are required by their religious law to obey the laws of the country in which they live, provided that those laws do not oblige them to do something contrary to Islam. Therefore, for the vast majority of Muslims, there is not much conflict between shariʿa and secular law. For the most part, Muslims are free to follow the shariʿa in their private lives, while at the same time adhering to Australian law in all the areas it covers.

This is true of family law, as well as of other aspects of life. The requirements of the Commonwealth Marriage Act 1961, which governs all marriages in Australia, are broadly expressed. Provided that the required notice is given,[19] the correct forms are filled in and the marriage is performed by an authorized marriage celebrant, there is no restriction at all on the time,[20] place,[21] or type of ceremony[22] a couple may choose to conclude their marriage. Many *imams* are authorized marriage celebrants and can conduct a marriage ceremony that is valid in both Islamic and Australian law. Imams cannot validly conduct polygamous marriage ceremonies, since polygamy is forbidden in Australian law. However, since the shariʿa permits, but does not require, polygamy, this issue does not create any tension.

The requirements for concluding a marriage under shariʿa can therefore be met within the framework of Australian law. A contract, whether oral or written, can be made. The *mahr*, an essential part of an Islamic marriage, can be paid in whatever form the parties choose. Muslims can choose not to marry anyone who is not a Muslim, or, for men, a woman who is not a Muslim, Jew or Christian.[23]

Traditionally, the common law in Australia did not regulate relationships within the family to any great extent. In recent times, however, laws have been introduced as deemed necessary for the protection of children, and to criminalize domestic violence. The shariʿa does regulate family life to a greater extent but, as mentioned, observing Muslims can adhere to shariʿa requirements in their private lives without offending against Australian law.

In the area of divorce, on the other hand, there are more zones of conflict between shariʿa and Australian law. There are several different forms of divorce in Islamic law. A man may divorce his wife by pronouncing *talaq*. This option is available only to men (unless they cede this right to their wives), and traditionally did not require any overseeing by a court. Today, many Muslim countries require some official processes to regulate *talaq* divorce.

It is not so easy for a wife to secure a divorce unless she has it provided in her marriage contract that she retains the right to divorce herself. In Muslim countries, the wife may apply to the shariʿa court for a divorce by *khulʿ*, in which case she normally agrees to return her marriage gift (*mahr*) to her husband in exchange for his divorce by *talaq*. Another form is divorce by *fasakh*, which is more in the nature of an annulment and depends upon establishing grounds for fault. Accepted grounds differ among the various schools. The parties may also mutually agree to divorce.

Since the introduction of the Family Law Act in 1975, divorce under Australian law has not required proof of fault, and has become a simple procedure. Muslims do obtain dissolution of civil marriages from the Family Court but must resort to shariʿa to dissolve their marriages also according to religious law. This alternative can be required when a person has property or inheritance rights in an overseas country (for example, Lebanon) which does not recognize civil divorce. It is also of importance for those men and women who regard their religion as a vital part of their lives and who would not wish to depart from its teachings in matters concerning their family life.

Some Muslim women find themselves in a 'limping marriage' after a civil divorce. When a woman cannot persuade her husband to grant her a religious divorce as well, she is then divorced according to civil law but still married according to religious law. There is no shariʿa court in Australia to grant a religious divorce to such a woman, nor any central Islamic authority that might confirm her divorced status. Some *imams* feel that they are qualified to grant a divorce in these circumstances, but this is entirely at the discretion of the *imam*. There is some anecdotal evidence that some men who have promised to pay extravagant amounts of deferred *mahr* sometimes refuse their wives a religious divorce in order to avoid the obligation to make this payment. The result is that the wife cannot re-marry within her community since she is still married according to her religion, but since Islam allows polygamy for men, the husband is under no such constraint and can re-marry at will without sanction from either Australian or Islamic law.

A further problem for women is that until very recently, there had been no instance of Australian courts enforcing the *mahr*, which left the divorced wife without the financial provision she would have expected from the terms of her marriage contract. However, in May 2012, the

NSW Supreme Court ordered a husband to pay his former wife the sum of AUS$ 50,000 which in their marriage contact he had promised her in the event that he initiated divorce. The court applied principles of contract law. The couple had married according to religious law only and the Family Law Act 1975 did not apply to their case.[24]

Rules concerning the custody of children vary considerably between shariʿa and Australian family law. Under shariʿa, the mother is entitled to the care and control of small children (the right of *hadhanah*). The father retains guardianship and may assume care and control of children at various ages, which vary according to different schools of thought (*madhabs*). However, in practice, it seems that these rules are not always implemented.

Australian Family Law and Islamic Arbitration

Alternative types of dispute resolution are now well recognized in Australian family law. The Family Law Act introduced a greater emphasis on counselling in cases concerning children. In 2004, the Family Court Rules were amended to adopt a new system of case management, with greater emphasis on counselling, conciliation and arbitration in family law disputes. Parties are now obliged to explore avenues for dispute resolution before commencing proceedings in court. This procedure is in line with shariʿa law, and is regulated accordingly in many Islamic family laws in Muslim countries.

The Jewish community has for many years maintained a Beth Din, a Jewish religious tribunal, in both Sydney and Melbourne, where Jewish people can seek resolution of problems involving family law. Similarly, the Catholic Church maintains its own tribunal, with power to declare annulment of marriages that are not in accord with the Catholic faith, and there are tribunals for other Christian denominations in Australia. These bodies allow those who approach them to obtain a mutually agreed settlement of their family problems, in accordance with their religious beliefs. At present, there is no national shariʿa family law council or tribunal like those of the Jewish and Christian communities. The services of individual *imams* or groups of *imams* are available in this field, but these are uncoordinated and unsupervised at present.

Recent Attempts to Bring Shariʿa into the Public Sphere: Two Case Studies

Case study 1: Australian Federation of Islamic Councils (Ikebal Patel)

On 4 April 2011, in response to an inquiry into multiculturalism held in that year by the Federal government, Ikebal Adam Patel, the president of the Australian Federation of Islamic Councils (AFIC), made a submission titled 'Embracing Australian Values, and Maintaining the Rights to be Different'. In this document he underlined the fact that Muslim countries differ in their use of shariʿa. In his submission Islamic law is viewed as being able to change according to the requirements of different places and times. It is thus implied, without being specific enough, that Australian Muslims can adopt and adhere to the same values shared by all Australian people. Using the active involvement of the Australian government with regard to Islamic finance and halal food as examples of positive sites of cooperation (for example, the exportation of AU$1.5 billion worth of *halal* frozen meat to Indonesia),[25] Patel recommended that multiculturalism in Australia should lead to 'legal pluralism'.

The Attorney-General, Robert McClelland, rejected the submission and claimed that there was no place for shariʿa in the Gillard government's debate about multicultural policy or in Australian society. This claim led to the publication in *The Australian* on 17 May 2011 of an article titled 'Muslims to push for shariʿa', and in the following week, thirteen articles on the topic were published in three leading newspapers, *The Australian*, *The Daily Telegraph* and the *Sydney Morning Herald*. Of these articles, eight portrayed a neutral view on the issue, four were somewhat negative, and one was somewhat positive. Of the 262 readers' comments published on the Internet sites of *The Australian* and *The Daily Telegraph*, 78 per cent were pro-secular and/or against shariʿa, 6 per cent were pro-shariʿa, and the rest tended to be off-topic statements without any clear meaning. Of the negative comments, 34 per cent were virulent comments and/or expressed racist tensions. Examples of comments of that type were: '[w]e have our laws in Australia to protect anyone who lives in Australia. If you don't like our laws leave, it's that simple', and '[i]f Muslims want shariʿa law, they should go back to Saudi Arabia'.[26]

On 17 June 2011, after an interview with *The Australian*,[27] Ikebal Patel claimed that it was a mistake to have mentioned shariʿa law and legal pluralism. He pointed out that there had also been criticism from inside the Muslim community, which was concerned by the lack of consultation with regard to his submission, and he underlined that in family matters, civil law should always take precedence.

On 24 November 2011, Luke Simpkins, Liberal MP for the Cowan electorate, claimed in the House of Representatives that a poll conducted in his electorate in Western Australia had found that almost all animals raised for meat, apart from pigs, are killed according to Islamic requirements. He argued that every business involved should clearly label halal meat. He stated:

> So, when you go to Coles, Woolworths, IGA or other supermarkets, you cannot purchase the meat for your Aussie barbecue without the influence of this minority religion. You have no choice. And the point is that almost no Australians are aware of this, because it is not labeled. … By having Australians unwittingly eating halal food we are all one step down the path towards the conversion, and that is a step we should only make with full knowledge and one that should not be imposed upon us without us knowing.[28]

Case study 2: Divorce in Australia: from an Islamic law perspective[29]

In 2011, an article written by Essof, a solicitor and migration agent, sparked a national debate on Islamic divorce. According to Essof, the current informal Muslim divorce process in Australia, combined with civil law divorce requirements, allows men to distort and abuse the cultural system.[30] Essof does not advocate a separate legal system for Australian Muslims, but rather argues for the incorporation of the single aspect of Islamic divorce law. Islam, he argued, does not condone this behaviour. Rather, it is a consequence of the current inconsistency between civil and religious law in Australia, and of the recalcitrance of husbands who decline to finalize their religious divorces with their estranged wives. Essof acknowledges that Islamic law operates on an informal basis via *imams*, or community religious leaders, especially with regard to family law matters.

He points out that there are no existing formal structures in the Family Law Act to deal with individuals or couples seeking divorce according to an Islamic perspective. Although a Muslim man who receives only a civil divorce would be at liberty to re-marry, a Muslim woman receiving only a civil divorce, and not an Islamic one, would not, within her religion, have that same right to re-marry, even though she would be allowed it under Australian law.

To address this issue, Essof proposes the establishment of a council of recognized *imams* and legal practitioners who have knowledge and understanding of divorce under both Islamic and Australian law, and the formalization of the divorce process in a way that it can be recognized under Australian law. The final recommendation of his article is the inclusion of an extra criterion in the divorce application: the applicant should be asked if he or she was married through a religious Muslim ceremony. If the applicant responds in the affirmative, then s/he is required to prove to the Registrar that the couple has been divorced under shariʿa law. Contrary to Patel's retraction, wherein he stated that civil law should take precedence in family matters, the case presented here seems to advocate the reverse.[31]

Shortly after the publication of Essof's article, a newspaper article entitled 'Local Islamists draw on British success in bid for sharia law',[32] written by the same journalist who reported the retraction by Patel, claimed that Essof's article was the latest move to give shariʿa priority over Australian divorce law under the guise of helping Muslim women, and pointed out that this would mean that Muslims would not be able to obtain a civil divorce unless they were first divorced under Islamic law. In this article the journalist argued that Australia had entered an 'ambitious new phase that draws on the tactics that have handed success to Islamists in Britain', thus claiming that there was a hidden agenda behind Essof's argument.

The two case studies we have discussed offered a moderate approach to legal pluralism in the public sphere. Although we are not discussing the nature of their arguments here, we want to underline the fact that in Australia and especially in the Australian media, there has not been a public dialogue of the Habermasian type (that is, engaged in communicative action; see below) concerning the application of legal pluralism, specifically as it applies to shariʿa.

The New Australian Conservative Modernity and Its Obstacles to Post-Secularism

The social scientist Jakubowicz[33] uses the expression 'the new Australian conservative modernity' to refer to the country's resurgent social values of Christian conservatism, the active government priorities of disengagement and a rapidly expanding culture of surveillance and obedience. In this new phase of modernity, there is a process of delegitimization of diversity, especially concerning Muslims – meaning that the process 'does not deny diversity, but rather seeks to reassert a traditional hierarchy of cultural power within which diversity is only acceptable within the dominant moral order.[34] In this process, Fozdar[35] sees a retreat from multiculturalism resulting from the policies of the conservative Howard government (1996-2007). In this new Australian modernity, political leaders portray 'Christianity as the norm, as a non-migrant religion, and as the taken-for-granted foundation for the nation's values and laws.'[36]

However, one must be aware of the current situation in Australia with regard to its Christian heritage. Randell-Moon[37] and Maddox[38] recently demonstrated that in the Australian case (a secular liberal society where a strong division between church and state is supposedly definitive), religion still has a part to play in politics. In this 'secular' liberal culture, where religion is often actually a significant factor in voting decisions and has increasingly intruded into the public sphere since the beginning of the 21st century, one should not be surprised to witness the many social and cultural bleeds across the border between state and religion. Granted that Christianity was for many years a silent backdrop to Australian national identity, Fozdar[39] observes that there is now an even stronger sense of the legitimacy of the public status of Christianity, and one of the illegitimacy of other religious traditions.

Bearing in mind the relationship between the mass media and the way political agendas are constructed,[40] this new religious project of the 'new modernity' also affects (and/or is affected by) the media. Black and Sadiq[41] cite the national newspaper, *The Australian*, as highlighting 'differences' between Muslims and non-Muslims in some Muslim countries (with topics such as stoning for adultery, forced marriages and female genital mutilation), and as feeding into the fear of what shariʿa family law would be in Australia if a dialogue on the subject were allowed. While there are demands from some groups in Australia for the adoption of full shariʿa,[42] Saeed[43] states that the large majority of Muslims advocating the use of shariʿa are only seeking its recognition in a few areas (such as marriage, burial practices, and interest-free financing) and are working towards a compromise between the demands of their religion and the Australian legal system.

Their detractors tend to present the religion of Muslims as unchanging and as representing a pre-modern and patriarchal value system.[44] These detractors also tend to characterize the Muslim community as bounded, fixed and stable.[45] This, of course, is far from being the case. Akbarzadeh and Roose[46] discuss three ideal types of Muslims in Australia, in order to provide a lens through which to look at this religious group. These are: an Islamist type who would embrace shariʿa in line with the historic experience of the caliphate; a moderate Muslim type who engages with the secular West; and a cultural Muslim type – those who define themselves as Muslims but do not actively follow Islamic principles. Cultural Muslims often have a pragmatic approach to religion. Islam is celebrated when it helps consolidate a community, but is not allowed to interfere and interrupt the daily routine of life, which to all intents and purposes may be called secular.[47]

In Australia, these cultural Muslims are the silent majority of the Muslim minority group, not much engaged with advocacy for legal change. Those Muslims mainly engaged in working out shariʿa in Australia in line with (and not in opposition to) the Australian legal system are of the moderate type. Some moderate Muslims are already working within a type of unofficial parallel legal system (as detailed above) in the private sphere. But when some moderate voices attempt to discuss, in the public sphere, how the two legal systems could interact, it appears the dialogue is not allowed to proceed. The 'extreme right' is already seeing the moderate Muslim as a 'Trojan horse' for radical Islamists, as if they were harbouring a hidden Islamic agenda.[48] It might be argued that in the public sphere, debate about the partial use of shariʿa leads its detractors (who are not necessarily from the extreme right) to believe that this might be a first step towards implanting full shariʿa law, as if shariʿa were a homogenous and timeless law straight from the caliphate. This belief is not conducive to a fruitful dialogue about the future of religion in Australia that would be helpful in advancing a post-secular project.

By post-secularism, we refer to the process of the de-privatization of religion, and to the current dialogue about managing the presence of religious groups within secular frameworks in the public sphere. As Habermas[49] has underlined, the challenge today is to draw the 'delimitations between a positive liberty to practise a religion of one's own and the negative liberty to remain spared from the religious practice of the others'. In other words, how do we work with post-secular societies' religious toleration in ways that celebrate religious diversity but that do not preclude the freedom to be atheist? And, more specifically to this chapter, how far should our own and others' religious practices be implicated within the legal system?

However, as already indicated in this chapter, one should be aware of the difficulties of entering into such a dialogue. Michele Dillon, in her 2009 presidential address to the Association for the Sociology of Religion, stated quite sharply that 'independent[ly] of whether an individual is religious or not, tolerance of otherness does not come easily',[50] that openness to alternative beliefs is more complicated than Habermas might have us believe, and that the idea that all religious and atheist groups can live in a self-reflective manner 'is attractive but hard to imagine'.[51] Part of the solution for Habermas is to have neutral and secular governments that can ensure that communities of various beliefs can coexist on an equal basis. His post-secular project is based upon the notion that the state is neutral and objective,[52] yet we know from studies in sociology how the state usually and instrumentally serves certain groups over others, as has already been alluded to in the above discussion of Australia and its new conservative modernity.

It appears that in Australia, one aspect of the trend towards post-secularism, that is the focus on religious and legal pluralism, is not allowed to be fully aired in the public sphere, unless to be shown in a negative light. On that point, it can be argued that Australia is failing to meet or implement the post-secular project. The issue here is not solely about including shari'a in the legal system or preventing its use in the private or public sphere, but about having a fruitful dialogue of the Habermasian type in the public sphere. This is not happening in Australia's new conservative modernity.

Notes

1 Z. Anwar, CEDAW *and Muslim family laws: In search of common ground*, Selangor, Malaysia: Musawah, 2011.

2 J. Ali, 'A dual legal system in Australia: The formalisation of Sharī'ah', *Democracy and Security*, 2011 (Vol. 7, No. 1).

3 A. Black, 'In the shadow of our legal system: shari'a in Australia' in: R. Ahdar and N. Aroney (eds.), *Sharia in the West*, Oxford: Oxford University Press, 2010, pp. 239-254.

4 Ahdar and Aroney (eds.), *Sharia in the West*, 2010, pp. 239-254; J. Hussain, *Islam: Its law and society* (3rd ed.), Sydney: Federation Press, 2011; A. Saeed, 'Reflections on the establishment of shari'a courts in Australia' in: Ahdar and Aroney (eds.), *Sharia in the West*, 2010, pp. 223-238.

5 Hussain, *Islam: Its law and society* (3rd ed.), 2011; Ahdar and Aroney (eds.), *Sharia in the West*, 2010, pp. 223-238.

6 A. Black and N. Hosen, 'Fatwas: Their role in contemporary secular Australia', *Griffith Law Review*, 2009 (Vol. 18, No. 2), pp. 420.

7 Ahdar and Aroney (eds.), *Sharia in the West*, 2010, pp. 223-238.

8 Black and Hosen, 'Fatwas', 2009, pp. 422.

9 Black and Hosen, 'Fatwas', 2009, pp. 423.

10 Hussain, *Islam* (3rd ed.), 2011.

11 S. Dagistanli, '"Like a pack of wild animals": Moral panics around "ethnic" gang rape in Sydney', in: G. Morgan and S. Poynting (eds.), *Outrageous! Moral panics in Australia*, Hobart, Tasmania: ACYS Publishing, 2007, pp. 181-196.

12 See: S. Poynting and G. Noble, *Living with Racism: The experience and reporting by Arab and Muslim Australians of discrimination, abuse and violence since 11 September 2001*. Report to the Human Rights and Equal Opportunity Commission, 19 April 2004, Sydney: HREOC, 2004.

13 A. Jakubowicz, 'Anglo-multiculturalism: Contradictions in the politics of cultural diversity as risk', *International Journal of Media and Cultural Politics*, 2006 (Vol. 2, No. 3), pp. 249-266; F. Fozdar, 'The "choirboy" and the "mad monk": Christianity, Islam, Australia's political landscape and prospects for multiculturalism', *Journal of Intercultural Studies*, 2011 (Vol. 32, No. 6), pp. 621-636.

14 R. Williams, 'Civil and religious law in England: A religious perspective', *Archbishop's home page*, 2008, http://www.archbishopofcanterbury.org.

15 David Humphries, 'Live here and be Australian, Howard declares', *Sydney Morning Herald*, 25 February 2006, http://www.smh.com.au/news/national/live-here-be-australian/2006/02/24/1140670269194.html.

16 P. Osborne and J. Turnbull, 'Government rejects call for Islamic courts', *Sydney Morning Herald*, 8 February 2008.

17 A. Black and K. Sadiq, 'Good and bad sharia: Australia's mixed response to Islamic law', *The University of New South Wales Law Journal*, 2011 (Vol. 17, No. 1), pp. 383-412.

18 Black and Sadiq, 'Good and bad sharia', 2011, p. 388.

19 Section 42 Marriage Act 1961.

20 Section 43 Marriage Act 1961.

21 This is different from the situation in the United Kingdom, where marriages must take place in a registered building and only some mosques meet this requirement.

22 Section 45 Marriage Act 1961.

23 Jews and Christians are considered 'People of the Book' who may legitimately marry Muslim men.

24 Mohamed v Mohamed, 2012, NSWSC 852.

25 Hussain, *Islam* (3rd ed.), 2011.

26 The authors would like to thank Morgane Dupoux who analysed these articles and comments while undertaking an internship, in 2011, at the Centre for the Study of Contemporary Muslim Societies, University of Western Sydney.

27 C. Merrit, 'It was a mistake to mention sharia law, admits Australian Islamic leader', *The Australian*, 17 June 2011.

28 L. Simpkins, 'Cowan Electorate: Halal foods', *Commonwealth of Australia Parliamentary Debates, House of Representatives*, 24 November 2011, p. 75.

29 I. Essof, 'Divorce in Australia from an Islamic law perspective', *Alternative Law Journal*, 2011 (Vol. 36, No. 3).

30 Essof, 'Divorce in Australia', 2011.

31 Research from Bano (2007) in the United Kingdom points out that in processes of dispute resolution, women are encouraged to reconcile and to conform to cultural dictates and acceptable patterns of behaviour if they are to be issued a divorce certificate. Drawing on a sample of ten women, her study found a process of marginalization of women.

32 C. Merrit, 'Local Islamists draw on British success in bid for sharia law', *The Australian*, 7 October 2011b.
33 A. Jakubowicz, 'Hard shell and soft centre: Australia as a truly modern nation', *International Journal of Diversity in Organisations, Communities and Nations*, 2003 (Vol. 3), pp. 337-350.
34 Jakubowicz, 'Hard shell and soft centre', 2003, p. 344. Discussion of shari'a and the thesis of multiple modernity is extended in M. Voyce and A. Possamai, 'Legal pluralism, family personal laws and the rejection of shari'a in Australia: A case of multiple or "clashing" modernities?', *Democracy and Security*, 2011 (Vol. 7, No. 4), pp. 338-353.
35 Fozdar, 'The "choirboy" and the "mad monk"', 2011, pp. 621-636.
36 Fozdar, 'The "choirboy" and the "mad monk"', 2011, p. 632.
37 H. Randell-Moon, 'Tolerating religious "others": Some thoughts on secular neutrality and religious tolerance in Australia', *The Australian Religion Studies Review*, 2009 (Vol. 22, No. 3), pp. 324-344.
38 M. Maddox, 'An argument for more, not less, religion in Australian politics', *The Australian Religion Studies Review*, 2009 (Vol. 22, No. 3), pp. 345-367.
39 Fozdar, 'The "choirboy" and the "mad monk', 2011.
40 P. Van Aelst and S. Walgrave, 'Minimal or massive? The political agenda-setting power of the mass media according to different methods', *The International Journal of Press/Politics*, 2011 (Vol. 16, No. 3), pp. 295-313.
41 Black and Sadiq, 'Good and bad sharia', 2011.
42 Black and Sadiq, 'Good and bad sharia', 2011.
43 Ahdar and Aroney (eds.), *Sharia in the West*, 2010, pp. 223-238.
44 S. Akbarzadech and J. Roose, 'Muslims, multiculturalism and the question of the silent majority', *Journal of Muslim Minority Affairs*, 2011 (Vol. 31, No. 3), pp. 309-325.
45 S. Bano, 'Islamic family arbitration, justice and human rights in Britain', *Law, Social Justice & Global Development*, 2007 (Vol. 1), http://www.go.warwick.ac.uk/elj/lgd/2007_1/bano.
46 Akbarzadech and Roose, 'Muslims, multiculturalism and the question of the silent majority', 2011, pp. 309-325.
47 Akbarzadech and Roose, 'Muslims, multiculturalism and the question of the silent majority', 2011, p. 320.
48 Akbarzadech and Roose, 'Muslims, multiculturalism and the question of the silent majority', 2011, pp. 309-325.
49 J. Habermas, Religion in the public sphere. *European Journal of Philosophy*, 2006 (Vol. 14, No. 1), p. 4.
50 M. Dillon, '2009 Association for the Sociology of Religion presidential address: Can post-secular society tolerate religious differences?', *Sociology of Religion*, 2010 (Vol. 71, No. 2), p. 149.
51 Dillon, '2009 Association for the Sociology of Religion presidential address', 2010, p. 152.
52 J. Barbalet, A. Possmai and B. Turner, *Religion and the state: A comparative sociology*, New York: Anthem Press, 2011.

4 United Kingdom

An Early Discussion on Islamic Family Law in the English Jurisdiction[1]

Jørgen S. Nielsen

Background

In 1975 the Union of Muslim Organisations of the United Kingdom and Eire (UMO) called a conference in Birmingham to discuss the place of shari'a family law in England. In January 1977 the UMO, together with the Anglo-Conservative Society, held a further meeting, this time in the House of Lords. The meeting discussed a number of practical issues facing Muslims, in particular those relating to schooling. But the main item on the agenda was a demand for the 'domestication' of Islamic family law for Muslims in Britain.[2]

In 1975 the Muslim case for the demand had been formulated by Sheikh Syed M. Darsh, an Azhar-educated Egyptian who had recently been seconded by the Egyptian authorities to the Regent's Park Mosque in London:

> When a Muslim is prevented from obeying this law he feels that he is failing a religious duty. He will not feel at peace with his conscience or the environment in which he lives.... They firmly believe that the British society, with its rich experience of different cultures and ways of life, especially the Islamic way of life which they used to see in India, Malaysia, Nigeria and so many other nations of Islamic orientation, together with their respect for personal and communal freedom, will enable the Muslim migrants to realize the identity within the freedom of British society. When we request the host society to recognize our point of view we are appealing to a tradition of justice and equity well established in this country. The scope of the family law is not wide and does not contradict, in essence, the law here in this country. Both aim at the fulfillment of justice and happiness of the members of the family. Still, there are certain Islamic points which, with understanding and the spirit of accommodation, would not go so far as to create difficulties in the judiciary system. After all, we are asking for their

> application among themselves, the Muslim community, as our Christian brothers in Islamic countries are following in the family tradition and the Christian point of view. The Qur'an itself has given them this right.[3]

At the time, the UMO initiative attracted only fleeting interest in the media, and within the legal institutions there was no significant response. Dr Zaki Badawi, the then director of the Islamic Cultural Centre, part of the Regent's Park Mosque complex, while not supportive, decided to test popular demand. In English law there was no reason why someone could not write a will requiring that his or her property be disposed of according to Islamic principles. It just had to be clear as to which version of Islamic law (or shariʿa) to use, so that there was no room for ambiguity. Such a will would be valid unless a relative contested it. Dr Badawi had a will form prepared by competent lawyers and made it available to worshippers. No one took advantage of the service.[4] Perhaps this was not all that surprising, as the Muslim community in Britain, as in the rest of Europe, was at the time still relatively young of age. Only a decade later did questions of disposition of property at death start to become a practical issue for a growing number of people. Thus, we saw tensions begin to be recorded in France between the expectations of Algerians and the demands of French law with regard to the disposition of immovable property.[5]

At the time, evidence of Muslim demand for the application of Islamic family law was patchy and remained so until the end of the 1980s. A quick check through a few Islamic magazines published in Europe during the 1980s found little evidence of interest in the subject. *The Straight Path*, published in Birmingham from the Green Lane Mosque, and closely associated with the Ahl-i-Hadith movement, only mentioned an interest in Islamic family law in response to external events. During this same period, the question of Islamic family law did not feature in the pages of *Al-Fadschr*, published by the Shi'ite Islamic Centre in Hamburg, nor was it raised in the Dutch monthly *Qiblah*, published in The Hague. Even the journal of the network of German-speaking Muslims, *Al-Islam*, published in Munich, did not deal with the question, even though it regularly carried general articles about shariʿa. In the late 1980s the UMO's initiative remained, to the best of my knowledge, the only one.

The impression was that the demand for implementation of Islamic family law for Muslims in Europe was usually only expressed by Muslim leaders when offered an opportunity to do so, or when reacting to particular events. Much attention was paid to the overarching role of the shariʿa, but when interpreted in practical terms, the magazines concentrated on the core ritual practices (the 'five pillars'), economic life and the ethics rather than the law of family life, especially as regards the position of women.

However, a Muslim 'demand' for the implementation of Islamic family law can be registered in ways other than direct expressions by leaders and in their media. Throughout this early period, it was clear that the practice of paying a dower, *mahr*, remained commonplace. English legal expertise suggested at the beginning of the 1980s that English law would condone it when it appeared in a Muslim marriage contract.[6] Rude-Antoine, writing in the mid-1980s, indicated that over three-quarters of marriages between North Africans living in France involved payment of *mahr*.[7] The recurring problem in Britain of so-called limping marriages (that is, where a civil divorce has taken place but the absence of a religious divorce prevents the woman from remarrying in a form acceptable to her community) was another indicator, as was the high proportion of Muslim marriages that were formalized both in civil law terms and in Islamic terms. The breakdown of marriages, in particular, was an early matter of concern. Unpublished research conducted in the Birmingham family courts in the early 1980s showed that four out of five divorce applications from parties with Muslim-sounding names were initiated by women, and the two most common grounds for divorce applications were the husband's violence against the wife or his abandoning or deserting her.[8]

That there was a growing demand for some kind of shariʿa-related provision, or at least a perception that there was such a demand, was indicated by the formation in the early 1980s of the first two – rival – United Kingdom Islamic Sharia Councils, both located in London. These councils made themselves available to advise individuals on correct shariʿa solutions to personal and family problems and, if necessary, to issue a decision which, at least in the community if not in civil law, might have the weight of authority. There were also other, more visible indications that Muslims were expecting the institutions of the countries of residence to adapt to some of their religious requirements, other than those of family law. The issue that had been most common was that of access to halal food. Furthermore, English schools were in the main adjusting well to Muslim girls wearing some form of Islamically acceptable dress, while the question of the *hijab* in mainland Europe was still a few years off. Also, local governments in the United Kingdom were beginning to meet requests for burial facilities, and employers and local planning authorities were being faced with requests for prayer facilities.[9]

Seeking clarification

It was the question of family law in particular that contributed to setting the agenda for a three-year project which had been instigated by the Brussels-based Churches' Committee for Migrant Workers in Europe (CCMWE) to consider the significance of the shariʿa for Muslim communities in Europe.[10] The working group started work in 1983 and consisted of four members nominated by the CCMWE: Jan Henningsson (Sweden), Michael Mildenberger (West Germany), Jan Slomp (Netherlands), and myself (United Kingdom). Two Muslim members were invited to join the group, namely Syed Darsh (UK) and Mehdi Razvi (West Germany).

Given the limited resources of a European (Protestant) church network working in this field, the possibility of a study that would meet academic criteria was never considered. Instead, the project was conducted as a 'listening exercise' consisting of three parts: a questionnaire sent to interested 'experts' known to the members of the working group; a series of four seminars, two each at the Quaker Woodbrooke College, Birmingham, United Kingdom, and at the Evangelische Akademie, Arnoldshain, West Germany; and correspondence with invited religious and academic experts at the drafting stage of the final report. In this way, by the end, the exercise had involved a total of 95 individuals. Most were from Germany and the United Kingdom, but a few were also from France, the Netherlands and Sweden. They included not only Muslim and Christian religious leaders and scholars, but also practising lawyers and local and national government officials.

The first stage of the work was to draft a questionnaire to be sent to a number of significant Muslim individuals and organizations around Western Europe to get their views on shariʿa generally and, more specifically, its family law dimensions. The questionnaire asked five questions:

1 What does shariʿa mean for you personally?
2 What does shariʿa mean for your community in this country?
3 What do you see as the function of shariʿa in your home country and in the Muslim world generally?
4 Does your understanding of shariʿa create problems for yourself and your community in this country? If so, which?
5 What contributions do you see shariʿa making to European society?

The questionnaire was answered by sixteen persons, of whom eleven were Muslims from three different European countries (the United Kingdom, West Germany and the Netherlands) and originating from eight different Muslim countries, and with a variety of different backgrounds and occupations. There is no space here to analyse the responses in detail,[11] but they covered a broad spectrum of views, ranging from those that required a comprehensive implementation of shariʿa to those that suggested that it cannot apply in a non-Muslim environment such as that of Western Europe, or that shariʿa needs a thorough rethink in relation to the modern world before any consideration of its implementation. Many of the respondents preferred to talk of shariʿa as an ethical system rather than something with legal implications.

Worth noting is that none of the respondents wanted to define shariʿa as a legal code, although the implications of some of the answers to the subsequent questions suggested that in an ideal world this might be close: shariʿa to one respondent meant 'the Law of God which was revealed by Him to mankind through His Prophet and Apostle Muhammad in order to be observed by them in every time and place as any individual (or group) with faith in Islam as his (its) religion.' But others simply equated it with religion, giving 'the direction to life and formulating one's disposition'. Many of the respondents pointed out that the implementation of shariʿa should take account of the context, and some particularly stressed the necessity of this in the context of modernity, not least in the minority situations of Europe: 'new *fiqh* has to be written for the Muslim countries themselves and much more so for Muslim minorities living now in non-Muslim countries.'

One response described the process of a growing consensus among the manifold Muslim community which ought to be brought about by concentrating upon the essentials of shariʿa and carefully adjusting them to the new situation, according to methods provided by the Islamic tradition. Such processes may suffer from the confusion 'between the permanent divine law … and the human elaboration' and, consequently, by 'some hasty and mistaken judgments' hinder the 'healthy mutual interaction with the society' of the host-country. It should be kept in mind that 'Islam indicates its basics and characteristics, but it does not meanwhile reject any other intellectual or social outcome which is not against its principles'. Moreover 'a clear distinction may be kept between the application of shariʿa in a Muslim country and society, and its application among a Muslim community which lives as a minority in a non-Muslim country.' Accordingly, two answers emphasize that in such a case, shariʿa can only be applied within a scope determined by the constitution and the laws of the host country. By contrast there is a group of Muslims (among them mainly converts) which 'will take the shariʿa "lock, stock and barrel" … and defying British law where they don't feel it is Islamic, e.g. marriage and divorce laws'.[12]

A significant concern was voiced by a number of the respondents who pointed to secularization as the big challenge; the 'real problem', however, is 'far more serious and fundamental'. Western Europe is increasingly becoming a 'non-religious and even irreligious society with norms which a Muslim finds difficult to comprehend, let alone accept'. This is a second level of problems that Muslims – as they remind us – share with their Christian brethren and sisters. 'The secular society emits values which a Muslim does not share or accept'.[13]

As a next step, the working group organized four seminars, two in Germany and two in Birmingham. The participants comprised Muslim and Christian intellectuals and community leaders, legal experts, and government officials. Given that the issue had been raised in the United Kingdom and at that time was not really exciting any interest outside the United Kingdom, the following account will be limited to the discussions at the two seminars that took place in Birmingham over two weekends in February and September 1985. The first event was attended by about twenty people, who had been personally invited, while the second attracted thirty people following a public announcement. The first seminar focused on family law, while the second one looked at implications for legal institutions and processes, as well as at broad, practical issues of integration in a multi-faith society (including education and religious practice in the workplace) which I will not deal with further here.

Considering family law, this was examined in the first seminar under the standard headings of marriage, divorce, inheritance, and the maintenance and custody of children. The participants first surveyed the general principles of English law as it stood at the time and of the Islamic legal tradition, before going on to an item-by-item comparison. As an example, the participants compared the principles of the Hanafi tradition of divorce as it was being applied in Pakistan after the Muslim Family Law Ordinance of 1961, and the English Matrimonial Causes Act of 1973 (see Table 1). A similar exercise was conducted on the basic principles of marriage (see Table 2). They concluded that in general terms, there was little dispute in principle between the two sets of principles. But there remained two major tensions.

With reference to divorce, Muslim participants wanted the collection and evaluation ('due consideration') of the facts required by English law to be conducted by a Muslim panel for Muslim litigants. The panel, it was argued, could function under the existing law as an extension of the Family Division of the High Court. This was an option on which the non-Muslim participants were divided.[14]

In the case of marriage, it was the Muslim participants who were divided, in that some did not wish to give up the age of puberty as being sufficient to enter into a marriage, while others, following the legislation of most Muslim countries, were happy to accept the minimum age set down in English law. The question of marriage guardians for women, required by the traditional shariʿa though under varying conditions depending on the school, was quietly ignored.

TABLE 1 *Grounds for dissolution of marriage*

England	Pakistan
Grounds:	
Irretrievable breakdown of marriage	Incompatibility
Facts:	
- unreasonable behaviour	- unreasonable behaviour
- adultery/intolerable	- intolerable
- desertion	- imprisonment for 7 years or more
- separation for 2 years (consent)	- disappeared for 4 years or more
- separation for 5 years	- husband's inability to maintain
Grounds for nullity:	
- physical/mental disorder	- physical/mental disorder
- lack of consent	- lack of consent
- under age	- under age

TABLE 2 *Conditions for marriage*

England	Pakistan
- free consent	- free consent
- sound mind	- sound mind
- public announcement	- public announcement
- witnesses	- witnesses
- age 16-18 (parental or court consent)	- age: puberty
- unmarried	- unmarried if woman: husband max. 4 wives
	- dower (*mahr*)

Interestingly, the issue of polygamy was not one that raised tempers. There was consensus among the participants that 'polygamy is, of course, impermissible in English law.' However, looking at the practice of English law relating to cohabitees ('common law spouses'), the participants did 'not feel the discrepancy between English and Islamic family law in this regard is insurmountable.'[15] Other Muslim participants took the view that since polygamy is not obligatory in Islam, living in a system in which it is banned should not be a problem for Muslims.

A practical problem on both sides, Muslim and non-Muslim, seemed to be the general popular ignorance of the law of Islam. In the Muslim community this manifested itself typically in a popular equation of social custom, often very strongly held, with shari'a. What are often broadly perceived by the English population as strongly male-dominant practices are, as often as not, just as much in conflict with shari'a as they are with English law and expectations. A point made with some effect by the Muslim participants was that the application of Islamic family law to the Muslim community would lead to a major improvement in the actual social status of women within many Muslim communities. Of course, this is, on the whole, correct, but by European standards of gender equality it would be insufficient, as some basic distinctions and inequalities would be retained in the fields of divorce and inheritance.

The issue of how to introduce some form or other of shari'a into the English legal system revolved around two main approaches. For some Muslims, the nature of the shari'a as a total, integrated system based on sources divinely revealed makes it extremely difficult to accept anything other than a separate system of family law, with its own autonomous judiciary. Parliament's role would be to make the space in the country's law and to establish the necessary courts. But the specific content of the law could not be under the control of Parliament, nor could there be appeal to higher, non-Muslim courts. The system envisaged would be much like that which functions in countries like Lebanon, Syria and Israel, which still retain elements of the old Ottoman *millet* system, with its self-governing confessional communities. At the other extreme is the model of a continuing unified system, but with the law opened up in a number of directions so as to create a generally permissive legal context in which different groups could voluntarily live according to their particular wishes. An example could be the theoretically possible legalization of polygamy, within which framework a Muslim could, if he so wished, enter into a polygamous marriage.

Another view expressed by some Muslim participants looked to the contents of the law, rather than its theologically overriding nature. In their view it was possible to build on the identified convergence of legal principles and look to some method of building consideration of Islamic rules and expectations into the existing system of law. The concept of a tribunal became central in the discussions, although clearly, different kinds of tribunal were intended by different participants. Some saw potential in distinct Islamic family tribunals before which Muslims could opt to appear. It was accepted by some, but not all, that the decisions of such tribunals could be subject to appeal into the general English system. Another view of such tribunals was one of a quasi-judicial body that would deal with cases with the purpose of presenting to the English family courts a settlement which takes into account consideration of Islamic rules. It was felt that one of the advantages of some form of tribunal was that it could be seen as a method to be utilized by other communities, such as Jews and Catholics, with a similar attachment to religious family law.

The possibility that a reform of the adversarial court procedures, which in the mid-1980s still prevailed in the family courts but were under discussion, was seen as providing a context in which some variation of the tribunal approach might become practicable. In a uniform system of family courts based on arbitration and reconciliation, a particular bench might be identified as Muslim, and parties could opt to appear before a bench of their choice. This might ensure that Muslim expectations were taken into account within a legal system that remained essentially unified.

Issues and implications

Despite the passing years, the discussion then, just as similar discussions now, raises a number of substantial questions. For a start, questions can be raised about the degree of consensus needed to be able to reach a unified Muslim family code. In fact, it depended on a number of assumptions: first, that the discussion of philosophical and ideological foundations was suspended; second, that both sides accepted the context of a plural and diverse society with room for all; and third, that the Muslim participants, although generally traditionalists, did not feel bound by the results of classical jurisprudence (*fiqh*) and were prepared to exercise their personal judgment (*ijtihad*) in the light of the current environment.

Some observers might argue that such assumptions by themselves contribute to making the results of no operational interest, because such assumptions will generally not be met in actuality. The second assumption, that of living together in a diverse society has, I would suggest, become broadly accepted, despite the recent attacks on multi-culturalism from certain political quarters. The arguments today are more about concepts and ideological polemics than about the ordinary practicalities of everyday life in the cities. The third assumption, the Muslim readiness to use *ijtihad*, is one that has a sound classical foundation and is one of the key characteristics of most contemporary Islamic movements, even when they are of the more conservative kind.

More problematical is the first assumption, namely that the discussion of philosophical and ideological foundations of a unified Muslim family code is suspended. The apparent contradiction is between a secularized Europe, whose legislative and judicial processes are primarily empirical in nature and rest on the foundations of popular sovereignty (although the historical foundations are clearly Christian), and on the other hand an Islamic system which is founded on the revelation of the word of God in the Qur'an and on the guiding behaviour and sayings of an inspired prophet, a system in which the law rests on the sovereignty of God. In fact, I would suggest that the difficulty here is more apparent than real. Even though God is the sovereign lawgiver, his authority still has to be interpreted, and this is a human process. This issue lies at the very centre of much current Muslim discussion about the role of Islam in the state. The real difficulty is not to be found in the clash between secularism and divine sovereignty but in the question of the identity of the judicial authority and its legitimacy. This is a dimension of an area of Islamic thinking which has undergone a radical transformation in recent generations – and which is still contested.

This transformation can be briefly described as follows. In the classical tradition the shariʿa and its institutions had been the primary field of confrontation between the political power and the Islamic authorities, the former in the shape of an often militarized state and the latter in the shape of the religious scholars, or *ʿulama*, and their institutions. The conception that God was the lawgiver in a polity or community defined primarily by its shared religion was the focal point of public legitimacy. Early attempts by the political leadership in the shape of the Umayyad and then the early Abbasid caliphs to present themselves as the representatives of that divine legislative power failed. It was the *ʿulama* who came to be accepted as those who held the authority to interpret, develop and refine the human understanding of the divine will. One of the most remarkable aspects of developments in shariʿa in the modern period has been the extent to which the state has succeeded in gaining control of legislation, including family law. It has done this partly by manipulating the various instruments of power, hard and soft, and partly by pursuing the one technique that had traditionally been available, namely control over the incomes of the *ʿulama*. In the modern period this has been done by co-opting them as judges and experts in family law in the now government-controlled courts and by sponsoring training in the Islamic religious sciences, including law/*fiqh* in government-funded universities. In historical terms, this intrusion of the state in the field of shariʿa is truly radical. This contributes to complications in Europe, where some Islamic tendencies will refuse to lend the state legitimacy, at least in core sectors of the shariʿa such as family law, while others will seek to co-opt the official institutions to legitimize practices whose validity in the community rest on a reference to the shariʿa.

Other significant changes have taken place in the practice and thinking of shariʿa, all in one way or another related to that basic revolution. One is the culmination of a long process whereby the shariʿa had been increasingly restricted to the domain of family law. However, there was a shift around the 1960s, when Islamic thinkers and movements began to try to regain ground. In various instances, one saw attempts to reintroduce aspects of shariʿa beyond the family chapters, as is illustrated by the growth of Islamic banking and economics both in practice and as an intellectual discipline across the Muslim world and into the major international banking centres outside the Muslim world.[16] In all of these innovations, the state has been an active partner. In some cases the political leadership has been the initiator, and in other cases the innovators have made what are often great efforts to get the state on board. In such an environment, it is the more radical-puritanical movements[17] which have marked out their claims to legitimacy by distancing themselves from the state, reasserting the independence of Islamic teaching, above all the shariʿa, from the control of the political authorities.

But these radical movements themselves also represent a revolutionary break with the classical tradition's division of the world into the 'territory of Islam' (*dar al-islam*) and the 'territory of war' (*dar al-harb*). Generally this division of the world lost its significance, except for possibly a symbolic dimension, in the course of the 20th century, as traditional Islamic states were first colonized and then replaced by modern national states (although the national substance of such states has tended to remain weak). In the classical tradition it was generally agreed that shariʿa only applied in *dar al-islam* where there was a legitimate Islamic authority, and where there were Islamic courts that could adjudicate disputes in the correct manner and legitimately. This meant that when Muslims travelled outside the Islamic lands, they were no longer subject to shariʿa, or at least not to those parts which had to do with human and social relations. If possible, the religious rituals were still to be performed, although a few voices suggested that even this was not necessary.

The main difference between the majority of Muslims and the minority of radical-puritans today is that the latter regard the modern state as irrelevant and lacking legitimacy.[18] They have often discarded the traditional geographical distinctions of *dar al-islam/al-harb* and personalized them: *dar al-islam* is where they are, while *dar al-harb* is the fallen world around them.[19] The authors of the CCME project report were perhaps being premature when they concluded that, 'Most Muslim leaders in Europe today regard the old concepts of *dar al-harb* and *dar al-islam* as outmoded and irrelevant.'[20] Although the terminology is mainly used in small, mostly politically extremist circles, elements of such thinking can be found more widely. With the shift from a territorial towards a personal paradigm, it has become possible to argue within the traditional Islamic frameworks that shari'a (or perhaps more correctly here, *fiqh*) potentially applies to Muslims wherever they are, thus making possible claims that Muslims in new minority contexts should also strive to practise the shari'a, not only in rite but also in other chapters. First and foremost, this includes family and personal status law, but also economic law – and, the hard-liners would argue, also in such areas as tort and possibly criminal law.

In the context of such a discussion, it is the authority under which a judicial process functions, rather than the substance of the law itself, which becomes a key consideration. This partly accounts for the internal Muslim disagreement in the 1985 seminars about the nature of a tribunal or a court that might be asked to adjudicate Muslim family law disputes. For some participants it was clearly not enough that the existing English family court system takes Islamic expectations into account. The court dealing with Muslim family disputes should itself be Muslim in its character and staffing. There was further disagreement on the matter of appeal among those who took this view, some insisting that an appeal either not be allowed or be allowed only to a higher Muslim tribunal. In fact, this view was probably also a reflection of the experience of Muslim family courts under British rule in India before 1947. Muslim family cases, like all other cases, could in those days ultimately be appealed to the Judiciary Committee of the Privy Council in London. There were instances of the higher courts in India, and of the Privy Council, either over-ruling a decision with reference to common law principles of equity or holding to a decision which was in effect a misunderstanding of rulings in the classical Hanafi tradition.[21] Such unhappy results for Muslim scholars should be avoided, if possible.

Such lack of trust in the intent of European authorities can clearly be traced back to colonial experiences. The suspicions vary in strength and character in different parts of the Muslim world and are probably stronger among, for example, Algerians than among Muslims from the Indian subcontinent. Basically this leads to the conclusion that European authorities cannot be trusted to consider Muslim practices fairly and correctly. This suspicion is mirrored from the European side. The implementation of Islamic family law is often interpreted as a political manoeuvre with a variety of purposes. There is little doubt that the demand for shariʿa has been voiced from some quarters as part of an internal rivalry for leadership among the Muslim minorities. Equally there is little doubt that the demand is also part of the process of cultivating links between European Muslim communities and major foreign Muslim sponsors, some but not all of them being states.

The Discussion Continues

The seminars of 1985 and the project of which they were part have not lost their relevance. The issues that were identified then are still with us today:

- What is meant by Islamic family law?
- How compatible are shariʿa family law rules with European practice?
- Who decides what Islamic family law rules are in a particular country?
- Who would be responsible for implementation?
- Who might be subject to it?
- How far is the demand driven by sectional interests?
- How do European democratic and human rights traditions deal with this issue, especially with regard to gender equality?

Most of these questions are far more technical than can be dealt with in the remainder of this chapter, but several of the other chapters in this volume touch on them. Let me here elaborate on the current disagreements among Muslims regarding the legitimacy of the authority seeking to implement family law.

Just as it was in England that the issue was first raised, so it is in England that it has remained most acute, and certainly where it has attracted most attention. Not long before the 1985 seminars were held, the first two UK Islamic Sharia Councils were established in London. They reflected both political and doctrinal differences, although a few of the members served on both councils. One represented a modernizing approach to the field and was an initiative of Dr Zaki Badawi, well-known for looking for constructive ways of integrating Islam into the European environment. The other was sponsored by the Muslim World League, representing a line close to Saudi Arabia's Wahhabi version of Islam. Numerous anecdotal accounts indicate that they were primarily engaged with cases of women seeking an 'Islamic' approval of a divorce. Since then, there has been a multiplication of Sharia Councils and, in the most recent decade, also the innovation of the Muslim Arbitration Tribunal.[22] Whereas the legal status of the decisions of the Councils is unclear, the Tribunal explicitly operates under English law, particularly the Arbitration Act of 1996. The issue of contention is the following.

Since an Islamically conducted marriage (*nikah*) has no legal standing in England, it follows in principle that such a marriage cannot be dissolved in the usual way through the family courts. In effect, it is up to the parties to decide how seriously to take their *nikah* if they decide to end the relationship. It appears that a majority of Muslim couples who get married in the civil process also get married by *nikah*. Among many of the Muslim cultural traditions, the civil marriage is regarded as something akin to an 'engagement' which only becomes a full marriage with the *nikah*.[23] It is with respect to this background that problems arise with divorce, as many will regard a divorce by the normal civil procedure to be inadequate. They will therefore want an Islamic divorce both for their own satisfaction and for the divorce to be recognized in the community. Traditionally such a divorce can be pronounced unilaterally by the husband (*talaq*), while the wife needs to go through some form of judicial process (*khul'*).

Different Islamic bodies have different views on this. According to research carried out at Cardiff University, the Birmingham Sharia Council accepts a civil divorce as valid and simply offers confirmation, if the parties so wish:

> ... the shari'ah Council regard the obtaining of a civil divorce as clear evidence of the parties' view that the marriage is over, and for the shari'ah Council, this is conclusive, such that it does not deem it necessary to grant a religious divorce to enable the parties to remarry under shari'a (although it will do so to reflect the parties' wishes for 'recognition' by the Council of the ending of their marriage).[24]

This degree of accommodation is unusual. Much more common is the view that for a divorce to be valid in Islamic terms it needs to be conducted under an Islamic authority, particularly if it is initiated by the wife in the form of a *khul'*. This is stated unequivocally in a *fatwa* on the Internet:

> I would like to affirm that the divorce issued by the civil court in response to the wife's request is neither a valid divorce nor legitimate marriage dissolution. This means that such a wife remains a wife and is not free to marry another man. Marrying another man while the original marriage is still in place is a violation of Islamic law and a crime.[25]

The UK Islamic Sharia Council takes a similar view but is more careful in its invitation to Muslims to use its services:

> The Council conducts Islamic divorces only: it does not conduct cases as part of the UK legal or judicial systems: for advice regarding a civil divorce, please consult a qualified, legal representative.[26]

The Muslim Arbitration Tribunal (MAT), established in 2007, has set out to solve the problem of tensions between shari'a expectations and the English judicial process by seeking to operate under the terms of the 1996 Arbitration Act. Ultimately its decisions are therefore subject to the English courts, should a party be dissatisfied with the process or the result. The language used by the MAT is ambiguous. Its description of its procedures refers to 'the Tribunal'.[27] However, in a recent document on forced marriages it regularly uses the term 'Judges'.[28] It is also clear from this document that the MAT sees itself not just as a forum for Alternative Dispute Resolution,[29] but also a potential partner or advisor to the authorities in solving difficult problems, in this case forced marriages.[30] MAT has thus formally located itself under the ultimate judicial authority of the English (non-Muslim) courts. This lies close to the main option suggested by the participants in the 1985 seminars, namely an attempt to create a judicial forum, in the MAT case a quasi-judicial one, which would have Islamic authority while situated within the formal English system, although one step removed by seeking to function as arbitration. For the same reason, the MAT project is opposed by the various shari'a councils for theological reasons – MAT is simply not sufficiently independent of the non-Islamic state – although one is entitled to suggest that political rivalries also have a role to play.

But England is no longer alone in facing this challenge. In his recent study on Muslims in France, John Bowen refers to French Muslim debates about *halal* and *haram* marriages.[31] At one end of the spectrum are those Muslims who refuse to have anything to do with '*kafir* marriage' and live together solely with a *nikah*. At the other end of the spectrum is a practice pursued by many *imams*, also in Belgium, namely agreeing to perform a *nikah*, so long as a civil marriage has already been conducted[32] – thus accepting to operate within the civil legislation. There is also evidence that a number of *imams* give in to parties who insist on having what they call a *halal* marriage, and then possibly going on to a civil marriage at some time later, a practice which carries a possible prison sentence for the *imam*. Some French Muslim scholars argue that the conditions for a valid French marriage are quite valid also in Islamic terms, so there should not be a problem – but again it is the question of whether the authority formalizing the marriage can be regarded as Islamically legitimate.

Recently conducted research in Denmark (unfortunately only in Danish) shows that these questions are also relevant there.[33] The most common practice in all generations and across the ethnic groups, according to this report, is that an Islamic marriage is conducted. Many of these are not formalized as valid civil marriages, although here there are substantial ethnic differences, with the absence of civil marriages being most common among Somalis and least among Turks. Dissolution of such *nikah* marriages, with or without an accompanying civil marriage, is usually conducted through some form of informal arbitration involving family members and/or an *imam*. This can be particularly difficult for women, especially in cultural contexts that are often very unhappy about divorce of any kind. This situation is encumbered by a Danish political-legal environment which is much more reluctant than that of England to countenance cultural flexibility in this area.

In conclusion, it could be argued that the tensions regarding the wish for some form of shari'a family law principles to apply among Muslims living in Europe are – yet another – consequence of Europe's past imperial adventures. The shift of political, legal and cultural primacy to the European imperial centres from the mid-18th century until the late 20th century contributed, firstly, to the freezing of the historically natural evolution of family law with changes in Muslim society and, secondly, to Islamic family law becoming the symbol *par excellence* of Islamic resistance to the imperial projects and their consequences. The arguments over the place of shari'a in Europe therefore have deep symbolic meanings associated with minority identities, which we can only hope to overcome during a long period of negotiation and trial and error.

Notes

1 An early version of some parts of this chapter have previously been published in my paper "Il diritto familiare nelle rivendicazioni dell'inserimento nei paesi europei', in J. Waardenburg (ed.), *I musulmani nella societa europea*, Turin: Fondazione Giovanni Agnelli, 1994, pp. 79-89.

2 Pasha, Syed Aziz, 'Muslim family law in Britain', unpublished paper presented at a meeting at the House of Lords, 20 January 1977, p. 1.
3 Ibid, p. 2.
4 Based on the account given to me by the late Dr Badawi himself in 1980.
5 E. Rude-Antoine, 'L'héritage et les familles maghrébines en France', *Hommes et migrations*, 1097 (15 November 1986), pp. 34-42, originally published in Italian in *Sociologia del dritto*, 1 (1986).
6 D. Pearl, 'Islam in English family law', *Research Papers: Muslims in Europe*, 9 (March 1981), pp. 6-10.
7 Rude-Antoine, 'L'héritage', p. 41.
8 The research was conducted by one of my MA students for a thesis that was never completed. It was based on a survey of the court case files covering 1982 and 1983.
9 See J.S. Nielsen, 'Muslims in Britain and local authority responses', in T. Gerholm and Y.G. Lithman (eds.), *The new Islamic presence in Europe*, London: Mansell, 1988, pp. 53-77.
10 I was the rapporteur of the final report 'Islamic law and its significance for the situation of Muslim minorities in Europe', *Research Papers: Muslims in Europe*, 35 (September 1987). It was also published in German as 'Das islamische Recht und seine Bedeutung für die Lage der muslimischen Minderheiten in Europa', *Evangelische Pressedienst*, 34/87 (3 August 1987), and in French as 'La loi islamique et son importance pour la situation des minorités musulmanes en Europe', Brussels: Comité des églises auprès des travailleurs migrants en Europe, 1987.
11 This was done in an unpublished five-page paper by Michael Mildenberger, dated 31 August 1983. The full file of all this material was never published but I have a copy in my personal possession.
12 Mildenberger, p. 3.
13 Mildenberger, p. 4.
14 See further below.
15 From the unpublished 'Report of a seminar held at Woodbrooke College, Selly Oak, 22-24 February 1985', p. 3.
16 In the United Kingdom, Islamic banking has gone into the retail market. See for example, the Islamic accounts at Lloyds TSB Bank: http://www.lloydstsb.com/current_accounts/islamic_account.asp, accessed 11 November 2011.
17 Here I refer particularly to those trends which are often referred to as Wahhabi or Salafi, rather than to political-radicals sympathetic to networks such as Al-Qa'ida.
18 In this, of course, they follow in a minority tradition within Islamic political thought that has often been opposed to the state, whether in the form of Kharijism and its successive 'rejectionist' cousins or in the form of the refusal of *'ulama'* to take public employment.
19 This can be seen as a spiritualized and pietistic version of the political dualism of people such as Syed Qutb and Abu'l-A'la Maududi.
20 Nielsen, 'Islamic law and its significance', p. 19.

21 A classic example of this, in the area of gifts and endowments, is referred to in N.J. Coulson, *A History of Islamic Law*, Edinburgh: Edinburgh University Press, 1964, pp. 167-170. A similar situation prevailed in Bosnia-Hercegovina after it became a protectorate of Austria in 1878, see Fikret Karčić, 'Secular state and religion(s): Remarks on the Bosnian experience in regulating religion and state relations' in European Abrahamic Forum, *Religion and Secular State: Role and Meaning of Religion in a Secular State from Jewish, Christian and Muslim Perspectives*, Zürich: European Abrahamic Forum, 2008, pp. 15-25.

22 www.matribunal.com, accessed 28 November 2011.

23 For a similar understanding in France see John Bowen, *Can Islam be French? Pluralism and Pragmatism in a Secularist State,* Princeton: Princeton University Press, 2010, pp. 160f. For England see Samia Banno, 'Muslim women, divorce and Shari'ah councils in Britain' in Rubya Mehdi *et al.* (eds.), *Interpreting Divorce Laws in Islam*, Copenhagen: DJØF, 2012, pp. 259-288.

24 Gillian Douglas *et al.*, *Social Cohesion and Civil Law: Marriage, Divorce and Religious Courts Report of a Research Study funded by the AHRC*, Cardiff University: Cardiff Law School, 2011, pp. 47f., accessed 28 November 2011 at http://ssrn.com/abstract=1940387. I am grateful for the steady feed of relevant information provided by colleagues on the mailing list 'Accommodation in Pluri-Legal Europe' (pluri-legal@jiscmail.ac.uk).

25 http://www.islam21c.com/islamic-law/912-fatwa-a-civil-divorce-is-not-a-valid-islamic-divorce, accessed 27 November 2011. The author, Sheikh Haitham al-Haddad, is a member of the UK Islamic Sharia Council but is here writing in his personal capacity, http://www.islamic-sharia.org/about-us/about-us-4.html, accessed 28 November 2011.

26 http://www.islamic-sharia.org/how-it-works/how-the-isc-works-3.html, accessed 28 November 2011.

27 http://www.matribunal.com/procedure_rules.html, accessed 1 December 2011.

28 http://www.matribunal.com/downloads/MAT%20Forced%20Marriage%20Report.pdf, accessed 27 November 2011. On its main page (see next note) it is more careful when it says that its 'arbitrators act like judges.'

29 The MAT explicitly associates itself with this concept; see http://www.matribunal.com/alt_dispute_res.html, accessed 27 November 2011.

30 http://www.matribunal.com/downloads/MAT%20Forced%20Marriage%20Report.pdf, especially section 6; accessed 27 November 2011.

31 John Bowen, *Can Islam be French? Pluralism and Pragmatism in a Secular State*, Princeton: Princeton University Press, 2010, pp. 158-165.

32 To conduct a religious marriage before the civil marriage is a criminal offence in Belgium, France and the Netherlands.

33 Annika Liversage and Tina Gudrun Jensen, *Parallelle Retsopfattelser i Danmark*, Copenhagen: SFI, 2011, also accessible at http://www.sfi.dk/rapportoplysninger-4681.aspx?Action=1&NewsId=3144&PID=9267.

5 The Netherlands

Applying Shari'a to Family Law Issues in the Netherlands

Susan Rutten

Introduction

According to the latest official count, there were 837,000 Muslims in the Netherlands in 2007.[1] Muslims therefore make up between 5 and 6 per cent of the entire population. The majority still possesses a foreign nationality, often in addition to their Dutch nationality.[2]

When considering the application of shari'a to matters of family law in the Netherlands, a distinction may be made between the application of shari'a by the authorities under the Dutch national legal order, on the one hand, and application of shari'a among Muslims themselves within the informal social legal order, on the other hand. In the former situation, Muslims are subjected by the State to shari'a family law; in the latter, Muslims are subjected to Dutch secular law, but observe shari'a principles within the informal social legal order.

Formal application of Shari'a

With regard to the first category, application of shari'a under the national legal system, two features of the Dutch legal order must be taken into account. The first is that religious legal systems, which may exist and co-exist in other countries, are not allowed in the Dutch legal order, as Dutch law is secular law. There is separation of Church and State, meaning that State law cannot be based on religious principles and State authorities may not impose religious norms on citizens. The second feature concerns the way in which the law governing family issues is organized in the Netherlands, whereby family disputes may be resolved at different levels.

First, they may be resolved according to the rules of private international law. Rules of private international law apply where a case relating to family law is considered to have an international character. As a result, foreign law may enter into the Dutch legal order in two ways: either through recognition of relationships or decisions established abroad or through application of foreign law by the Dutch authorities. Quite often, Dutch rules on private international family law still refer to the law of a person's nationality. If that foreign law still observes, or is based on, shariʿa law, the Dutch authorities apply shariʿa rules indirectly.

The second level at which family law is applied is that of foreign diplomatic authorities. These can be consulted by foreign nationals in relation to all kinds of matters, such as the conclusion of a marriage and the establishment of a marriage contract, including agreement between the spouses on such matters as the dower, the establishment of parentage, reconciliation attempts, other family disputes, and matters of succession. The fact that diplomatic authorities can intervene in all kinds of family affairs and mediate or, to a large extent, indirectly decide in accordance with the principles of shariʿa, seems to diminish the need among Muslims to have their disputes resolved by Islamic religious authorities in informal settings.

The third level is the level of Dutch substantive law, which in itself offers a variety of possibilities for introducing shariʿa concepts.

Informal application of Shari'a

With regard to the informal application of shariʿa among Muslims themselves, there is no general legal impediment to this practice. So long as the limits set by the national legal system are respected, people are free to conduct themselves as they wish. Acting in accordance with shariʿa law is therefore permitted, on condition that Dutch law is observed. Muslims are even permitted to consult religious authorities, providing that Dutch law is not violated. Only in relation to a very small number of issues does Dutch law prescribe a certain sequence of actions, in the sense that religious activities may only take place after obligations under civil law have been fulfilled. The most explicit rule is the one governing marriage: a religious marriage may not take place unless a civil marriage between the spouses has already been concluded.[3]

However, acting in accordance with shariʿa principles may give rise to legal disputes. In that event, the informal and the national legal order may converge. Although shariʿa rules respected within the informal social order will not be officially recognized under the national legal system, the fundamental rights of Muslims, such as women's rights, may be at stake. Protection of these fundamental rights might be disrespected within the informal social order. The question arises as to what role human rights can play in protecting the social position of Muslims within their informal social order.

In this article, the application of shari'a as a legal system will not be discussed. In what follows, I focus on describing the legal instruments that may be used to either accept or reject shari'a as rules of conduct for Muslims in their daily life. As a result, I will reflect neither on issues of private international law, nor on the application of shari'a law by foreign consular authorities. In the following I will therefore first discuss the application of shari'a concepts within Dutch substantive law and, second, the legal attitude towards the use of shari'a in informal social settings. After having described the legal framework and the legal instruments available, I will conclude the article by briefly discussing the relevance of the political climate and political policy towards migration and integration, and the way in which this may affect the issue of applying shari'a in the Netherlands.

Applying Shari'a Under the Dutch Legal System

In this section, I will discuss the extent to which Dutch law enables Muslims to apply shari'a to family law issues. This will be explained by describing the legal instruments available to accommodate religious family law values. The following instruments will be discussed: 1. party autonomy; 2. the favour-principle; 3. the use of open norms by the legislator; 4. express legal provisions to accommodate expressions of religion; and 5. the fundamental right to freedom of religion.

Party autonomy

Many family disputes may be settled by the parties themselves, either by bilateral agreement or unilateral declaration, or by merely fulfilling religious obligations, for example within the context of bringing up children. However, the formal requirements set by Dutch law must be met. For instance, divorce can only be pronounced by a court of law,[4] and marriage can only be concluded before the civil authorities.[5] The divorce or marriage of Muslims carried out by an *imam* in the Netherlands will not be recognized by law. Where there are no formal requirements set by law, the parties are free to organize their family issues as they wish, with or without the involvement of an Islamic authority.

A second restriction is found in the applicable substantive legal rules themselves. It must be borne in mind that the applicable substantive law will often be determined by rules of private international law. Since many Muslims in the Netherlands still possess a foreign nationality, private international law will always come into play in matters of family law. For the purposes of this article, I will only discuss *Dutch* substantive law. Agreements governed by private law are usually valid as long as they are not in contravention of the law, public policy, or good morals.[6] Future spouses are free, in principle, to agree for instance on the dower the man will have to pay to the woman according to shariʿa law.[7] Only where the agreement violates public policy will the autonomy of the parties be limited. Another example is the following: people are free to determine how their property should be disposed of after their death. Under the rules of private international law, the applicable substantive law will either be the law of the nationality of the deceased or the law of his last habitual residence.[8] Should the conflict rule refer to Dutch inheritance law, only a few restrictions must be taken into account and the disposition may not be contrary to good morals or public policy.[9] So long as these restrictions are observed, distribution of the estate according to shariʿa law is enforceable.

The favour-principle

In some instances, the parties may choose which one of several alternatives is to be applied. In these situations, a choice may be made for the alternative that mostly favours shariʿa principles. An example is found in the law governing names. The free choice of a child's first name is given to the parents.[10] They are allowed to choose 'one of the 99 beautiful names of Allah'[11] if they so desire. Parents are also afforded the possibility of opting for either the mother's or the father's family name as their child's family name.[12] Thus, in order to demonstrate the child's legal descent and to show its observance of Islamic religion, its parents may opt for the name of the Muslim father.

Express provisions and open norms

Dutch family law does not include provisions that expressly accommodate the application of shariʿa or other religious principles.[13] On the other hand, the Dutch legislator has deliberately laid down open norms in several family law provisions, so that the specific circumstances of each case, changing circumstances and other developments may be taken into account.[14] The 'interest' or the 'best interest' of the child is such a concept. It is used in all custody cases and in cases of child protection and needs to be construed depending on the factual circumstances of the case. It is debatable whether a child's upbringing in accordance with shariʿa would be in its interest, or whether circumcision is in the interest of the Muslim child concerned. It follows from Dutch case law that, if parents disagree on the circumcision of their child, circumcision is not readily considered to be in the interest of a Muslim boy.[15] However, the Dutch courts will only arrive at such a conclusion after having weighed up the various interests and circumstances involved in the case. One consideration is the religious and social interests of the parents and the child in having him circumcised.[16]

Freedom of religion

Freedom of religion and the practice of religion are fundamental rights, guaranteed, *inter alia*, in Article 9 of the European Convention on Human Rights. Although the provisions of this article are applicable in the Netherlands, invoking freedom of religion has hardly ever been successful in matters of family law. In family law issues, freedom of religion usually has to be balanced against other interests at stake, such as the gender equality principle, the interest of the child and public interests. Since it is common sense that the gender equality principle in Europe is of fundamental value and that the interest of a child should be given predominant weight as far as children are involved, balancing the interests often results in attaching more weight to these latter interests.[17]

The Use of Shari'a in Informal Social Settings and the Role of Human Rights

Human rights may have a variety of functions where the application of shari'a is concerned. On the one hand, human rights may serve as a shield *against* the application of certain shari'a family law rules. Where shari'a violates the principle of gender equality, the principle of equality between spouses, the principle of equality on the basis of birth, or the principle of equality on the basis of religion, its application is not accepted as a rule. In this event, application and recognition of foreign shari'a family law rules may be refused. These grounds are also invoked in the debate about shari'a councils (see discussion below). Furthermore, they impede the operation of shari'a in all other areas of domestic law, for example where shari'a condones violence or prescribes circumcision.

On the other hand, human rights, primarily the right to freedom of religion, may be used to *accommodate* the application of shari'a. However, as we have seen above, this freedom of religion is rarely successfully invoked in Dutch family disputes.

And finally, human rights may be used as a tool to offer protection against human rights violations brought about in the informal social religious order. This last function of human rights will be discussed in more detail in the next section.

The example of the 'chained wife'

The example of the 'chained wife' concerns the following situation: a Muslim wife has married a Muslim husband in both a religious and a civil ceremony. Only the civil marriage is legally valid in the Netherlands. In the case of divorce, it is the Dutch court, and the Dutch court only, which can rule on the divorce. The court will only dissolve the civil marriage, not the religious one. The latter can only be dissolved in religious proceedings. To obtain such a divorce, Muslims must apply to religious or consular authorities. To acquire a religious divorce, the cooperation of the husband is usually required. If the husband refuses to cooperate, the wife will remain in her religious marriage. As a result, she will not be free to enter into a new relationship. Her right to marry, her right to start a (new) family, and her right to develop and participate freely in society (her right of self-determination), are some of the rights that may be thwarted. The phenomenon of the 'chained wife' first emerged within Jewish communities, where it is presumably better known. The term 'chained wife' stems from the *aguna*, the chained wife under Jewish law who was not able to receive her *get*, the Jewish letter of divorce her ex-husband had to hand over to her. Nowadays, this issue has been extended to Muslim women.

In fact, Dutch case law does permit women to apply to the court for an order to force the ex-husband to cooperate with a religious or consular divorce. Already in 1982, the Netherlands Supreme Court recognized the possibility of ordering a Jewish ex-husband to deliver a *get* to his ex-wife before rabbinical authorities in the Netherlands.[18] In 1989, the same Court recognized the possibility of ordering a Muslim ex-husband to cooperate with a consular divorce so that the divorce would be valid in the state of origin as well.[19] In a case in 2010, a Pakistani Muslim woman, who applied to a Dutch Court of First Instance to force her husband to cooperate with an Islamic divorce carried out by an *imam*, was granted her request.[20]

In all these cases, the application was based on tort: depending on the circumstances of the case and the interests involved, failure to cooperate with a religious divorce after a civil divorce has been obtained may be regarded as a civil wrong (negligence) committed against the ex-wife. The issue was thus resolved in accordance with the provisions of Dutch substantive private law.

The question may arise as to whether the wife, to have the matter resolved, could also have successfully invoked human rights and thus be released from her marriage.[21] It can be argued that the human rights of a chained wife, as summed up previously, had been violated. However, at least three dilemmas would have to be overcome. The first dilemma is that, since shari'a represents informal law, the wife is only informally chained to the marriage. Legally, she is divorced; formal impediments to entering into a new relationship no longer exist. Should human rights be invoked for the sole purpose of resolving the social problems women face within the informal legal order? My answer would be in the affirmative. Human rights protect real-life situations regardless of how these have come about. In a democratic, pluralist society, authorities should recognize that problems may exist within the informal legal order. Recognition of the existence of informal religious marriages and the social results of such marriages is a precondition for the will to have it solved by legal means. In a case concerning a Jewish *aguna* decided by the Canadian Supreme Court in 2007, the Court considered the following:[22]

> Recognizing the enforceability by civil courts of agreements to discourage religious barriers to remarriage, addresses the gender discrimination those barriers may represent and alleviates the effects they may have on extracting unfair concessions in a civil divorce. This harmonizes with Canada's approach to equality rights, to divorce and remarriage generally, to religious freedom, and is consistent with the approach taken by other democracies.

The second dilemma concerns the following question: should a secular state and secular courts intervene in religious disputes? My answer to this question would again be in the affirmative.[23] Although States must exercise restraint in intervening in religious affairs, secular authorities may intervene if human rights are not observed in the application of religious rules. This was the argument used by the European Court of Human Rights in the case of Pellegrini v Italy, where the procedural fundamental rights of one of the spouses had been violated during the Christian Court proceedings,[24] and more recently in two cases where churches were not allowed to dismiss one of their employees because they maintained an extramarital relationship.[25]

The third dilemma reads as follows: must the parties themselves respect human rights in their private relationships? Not the State as public authority, but the ex-husband himself, is ordered by the court to cooperate in a private legal act, that is, a divorce, within the private marital relationship. Of the three dilemmas, the last one may be the hardest to solve. Although human rights are primarily invoked against State authorities, there is a tendency to accept that human rights are enforceable in private relationships as well.[26] Direct application of human rights in the situation of the chained wife is an interesting option that deserves to be examined more thoroughly. Should direct application not yet be accepted, human rights could at least be used to support the wife's civil claim aimed at having her chained position terminated. For one could at least argue that neglecting the fundamental rights of the wife would easily constitute an act of tort.

Application of Shariʿa: Politically Sensitive

Application of shariʿa in the Netherlands does not seem to be merely a legal question that can be answered by legal reasoning alone. Rightly or wrongly, it seems to be inextricably intertwined with policies on migration and integration. In the course of time, however, these policies have taken different forms. In the 1970s, the presence of migrants in the Netherlands was supposed to be temporary.[27] Since it was assumed that migrants would return to their countries of origin, they were allowed to fully keep their identities.[28] From the end of the 1970s onwards, there was growing awareness that migrant residency had assumed a permanent nature. The objective then became for minorities to participate fully in society.[29]

The integration of migrants required mutual adaptation and recognition of existing diversity. In the Integration Memorandum 2007-2011, social cohesion, social integration and participation are deemed essential conditions for integration.[30] Very diverse ideas on ethnic, cultural and religious differences within society would have to be bridged. Society realized that integration would be a long process spanning several generations. On several occasions, the European Court of Human Rights stressed the importance of tolerance and acceptance of religious pluralism in present-day democratic pluralist societies.[31] But by 2010, the government's patience suddenly seems to have run out. Multicultural society has failed, a Dutch Minister has proclaimed.[32] Specific integration policy was put on hold. It was felt that many aspects of foreign cultures hamper the process of integration. The political majority's policy of that time seems to be barring foreign elements from society.

In June 2011, in a paper entitled *Integratie, binding, en burgerschap* (Integration, bonding, and citizenship), the Dutch Minister of Internal Affairs launched the government's new perspective on integration.[33] In this paper, the government endeavours to establish a common and recognizable basis for all its citizens. This common basic foundation is first of all shaped by the social achievements of Dutch society and by such fundamental values as freedom, equality, equal respect for all citizens, tolerance and solidarity. However, according to the Minister, existing unwritten codes of conduct also form part of this common basis. The Minister furthermore states that the Dutch government is also aware of the concerns about the incompatibility between the Western and the Islamic way of life among the traditional population,[34] and its attitude towards symptoms of radicalization, violence, and other antidemocratic acts.[35] The government also states that it considers itself responsible for allaying these concerns.[36] This is a crucial, but worrisome point, as policy is no longer determined by existing incompatibilities and real dangers, but by fear; the fear that incompatibilities and dangers will be the decisive factor, whether such fears have a basis in reality or not.

Measures are to be developed in the area of family law in relation to foreign marriages. Marriage immigration is blamed as one of the reasons for migrants' failure to integrate. In particular, marriages entered into abroad with spouses not prepared for Dutch society are deemed to cause problems of integration and oblige society to make costly efforts to overcome the disadvantaged position of women and children. The government therefore intends to tighten the rules on marriage immigration, in particular as regards forced and polygamous marriages. In this respect, the government is pursuing a multidisciplinary approach, opting for both legal and non-legal, often social, measures. The intended legal measures are in the areas of family law,[37] private international law,[38] and criminal law,[39] as well as in the area of migration law.[40]

It is interesting to see that the issue of forced and polygamous marriages is nowadays approached from a totally different angle than previously. In the past, the issue was regarded as either a gender or human rights issue, or from the perspective of multiculturalism. As a gender and human rights issue, the most important goal used to be the provision of legal instruments to protect the interests of the wife in a forced or polygamous marriage. These instruments were found in family law (marriage impediments), in private international law (refusal to recognize such marriages), and sometimes in criminal law (penalization of such marriages). Nowadays, what seem to have become of paramount importance are the consequences of such marriages for migration and integration. This change in attitude is to be regretted, since it implies a high risk of overlooking the specific interests of the parties concerned and of attaching too much weight to public interest. If the proposals are implemented and prove to be successful, the result will be less acceptance of shari'a in the Netherlands.

Conclusion

The Dutch legislator has expressly and deliberately allowed the application of foreign law – by rules of private international law and by accepting the competence of foreign diplomatic authorities – and the practice of religion. Furthermore, legal instruments are employed, such as party autonomy, open norms, and the favour-principle, so that all kinds of interests may be taken into account. By means of these techniques, shari'a has been formally included in the Dutch legal order. At the same time, the Dutch legal system offers a number of principles restricting the use of shari'a: the secular nature of the Dutch legal system, the prevalence of human rights, and the legal constraints of 'good morals' and 'public policy', which function as 'shields'.

Although the Dutch legal system may be well equipped to cope with legal and religious pluralism and consequently with shari'a, some issues remain to be resolved. There is room for improvement in the application of existing legal instruments, which could be refined. The question is how to achieve this. If shari'a manifestly infringes human rights or public policy, shari'a may not be applied. Where the application of shari'a does not violate Dutch legal standards, it may be readily accepted. From a legal perspective, less clear situations, such as the question of whether Muslim parents are allowed to have their sons circumcised, are the most challenging and open to debate. The instruments provided by Dutch law to cope with these situations seem to be appropriate. However, correct application of the instruments often requires more understanding of the relevance and significance of shari'a principles for those Muslims concerned.

Another problem results from the way in which the gap between the application of Dutch laws and the application of shari'a family law to Muslims and their observance of shari'a family law within the informal legal order is to be bridged. A precondition for resolving this dilemma is recognition of the informal legal order as a social reality. Legal recognition of this social reality, in the sense of legitimizing informal conduct, is not necessary, however, nor is it desirable in general. However, denial on principle of any legal relevance of the informal setting would entail not taking into account genuine, existing interests. Dutch secular rules already allow a certain degree of observance of shari'a.

In addition, human rights are a potential instrument for coping with difficulties ensuing from the informal application of Islamic family law. These often concern the position of women and that of related persons in non-marital relationships, such as partners and their children. Human rights could be an interesting instrument in protecting the position of women and children against unfair consequences of their observance of shari'a. Thus far, human rights have rarely played such a role, and the further development of this role should thus be encouraged.

Notes

1 http://www.cbs.nl/NR/rdonlyres/ACE89EBE-0785-4664-9973-A6A00A457A55/0/2007k3b15p48art.pdf.
2 http://www.cbs.nl/nl-NL/menu/themas/bevolking/publicaties/artikelen/archief/2012/2012-3578-wm.htm.
3 Article 68 of Book 1 of the Dutch Civil Code.
4 Article 55 of Book 10 of the Dutch Civil Code (in force since 1 January 2012). In earlier jurisprudence: Netherlands Supreme Court (HR) 31 October 1986, *Nederlandse Jurisprudentie* (*NJ*) 1987, 924.
5 Article 68 of Book 1 of the Dutch Civil Code.
6 Article 40 of Book 3 of the Dutch Civil Code.
7 Agreements on a dower often gave rise to questions of characterization. Should such an agreement be classified as a marital agreement, a maintenance agreement or a contract *sui generis*? For a more extensive discussion of these questions, see the contribution by N. Yassari in chapter 9 of this volume.
8 Articles 145 and 146 of Book 10 of the Dutch Civil Code and the 1989 Hague Convention on Succession.
9 Article 44 of Book 4 of the Dutch Civil Code.
10 Article 4 of Book 1 of the Dutch Civil Code.
11 K.M. Sharma, 'What's in a Name? Law, Religion, and Islamic Names,' *Denver Journal of International Law and Policy* 1997-1998 (Vol. 26, No. 2), pp. 151-207; A. Schimmel, *Islamic Names*, Edinburgh University Press 1989 (series: Islamic Surveys).
12 Article 5 of Book 1 of the Dutch Civil Code.
13 The last provisions that expressly referred to religious interests were repealed on 1 January 2005. These articles prescribed that the religious character of a foster institute and the religion of the child should be taken into account when placing a child in a foster family.
14 R.J.S. Schwitters, *Recht en samenleving in verandering. Een inleiding in de rechtssociologie*, Deventer: Kluwer, 2008 (2nd ed.), pp. 56-57.
15 S.W.E. Rutten, 'Besnijdeniszaken voor de Nederlandse rechter,' in: Pauline Kruiniger (ed.), *Recht van de Islam 24*, Den Haag: Boom Juridische Uitgeverij, 2010, pp. 67-78.
16 Court of Appeal 's-Hertogenbosch, Judgment of 26 November 2002, LJN: AF2955.
17 Supreme Court 1 July 1982, *Nederlandse Jurisprudentie* (NJ) 1983, 201 (child protection measure); Court of Appeal 's-Hertogenbosch 26 November 2002, LJN: AF2955 (circumcision of a male child); ECtHR 29 November 2007, appl.nr. 37614/02 (Ismailova t. Rusland) (upbringing by Jehovah's Witness and awarding of custody); Supreme Court 9 November 2001, NJ 2002, 279 (unilateral

repudiation); Court of First Instance Rotterdam 27 January 2010, LJN: BL1502 (unequal positions of men and women with regard to denial of paternity).

18 Supreme Court 22 January 1982, *Nederlandse Jurisprudentie* 1982, 489. More recently: Court of First Instance Amsterdam 10 April 2012, LJN: BW3800.

19 Supreme Court 10 November 1989, *Nederlandse Jurisprudentie* 1990, 112.

20 Court of First Instance Rotterdam 8 December 2010, LJN: BP8396.

21 See also Susan Rutten, 'Protection of spouses in informal marriages by human rights,' *Utrecht Law Review* 2010, 2 (Special Issue: Human Rights Law as a Site of Struggle over Multicultural Conflicts. Comparative and Multidisciplinary Perspectives), pp. 77-92.

22 Canadian SC 14 December 2007, No. 31212, *Bruker v. Marcovitz.*

23 I wrote extensively about this question in a Dutch-language article entitled 'Het recht van de gescheiden vrouw om verlost te worden uit het huwelijk', *NJCM-Bulletin* 2008 (33)/6), pp. 755-769.

24 ECtHR 20 July 2001, appl.no. 30882/96 (*Pellegrini v Italy*).

25 ECtHR 23 September 2010, appl.no. 425/03 (*Obst v Germany*) and ECtHR 23 September 2010, appl.no. 1620/03 (*Schüth v Germany*).

26 See, for example, article 16 CEDAW. More extensively on this point: Susan Rutten, 'Het recht van de gescheiden vrouw', 2008, 'Protection of spouses', 2010.

27 Report of the WRR (Wetenschappelijke Raad voor het Regeringsbeleid), 2001, p. 168; Report of the Tijdelijke Commissie Onderzoek Integratiebeleid "Bruggen bouwen", TK 2003-2004, 28689, nrs. 8-9, p. 28.

28 Idem.

29 Ministerie van Binnenlandse Zaken, 1983, *Minderhedennota*, TK 1982-1983, 16102, nrs. 20-21, Den Haag; Ministerie van Binnenlandse Zaken, 1994, *Integratiebeleid etnische minderheden; contourennota*, TK 1993-1994, 23 684, nrs.1-2.

30 Integratienota 2007-2011, TK 2007-2008, 31268, nrs. 1-2, pp. 11-18.

31 See: Eva Brems, 'Human Rights as a Framework for Negotiating/Protecting Cultural Differences – An Exploration of the Case-Law of the European Court of Human Rights', M-Cl. Foblets *et al.* (eds.), *Cultural Diversity and the Law*, Bruxelles Bruylant 2010, pp. 663-715.

32 TK 2010-2011, 32824, nr. 1, p. 3.

33 TK 2010-2011, 32824, nr. 1.

34 41% of these citizens.

35 No numbers are given.

36 Integratienota 2011, pp. 5-6.

37 Attributing authority to the Public Prosecutor to suspend a forced marriage, facilitating the nullification of forced marriages, extending the persons who may nullify a forced marriage by attributing this competence also to the Public Prosecutor, prohibiting marriages between nieces and nephews unless the partners can prove that there is no forced marriage, and increasing the marital age to 18 years.

38 Forced marriage as an express ground for invoking public policy, in case of a threat: Dutch law always applies where there is a ground for invoking public policy; removing the attributive rule that refers to foreign law, listing age as a ground for invoking public policy, strengthening recognition policy with regard to polygamous marriages.
39 Increase in the number of prosecutions, instituting extraterritorial criminal authority; penalizing forced marriages abroad, not only when committed by own nationals but also by foreigners with durable residence in the Netherlands, extending the period of prescription.
40 Refusal of residency permits in case of forced marriages, arranged marriages between nieces and nephews, child marriages, polygamous marriages, and marriages of convenience.

6 Albania and Kosovo

The Return of Islam in South East Europe: Debating Islam and Islamic Practices of Family Law in Albania and Kosovo

Besnik Sinani

Introduction

Albania emerged at the end of the communist era in Eastern Europe as the only country where the communist regime had completely banned and penalized the practice of religion. It is also the only Balkan country to have emerged from the collapse of the Ottoman Empire with a mainly Islamic population: an estimated 70 per cent of Albanians are Muslims. Following the fall of communism, Albania has been seeking integration in the European Union and it is often feared that any revival of its Islamic identity will be an impediment to that endeavour.

Kosovo, the other Albanian-populated country in the Balkans, declared independence from Serbia in 2008 and has been seeking Western support and European integration. Although religion was not banned in Kosovo under the Yugoslav Federation, as happened in Albania, the communist regime discouraged the practice of religion. Nevertheless, Kosovo is facing dilemmas very similar to those faced by Albania regarding its religious tradition.

In both these countries, the Albanian Muslim Community (AMC) in Albania and the Islamic Community of Kosovo (ICK) in Kosovo represent Islam in relation to the governments and hold control and ownership of the mosques and educational institutions. Both these institutions have suffered from inherited weakness due to the long suppression of religion in Albania during the communist regime and the strict control of religion in Kosovo under the Yugoslav Federation. It is believed that this weakness created the conditions for the presence of Middle Eastern charity organizations in the 1990s that were instrumental, among other things, in providing scholarships for a new generation of Albanians to study at Middle Eastern Islamic universities. Upon their return, many of them questioned the legitimacy and the religious credentials of representatives of the older generation who led the representative institutions.

In more recent years, however, both these institutions have become stronger, due to a number of factors: first, governments in both Albania and Kosovo have preferred to negotiate with these institutions than with other Muslim organizations; second, Muslim activists in various Muslim civil society organizations, even those critical of the leadership, seem to have recognized that the strength of these institutions is beneficial for the whole community; and a third factor in Albania relates to representatives of the Gülen Movement, an organization with Turkish roots, having taken control of the leadership of the AMC. Despite criticism from other Muslims, followers of the Gülen Movement in Albania have concentrated their efforts on strengthening the AMC and on taking control of mosques and other religious institutions in the country.

Today, in both of these countries with Albanian majority populations, questions are often raised in public debates regarding the way Western Europe perceives the Islamic identity of Albanians and whether Islam is a hindrance to integration in Europe. These questions are part of a common debate in Kosovo and Albania on identity, perceptions of the Ottoman past, and political and cultural orientation.[1] These concerns have affected attitudes towards Islamic practices and particularly the novelty of women wearing headscarves and men growing beards is perceived as tarnishing the image of Albanians in the West.

This chapter will discuss some of the debates that have emerged from the political elites regarding Islam in both Kosovo and Albania; debates that are mutually informed and influenced by one another. Furthermore, I will examine some examples of practices in matters of Islamic family law, whereby I will limit myself to those from Albania.

Under the Gaze of Europe

On 15 October 2011, the President of the newly independent Republic of Kosovo, Atifete Jahjaga, gave a speech in a remote region of her country, near the border with neighbouring Albania, in honour of Shtjefën Gjeçovi (1873-1929), a Catholic priest of the Franciscan order who is known for having recorded the tribal code that governed the highland regions, known as the *Kanun of Lekë Dukagjini*. Speaking about the *Kanun* and the role of the Catholic Church in the forefront of the struggle for freedom and progress in the history of the Albanian people, she added:

> Through the *Kanun* of the Mountains, known as the *Kanun of Lekë Dukagjini*, the descendants of Scanderbeg in their national resistance

> against the Ottoman invasion regulate the lives of people and this made it impossible for the implementation of *shari'a* in these lands and among our people of the Catholic or of the Muslim faith. In our lands it was unconceivable for the Ottoman authorities to cut off the hand of someone accused of stealing or to apply fifty lashes to someone's body in public. So this *Kanun* preserved the honour and dignity of the individual and the national dignity for over five hundred years.[2]

Anti-Ottoman rhetoric is common in Albanian nationalist discourse and Albanian nationalism considers mountains 'as sanctuaries of the nation' where national values were preserved. The *Kanun* is perceived as a particularly Albanian institution instrumental in this preservation of the national character.[3] Juxtaposing Christianity and particularly Catholicism as the opposite 'other' of Islam – one representing Europe, progress, liberty and an indigenous religious experience, and the other representing a backward, eastern, foreign threat – has also been part of Albanian political rhetoric since the fall of communism. This situation, in which the leaders of a Muslim-majority country reject Islam and allude to Christianity as the true legacy of the people of Albania and Kosovo, has occurred repeatedly in recent years.

Six years earlier, in 2005, addressing an audience at the Oxford Union in the United Kingdom, the former President of Albania (2002-2007), Alfred Moisiu, declared that in essence, Albanians are Christians and Islam is not an original religion of the Albanians.[4] In a similar vein, former deputy Prime Minister of Albania, Gramoz Pashko (1991-1995), stated in a paper he wrote on Christianity that the only hope for Albania is its young generation, 'which has loved European Civilization and Christian values.' Commenting on Mr. Pashko's writing, the scholar Maria Todorova points out that '[this] frank appeal to Christian values from a country that before it became atheist was 70% Muslim bespeaks the naiveté and straightforwardness of the Albanian political discourse that has not yet mastered the ennobling façade of the pluralist vocabulary.' She further adds: 'It is, however, also a tribute to the sound political instincts of the new Albanian political elites who have not been duped by the pretence of supra-religious, non-racial, and non-ethnic universalism and pluralism of the European or Western discourse.'[5]

In her speech on the *Kanun*, Kosovo President Jahjaga has joined other representatives of the Albanian political elites in Kosovo and Albania in affirming a self-designation of European-ness permeated by Christian values and distancing itself from, if not completely rejecting, Islam.[6] The novelty of President Jahjaga's speech, however, is the reference to shari'a law. The Ottoman past and Islam are often blamed for the backwardness of the Albanians, for being the cause of historical misfortunes and for keeping Albanians away from their natural family of European nations. Shariʿa law, however, has not been part of this tradition of nationalist discourse. The images of the cutting off of hands and flogging in public seem to have been transported from current events in distant territories into threats in the Albanian historical imagination and into the current political discourse, as part of this politically engendered identity construction of being European.

As Talal Asad has pointed out, since the last decades of the twentieth century, Europe has witnessed a shifting of borders that aims to represent what European Civilization is. 'They reflect a history whose unconfused purpose is to separate Europe from alien times ("communism," "Islam") as well as from alien places ("Islam," "Russia").'[7] It is under this configuration of the European identity map that Albanian politicians position themselves in the 'right place' of the dividing line between East and West, Islam and Christianity, where the affirmation of European-ness comes with the rejection of Islam, the Ottoman past and shariʿa law. President Jahjaga's anti-shariʿa rhetoric does not relate to shariʿa per se, since the draconian punishments that she refers to were not part of the Albanian Ottoman experience, and we have not witnessed any calls in Albania or Kosovo for a 'return to shariʿa,' the cutting off of the hands of thieves or the flogging of adulterers. Her reference to shariʿa reflects the fears and anxieties of the West in relation to its former colonial subjects and Muslim migrants, as projected in the political profile of countries in the Balkans that seek to affirm their place in Europe.

On the other hand, Albanian Muslims in their daily life and in their religious practices make attempts to live according to the teachings of their religion, teachings that are known to be part of the corpus of Islamic law, or shariʿa. As I have attempted to show above, there are important similarities, overlapping issues and mutual influences in the discourse of the political elites in both Albania and Kosovo regarding religion. Despite similarities, however, there are differences in religious practices and discourse in Albania and Kosovo. In the next paragraph I will illustrate this discussion with examples of Islamic family law practices, whereby I will restrict myself to the situation in Albania.

Certainly, there is another discourse on shariʿa law emerging in Western Europe that seeks to accommodate aspects of shariʿa family law in the framework of multicultural citizenship.[8] Albanian elites have made clear, however, that their countries will follow a French model of republicanism[9] that sees multiculturalism as equal to a 'balkanization' of society. The dominant and unchallenged notion of citizenship in post-communist Albania and newly-independent Kosovo is permeated with the notion of national interest. However, Muslims are often challenged to answer whether their primary loyalty stands with the nation or with the *Ummah*, the global Muslim community. The assumption embedded in the question is that Muslim loyalties stand with a foreign entity in opposition to the national interest and European identity. The assumption is that young Muslims that embraced Islam after the collapse of communism are loyal to religious agendas originating from the Middle East.[10]

Muslim responses to these challenges have been diverse. Some have appealed to an Anglo-Saxon understanding of secularism when arguing for the right of women to wear the headscarf in public schools. However, there have not been attempts to go as far as to claim separate Muslim judiciary systems or to articulate a notion of similar forms of 'privatized diversity.'[11] Ayelet Shachar points out that 'the main claim raised by advocates of "privatized diversity" is that respect for religious freedom or cultural integrity does not require inclusion in the public sphere, but *exclusion*.'[12] The dominant tendency of Muslims in Albania, however, has been one that seeks inclusion in the dominant societal paradigm and rather than claiming a distinctive place as a tolerated minority, they claim a place for Islam under the national umbrella. Muslim practices related to shari'a, including those practices that incorporate matters of family law, have to be understood through the lenses of a post-communist society that often perceives its Islamic past and current Muslim practitioners as a liability in their bid to join 'the European family'; they have to be understood, also, in terms of a Muslim community that seeks a place for Islam in contemporary Albania, rejecting marginalization.

Islamic Marriage and Divorce in Secular Albania

A question was presented to *imam* Ahmed Kalaja, *imam* of Dine Hoxha Mosque in Albania's capital, Tirana, during a question and answer session in the mosque: 'Am I permitted to hit my wife? Although I haven't got married yet, I have performed the *nikah*.'[13] The *imam* criticized the questioner, advising the congregation to lead a marital life of common understanding and affection, and to overlook shortcomings. He affirmed the permission granted in the sacred texts for such punishment, but he clarified that physical punishment is only allowed in extreme cases when the behaviour of the spouse is posing a threat to the religion and the wellbeing of the children and the family in general. He stressed, however, that the Prophet Muhammad advised against hitting women and mentioned the example of the Prophet who is reported to have never hit a woman or a child.

Next, he addressed the rather awkward situation of the questioner's status of being engaged but not married, although he had performed the Islamic contract of marriage, the *nikah.* A number of couples that intend to build a family and a home together are often, mostly for economic reasons, unable to have their own house and, by consequence, are unable to have a wedding, which is customarily the event after which a couple will live together. The performance of a religious marriage – *nikah* – rather than a civil marriage, however, enables the partners to be in each other's company without the presence of a chaperone. This distinction between being married and not being married, but having performed the *nikah,* seems to worry many *imams.* First of all, it leads to an understanding of *nikah* as somehow less than 'a real marriage.' In these cases, *nikah* seems to resemble what is customarily known in contemporary Albania as the status of being engaged.

The *imam* who answered the question, therefore, emphasized that once the *nikah* has been performed, the couple is considered married and that prior to this, the couple is not allowed to be secluded or have any physical contact. The *imam* emphasized that *nikah* is marriage. A number of *imams* that I interviewed in Tirana insisted that prior to the act of *nikah,* the couple ought to present the marriage certificate from the municipal office. There seem to be two main reasons for taking this approach. According to *imam* Ferid Piku, *hatib* of the Medrese Mosque in Tirana, Islamic law recognizes marriage contracts conducted by non-Muslim entities. If a couple that has been married in a Christian church, for example, later becomes Muslim, they don't have to repeat the marriage, since their marriage is considered valid in Islamic law. Similarly, if a couple is married in the municipal office according to secular law, the marriage is still valid according to Islamic law. Therefore, a couple that is married in the municipal office of a secular state is also considered married by the community of Muslims.[14] According to *imam* Tahir Zeneli, who served as deputy head of the AMC in the 1990s, the Islamic validity of civil marriage contracts is the reason why the AMC did not take any steps to ritually recognize the marriages conducted during the communist regime, as was done by other religious communities, since those marriages were deemed legal and acceptable from an Islamic point of view.[15]

Another important reason, however, why Muslim *imams* in Albania insist that a couple should present a marriage certificate from the municipal office prior to performing the *nikah* contract, is to do with the potential for divorce. According to the abovementioned *imams*, under current conditions, the act of *nikah* or the marriage contract according to Islamic law is more of a religious ritual. An *imam* that concludes a *nikah* has no power in the case of divorce to enforce the consequences of such a divorce, such as the conditions of the financial obligations on husbands as envisioned by Islamic law. In the case of a marriage contracted in the municipal office, however, the divorce litigation can be taken to court. Indeed, the result of such litigation could be very different from that which would be envisioned in Islamic law. However, according to the *imams* that I interviewed, this is preferable to not having any legal recognition of the marriage or any legal protection at all. While quite often, when discussing marital conflicts, these *imams* exposed a gendered view of the relations within the family, when discussing divorce, their main concern was related to securing legal protection for women. Their concern relates to an understanding that in the case of divorce, women are in a position of disadvantage and that the court can provide legal and financial protection.

Certainly, shari'a religious law retains moral strength, but these *imams* argue that matters of marriage and divorce should not depend on the strength of the participants' religious convictions at the time of the marital conflict. In the absence of a system in which Islamic law can impose the obligations ensuing from a divorce settlement, they instead have the laws of the secular state impose a system of safeguards and obligations in the case of divorce, even though these legal obligations do not reflect or otherwise refer to Islamic family law.

According to these *imams*, in almost all cases of marital conflicts where they were asked to serve as mediators, the process of mediation was requested by women. This process of mediation is not recognized by the courts and has no legal weight. The *imams* themselves referred to these processes as 'offering advice;' that is, advice that the couple was free to follow or reject. The approach taken in these mediation processes also differed. Some *imams* preferred to remind the couple of the words of God in the Qur'an and the teaching of the Prophet, the Sunna, in matters of marriage, reminding the couple that although Islam recognizes divorce, 'it is the most hated of the matters that have been allowed.' Other *imams*, however, insisted that the best approach is to counsel on the basis of the standard ethical norms in society for maintaining a healthy marriage. Regarding the models offered in contemporary Albanian society, these *imams* were referring to 'traditional' norms, and they envisioned a gendered understanding of the obligations of women and the responsibilities of men.

It is interesting to note that while traditionally in Islamic law and in many Muslim societies around the world today, the question of divorce is often discussed in relation to the deferred *mahr*, or dowry, and the financial settlements, particularly when the *mahr* amounts to a considerable sum of money and valuable assets, the *mahr* does not seem to carry an equal weight among Albanian Muslims. The concept of *mahr* was abandoned in Albania with the abolition of religion in 1967, but was reintroduced in the 1990s with the re-emergence of religion. The first generation of *imams* that graduated from Islamic universities in the Middle East favoured and preached an idea of *mahr* that avoided large sums of money. Even in conversations with devout Muslims, the idea of large sums of money as *mahr* is scorned as indicating greed, monetizing marriage and as standing in contradiction to the religious principles of Islamic marriage. Albanian *imams* have quoted the prophet Muhammad as stating that even a ring can be given as *mahr*. In most cases, giving a ring as *mahr* has given an additional meaning to the custom, followed by most Albanians regardless of religious affiliation or lack of it, of offering the ring during the engagement party, known as 'the exchange of rings.'

During the early years of the re-introduction of religion in post-communist Albania, one would often hear about conflicts between a young generation of devout Muslims who had discovered a new religious identity and their parents and relatives, who had grown up under communism. The way in which the 'exchange of rings' has been transformed to also represent the offering of *mahr* is one of the ways in which some of these conflicts have been resolved.[16] It is quite common, however, for the *mahr* to constitute the groom's promise to provide for the bride's expenses when performing Haj, the Muslim pilgrimage to Mecca in Saudi Arabia. Since this journey is to be undertaken under the condition that it is financially possible, it is understood by the *imams* in Albania to be a deferred *mahr*. Contrary to the stipulations of the deferred *mahr*, however, it is unheard of for a divorced wife to request that the sum of money needed to pay for the pilgrimage be given to her as part of a divorce settlement.

When it comes to child custody, *imams* in Albania seem to encourage accommodation, arguing that there are no major differences between Islamic law and the secular law that favour the mother, particularly in regard to female children. Certainly, these *imams* are aware that the discussion in Islamic law, particularly regarding male children, is more complex (at a certain age, the custody switches from the mother to the father), yet this position seems to be motivated by the personal conviction that the interests of children will be better served under the care of their mothers – reflecting a gendered view of the role of women as caregivers – as well as by reluctance to take a stance against the law of the land.

This accommodating attitude to the laws and customs of a deeply secularized society is not articulated in religious treatises as a response to living in the context of a secular state. It is in the religious answers to individual cases reflecting the complex realities of devout Muslims that one can see a general tendency to avoid a confrontation with the laws and norms of Albanian society.

There has been more prominent confrontation between religious law and secular state law in matters of political participation. Some *imams* argue against participating in elections, since this amounts to recognizing and supporting a system that is not founded on the laws of God.[17] These voices, however, constitute a very small minority that carries little weight in the community. This stance is even more striking when one considers that the majority of *imams* in Albania were educated in Saudi Arabia in the 1990s, where the religious establishment insisted on preaching an apolitical approach to politics in response to the political opposition of the *Sahwa* movement in Saudi Arabia, following the first Gulf War.[18] Politically active *imams* explain their political engagement in terms of *maslaha*, or public interest, arguing that it is in the community's best interest to be politically active as a way of combating marginalization and achieving better integration in society.[19]

In an interview given to the US-based *Slate* magazine, *imam* Ahmed Kalaja of the Tirana mosque is quoted as saying that 'he tries to "adapt to the peculiarities of the Albanian tradition." He says Albania will always be a society of tolerance, where religion and state are separate.'[20] In arguing for the right of Muslim school girls to wear the headscarf, for example, Albanian Muslims have not argued against the principles of secularism, but have instead appealed to those models of secularism that allow for more religious freedom.[21]

The latest debates between Muslim groups and the governments of Albania and Kosovo have focused on the very same topics: Muslim groups demanded permission to build new mosques[22] in the centres of the capitals of Kosovo and Albania, Prishtina and Tirana, protested against the state's promotion of Mother Teresa, the former Catholic nun and Noble Peace Prize laureate, and also protested against the ban on Muslim female students wearing headscarves in public schools. The building of new mosques was debated in relation to new Christian cathedrals recently built in both capitals. Muslims in both Albania and Kosovo feel that their governments are favouring and supporting Christianity at the expense of Muslims, as part of their attempt to show a more European face. In the view of many Muslims in Albania and Kosovo, the debate over the headscarf is motivated by the same concerns.[23] As shown by the debate about the state's promotion of the legacy and missionary activities of Mother Teresa, Muslims in both Albania and Kosovo have argued that the governments in both countries are acting contrary to the principles of secularism. Many have questioned the sincerity of these Muslim appeals to the principles of secularism and have interpreted them as indications of Islamic fundamentalism and intolerance. What people tend to overlook, however, is that Muslim activists regard secularism as protection from those government policies that they believe favour other religious communities.

Despite the similarities and parallel debates in both countries, Muslims in Albania have not followed the example of Muslims in Kosovo, who, on numerous occasions, have taken to protesting in the streets, sometimes leading to violent confrontations with the police. Imams and Muslim activists in Albania seem to have found their numerical strength to be the most suitable basis for addressing their concerns. The head of one of the major Muslim non-governmental organizations (NGOs) in Albania told me about his conversation with a political candidate in the most recent municipal elections. After the politician had promised support for the building of a new mosque in the capital, the head of the Muslim NGO had responded that the building of the mosque is not the most important priority for Muslims. What Muslims want is not to be made to feel like foreigners in their own country. The common complaint of many Muslims is that many politicians have adopted the European right-wing rhetoric about Muslim immigrants and are using it against Muslims in Albania.[24]

The Reflection of Europe

In October 2011, Albania completed a controversial census of the population that included an optional question on religion. Many people have questioned the results of this census, particularly with regard to the matter of the self-declaration of ethnicity. The census is largely believed and openly celebrated, however, as an opportunity to remove, in the eyes of the outside world, the stigma of Albania as an Islamic country. The AMC called upon the government to remove the questions relating to ethnicity and religion from the census.[25] In October 2011, the AMC restated its reservations regarding the process, but also called on Muslims to freely and proudly declare their ethnic and religious identity.[26]

At the time of writing the results have not been announced, and they are expected to be made public some time in February 2013.

In any case, the manner in which the Albanian Muslim community will deal with the challenges of a society still uneasy about its cultural identity will depend much on how Western Europe deals with its own Muslim communities, on the rhetoric that its leaders adopt when addressing issues related to the Muslim presence in Europe, and on the kind of image Europe reflects for countries such as Albania and Kosovo, that want to emulate Western political and economic systems.

As shown by many debates on social media networks, Muslims in Albania will have to address a number of issues that are today being debated within the community. The place of women in the mosques and their representation in community institutions are only some of the contemporary concerns of devout Muslims. They are also looking for ideas and answers from the West, as is shown by increased interest in the translation and the study of the works of Western Muslim thinkers such as Timothy J. Winter and Tariq Ramadan, who recently visited Kosovo and Albania.[27] There is an increased awareness that Muslim identity and practices will have to reflect the national consensus of modelling their society on the European model. The question remains, however: will Europe reflect a vision that represents its Muslims?

Notes

1 In 2006, a debate on the identity of Albanians between Dr. Rexhep Qosja, a political activist and member of the Academy of Science of Kosovo, and Ismail Kadare, the best-known Albanian writer and many times candidate for the Nobel Prize for Literature, dominated the headlines in the media for four months. Dr. Rexhep Qosja held the view that the cultural identity of the Albanians has been influenced by both Eastern and Western cultures and that this experience has enriched Albanian cultural identity (Dr. Qosja's main contribution in this debate was later published in a book titled *Realiteti i Shperfillur* [The Neglected Reality], Toena: Tirana, 2006). Ismail Kadare held that Albanians are solely Europeans and that any ambiguity in this regard is detrimental to the interests of the Albanians (his main contribution to this debate was also published that same year as a book titled *Identiteti Evopian i Shqiptareve* [The European Identity of the Albanians] Onufri: Tirana, 2006).

2 "Bashkohu: Presidentja të kërkojë falje, ofendoi Sheriatin." [Join us: the President should apologize, she offended the shari'a]. *Express*. 18 October 2011. http://www.gazetaexpress.com/?cid=1,15,65319.

3 See Ulf Brunnbauer and Robert Pichler. "Highland Values and Nation-Building in the Balkans." *Balkanologie* VI [1-2], December 2002, pp. 77-100.

4 Alfred Moisiu, "Fjala e mbajtur ne Unionin e Oxfordit." [Speech presented at the Oxford Union]. http://www.president.al/english/pub/info.asp?id=1089 (the speech cannot be currently accessed from this link. Last accessed in January 2006).

5 Maria Todorova, *Imagining the Balkans*, Oxford University Press: New York, 2009, pp. 45-6.

6 The President of Albania, Bamir Topi, added his weight to this recent debate. In a visit to a remote region of Albania, Mirdita, hometown of Shtjefën Gjeçovi, the Franciscan Priest, Mr. Topi said that, 'Mirdita ... symbolizes the most precious Albanian tradition, the autochthon laws that inspired Father Shtjefën Gjeçovi, the cultural monument of the *Kanun* and the resistance to whoever attempted to violate it. Mirdita symbolizes the strong and unwavering faith and the European Identity... [and the people of Mirdita] built the positive and modern cult of the Albanian cleric.' See "Vizita e Topit në Mirditë." [Topi visits Mirdita]. Top Channel Web Page. 6.12.2011. http://top-channel.tv/artikull.php?id=224425.

7 Talal Asad, 'Muslims and European Identity' in Anthony Pagden (ed.), *The Idea of Europe: From Antiquity to European Identity*. Washington DC: Woodrow Wilson Center Press and Cambridge University Press, 2002, pp. 218-9.

8 See the speech by the Archbishop of Canterbury, Dr. Rowan Williams, at the Royal Courts of Justice. Dr. Rowan Williams, 'Civil and Religious Law in England,' and Tariq Modood, 'Multicultural Citizenship and the shari'a Controversy in Britain,' in Rex Ahdar and Nicholas Aroney (eds.), *Sharia in the West*, New York: Oxford University Press, 2010, pp. 293-308 and 33-42.

9 Arsim Bajrami, Head of the Commission for the Amendment of the Constitution, declared recently that Kosovo will follow a French model of republicanism. See 'Kosova me modelin francez te republikes.' *Telegrafi* 19 November 2011. http://www.telegrafi.com/lajme/kosova-me-modelin-francez-te-republikes-2-18431.html.

10 Piro Misha. *Arratisja Nga Burgjet e Historise: Cdo te thote sot te jesh Shqiptar*. [Escaping the prison of history: What does it mean today to be an Albanian?], Tirana: Toena, 2008, pp. 306-9.

11 By 'privatized diversity' Ayelet Shachar means 'the request by members of religious minorities on the territory of a secular state to *privatize diversity*. By this I refer to the recent proposals raised by self-proclaimed "guardians of the faith" to establish private arbitration tribunals in which consenting members of the group will have their legal disputes resolved in a binding fashion – according to religious principles – under the secular umbrella of alternative dispute-resolution.' In *Sharia in the West*, 2010, pp. 118-9.

12 Ayelet Shachar, *Sharia in the West*, 2010, pp. 118-9.

13 Ahmed Kalaja. 'Sjellja me Gruan.' [Behavior with the spouse], 19 January 2010, http://www.youtube.com/watch?v=xuMhgJRD5zg.

14 Interview with the author, November 2011.

15 Interview with the author, November 2011.

16 For most Albanians, the marriage party is an event that takes a long time to prepare for, and a lot of drinking is expected. This is obviously contrary to the

ethical concerns of a young generation of devout Muslims. In recent times, however, many such parties have been organized using non-alcoholic beer.

17 Besnik Sinani, *From Students of Knowledge to Hoxhas*, unpublished MA thesis, Hagop Kevorkian Center for Near East Studies, New York University, New York, 2010.

18 Stephane Lacroix, 'Between Revolution and Apoliticism: Nasir al-Din al-Albani and his Impact on the shaping of Contemporary Salafism,' in Roel Meijer (ed.), *Global Salafism: Islam's New Religious Movement*, New York: Columbia University Press, 2009, p. 76.

19 Besnik Sinani, 'From Students of Knowledge to Hoxhas.'

20 See Nathan Thrall, 'Albania, the Muslim World's Most Pro-American State,' *Slate*, 3 September 2009. http://www.slate.com/articles/news_and_politics/dispatches/features/2009/albania_the_muslim_worlds_most_proamerican_state/the_muslim_worlds_most_tolerant_nation.html.

21 Besnik Sinani, 'Ajatollahet e Sekularizmit [Ayatollahs of Secularism],' *Shekulli*, 29 April 2009.

22 See Kerem Oktem, 'New Islamic Actors After the Wahabi Intermezzo: Turkey's Return to the Muslim Balkans,' European Studies Center, University of Oxford, December 2010, http://balkanmuslims.com/.

23 Mark Lowen, 'Headscarf ban sparks debate over Kosovo's identity,' BBC *News*, 24 August 2010. http://www.bbc.co.uk/news/world-europe-11065911.

24 Field notes from interviews with Muslim congregants in Tirana, winter 2010 and autumn 2011.

25 AMC, 'Deklarate per Shtyp e Keshillit te Pergjithshem te KMSH-se. [Press announcement of the General Council of AMC],' March 2011. http://www.kmsh.al/aktualitet/410-deklarate-per-shtyp-e-keshillit-te-pergjithshem-te-kmsh-se.html.

26 The census was largely debated because it was perceived as the result of Greek pressure to artificially inflate the size of the Greek minority in Albania. For the second press announcement of AMC see AMC: 'Mblidhet Keshilli i Pergjithshem i Komunitetit Mysliman. [Meeting of the General Council of AMC],' October 2011. http://www.kmsh.al/component/content/article/15-faqja-e-pare/616-mblidhet-keshilli-i-pergjithshem-i-komunitetit-mysliman-te-shqiperise.html.

27 Tariq Ramadan in a speech held in Tirana, Albania, in June 2011, with Albanian translation, titled 'Muslimanet ne Evrope: Sfida dhe Perspektiva. [Muslims in Europe: Challenges and Perspective].' http://www.youtube.com/watch?v=kQY8zQrq1os&feature=player_embedded. See also Tariq Ramadan's interview on Albanian television during the same visit: Interviste ne TV Al Sat: Studio e Hapur me Eni Vasili. [Interview on TV Alsat: Open Studio with Eni Vasili], June 2011. (http://www.youtube.com/watch?v=oziPox-5XPU&feature=player_embedded).

7 Greece

Debate and Challenges

Angeliki Ziaka

Introduction

Within Greece today, the Muslim community makes up almost 2 per cent of the total population and can be found mainly in the region of Western Thrace. It is the legacy of the long-lasting co-existence between Greeks and Ottoman Muslims, along with certain historical situations created both in Greece and the rest of South East Europe. This Muslim community, which is officially recognized by the Greek state, enjoys a unique legal status with regard to familial, hereditary and religious matters, along with a right to implement shari'a law, particularly in accordance with the school (*madhhab*) of Hanafiya.

Perhaps the only example of the implementation of shari'a in Europe, this situation has existed for many years in Greece, but has only recently (that is, in the last few decades) begun to spark discussion between Greek and European jurists, as well as supporters of human rights.[1] For its part, the Muslim community in general seems to be satisfied with this particular status, although they sometimes appeal to the Greek civil courts for relief from decisions by Islamic court functionaries (muftis) that are based on the principles of shari'a, usually ones involving family or inheritance.

In order to further our understanding of the particular situation of the Muslim community in Greece, we need to look at its historical circumstances, as well as the legal and social problems that have arisen from these. We also need to consider the perspectives and possible challenges resulting from the implementation of shari'a in the region of Western Thrace. For many observers, the special status of Muslims in Greece should be regarded as a kind of Ottoman 'neo-milletism', in that it is not only anachronistic, but also contrary to the wording of the Universal Declaration of Human Rights in terms of religious-legal decisions. For others, however, it represents a positive acceptance of religious diversity and constitutes an effective paradigm of skilful co-existence. In the latter case, though, it may be argued that legislators from both sides (from both the Greek-secular and the Muslim-religious sphere) need to modernize and harmonize this situation with regard to current conceptions of human rights, especially in matters that involve family law, the relations between husbands and wives, divorce, inheritance and gender equality.

Geographical, Historical and Legal Overview

A survey of the history and emigration background of Muslims in Greece reveals that Greece, as well as the neighbouring Balkan countries, has a longstanding relationship of co-existence with Islam, mainly because of the special historical conditions in the region and the Greeks' subjugation to the Ottoman Empire from the late fourteenth to the first half of the twentieth century. In other words, nearly five centuries of co-existence have occurred. Independence was a gradual process that started in 1821 with the Greek Revolution against the Ottoman Empire, resulting in the establishment of the first independent nation state in South East Europe (1829-1831).

Ever since the Greek state was established, the Orthodox Christian religion has been predominant and therefore recognized as the official state religion. Christians of other confessions, as well as Muslims and Jews, were recognized as religious minorities in the protocols that were successively signed in London in 1829, 1830 and 1832, reflecting the Great Powers' interest in protecting religious minorities living within the borders of the first independent Greek state.[2] In this Greek state (which covered one-third of the area of modern Greece) there were only a few Muslims, and they were subject to the general Greek legislation without any special legal provisions. Their number rose with the annexation of Thessaly by Greece in 1881. The first international legal document that gave a detailed definition of Greece's obligations towards the Muslim community was the Convention of Constantinople, signed between Greece and the Sublime Porte on 2 July 1881.[3] Tsitselikis notes that 'For the first time, a Muslim minority was protected as a legal entity enjoying religious and educational autonomy.'[4]

After the end of the Balkan Wars (1912-1913), when Greece's borders were extended, the number of Muslims rose again and the legal status of the Muslim minority was regulated by the Convention of Peace between Greece and Turkey (1-14 November 1913 in Athens).[5] Article 11 of the Convention provided additional rights to Muslims with Greek citizenship, such as equality before the law, religious freedom and religious autonomy, and guaranteed their legal status as a community. Article 9 of the Convention also recognized their religious leaders *(muftis, imams, hatibs* and *muezzins)*, and provided special administrative autonomy regarding Muslim property (*waqf* or *vakf*). The Convention safeguarded the freedom to practice Islamic worship, and institutionalized communication between the religious leader of Thrace and the higher Muslim religious leader, Sheikh al-Islam of Constantinople. Several years later, in 1920, when the Kingdom of Greece acquired large portions of Ottoman territory (including Eastern Thrace up to 30 kilometres from Constantinople, and Smyrne [Izmir] and its wider administrative area), it confirmed its obligations concerning the protection of minorities under the Treaty of Sèvres of 10 August 1920.[6]

The legal status provided by the Convention of Athens lasted until 1923, when at the end of the Greek-Turkish War (1919-1922) the Lausanne Conference[7] created a new geographical map for Greece and Turkey. The first issue discussed at the Conference was the final settlement of Greek-Turkish borders. The concept of a homogenous nation state dominated the Conference and resulted not only in a re-affirmation of the previous massive and compulsory exchanges of population between the two states, but also the implementation of a final exchange that had no precedent throughout the geographical extent and history of the area.[8] The massive Greek-Turkish exchange meant a permanent uprooting of the Greek population of Turkey, and in particular of Asia Minor and Eastern Thrace, from ancestral homelands that they had inhabited since the 8th-6th centuries BC. It also resulted in the obligatory expatriation of Muslims who resided in Greece; that is, indigenous peoples (Greeks Valaades or Vallahades, Muslims of Crete, Pomaks and Roma) who had converted to Islam under the Ottoman Empire, or Turks who had resided in the area since the end of the 14th and beginning of the 15th century.[9] The Muslims of Western Thrace were exempt from this exchange, and later, when Greece annexed the islands of the Dodecanese from the Italian occupation in 1947, a small Muslim population of Turkish origin was allowed to remain on the islands of Rhodes and Kos.[10]

The migration of the Muslims of Greece to Turkey and of the Christian Greeks from Turkey to Greece altered the demographic map of the two countries. This migration also caused Greece to change its legislation to accommodate the needs of the Muslims of Western Trace, who were guaranteed security by the Convention of the Treaty of Lausanne, according to which they received the official status of a 'Muslim minority'. According to the Proceedings of the Acts of the Conference,[11] the Turkish delegation objected to the use of 'racial' or 'ethnic' categories, instead emphasizing the religious character of the Greek minority in

Turkey.[12] Despite the Turkish delegation's arguments, the Convention of Lausanne (30 January 1923) made explicit reference to Greek inhabitants of Constantinople and Muslim inhabitants of Western Thrace.[13] Likewise, the Greek Christians of Constantinople, Imbros, and Tenedos, referred to by the Turkish State as the 'non-Muslim minority-Rum Orthodox Christians,' were protected by the Treaty of Lausanne.[14] The minority provisions of the Treaty of Lausanne remain in force today. Consequently, the faith, worship, customs, traditions, and education of Muslims of Greek citizenship are protected by the Greek Constitution and by special Greek legislation in accordance with the Treaty of Lausanne.[15]

In order for an outsider to understand what took place and what continues to take place at a political, legal and educational level in Greece, one has to consider the position of the minorities (both Christian and Muslim) that remained in Greece and Turkey in accordance with the Treaty of Lausanne.[16] It is very important to point out that, on top of the charged historical background, there is also a constant debate over the *ethnic* as opposed to *religious* identity of the minorities.[17] With regard to the Muslim minority of Western Thrace, recent decades have seen many appeals from formerly Muslim associations in the area to the European Court of Justice, in order to claim their right to be characterized as Turkish associations.[18] The Greek state insists on characterizing them as 'Muslim associations', based on the Treaty of Lausanne, emphasizing that these associations are not exclusively Turkish, but also include Pomaks and Roma. The fact remains, however, that the other ethnic groups, Pomaks and Roma, have been and still are forced to learn the Turkish language in the minority schools, which has led to their 'Turkification.'[19] Regardless, though, of the dispute about religious and ethnic identity, the vibrant Muslim community of Thrace (which is estimated to have between 100,000 and 130,000 residents) certainly shares all the privileges enjoyed by every Greek citizen, while at the same time, its religious identity is protected by the Treaty of Lausanne. This is not entirely the case for the Greek minority that remained in Istanbul after the events of 1955. The prosperous Greek community in Istanbul, which then numbered 80,000 to 100,000, has today dwindled to approximately 2,000 to 4,000 people, mainly because they are denied their minority rights under the Lausanne Treaty.[20]

The Mufti and So-Called Neo-Milletism

The faith, worship, customs, traditions, and education of Muslims of Greek citizenship are protected by the Greek Constitution and by special Greek legislation in accordance with the Treaty of Lausanne. This regulation of the relation between Greece and its Muslim citizens of Western Thrace is largely based on the ancient Ottoman system of *millets*. In effect, this system continues to create a kind of 'neo-milletism.' The Muslim community, which has been recognized by the Greek state since 1881 and which is defined by its religion, has retained certain privileges. This is the reason why certain regulations of shariʿa – in particular, religious rituals and family and inheritance law – remain in effect in Greece. These aspects of shariʿa are applied by the mufti, the religious leader and judge of the Muslim community.[21]

The Greek state has special provisions for the religious needs of the Muslims of Thrace, although the legal decisions of their religious courts are restricted in this area. Muslim Greeks in Athens, for example, who wish to be married in a Muslim marriage, must go to the mufti appointed for their region. Muslim marriage is thus recognized by the Greek state.[22] Muslim Greeks have approximately 300 mosques and *metjitia* (from *masjid*), smaller mosques for daily prayer (except for Fridays), and approximately 400 spiritual leaders (*imam, hatib, muezzin*). The mufti-ship is divided over three muftis, in Xanthi, Komotini and Didymotikhon, who together have the highest religious authority in Thrace. In addition, on the islands of Rhodes and Kos, there are three mosques with two *imams* and one mufti. The individual mufti-ship of Kos ceased to exist on 1948, and that on the island of Rhodes in 1974.

The mufti is the religious leader of the Muslims of Greek citizenship of Western Thrace; he also has the jurisdiction of *qadi*, that is, a judge who also acts as the highest religious teacher and interpreter-judge of Islamic Law, or shariʿa. He presides over special courts, Religious Courts, where he rules on familial, inheritance, and religious matters (including marriages, divorces, tutelage, alimony, emancipation of minors, Islamic wills, and intestate succession) of the Muslim community according to the Hanafi school of shariʿa. The mufti must be a graduate of Muslim Studies in theology and law, usually from the cities of Mecca or Medina, and be versed in the old Ottoman language, in which the decrees (*fatwa-fetva*) are written and redacted (which makes Thrace one of the few places where this old language from the Ottoman Empire is still practised). Other prerequisites for his appointment are that he must have served as an *imam* for at least a decade, be the epitome of morality, and possess excellent theological qualifications.

In his capacity as *qadi* (judge and religious teacher), the mufti is a civil servant of the Greek state. According to article 11 of the Convention of Athens, the mufti is appointed by the Greek state with a Presidential Decree after nomination by the Greek Ministry of Education and Religion. He receives a salary from the Greek Treasury, with the rank of General Director. The rulings of the mufti in the religious court are translated from Ottoman into Greek and are then validated by the Greek Courts of Law.[23]

Due to the constant antagonism between Greece and Turkey on the issue of the Muslim minority, the issue of the election of the mufti of the Muslim community has remained prominent, primarily since 1980. Correspondingly, there are two views concerning the selection of the mufti. The first one is that the mufti is nominated by a committee of experts and is appointed by the Greek state.[24] This procedure follows the custom of Muslim states in which the mufti is appointed by the state. The other view is that the mufti should be elected. According to the second opinion, which is expressed by a number of Muslims, the election of the mufti should be a matter for the Muslim community. This latter view represents the new political tendencies of Islam, which are influenced by Turkish policy in the area.[25] Some contemporary legal scholars are in favour of the Muslim community electing their mufti. However, these researchers also suggest that the election would entail the abolition of shariʿa. The rationale behind the claims of these legal experts is that Greece is the only European country in which shariʿa is applied. In many cases, the application of shariʿa is not compatible with the Universal Declaration of Human Rights and modern views, such as those concerning the equality of the sexes. What seems to be the main problem for these legal scholars is the fact that shariʿa is considered antiquated, and the articles of the Convention of the Treaty of Lausanne should be modernized to benefit the Muslim community and its equality before the law.[26] The Council of Europe Parliamentary Assembly has moved towards this perspective in reference to the Greek and Turkish positions vis-à-vis minority issues. In regard to the issue of the implementation of shariʿa in Greece, a report produced by the Council of Europe calls on Greece, among other things, to

> "allow the Muslim minority to choose freely its Muftis as mere religious leaders (i.e., without judicial powers), through election or appointment, and thus to abolish the application of shariʿa law – which raises serious questions of compatibility with the European Convention on Human Rights – as recommended by the Commissioner for Human Rights."[27]

The problem, though, of the election of the *mufti* is complicated by the broader political goals of the area's political representatives and deputies, who believe that the mufti's spiritual and legal powers restrict and undermine their authority. Depending on the region and political context, whole areas of residents are split on the issue of the 'election' of the mufti. The problem dividing the Muslims of the region is political. Turkey supports the elected muftis and their proponents,[28] while Greece appoints those who recognize their judicial authority. A consequence, therefore, of the proposed election of the mufti, rather than his appointment, would be the Greek state's refusal to recognize the implementation of shariʿa.[29] The paradox is that the muftis and those advocating for their election do not seem willing to lose the legal rights that are provided to them by shariʿa and to be deprived of their legal jurisdiction.

Another issue is the interaction between the internal legal system of shariʿa family law and the Greek legal system. As a matter of principle, the civil courts do not have jurisdiction over cases that are under the jurisdiction of the mufti, according to the current legislation.[30] However, wherever there are cases involving the violation of basic human rights, such as underage marriage (according to article 1350 of the Civil Code, underage marriage is not allowed), divorce without both parties being present, marriage through representatives, and so forth, the mufti and the appointed judge in the area are obliged to find ways to safeguard the individual rights of the members of the Muslim Community (*lex ferenda*).[31] The truth is, however, that the number of Muslims of Greek citizenship who appeal to civil courts is small, and it is even smaller for Muslim women of Greek citizenship, most likely for reasons of stigmatization and social isolation.

Despite the existence for many decades of a special Muslim minority education system, the most appropriate way to empower new generations of Muslims in Western Thrace would be to once again discuss issues concerning education, so that brave decisions could be made in favour of the Greek Muslims.[32] We should note that for the last ten years, a pilot educational programme has been in place for the children of the minority community, with positive results.[33] Certainly, citizens educated in a wider European framework, whether it be the 'majority' or the 'minority', are more capable, at a psychological, political and social level, of achieving self-determination for their community.

In the light of the aforementioned debates, however, we should note that the majority of the Muslim community is generally satisfied with the unobstructed functioning of shariʿa in Thrace. The people of the Muslim community seem to appreciate their freedom to apply shariʿa within European territory, especially when such a thing is impossible in modern Turkey. Even those who resort to elected and not appointed mufti prefer to perform Islamic religious marriages and to settle other family and inheritance matters according to the Muslim ethos, although the judicial acts of the elected mufti are typically not recognized by the Greek state. Through the application of shariʿa, the Muslims of Western Thrace feel closer to their Islamic obligations and preserve the Islamic *umma* and its justice.

Immigration and New Challenges

All of the above, of course, concerns the Greek Muslims of the 'old' Islam, that is, Muslims with Greek citizenship in Western Thrace. The 'new' Islam is that of Muslim immigrants who have come to the country more recently, particularly since the 1990s, and who originate from all over the world (Asia, the Middle East, Africa, and so forth). They do not enjoy any special religious legal status and they are subject to Greek laws that apply, without any exception, to all immigrants.[34] They are not dealt with on the basis of their religion, but their nationality, and as such fall outside the privileged measures for Muslims with Greek nationality. Consequently, the special minority rights applying to 'old' Muslims do not apply to the 'new' Muslims, who are mostly concentrated outside Thrace. This has created a host of problems regarding the lack of mosques and Islamic cemeteries in these areas (especially in the city of Athens), and the Greek government has been slow in keeping its promise to allow the construction of a mosque in Athens and the creation of Muslim cemeteries. Consequently, there are now unofficial Muslim places of worship, which, according to the president of the Muslim Union in Athens,[35] number as many as a hundred; while there is no provision for the education and training of their religious teachers, the *imams*, as there is in other European countries, even though 'their quality is sometimes put under question.'[36] In some cases, such as in relation to the issue of burial, services are performed by the muftis of Western Thrace in Thrace, since there is no other place in Greece for Muslim burial. The legal jurisdiction of the mufti on familial and inheritance issues applies exclusively to Muslims of Greek citizenship and especially to those of Western Thrace, although this aspect is under consideration vis-à-vis article 13 of the Constitution regarding religious freedom.[37] Any other legal action between non-Greek Muslims can be impugned.

There is no special legislative accommodation for Muslim immigrants with regard to the teaching of Islam. In accordance with the introductory report for the Law on Multicultural Education prepared by the Greek Parliament's Scientific Council in 1997, the focus of modern multicultural education is not necessarily on support of religious difference, but on 'strengthening the ethnic identity of the various groups of foreigners living in the country.'[38] Greek schools, which found themselves unprepared in many areas, particularly in language training for foreign students and the management of multiculturalism, quickly began to adjust. Both legislators and the Ministry of Education hastened to resolve these issues, to the extent that it was possible, through the creation of so-called intercultural or multicultural schools as early as 1996.[39] At any rate, the children of all immigrants – regardless of their religion – study alongside Greek children in public schools from kindergarten to high school, without exception.

The Greek case could represent not a retrogressive example but one that expresses a smooth symbiosis and demonstrates respect for the various religious expressions of minorities. The main challenges that still exist are whether the implementation of shariʿa can operate as a cohesive or a segregating bond between citizens, what European Muslims desire for themselves (is there only one will?), and how secular states can satisfy the many different tendencies within their societies.

Notes

1 The timing is not coincidental; parallel, intense and wide-ranging discussions about the possibility of Muslims in Europe implementing shariʿa law are taking place in various European countries.

2 On 30 August 1832, the London Protocol was signed to ratify and reiterate the terms of the Treaty of Constantinople (21 July 1832) in connection with the border between Greece and the Ottoman Empire. See Paraskevas Konortas, *Les musulmanes de la Grèce entre 1821 et 1912* (Mémoire de DEA), Paris: École des Hautes Études en Sciences Sociales, 1980, pp. 16-17.

3 According to article 3: 'La vie, les biens, l'honneur, la religion et les coutumes de ceux des habitants des localités cédées à la Grèce qui resteront sous l'administration hellénique seront scrupuleusement respectés. Ils jouiront entièrement des mêmes droits civils et politiques que les sujets hellènes d'origine.' Article 8: 'La liberté ainsi que la pratique extérieure du culte sont assurées aux Musulmans dans les territoires cédés à la Grèce. Aucune atteinte ne sera portée à l'autonomie et à l'organisation hiérarchique des communautés musulmanes existantes ou qui pourraient se former, ni à l'administration des fonds et des immeubles qui leur appartiennent. Aucune entrave ne pourra être apportée aux rapports de ces communautés avec leurs Chefs spirituels en matière de reli-

gion. Les Tribunaux du Chéri locaux continueront à exercer leur juridiction en matière purement religieuse.' Retrieved from the Greek Ministry for Foreign Affairs: http://www.mfa.gr/ (accessed June 10, 2011).

4 Konstantinos Tsitselikis, 'The Legal Status of Islam in Greece', *Die Welt des Islams*, 2004 (Vol. 44, No. 3), pp. 402-431.

5 The Convention of Peace between Greece and Turkey, also known under the name The Treaty of Athens, was ratified by the Law (ΔΣΙΓ') 4213/1913.

6 Article 2 states: 'Greece undertakes to assure full and complete protection of life and liberty to all inhabitants of Greece without distinction of birth, nationality, language, race or religion. All inhabitants of Greece shall be entitled to the free exercise, whether public or private, of any creed, religion or belief, whose practices are not inconsistent with public order or public morals.' The mentioned minorities are Jews, Vlachs and Muslims. See *Traité concernant la Protection des Minorités en Grèce*, signé à Sèvres le 10 Août 1920, *Recueil des Traités de la Société des Nations*, No. 711, pp. 243-265. Retrieved from http://untreaty.un.org/unts/60001_120000/14/30/00027489.pdf (accessed December 29, 2011).

7 13 November 1922 – 24 July 1923.

8 The majority of the Muslim populations of the Balkan Peninsula were forced to abandon the region during the Balkan wars (1912-1913). The persecution of non-Turkish populations, who had lived for centuries on the coast of Asia Minor and the Black Sea, began at the dawn of the First World War (1914) on the pretext of the security of the collapsing Ottoman Empire and the emerging Turkish State of the Young Turks.

9 'Following the defeat of the Greek Army in 1922 by nationalist Turkish forces, the Convention of Lausanne in 1923 specified the first compulsory exchange of populations ratified by an international organization. The arrival in Greece of over 1.2 million refugees and their settlement proved to be a watershed with far-reaching consequences for the country'; See Elisabeth Kontogiorgi, *Population Exchange in Greek Macedonia*, Oxford: Clarendon Press (Oxford Historical Monographs), 2006.

10 *Treaty of Peace* with Italy, section V, article 14.

11 *Proceedings of the Acts of the Conference* No 6, 1922, p. 445.

12 'En Turquie, il existe des minorités de religion, non des minorités de race. La délégation turque n'accepte donc pas le principe de la protection des minorités de races ou de langue.' Retrieved from Photini Pazartzis, 'Le Status des Minorités en Grèce', *Annuaire Français de Droit International*, 1992 (issue XXXVIII), pp. 377-391, here 388 (58). The Treaty of Lausanne brought into force the Treaty of Sevres (1920) on the topic of 'minorities in Greece', that regulated the legal obligations of Greece towards ethnic, religious, and linguistic minorities. See Tsitselikis, 'The Legal Status of Islam in Greece', p. 5: 'Muslims of Greece and non-Muslims of Turkey were granted special legal protection' according to articles 37-45 of the Treaty.' Cf. also FEK 238/25.9.1923.

13 See article 2 of the Convention concerning the Exchange of Greek and Turkish Populations and Protocol, signed at Lausanne, 30 January 1923. Retrieved from http://www.worldlii.org/int/other/LNTSer/1925/14.html (accessed December 29, 2011).

14 See article 14 of the Treaty: 'The islands of Imbros and Tenedos, remaining under Turkish sovereignty, shall enjoy a special administrative organization composed of local elements and furnishing every guarantee for the native non-Moslem population in so far as concerns local administration and the protection of persons and property. The maintenance of order will be assured therein by a police force recruited from amongst the local population by the local administration above provided for and placed under its orders. The agreements which have been, or may be, concluded between Greece and Turkey relating to the exchange of the Greek and Turkish populations will not be applied to the inhabitants of the islands of Imbros and Tenedos.'

15 On the legal issues that have arisen from the application of the Treaty of Lausanne until now, and interpretations of its provisions during the intervening period, see Vermund Aarbakke, *The Muslim Minority of Greek Thrace*, (Ph.D. Thesis), Vol. 1 & 2, Bergen: University of Bergen, 2000; Tsitselikis, 'The Legal Status of Islam in Greece', pp. 7-9; Konstantinos Tsitselikis, 'Muslims in Greece' in: R. Poz & W. Wieshaider (eds.), *Islam and the European Union*, Leuven-Paris-Dudley: Peeters, 2004, pp. 109-132; Dimos Tsourkas, 'Les juridictions musulmanes en Grèce', *Hellenic Review of International Relations*, 1981-1982 (Vol. 2, No. 11), pp. 582-598; Pazartzis, 'Le Status des Minorités en Grèce', pp. 377-391.

16 Here we should also add the Istanbul Pogrom (or September riots) of 1955 and the Cyprus issue. See Speros Vryonis, *The Mechanism of Catastrophe: The Turkish Pogrom of September 6-7, 1955, and the Destruction of the Greek Community of Istanbul*, New York: Greekworks, 2005. On the Cyprus issue, the September riots and their effects on the Muslims of Thrace (1955-1957), see the work of Kostis Tsioumis, *Η Μουσουλμανική μειονότητα της Θράκης (1950-1960)* (*The Muslim Minority of Thrace [1950-1960]*), Thessaloniki: Stamoulis, 2006, pp. 127-193.

17 According to Kostis Tsioumis, 'The case of Greece could not be excluded from the attitude of modern-nation states of the Balkans, where ethnic identity developed as opposed to the identity of the "other" and this reality has affected also the management of minority educational policy [...] This criterion, adopted by governmental and educational institutions, regarding the management of minority identity, was that of national security rather than its integration into the Greek society [...] The influence of the Cold War and the newly formed political and global circumstances (U.S. and NATO influence) were a catalyst [...] In this context can be understood the use of the terms "Muslim" and "Turk", the attitude of the Greek state and other social institutions on the issue of ethnic formation, and finally, the dynamics of the minority of Thrace and its identity management from the various ethnic components of the minority.' See Kostis Tsioumis' paper entitled "Η διαχείρηση της μειονοτικής ταυτότητας στον ελληνικό χώρο και η διαμόρφωση της εκπαιδευτικής πολιτικής: Η περίπτωση των μουσουλμάνων της Θράκης 1923-1974" ("The management of minority identity in the Greek milieu and the formation of educational policy: the case of the Muslims of Thrace, 1923-1974"), at the 4th Conference of the European Society of Modern Greek Studies (Granada, 9-10 September 2010). Retrieved from http://www.eens.org/?page_id=1761 (accessed December 29, 2011).

18 See the Report by Thomas Hammarberg, Commissioner for Human Rights of the Council of Europe, following his visit to Greece on 8-10 December 2008. Issue reviewed: *Human rights of minorities*, Retrieved from https://wcd.coe.int/ViewDoc.jsp?id=1409353 (accessed December 29, 2011).

19 Photini Pazartzis, 'Le statut des minorités en Grèce', pp. 388-389. For a detailed description of a) Turkish nationalism in Western Thrace, b) the Greek policy towards the educational function of the Muslim minority and c) the competition between old-Muslims and Kemalists in the region of Western Thrace in 1954, and the Kemalists' dominance in imposing the Latin rather than Arabic system of writing the Turkish Language as well as their reinforcement of the Turkish national identity, see Tsioumis, *Η Μουσουλμανική μειονότητα της Θράκης (1950-1960)* (The Muslim Minority of Thrace [1950-1960]), pp. 112, 117-118, 121. See also Aarbakke, *The Muslim Minority of Greek Thrace*, pp. 139-140.

20 See the Minority Rights Group International report on Rum Orthodox Christians in Istanbul, Retrieved from http://www.minorityrights.org/4412/turkey/rum-orthodox-christians.html (accessed December 29, 2011).

21 The special courts applying the jurisdiction of the mufti were organized in detail by Law 2345 of 1920.

22 Only Greek Muslims residing in Thrace can, according to the prevailing opinion, bring their case before the mufti. See Aspasia Tsaoussi, Eleni Zervogianni 'Multiculturalism and Family Law: The Case of Greek Muslims', in: K. Boele-Woelki and Tone Sverdrup (eds.), *European Challenges in Contemporary Family Law*, Antwerp-Oxford-Portland: Intersentia, 2008, pp. 209-239, esp. 213 (20). However, according to other opinion, Muslim religious law can be applicable to all Greek Muslim citizens hailing from Thrace. See Ioannis Ktistakis, Ιερός Νόμος του Ισλάμ και Μουσουλμάνοι Έλληνες Πολίτες (Sacred Islamic Law and Greek Muslims), Athens: Sakkoulas, 2006, p. 36 (3).

23 Law 1920/1990 (on Muslim Religious Functionaries), especially article 5, paragraphs 1-3.

24 As part of the implementation of the Convention of Constantinople of 1881 between Greece and the Ottoman Empire, the Law (ΑΛΗ') 1038/1882 was promulgated, concerning the spiritual leaders of the Mohammedan (sic) communities, according to which the mufti is recognized as a public servant of the Greek state. The provisions of this law were abolished in accordance with article 15, paragraph 1 of the Law 2345/1920. The 24.12.1990 legislative act (FEK A' 182), which was ratified by the Law 1920/1991, introduced a procedural law rule by specifying the mufti's legal jurisdiction. Thus, the decisions of the mufti in cases that are contested within his jurisdiction become applicable and create a *res judicata*, if declared applicable by the local pertinent First Instance Court, in the process of the voluntary jurisdiction. Here, the court investigates whether the decision was issued within the geographical limits of the mufti's jurisdiction and whether the provisions that were applied were contrary to the Constitution. George Doudos, 'H shariʿa, ένα σύστημα δικαίου με δυναμική και μέλλον ("shariʿa, a legal system with dynamics and future), *Azinlikça*, 2009, (Vol. 53), available online at http://www.azinlikca.net/ellinika-arthra/2010-01-07-15-30-25.html.

25 Alexis Alexandris, 'Religion or Ethnicity. The Identity of the Minorities in Greece and Turkey', in R. Hirschon (ed.), *Crossing the Aegean*, Oxford, N.Y.: Berghahn Books, 2003, pp. 117-132, esp. 123-124.

26 See some related articles: Ioannis Konidaris, 'Greek-Turkish sacred (issues)', newspaper TO VIMA (27/6/2010): http://www.tovima.gr/opinions/article/?aid =340293; Report on Religious Freedom of the COE: http://assembly.coe.int/ main.asp?Link=/documents/workingdocs/doc09/edoc11860.htm (§55). Lina Papadopoulou, 'Trapped in History: Greek Muslim Women Under the Sacred Islamic Law', *Annuaire International des Droits de l'Homme*, 2010 (Vol. 5), pp. 397-418. Retrieved from: http://papers.ssrn.com/sol3/papers.cfm?abstract_id= 1877048 (accessed June 13, 2011).

27 Par. 18.5 of Working Document 11860, titled "Freedom of religion and other human rights for non-Muslim minorities in Turkey and for the Muslim minority in Thrace (eastern Greece)", April 21, 2009 (The Reporter was Michel Hunault). Retrieved from http://assembly.coe.int/ASP/Doc/XrefViewHTML. asp?FileID=12681&Language=EN (accessed June 13, 2011).

28 TURKEY-GREECE – Turkish foreign minister visits Xanthi Turkish Association and Xanthi's elected mufti. Retrieved from http://www.thefreelibrary. com/TURKEYGREECE+Turkish+foreign+minister+visits+Xanthi+Turkish.. .-a0251124226 (accessed December 29, 2011).

29 Ilhan Ahmet, 'Ilhan Ahmet'ten Ksinidis'in müftü kanunuyla ilgili sözlerine cevap' (Ilhan Ahmet replies to Xynidis' statements for the Muftiship), in the bilingual journal *AZINLIKCA* (Turkish-Greek), 17 Ocak 2012; retrieved from http://www.azinlikca.net/eidhseis/ilhan-axmet-ksinidis-mouftidwn-1252012. html (accessed October 5, 2012).

30 Article 4 of Law 147/1914, act of legislation 24.12.1990 which has been in effect with the enactment 1920/1991.

31 George Doudos, "Το υποστατό των μουσουλμανικών γάμων που τελούνται δια πληρεξουσίου στα πλαίσια της ελληνικής έννομης τάξης" ("Muslim Marriages by Proxy in the Greek Legal system"), *Nomokanonika*, April 2004 (Vol. 3), Athens: Sakoulas, pp. 331-337. For the opposing legal opinions, see the Report by Thomas Hammarberg, on Human Rights of Minorities, (Strasbourg 2009); retrieved from https://wcd.coe.int/ViewDoc.jsp?id=1409353 (§ 31) (accessed December 29, 2011).

32 Minority education does not refer only to religious education, but also to general education.

33 For the diplomatic-political processes and the educational policy concerning the Muslims of Western Thrace from 1923 onwards, see the submentioned works by Kostis Tsioumis. The directors of this programme, which is entitled *Project Enhancing Education for Minority Children (PEM)*, are Anna Frangoudaki and Thaleia Dragona. See the Programme for the Education of Muslim Children 1997-2008: Retrieved from http://www.museduc.gr/en/index.php?page=1 (accessed June 10, 2011). For further details on the Muslim minorities issue, see my article: A. Ziaka, "Muslims and Muslim Education in Greece", in Ednan Aslan (ed.), *Islamic Education in Europe*, Vienna: Böhlau Verlag, 2009, pp. 141-179.

34 See the related Laws: 4310 (6/16 of August 1929), 1975/1991, PD 358 & 359/1997, Law 2910/2001 and 3536/2007. The issue of immigration was sudden and massive and the Greek state, despite the measures taken, has so far been unable to satisfactorily resolve the problem which is growing due to the daily influx of immigrants in the country.

35 Naim Elghadur, president of the Muslim Association of Greece, in a recent interview conducted by the reporter Georgia Dama for the *Eleftherotypia* newspaper (1 November 2011) notes the following concerning our topic: '[...] The Muslim Union is very concerned because it fears that the radical groups on the one hand and the extreme rightwing fanatics and Islamists on the other can agitate the social peace. And if the Muslims are aroused they will not be able to be restrained, because they are hopeless, unemployed and because they believe that if you are killed defending your right, you will go to heaven. This is why those who want the implementation of shari'a ought to immigrate to countries where it is implemented.' He concludes with a very interesting personal remark on the issue: 'today, shari'a cannot be in effect in any country, because there is no social protection and justice. Some,' he says characteristically, 'are forced to steal because they are hungry. It is unthinkable to cut off their hand.' Retrieved from *Eleftherotypia*: http://www.enet.gr/?i=news.el.article&id=219088 (accessed June 1, 2011).

36 Jean-François Husson, *Training Imams in Europe. The Current Status*, Belgium: King Baudouin Foundation, 2007, p. 30; retrieved from King Baudouin Foundation: www.kbs-frb.be (accessed October 13, 2012).

37 On religious freedom in Greece, see Ch. Papastathis, 'Η Θρησκευτική Ελευθερία στην Ελλάδα' ('Religious Freedom in Greece'), Charalambos Papastathis & Rev. Gregory Papathomas (eds.), *Πολιτεία, Ορθόδοξη Εκκλησία και Θρησκεύματα* (*The State, the Orthodox Church and Religions in Greece*), Athens: Epektassi, 2006, pp. 289-326 (the same article has also been published in the Revue *L'Année Canonique* 45 (pp. 295-309).

38 George Mavrommatis and Konstantinos Tsitselikis, 'Η Εκπαίδευση των Μεταναστών στην Ελλάδα (1999-2003). Πολιτικές και Πρακτικές' ('The Education of Immigrants in Greece (1999-2003). Policies and Practicies'), in: Pavlou M. and Christopoulos D. (eds.), *Η Ελλάδα της Μετανάστευσης* (*Greece of Migration*), Athens: Kritiki, Series of Studies KEMO, 2004, pp. 121-140, esp. 135-136.

39 Ziaka, "Muslims and Muslim Education in Greece," pp. 163-165; Konstantinos Tsioumis, "Εκπαιδευτική Πολιτική για τη διαπολιτισμική Εκπαίδευση στην Ελλάδα," (Educational Policy towards Intercultural Education in Greece), in: D. Syrri (ed.), *Συμβιώνοντας με τη Μετανάστευση* (*Living Together with Migration*), Athens: Ianos, 2011, pp. 143-150.

SECTION II

LAW VERSUS CULTURE

8 Unregistered Islamic Marriages

Anxieties about Sexuality and Islam in the Netherlands[1]

Annelies Moors

Introduction

Both in Europe and the Middle East, unregistered Islamic marriages cause a great deal of anxiety. Whereas the men and women who enter into these marriages consider them permissible under Islam, they are not registered according to the law of the country where they are concluded. In the Netherlands since 2005, such marriages (which are often referred to as 'Islamic marriages') have drawn the attention of the security services, and have become a topic of debate in both the media and in parliament. These marriages are seen as an indication of radicalization and as a means through which salafi *imams* are trying to build a parallel society, while the women involved are defined as the victims of men using them for their own dubious purposes. In Muslim majority countries, such as in Egypt, these marriages (often called *'urfi* marriages) were already the focus of public debate a decade ago.[2] In these countries, the state authorities often consider the women involved to have been duped by unscrupulous men who want to engage in sexual relations and then simply leave them, or deny that a marriage ever took place. In the following, I argue that the portrayal of the women who engage in such marriages as victims of irresponsible men is, at best, only part of the story. Instead, I investigate how the categories of *'urfi* and 'Islamic' marriages have been produced in Muslim majority countries and the Netherlands respectively, and how they circulate through fields of power. Whereas the state authorities consider these unregistered marriages illegal and some religious scholars hold them to be irregular, if not void, the multiple and varied ways in which these marriages are concluded and lived indicate that the participants themselves draw on multiple discourses of permissibility.[3]

In the first section of this chapter, I discuss the shifting meanings of *'urfi* marriages in Muslim-majority countries in the Middle East. Starting with a brief reflection on the conclusion of marriages in classical Islamic law, I discuss how the emergence of the nation state and the concomitant codification and reform of Muslim family law have turned *'urfi* marriages into unregistered marriages. Next, I analyse how the meanings of *'urfi* marriages further diversified in the course of recent decades and become the topic of public debate. In the second section, I analyse how 'Islamic marriages' have emerged as a category of concern in the Netherlands, and investigate the highly diverse motivations young women have for concluding such marriages and the multiple meanings these may hold for them. Whereas in both contexts, state authorities are particularly concerned about the effects of such marriages on women, different issues underlie their anxieties about unregistered marriages. In Muslim majority settings, the main concern is undesirable forms of sexuality, while in the Netherlands, the major target is undesirable forms of Islam.

Muslim Majority Countries: Towards the Registration of Marriages

Prior to the emergence of the modern nation state, unregistered (*'urfi*) marriages, widely known in the community through various rituals and celebrations, were the norm. According to Islamic law, marriage is a contract that makes sexual relations permissible (*halal*); pre- or extramarital relations are considered *zina* (unlawful sexual intercourse). The marriage contract is similar to other contracts in that it is concluded through offer and acceptance; for it to be valid, two male Muslim witnesses (two women may replace one man) need to be present. Fathers can conclude such a contract for minors, while according to most schools of law adult women entering their first marriage should have their marriage guardian conclude the marriage for them. The Hanafi school of law, in contrast, holds that a woman who has reached her legal majority has both the right to refuse a marriage and to arrange for her own marriage.[4] The presence of a religious functionary is not necessary for a marriage to be valid, a written document is not required, and the marriage does not need to be registered to be valid under Islam. Publicity is required, however.

Whereas for most schools of law, the obligation of publicity is fulfilled through the presence of two witnesses,[5] in social practice, the normative requirements are both more gradual and more extensive. A publicly celebrated engagement (a commitment to marry which has no legal effects) often precedes the conclusion of the marriage contract. Whereas according to Islamic jurisprudence, once the marriage contract is concluded, the couple can no longer be accused of *zina*, from a social perspective, the consummation of the marriage (*dukhul*) and cohabitation are only considered licit after the wedding ceremony has taken place, which may be months or even years later. The new couple often use the period between the contracting and the celebration of the marriage to get to know each other better and to prepare for the wedding and marital life.

Marriage entitles men and women to different rights and obligations. A husband is obliged to maintain his wife (in terms of housing, food and clothing), independent of the latter's own means, and to pay a dower. Women are required to obey their husbands, at least as far as cohabitation is concerned. The relation between maintenance and obedience is evident in the ruling that if a wife leaves the marital home against her husband's wishes (and has no valid reason for doing so), the husband is no longer obliged to maintain her. However, some schools of law allow for a modification of gender relations through the inclusion of conditions in the marriage contract.[6] With the family law reforms of the past decades, in many Muslim countries marriages are only registered above a minimum age, while in some, the presence of the marriage guardian is no longer necessary and the requirement of obedience has been removed.[7]

There are some differences between Sunni and Shia Islamic law in concluding marriages. According to Shia jurisprudence, a marriage without witnesses is also valid, and it is possible to conclude a marriage for a specific period of time.[8] In the case of such a 'temporary marriage', a man needs to pay a dower to his wife, but he is not obliged to pay maintenance and the partners do not inherit from each other. Children, however, have the same rights as in a permanent marriage. Whereas temporary marriages are often called *mut'a* or *sigheh* (terms referring to sexual enjoyment), it is also possible for the partners to conclude a non-sexual temporary marriage. Especially in settings of strict gender segregation, non-sexual temporary marriages allow men and women to interact more freely.

Historically, religious authorities were rather flexible in recognizing marriages, using the notion of *shubha*; that is, assuming that the parties concerned thought they had concluded a valid marriage. In some cases, a child was even recognized as legitimate if a marriage was concluded up to one month before delivery.[9] Regulations about the need to *register* marriages have come with the emergence of the modern nation state.[10] The concomitant centralization of authority has engendered the codification and reform of Muslim family law. Also under the statutory obligation to register marriages, however, unregistered marriages that fulfil Islamic conditions are considered irregular rather than invalid. Still, religious authorities often argue that registering a marriage is desirable on Islamic grounds. Registration functions as a means to publicize a marriage and is beneficial for women, as only then can their rights be guaranteed. It is a means of checking whether the marriage meets the state regulations in question, such as the minimum age, the consent of both parties, and conditions for polygamy.[11]

In the course of the twentieth century, registration of a marriage has been normalized, as bureaucratic states increasingly require official documents for access to resources. Many countries have also developed means to register a marriage *post facto* through the 'confirmation of an existing marriage', especially in those cases where both partners act in unison. However, if one of the parties, usually the man, denies the marriage, the situation becomes far more complicated, and the religious establishment is particularly concerned about such cases. The media attention attracted by such cases and the sense of crisis they produce have engendered a trend towards stricter implementation of the legal obligation to register marriages, with the authorities imposing fines and other penalties to encourage the public to conform to statutory law.[12]

Unregistered marriages: new variations

Whereas prior to the emergence of the modern nation state, unregistered (*'urfi*) yet widely publicized marriages were the norm, contemporary *'urfi* marriages, by contrast, tend to be purposely concealed from particular categories of people, be it the state authorities, the parents or the husband's first wife and her family. Whether the public considers these marriages to be licit or illicit depends largely on the extent to which and from whom they are concealed.

The least controversial *'urfi* marriages are those that are widely known about in the community, but not registered with the state. In some cases, these marriages are not registered because registration is not possible. A paradigmatic example is the case of underage girls. In many countries, codification and family law reform have introduced minimum ages for marriage; if girls have not yet reached that age, the marriage cannot be registered. Sometimes, if families insist on such a marriage, they will conclude a marriage contract, but only register it once the girl reaches the minimum age.[13] In other cases, women refrain from registering their marriage because they consider it too disadvantageous to do so. For instance, if they officially register a new marriage after divorce, they run the risk of losing custody over their children, while if they do so after being widowed, they may lose their right to their deceased husband's pension.[14]

Other *'urfi* marriages are characterized by a far greater emphasis on secrecy and are thus more controversial. These *'urfi* marriages are often considered to be evidence of 'the family in crisis', and are part of a discourse that also includes concerns about single females and delayed marriage.[15] Some consider the great expense of getting married – the dower, gifts of jewellery, the cost of housing, and wedding parties, mostly paid for by men – as the main reason behind delayed marriage.[16] However, in the first decades of the twentieth century, Egyptian men were already complaining about the high cost of marriage.[17] Perhaps more important for the rise in the average age at which someone gets married is the spread of women's education and formal employment, which has provided young women with a valid reason for avoiding early marriage.[18] Getting married later stretches the time period between sexual maturity and married life. In a context in which sexual relations outside of marriage are considered both Islamically and socially illicit,[19] this places young adults in a difficult situation.

Under such circumstances, young people may consider an *'urfi* marriage as a means of making sexual relations permissible under Islam. Such *'urfi* marriages are usually kept hidden from the couple's families and are only known to a small circle of friends.[20] It is this type of *'urfi* marriage that the state and many religious scholars in Egypt are particularly concerned about, both because they may be concluded in a way that does not fulfil the statutory conditions for a valid Islamic marriage (such as the agreement of the woman's marriage guardian) and because they transgress social norms of deference to one's parents.[21] A common trope is that of an unscrupulous man who uses an *'urfi* marriage to trick a naive, young woman into a sexual relationship, pretending that such a marriage is a legitimate marriage. As soon as the woman is pregnant or once he has lost interest in her, he leaves her and denies that a marriage has taken place.[22] Equally challenging to parental authority is another motivation for concluding an *'urfi* marriage. If a woman's parents do not agree with her choice of partner, the couple may then use an *'urfi* marriage as a means to force her parents to agree with the marriage. This is similar to elopement, while remaining within the boundaries of Islamic law.[23]

Interestingly, in Turkey, where according to statutory law the registration of a civil marriage needs to precede a religious marriage, a very similar phenomenon is occurring. In the case that people first conclude an Islamic marriage, the levels of publicity or secrecy determine whether such a marriage is considered to be licit or illicit. Religious marriages that are not registered with the civil authorities, but that have the approval of the couple's parents and are publicly known in the community, are considered licit in the circles in which they occur.[24] The very same religious figures are, however, highly critical of *gizly* (secret) marriages that are concluded without the knowledge of the parents and that are only publicized to a very limited extent.[25]

Some unconventional non-registered marriages have, by contrast, gained a measure of acceptance, and religious leaders have used elements from existing Islamic traditions in novel ways to legitimize certain kinds of contemporary *'urfi* marriages. Amongst Shia Muslims, this is the case for temporary marriages. Whereas in Iran under the Pahlavi Shahs, temporary marriage had come to be considered an outdated institution, the practice was revived after the Islamic revolution. Moreover, within a decade, it was no longer only considered an instrument for regulating male sexuality. During a speech in 1990, former president Hashemi Rafsanjani redefined temporary marriages by also recognizing women's sexual desire, explaining that it is also legitimate for women to take the initiative in concluding such a marriage. In his view, a temporary marriage could function as a solution to the present-day problem of young people becoming sexually mature yet only being able to conclude a permanent marriage at a later age because of longer periods of study.[26] Rafsanjani was strongly criticized by the secular middle classes and by women's organizations, who considered the practice not only a relic of the past, but also a threat to the family and to women in particular, and an institution resembling prostitution. Based on her fieldwork in Iran, Haeri[27] concluded that temporary marriage could indeed enable poorer divorced and widowed women to engage in affective relations. Still, she also pointed to the risks such marriage entailed for young women who had not been married before. Because of the cultural value attached to virginity for a woman entering her first (permanent) marriage, these women may face great difficulties finding a respectable husband.

Unconventional forms of marriage have also emerged amongst Sunni Muslims. In Egypt, there are indications that the number of marriages in which the wife is older than her husband, and sometimes in a stronger financial position, is growing.[28] Whereas such marriages are commonly registered, under specific conditions, such as when foreign women are involved, they frequently remain unregistered. According to Karkabi,[29] when Western women and younger Egyptian men in the tourist resort of Dahab engage in a relationship, they often opt for an *'urfi* marriage.[30] For the men, such a marriage functions as a means to legitimize a longer-lasting sexual relationship, while the women concerned do not aspire to a 'real' marriage.[31] Another case is that of Russian-speaking female migrants in Hurghada, who, according to Walby,[32] are often better educated, slightly older, and more mobile than their partners. Also in this case, an *'urfi* marriage is a convenient solution, as neither of the parties concerned is interested in a state-registered marriage contract that limits women's freedom of movement and imposes the duty of maintenance on men.

Another form of marriage that has engendered much public controversy is the *misyar* (ambulant or visiting) marriage. In the case of a *misyar* marriage, the partners do not live together and the wife does not claim her right to maintenance and accommodation. Such marriages, which may or may not be registered, are often concluded by men who are already married. In that case, they are often kept secret from the first wife, but are publicly known amongst the family, friends and neighbours of the woman engaging in a *misyar* marriage. Debates about this form of marriage emerged in Saudi Arabia in the 1990s. The Grand Mufti (Ibn Baz) issued a *fatwa* in 1996 which considered *misyar* marriages permissible, but also stated that they needed to be made public.[33] In 1998 Shaykh Yusuf al-Qaradawi, a prominent scholar aligned to the Muslim Brotherhood, stated in Qatar that he considered such marriages licit, as long as the women involved agreed with the conditions.[34] In the following years, the debates continued. Some considered these marriages an infringement of the rights of women, while others saw them as a possibility for women who might not otherwise find a suitable husband with whom to enjoy marital relations and perhaps motherhood. References were made to well-educated women who could easily forego the right to maintenance.[35] In 2006, the Saudi Arabian Fiqh Council not only deemed *misyar* marriages licit, but also the so-called 'friend marriages' aimed at Muslim men and women who study in the West. These make sexual relations legitimate, but do not oblige men to cohabit with and provide accommodation and maintenance for their wives.[36]

Whereas such *misyar* marriages are often presented as a new phenomenon emerging in the Gulf, there are indications that they may have a longer history and wider geographical presence. For instance, Granqvist[37] describes some cases in rural Palestine in the 1920s in which women with some economic independence, usually widows with their own houses, opted for similar polygamous marriages. Also in poorer countries, such as in present-day Egypt, divorced women engage in such partially secret marriages. According to Sonneveld,[38] for them it is a way of dealing with the societal pressure they experience to re-marry. A divorced woman is usually only considered an acceptable wife for a man who has already been married. Rather than marrying a widower or a divorced man, which often comes with the obligation of caring for his children, they may prefer to become the second wife in a *misyar* marriage, which enables them to keep some of their autonomy. While they ensure that their own social circle, including their neighbours, is well-informed about the marriage, the first wife is not usually told. If such a *misyar* marriage is not officially registered, it can be kept hidden from the first wife more easily, especially in countries where the first wife is to be officially notified of her husband's subsequent marriages.

Another kind of marriage that frequently goes unregistered is sometimes referred to as a 'visiting marriage'. These are the marriages conducted during the summer vacation by older men from wealthy Gulf States with young girls from poorer families in countries such as Egypt, Morocco, India and Indonesia. Whereas such transnational marriages have a long history, it was after the oil boom, which created new and very stark inequalities between these oil economies and poorer countries, that such marriages became particularly exploitative, with young, sometimes underage girls forced into such marriages by their fathers and discarded by their husbands after the summer holidays when the latter had returned home. Such marriages have become a topic of debate and have also drawn the attention of government officials.[39]

In short, present-day unregistered marriages differ considerably from pre-modern *'urfi* marriages. The main point of difference is that the new *'urfi* marriages are often kept purposely hidden from at least some of the parties concerned, be it state officials, the couple's parents, or the first wife. Functioning as a means for young people to have sexual relationships without concluding an officially registered marriage, they are the topic of much anxiety, as there are disputes about their Islamic validity, they challenge social conventions, and they may, in some cases, be highly exploitative. For women who have previously been married, or are past the acceptable age for marriage, such marriages may be a means to acquire marital status while maintaining some measure of independence. In turn, these various forms of *'urfi* marriages release men from the responsibility to provide maintenance and accommodation. How such marriages affect women depends to a large extent on the resources women can draw on.

'Islamic Marriages' in the Netherlands: Gender and Securitization

Not only in Muslim majority countries, but also in the Netherlands, unregistered Islamic marriages have become a topic of debate and policymaking. According to the Dutch Civil Code, 'religious functionaries' are only allowed to conclude a religious marriage after a civil marriage has been concluded (Article 68 Book 1 Civil Code).[40] This regulation emerged in the course of contestations between state authorities and the Roman Catholic Church in the early nineteenth century. Except for occasional discussions about a possible infringement of the freedom of religion, this regulation hardly drew any public attention until it was revitalized in the course of the debates in 2008 about *imams* who concluded Islamic marriages prior to civil marriages.[41] This then raises the broader question of how such Islamic marriages have become a social and legal problem. Who are the main actors in this field, and when and under which conditions did this happen?

As a starting point for analysing how this issue emerged as a topic of public debate and contestation, I performed a search on 'Islamic marriages' in a number of Dutch dailies, covering the period from 1992 until 2010.[42] During the first thirteen years, very few articles were published referring to Islamic marriages. Moreover, these covered a wide range of topics and mainly concerned such marriages abroad. This stands in stark contrast to 2005 and 2008, when there were two distinct peaks in media attention (ebbing away in the following years), which related to two specific issues, the round-up of an alleged terrorist organization called the Hofstad network in 2005 and the debate on salafi *imams* concluding Islamic marriages prior to their civil registration in 2008.

The sudden hype about Islamic marriages in 2005 emerged in the context of the trial of the members of the Hofstad network, when journalists reported on the Islamic marriages that were concluded in the circles around this network. Not only were these marriages unregistered, but they were also concluded in a highly informal manner, with the parents of the young women concerned unaware of their involvement in such marriages. Many of the newspaper articles referred to information provided by the two Dutch civil security services, the Algemene Inlichtingen- en Veiligheidsdienst (AIVD) and the Nationaal Coördinator Terrorismebestrijding (NCTb).

Islamic marriages have indeed become a security issue. They are not only regularly and publicly referred to in the reports of the security services, but in February 2006, the NCTb also published a special report asserting that Islamic marriages formed a threat to national security.[43] The main arguments presented in this report were that these marriages may function as a means to recruit women for violent *jihad*, that they can be considered an indication of a man entering the last phase prior to dying as a martyr in a terrorist attack, and that they may in time be considered as a threat to the democratic rule of law. Whereas little evidence was provided to support these statements, they were regularly referred to in the press.[44] In fact, whereas journalists refer to information provided by the security services, the NCTb report, in turn, used newspaper articles as one of its sources. In this way, in a closely-knit web of mutual referencing, Islamic marriages – a phenomenon previously unknown to the large majority of the population – were linked to violent jihadism.

In 2008, Islamic marriages again became a topic of public debate and contestation. This time the target was salafi *imams*, who were accused of concluding an Islamic marriage between partners who had not yet performed a civil marriage. In this case, members of parliament, including the social democrats (PvdA), the Christian democrats (CDA), the right-wing liberals (VVD) and Geert Wilders' anti-Islam party (PVV) played a pivotal role in turning Islamic marriages into a matter of public concern. The press extensively reported on the parliamentary questions they posed and the investigations of salafi *imams* and mosques they requested. These Islamic marriages were first and foremost considered as evidence of and an instrument for the development of a strictly orthodox Islamic 'parallel society' that purposely distanced itself from Dutch society. As had been the case with the newspaper articles in 2005, the arguments presented by members of parliament resonated strongly with those of the reports produced by the Dutch security services (especially AIVD).[45] By contrast, little media attention was paid to later reports, commissioned by the security services and by the Ministry of Justice, which employed a more empirically grounded approach and came to less alarmist conclusions, at least as far as Islamic marriages were concerned.[46]

Although two different categories of Muslims were the target of these two periods of hype, first violent jihadist and later salafi *imams*, the women entering into these marriages were framed in similar terms. They were first and foremost defined as victims. During the first period of hype, it was argued that they were recruited by unscrupulous male extremists, who employed 'loverboy-like' practices to mobilize them for *jihad*.[47] In the case of salafi *imams*, they were considered the victims of those who intended to institutionalize the shariʿa in the field of family law in the Netherlands and hence propagate gender inequality.[48]

In addition to this dominant discourse that defined women as victims and as devoid of agency, the media also employed an alternative discourse that centred on sexuality. In some cases, these media debates give space to Islamologists, who describe Islamic marriages in neutral terms as a means to Islamically legitimize a sexual relationship. Journalists themselves have also picked up this theme, but tend to use a more normative, and at times sensationalist, tone, presenting these forms of sexuality as somewhat dubious. Especially in articles about the Hofstad network, Islamic marriages were often linked to polygamy, with the women involved described as playing an active role in arranging such polygamous marriages.[49] Journalists used normative terms such as 'loose marital morale',[50] while the NCTb commented in its report that it had the impression that 'behind the pious way in which the Hofstad network presents itself publicly, there is a world of unlimited licentiousness'.[51] Adopting a moral tone and also highlighting the fact that the parents of the young women were often unaware of these marriages, this alternative discourse on sexuality seems closer to the more conservative views of an older generation than to that of the young people involved. This is remarkable, because in mainstream Dutch society, the sexual autonomy of young adults is generally valued.

In short, it is evident that the sudden interest in Islamic marriages has been driven by the securitization of Islam, with the young women involved mainly considered to be victims of jihadist or salafi *imams* or, alternatively, as engaging in dubious Islamic sexual relations. This public attention has led to the criminalization of the *imams* involved in concluding these marriages. This raises a number of questions. Are these Islamic marriages a new phenomenon that emerged in 2005 with violent jihadism and then in 2008 with the growth of salafi Islam? Are the women who enter into such marriages indeed the victims of unscrupulous men and driven by ideological motivations to reject a civil marriage?

Dutch Islamic marriages in practice: multiple motivations and meanings[52]

As the discourse about the women involved in Islamic marriages underlines that they are 'the weaker party' (and therefore in need of legal protection), what might be their motivations for entering into such marriages? Before 2005, engaging in an Islamic marriage was not considered a societal problem or a legal concern, and hence, little attention was paid to such questions. Still, there are indications that the ways in which many migrants from Muslim majority countries concluded their marriages were rather similar to those they would have used in their country of origin. Also in the Netherlands, it was quite common for migrants from Muslim countries to use the gap between the conclusion of the marriage contract (whereupon the couple was married according to Islam) and the actual wedding (after which the couple would live together) as some kind of dating period.

There were a number of options as to where to conclude an Islamic marriage contract. If neither party had Dutch nationality, they could conclude the marriage contract at the consulate, and they also could opt for marriage in their country of origin. In countries where some form of Muslim family law was codified, such as in Morocco, for instance, marriages at the consulate, as in the home country, fulfilled both the conditions for an Islamic marriage and were recognized and registered by the state. These marriages were then also valid according to Dutch law.[53] When one of the parties had also acquired Dutch nationality, only marrying at the consulate was no longer an option. In this case, a Dutch civil marriage was required before the couple in question could be married at the consulate.[54]

The situation for those holding Turkish nationality is different, because in Turkey a distinction is made between a civil and a religious marriage, whereby the state only recognizes the former. As in the Netherlands, a civil marriage is required before a religious marriage can be concluded. For those who married at the consulate, the question was whether and when to conclude the religious marriage. As has been the case in parts of Turkey, some couples decided to conclude a religious marriage (*imam nikah*) before entering into a civil marriage (*resmi nikah*). In more conservative circles, where there was little space for the young couple to date before concluding the Islamic marriage contract, the main motivation for doing so was that the young couple would then be able to get to know each other better without having to commit themselves to an official state-registered marriage.[55] With the criminalization of Islamic marriages in the Netherlands, *imams* have become more hesitant to become involved in such marriages. As there is no Islamic ruling that an *imam* needs to be involved in the conclusion of an Islamic marriage, people who are aware of this may simply decide to marry in the presence of two witnesses.[56] In other cases, they try to find a middle way. Rather than looking for 'an *imam*', couples involve someone with 'enough Islamic knowledge' about how to conclude such a marriage. In some sense, this may be considered a way in which Islamic marriages are becoming more informal.

The above indicates that one reason for women to enter into an Islamic marriage before engaging in a civil marriage is that the traditional sequence of the arrangement and conclusion of a marriage is thereby followed, with the period between entering into the contract and the wedding itself, allowing for a degree of intimacy, for the preparation of the wedding and for setting up a new household. However, there are also more specific reasons why women in the Netherlands decide to first conclude an Islamic marriage. Below, I start by examining those cases in which the couple is not able or willing to conclude a civil marriage. Then I turn to the question that seems to haunt the Dutch authorities most: if no civil marriage is concluded, why enter into an Islamic marriage that has no legal effects in the Netherlands? Is it because the parties concerned are not aware of this? Are they perhaps under pressure to do so, or do they actively desire to enter into such a marriage?

Obstacles to concluding a civil marriage

In the course of the last thirty years, the Netherlands has witnessed a trend towards increasingly informal marriages. A growing number of couples simply cohabit without entering into a civil marriage or concluding another form of contract.[57] Some couples that conclude an Islamic marriage, however, would actually have preferred to register their marriage, but they face the problem that they are not able to enter into a civil marriage. For in order to conclude such a marriage, a number of documents are needed, such as a legalized birth certificate, valid proof of identity and proof of civil status (that is, evidence of not being married). Sometimes people do not have the required documents and are not able to acquire them, for instance if they are refugees. In other cases they do not have legal resident status and are thus very hesitant to even enter into the process of concluding a civil marriage, although this may be legally possible.

People are not only unable to conclude a civil marriage because they do not have the documents needed, however. Concluding a marriage may also be impossible because they do not fulfil the conditions for a civil marriage. In the Netherlands, marriages between relatives in the first or second degree are forbidden (which is also the case in Islamic law), forced marriages are forbidden, neither party may already be married, and both need to be eighteen years or older (unless the woman has already given birth or is pregnant; then the minimum age is sixteen and the permission of the parents is needed). Statutory Muslim family laws have also often emphasized the need for consent to marry, institutionalized minimum ages for marriage (for instance, in Morocco the minimum age is also eighteen years), and have curtailed polygamous marriages, although usually short of outright forbidding them. With respect to Muslim minorities in Europe, some Islamic scholars have argued strongly in favour of concluding a civil marriage contract, because only in that case are women's rights guaranteed.[58]

If one of the parties is underage or already married, couples cannot conclude a civil marriage in the Netherlands. How often couples conclude an Islamic marriage for such reasons is hard to say. A few of the women with whom I discussed marriage arrangements had entered into an Islamic marriage when they were sixteen years old. Polygamous marriages were occasionally mentioned, but only involved marriages abroad. Roex[59] also states that some of her salafi respondents married very young and that a few of her respondents were polygamously married, but most of them were eighteen or older and the number of polygamous marriages was very small.

An Islamic marriage has no legal effects under Dutch law, hence the parties concerned are seen as engaging in a sexual relationship outside of marriage, which is of no concern to the law.[60] Yet, the question remains whether such Islamic marriages may be unwanted by the women who enter into them. It is true that Islamic marriages may be used to bind youngsters at a young age, but there is no reason to assume that there is a direct relation between forced marriages and Islamic marriage.[61] Civil marriages as well as sexual relations outside of marriage may be unwanted, while Islamic marriages may be strongly desired. The underage girls entering into an Islamic marriage who were involved in the Hofstad network, those mentioned by Roex and those whom I interviewed, were not pushed into such marriages by their parents, but rather did so without asking their opinion or for their approval. The same seems to be the case with the women who enter into a polygamous marriage.

Legal obstacles are not the only reason why Muslims refrain from civil marriage. Some are able to conclude a civil marriage, yet prefer not to do so, because they would find such a situation disadvantageous. Entering into a state-registered marriage may, for instance, cause the loss of social security benefits and other financial entitlements. Such considerations may also be found amongst non-Muslims in the Netherlands as well as in Muslim majority countries, as the previous example of Egyptian widows indicated. There is also a category of women that faces no legal impediments to entering into a civil marriage, but that, at least for the time being, refrains from doing so for very different reasons. These are ethnic Dutch women (often, but not always converts to Islam) who want to marry a Muslim partner, usually from a migrant background, who face strong resistance from their own family. In order not to antagonize their families or hurt their feelings, they may opt to enter into an Islamic marriage only. Their parents do not need to be involved in such a marriage, or even know about it, as it does not have legal effects, while by concluding an Islamic marriage they themselves engage in a licit sexual relationship according to Islam.

Opting for an Islamic marriage

If some Muslims in the Netherlands are unable or unwilling to conclude a civil marriage, this still begs the question, why opt for an Islamic marriage? The narratives of women who enter into Islamic marriages point to two different lines of argumentation. Some do so in response to social pressure; to them, Islamic marriages are of little importance. Others, by contrast, actively desire to conclude an Islamic marriage. Due to their religious convictions, having an Islamic marriage is what counts most for them.

In more conservative Muslim circles in the Netherlands, parents may find it hard to accept that their son, or especially their daughter, has a relationship that is not quickly legitimized in the form of a marriage. Once some sort of relationship becomes apparent, the parents expect that marriage will soon follow. As a result, the couple may feel strong social pressure to enter into a marriage for which they themselves do not feel ready. In such cases, concluding an Islamic marriage may be a convenient solution. By doing so, they can show their consideration for the concerns of their parents, who consider an Islamic marriage to be crucially important, and avoid offending them. Having grown up in the Netherlands and being aware of mainstream Dutch ideas about relationships and marriage, they themselves may hold quite different ideas and may value the civil marriage as the real marriage. To them, concluding an Islamic marriage is a means to appease their parents and the larger Muslim community, while they consider the period between concluding the Islamic marriage and, if things work out well, registering a civil marriage as a 'try-out' period that is quite similar to dating.

However, these youngsters are faced with the criminalization of *imams* who conclude such Islamic marriages. While some will either do without an *imam* or find someone 'knowledgeable' about Islam to be involved in the Islamic marriage, others opt to marry in the country of origin. Often having spent most, if not all, of their lives in the Netherlands, they do not always take such marriages very seriously. However, as such a marriage in the country of origin is often officially registered, it is legally valid, not only there, but also in the Netherlands. If the marriage does not work out, and especially if the husband subsequently refuses to cooperate in the dissolution of the marriage, the wife may discover that it can take a lot of effort, time, and money to arrange a divorce.

An Islamic marriage may also function as a means for a woman to convince her family to agree to a marriage to a man of her own choosing. Although family pressure in Muslim migrant circles, especially those who have been in the Netherlands for a long time, has gradually diminished, and most parents would not push their children into a marriage they actively resisted, parents may refuse to accept the choice a daughter has made. Some families are, for instance, hesitant about a partner from another ethnic background, or one who is not a born

Muslim but has converted to Islam. If the couple can find an *imam* who is respected by their families and who is willing to conclude an Islamic marriage, this may solve the problem. Once they are married according to Islam, the parents may well decide that it will be of little use to exert further pressure.

Actively desiring an Islamic marriage

If for some couples, engaging in an Islamic marriage is simply a convenient solution to mediate between the normative ideas of older and younger generations of Muslims from migrant backgrounds, then those who enter into an Islamic marriage out of conviction follow very different lines of argumentation. Expressing a strong commitment to Islam, they tend to experience their religion in more strictly orthodox ways. Some of them may be part of the salafi Muslim circles that have been the focus of much public debate and political concern. For these Muslims, an Islamic marriage is their first priority, as it makes their relationship permissible under Islam.

Rather than a means to enable a form of dating (during the period between concluding the marriage contract and the public wedding), amongst women who actively desire an Islamic marriage, dating is often purposely rejected. This category, which includes both born Muslimahs and also a relatively large number of new Muslimahs (women who have converted to Islam), holds different convictions about the preferred way to conclude a marriage, from the moment of getting acquainted to the wedding ceremony. Their preferences differ not only from mainstream Dutch conventions, but also from those of many Muslims from migrant backgrounds. They often strongly support the normative notion of gender segregation. Before the marriage contract is concluded, the man and the woman only meet each other a limited number of times, and always in public; that is, in the company of others or in a public setting. They use these meetings to exchange ideas about how they would like to organize their marital relations, what they expect from each other, and sometimes write this down in the form of marital conditions. Then they search in their own circles for someone with Islamic knowledge to be involved in the conclusion of the marriage contract. This is especially important for a new Muslimah, because her non-Muslim father cannot function as her marriage guardian; this becomes the responsibility of an *imam*. Such Islamic marriages are not only very different from the Dutch notion of dating; born Muslimahs from migrant backgrounds also emphasize that such marriages differ greatly from traditional arranged marriages, where parents are also strongly involved in the choice of partner, but which focus more on family relations and material matters than on character and religiosity. The wedding itself is also often celebrated in a different way. With more gender segregation and with music that is limited to the singing of religious hymns (*anashid*), often by the female friends of the bride, the wedding festivities are generally smaller-scale and far less commercialized than is common in Muslim migrant circles.

Still, a commitment to an 'Islamic marriage and wedding' does not imply that the women concerned reject civil marriage. Rather, they deal with civil marriage in a pragmatic manner. At some point in time, they may well conclude a civil marriage, because it is the most convenient way to safeguard financial rights, such as entitlements to one's husband's pension, inheritance rights, and the relationship with their children. Such considerations are very similar to those made by non-Muslim Dutch when dealing with the question of whether to officially marry or not.

Temporary Shia marriages

Shia Muslims only make up about 10 per cent of the Dutch Muslim population. Mainly coming from Iranian, Iraqi, Afghan and Pakistani backgrounds, there are great differences in their level of commitment to Islamic law. For those who came to the Netherlands from Iran, often as refugees after the Islamic revolution, following the shari'a is often not a major concern in everyday life. To those who came from Southern Iraq, fleeing Saddam Hussein's regime after the failed uprising in 1991, Islamic law is often an important guideline.[62]

When Shi'ites in the Netherlands conclude a temporary marriage, this is a highly informal affair. Many of these marriages are concluded between Shia men and ethnic Dutch women, who are non-Muslim at the time of marriage. For the men involved, such a marriage has a strong religious meaning.[63] Whereas in a country such as Iran, some couples conclude a temporary marriage simply to avoid the accusation of *zina* and the risk of prosecution, in the Netherlands, pre-marital sex is not a concern of the legislature. If a Shia man in the Netherlands concludes an Islamic marriage with an ethnic Dutch woman, he does so because he does not want to engage in a relationship with a woman (which may well mean any kind of dating) with whom he has not concluded an Islamic marriage. The women involved in such marriages, who tend to be unfamiliar with the concept of a temporary marriage, may simply agree to them because they sense that such an arrangement is important to their partner. These temporary marriages are concluded in a highly informal manner, not only without a religious functionary, but also without witnesses, and the dower demanded by the woman – on the request of her husband – is usually insignificant. In fact, many of the women involved would not agree to conclude a more formal form of marriage, let alone a civil marriage, as it would be far too early in the relationship for them. It is precisely because a temporary marriage is so informal and has no legal effects that they agree to such marriage. The risks Haeri sees for women who engage in unregistered Shia marriages in Iran, where rights to maintenance are more important and non-virginity is culturally more problematic, are far less relevant in the Dutch context.[64]

Some Dutch women who initially conclude a temporary marriage for the sake of their partners gradually start to see its value and take it more seriously, especially when they feel attracted to Islam and convert. However, they may also express some ambivalence about this institution, because of their concerns that men may abuse it as an easy means to engage in a large number of sexual relationships with few obligations. Socializing in circles of born Shia women, they become aware of the fact that women from countries such as Iraq are far more hesitant to conclude a temporary marriage, as for them, temporary marriages often have negative connotations.

Conclusion

Both in Muslim majority settings and in the Netherlands, women who engage in unregistered Islamic marriages have been defined as the victims of men. It is true that some of these marriages do not work, or may even be highly exploitative, but this is not necessarily a consequence of how these marriages are concluded. Women have a wide variety of motivations for entering into and consenting to unregistered Islamic marriages prior to, or even instead of, a registered or civil marriage. They may be simply unable to officially register a marriage, find it too disadvantageous, or feel that they and their partner are not yet ready for an official marriage in either a material or an emotional sense. Instead, they may opt to conclude an unregistered Islamic marriage to legitimize their relationship. In some cases, women may enter into an Islamic marriage as a means to force their parents to agree with their choice of partner. For others, especially more strictly orthodox or salafi women, an Islamic marriage is what really counts.

In mainstream public discourse, however, unregistered Islamic marriages are considered to be highly undesirable. In Muslim majority countries, the main issue at stake is that such *unregistered* marriages undermine established structures of authority. Unregistered marriages amongst young people are a particular source of concern, as they challenge a whole set of strongly intertwined authority structures. They do not simply defy the state authorities, but also go against the grain of gender and generational hierarchies. They challenge the authority of the parents, which is especially problematic in the case of daughters, and go against the opinions of at least some religious figures. Unregistered marriages such as those conducted by older single women or women who have previously been married tend to be deemed less problematic, as these simultaneously function as a solution to social concerns about a 'woman without a man'. For these women, unregistered marriages may entail a level of autonomy that is not recognized in the conventional marriage contract, while men are not burdened with the obligations that such a contract brings. Whereas religious authorities are very hesitant about unregistered marriages and may consider them a threat to societal stability, they may also recognize that there are grounds for considering them permissible under Islam. Moreover, some also recognize that changing societal conditions, such as the tendency to delay marriage, require unconventional solutions.

The concerns in the Netherlands about Islamic marriages are very different. In this case, state authorities do not object to the fact that the couple does not conclude a civil marriage. Instead, they consider it problematic that they enter into an *Islamic* marriage, considering this an indication and instrument of radicalization and an attempt to develop a parallel society based on the shari'a. As has become evident, rather than finding themselves in the position of passive victims, young women often actively partake in the arrangement of an Islamic marriage, and may well enter into a civil marriage later. They have a great variety of reasons to do so. For some, it is because they consider the civil marriage 'the real marriage' that they do not yet want to conclude a civil marriage. Moreover, amongst those for whom an Islamic marriage is of paramount importance, there is no indication that they actively refuse a civil marriage for ideological reasons (or would do so more consistently than non-Muslim Dutch). After all, the Roman-Catholic Church also only recognizes Roman Catholic marriages as real marriages, and considers civil marriage to be a merely administrative act. In fact, these women deal with civil marriage in a way that is very similar to that adopted by their non-Muslims: they follow a pragmatic approach. The paradox is thus that whereas the Netherlands has witnessed a strong tendency towards more informal marriages in the last four decades, in the case of Muslims, an ideological commitment to civil marriage is required.

Notes

1 The research for this article was commissioned and funded by the FORUM Institute for Multicultural Affairs. FORUM is an independent knowledge institute. Its mission is to contribute towards social stability in the Netherlands on the basis of knowledge.

2 Mona Abaza, 'Perceptions of urfi marriage in the Egyptian press', *ISIM*, 2001 (Newsletter 7), p. 20.

3 These marriages are part of the wider field of acts that are considered illegal but licit. See Willem van Schendel, 'Illegal but illicit: Transnational flows and permissive polities in Asia', *IIAS Newsletter*, 2005 (Vol. 58, No. 32); Barak Kalir, Malini Sur and Willem van Schendel, 'Introduction: mobile practices and regimes of permissiveness' in: Barak Kalir and Malini Sur (eds.), *Illegal but licit: transnational flows and permissive polities*, Amsterdam: Amsterdam University Press, 2012. See also Oussama Arabi, *Studies in modern Islamic law and jurisprudence*, Den Haag/London/New York: Kluwer, 2001, pp. 147*ff*, who explains how non-conventional marriages emerged amongst the general public, provoking the religious and state authorities to respond.

4 Judith E. Tucker, *In the House of the Law: Gender and Islamic law in Ottoman Syria and Palestine*, Berkeley: University of California Press, 1998, p. 51.

5 Arabi, *Studies in modern Islamic law and jurisprudence*, 2001, pp. 160*ff*.

6 Such as, for instance, the option to divorce themselves and to determine where to live. See Lynn Welchman, *Women and Muslim Family Laws in Arab States: A Comparative Overview of Textual Development and Advocacy*, Amsterdam: Amsterdam University Press, 2007, pp. 99*ff*.

7 Welchman, *Women and Muslim Family Laws*, 2007, pp. 62*ff*; 70; 94. Statutory laws no longer allow a woman's marriage guardian (usually her father) to exert coercion with respect to her marriage, but in some cases they still require his consent or allow for his objection to her marriage. See Lynn Welchman, 'Muslim family laws and women's consent to marriage: Does the law mean what it says?', *Social Differences Online*, 2011 (Vol. 1), p. 68. Reforms have given women also a greater say with respect to divorce and custody, but have in some cases also burdened them with new obligations (contributing towards maintenance of the family) and have made it more difficult to claim paternity.

8 Shahla Haeri, *Law of desire: Temporary marriage in Iran*, London: I.B. Tauris, 1989.

9 Tucker, *In the House of the Law*, 1998, pp. 164; 173. In addition, the Maliki school of law allowed a claim of paternity for up to five years after a woman was widowed or divorced. See Willy Jansen, 'Sleeping in the womb: protracted pregnancies in the Maghreb', *The Muslim World*, 2000 (Vol. 90, No. 1-2), pp. 218-237.

10 The Ottoman Empire started to require registration by the end of the nineteenth century. J. Anderson, 'Recent developments in shari'a law III. The contract of marriage', *The Muslim World*, 1951 (Vol. 4, No. 2), p. 113; Welchman, *Women and Muslim Family Laws*, 2007, p. 53.

11 Welchman, *Women and Muslim Family* Laws, 2007, pp. 53*ff*.

12 For a discussion about registration on the West Bank, see Welchman, *Women and Muslim Family Laws*, 2007, p. 375;, for Morocco see Leila Jordens-Cotran, *Het Marokkaanse familierecht en de Nederlandse rechtspraktijk*, Utrecht: Forum, 2000, pp 87ff; for Indonesia see Adriaan Bedner and Stijn van Huis, 'Plurality of Marriage Law and Marriage Registration for Muslims in Indonesia: A Plea for Pragmatism,' *Utrecht Law Review*, 2010 (Vol. 6, No. 2), pp. 186ff; for Turkey see Ihsan Yilmaz, 'Non-Recognition of Post-modern Turkish Socio-Legal Reality and the Predicament of Women', *British Journal of Middle Eastern Studies*, 2003 (Vol. 30, No. 1), p. 34; and for Egypt see Shahreena Shahrani, *The social (re)construction of 'urfi marriage*, MA Thesis: Ohio State University, 2010, p. 68).

13 For the British Mandate period in Palestine see A. Moors, *Women, Property and Islam. Palestinian Experiences 1920-1990*, Cambridge: Cambridge University Press, 1995, p. 96).

14 Abaza, 'Perceptions of urfi marriage', 2001, p. 20; Shahrani, *The social (re)construction of 'urfi marriage*, 2010, p. 32.

15 Frances Susan Hasso, *Consuming Desires: Family Crisis and the State in the Middle East*, Stanford, CA: Stanford University Press, 2011.

16 (See Diane Dingerman and Barbara Ibrahim, 'The Costs of Marriage in Egypt: A Hidden Dimension in the New Arab Demography', *Cairo Papers in Social Science*, 2003 (Vol. 24, No. 1). Some NGOs have attempted to intervene and provide financial support for young people in order to enable them to marry. See Jad Chabaan, 'Youth and Development in the Arab Countries: The Need for a Different Approach' *Middle Eastern Studies* (Vol. 45, No. 1) 2009, pp. 33-55; Frances Susan Hasso, *Consuming Desires: Family Crisis and the State in the Middle East*, Stanford, CA: Stanford University Press, 2011.

17 Hanan Kholoussy, *For Better, For Worse: The Marriage Crisis that made Modern Egypt*, Stanford: Stanford University Press, 2010, pp. 24ff.

18 Hoda Rashad, Magued Osman and Farzaneh Roudi-Fahimi, *Marriage in the Arab world*, Washington: Population Reference Bureau, 2005

19 Bahgat, Hossam and Wesal Afifi, 'Sexuality Politics in Egypt' in: Richard Parker, Rosalind Petchesky and Robert Sember (eds.), *Sex Politics: Report from the Front Lines*, 2008, available online at http://www.sxpolitics.org/frontlines/book/pdf/sekspolitics.pdf.

20 Abaza, 'Perceptions of urfi marriage', 2001, p. 20; Saher el-Tawila and Zeinab Khadr, *Patterns of marriage and family formation among youth in Egypt, 2004*, Cairo: National Population Council and Cairo University, 2004.

21 However, the couple may find recourse in the Hanafi ruling allowing adult women to conclude their own marriages.

22 As in the paradigmatic case of Hind al-Hinnawy and the famous television star Ahmad al-Fishawi (Hasso, *Consuming Desires* 2011, pp. 1*ff*; Bahjat and Afifi, 'Sexuality Politics', 2008, p. 53).

23 Jordens-Cotran, *Het Marokkaanse Familierecht*, 2000, p. 93) makes this argument for the case of Morocco.

24 Ihsan Yilmaz, 'Marriage solemnization among Turks in Britain: The emergence of a hybrid Anglo-Muslim Turkish law,' *Journal of Muslim Affairs*, 2004 (Vol. 24, No. 1), pp. 62-3.

25 Yilmaz, 'Non-recognition of post-modern Turkish socio-legal reality' 2003, p. 39.
26 Haeri, 'Temporary marriage and the state in Iran: An Islamic discourse on female sexuality in Iran', *Social Research*, 1992 (Vol. 59, No. 1), pp. 201-2.
27 Haeri, *Law of Desire*, 1989.
28 Magued Osman and Laila Shahd, 'Age discrepant marriages in Egypt' in: Nicholas Hopkins (ed.), *The new Arab family*, Cairo: The American University in Cairo Press, 2003.
29 Nadeem Karkabi, *Couples in the global margins: sexuality and marriage between local men and western women in Dahab (South Sinai)*, MA thesis, University of Haifa, 2008.
30 In spite of the great economic inequality between the partners, Karkabi does not define this simply as exploitation or sex tourism, as, according to him, this may also entail an affective, romantic relationship.
31 Many marriages were polygamous, as the men often married younger Egyptian women with whom they had children.
32 Joanne Walby, 'Extended holiday in Hurghada: Russian migrant women and "urfi marriage"', *Surfacing*, 2010 (Vol. 3, No. 1), pp. 39-70.
33 Arabi, *Studies in modern Islamic law*, 2001, pp. 164*ff*.
34 Abaza, 'Perceptions of urfi marriage', 2001, p. 21.
35 Arabi, *Studies in modern Islamic law*, 2001, pp. 147-67.
36 Welchman, *Women and Muslim Family* Laws, 2007, p. 103.
37 Granqvist, Hilma, *Marriage conditions in a Palestinian village II*, Helsingfors: Akademische Buchhandlung, 1935, pp. 312*ff*.
38 Nadia Sonneveld, *Khul' divorce in Egypt. Public debates, juridical practices, and everyday life*, PhD thesis: University of Amsterdam, 2009.
39 Nadia Abou el Magd, 2009, 'Outcry in Egypt over "marriage tourism"', *The National* 17 August 2009. http://www.thenational.ae/news/worldwide/africa/outcry-in-egypt-over-marriage-tourism; Riham Adel, 2009, 'Married, or maybe not', *Al-Ahram Weekly Online*. http://weekly.ahram.org.eg/2009/976/feature.htm.
40 See also Joanne van der Leun & Avalon Leupen, *Informele huwelijken in Nederland; een exploratieve studie*. Leiden: Universiteit Leiden, Faculteit der Rechtsgeleerdheid, 2009, p. 7; Susan Rutten, 'Protection of spouses in informal marriages by human rights', *Utrecht Law Review* 2010 (No. 2), pp. 77-92.
41 This in spite of the differences between a Roman Catholic marriage (which requires a priest as it involves a sacrament) and an Islamic marriage (which is a contract, the conclusion of which does not require the presence of an *imam*). Van der Leun and Leupen, *Informele huwelijken in Nederland*, 2009, p. 8ff) describe debates in the field of law about the relation between civil and religious marriages.
42 I counted the number of articles that were published each year in four daily newspapers (*NRC*, *Trouw*, *de Volkskrant* and *De Telegraaf*), using the search term 'islamitisch! huwelijk!'.
43 NCTb, *Informele islamitische huwelijken. Het verschijnsel en de (veiligheids)risico's*, Den Haag: NCTb, 2006.

44 A non-specified hadith about the higher status of married over single men is mentioned as evidence for the willingness to die as a martyr, and the threat to the democratic rule of law is substantiated with the argument that ultra-orthodox Muslims refuse to register a civil marriage on ideological grounds NCTb, *Informele islamitische huwelijken,* 2006, pp. 26-7.

45 AIVD, *De radicale da'wa. De opkomst van het neo-radicalisme in Nederland,* Den Haag: AIVD, 2007.

46 C. de Poot and A. Sonneschein, *Jihadistisch terrorisme in Nederland. Een beschrijving op basis van afgesloten opsporingsonderzoeken,* Den Haag: NCTb, 2009; Ineke Roex, Sjef van Stiphout and Jean Tillie, *Salafisme in Nederland. Aard, omvang en dreiging,* Amsterdam: IMES (commissioned by the NCTb), 2010.

47 NCTb, *Informele islamitische huwelijken,* 2006, p. 22.

48 AIVD, *De radicale da'wa,* 2007, p. 68.

49 Groen and Kranenberg also included some of these articles in their book *Strijdsters for Allah,* 2006 (later translated as *Women warriors for Allah. An Islamist Network in the Netherlands,* Philadelphia: University of Pennsylvania Press, 2012).

50 *De Volkskrant* 11 November 2006.

51 NCTb, *Informele islamitische huwelijken,* 2006, p. 24.

52 The remainder of this chapter is based on explorative qualitative research conducted among young Muslims, focusing on the conclusion of Islamic marriages, which was started in 2009. It includes the gathering of topical life stories as well as many informal conversations about this topic with both born Muslimahs and new Muslimahs (converts), and information publicly available on the Internet (such as discussion fora). I thank Vanessa Vroom-Najem, Eva al-Haidari (also for allowing me to use her MA thesis), Khadija Amatallah, and Loubna al-Mourabet for sharing their insights with me.

53 That is, if there were no issues of public order, such as polygamy. See Van der Leun and Leupen, *Informele huwelijken in Nederland,* 2009, p. 16.

54 Van der Leun en Leupen, *Informele huwelijken in Nederland,* 2009, p. 31.

55 See Nathal Dessing, 'Continuiteit en verandering in de huwelijkssluiting bij Turkse, Marokkaanse en Surinaamse moslims in Nederland', *Recht van de Islam,* 1999 (Vol. 16), pp. 59-81.

56 However, Dutch models of the governance of religion that build on Christianity have given more weight to the position of *imams* than may be the case in Muslim majority countries. This has also influenced Muslims in the Netherlands, some of whom assume that the presence of an *imam* is required.

57 Jan Latten, 'Trends in samenwonen en trouwen. De schone schijn van burgerlijke staat', CBS *Bevolkingstrends,* 2004, (Vol. 52, No. 4), pp. 46-60; Van der Leun en Leupen, *Informele huwelijken in Nederland,* 2009, p. 10.

58 John Richard Bowen, *A new anthropology of Islam,* Cambridge: Cambridge University Press, 2012, p. 165*ff.*

59 Roex a.o. *Salafisme in Nederland,* 2010, pp. 147-8.

60 In the Netherlands, sexual relations may become a legal concern if one of the two parties is below the age of sixteen.

61 Forced marriages are generally decreasing in the Netherlands. See Oka Storms and Edien Bartels, *De keuze van een huwelijkspartner. Een studie naar partnerkeuze onder groepen Amsterdammers,* Vrije Universiteit Amsterdam, 2008.

62 Tayba Sharif, *Resistance and remembrance: History-telling of the Iraqi Shi'ite Arab refugees women and their families in the Netherlands*, PhD thesis: University of Amsterdam, 2003.

63 See also Eva Al-Haidari, *Vernuftige verhoudingen.Opvattingen over het tijdelijk huwelijk in West-Europa,* Universiteit van Amsterdam, 2001.

64 Haeri, 'Temporary marriage and the state in Iran', 1992.

9 Understanding and Use of Islamic Family Law Rules in German Courts

The Example of the *Mahr*

Nadjma Yassari

Introduction

This chapter will address the question of how domestic courts may accommodate foreign legal institutions within the scope of their own legal system. The example chosen is the Islamic dower (*mahr*), as it is the most prominent institution of Islamic family law adjudicated in German courts for over forty years.[1] For this purpose, the following questions will be raised: first, what is the *mahr*, and second, how is the *mahr* understood and interpreted by German courts?[2] These questions will be discussed by focusing on two aspects: first, the legal techniques at hand in order to fit the *mahr* into German law, and second, the ways parties argue their cases.

Generally speaking, the *mahr* is a legal institution of Islamic family law, consisting of an asset of monetary value that the husband gives his wife upon marriage.[3] Usually the payment of the *mahr* is split into two halves: one part, the so-called proper dower, is due at the time the marriage is concluded, and the other part, the so-called deferred *mahr*, is due at the time the marriage is dissolved. It may also be that the full payment of the *mahr* is deferred to the time of the dissolution of the marriage. The *mahr* can appear in a domestic court essentially by two means. First, in cases involving foreigners, the rules of private international law may point to the application of a foreign law under which the *mahr* has been contracted. In these cases, the German courts have to apply the applicable law and decide on the *mahr* according to those foreign rules. There are many examples of such cases in German courts. However, the conflict of laws rule may also point to the application of German domestic law. These cases particularly concern parties who are citizens of different (Islamic) countries, so that, according to the German conflict of laws rules, the law of habitual residence (that is, German law) applies. Additionally, cases have occurred where German Muslims had agreed on a *mahr*, which the wife then claimed under the provisions of German family law. As the *mahr* is foreign to German domestic law, courts often struggle to understand and appropriately accommodate it within their own legal framework.

The common thread running through the struggle to accommodate the *mahr* in a German setting is – in accordance with the German theory of functional approach (*funktionale Qualifikation*)[4] imported from the field of private international law – the search for the function of the *mahr*. In doing so one must, as a first step, determine the function and aims of the foreign institution according to its native law (the law under which it has been contracted) in order to be able, in a second step, to accommodate it within similar legal instruments available under domestic law.

In the following, we will first discuss the function of the *mahr*. This will be done in great detail, which is necessary to get a proper understanding of the problems we encounter in the German court rulings on this matter. In these rulings, we will limit ourselves to an analysis of the judicature of the German Federal Supreme Court, with a focus on its legal techniques as well as the cultural and religious arguments put forward by the parties.

Function of the *Mahr*

When analysing the many purposes and aims that have been attributed to the *mahr*, two categories can be distinguished: material and immaterial functions.

Immaterial functions

The *mahr* is said to be a token of the husband's respect for the wife and a sign of his commitment to marriage.[5] It furthermore touches upon the idea of prestige, as the *mahr* is considered to correspond to the level of desirability of the wife and the financial potential of the husband.[6] In addition, it is argued that a high *mahr* may deter the husband from a quick and thoughtless repudiation and prevent him from engaging in polygamy, since a new *mahr* is due for all subsequent marriages.[7] These functions are meant to influence the behaviour of the parties to act in a specific manner or are expressions of a certain status of the wife and/or the husband. As such, the *mahr* is seen as a bargaining tool in the negotiations of spouses of Islamic origin.[8]

Material functions

Additionally, there are material or economic aspects to the *mahr*: it is supposed to ensure financial security when paid as a prompt *mahr* at the time of the conclusion of the marriage, by providing the wife with a certain degree of economic independence and enabling her to build up her own property.[9] It has also been seen as a financial cushion after divorce, since in most Islamic countries, there is no substantial post-marital support for the wife.[10] And finally, it has also been argued that the *mahr* is conceived to counterbalance the lesser inheritance rights of the wife in the case of the husband's death.[11] This last function is particularly raised in view of the husband's potential polygamous marriages, as the inheritance portion of the wife will have to be divided between all wives. In the words of Indian scholar Asaf Fyzee, in a nutshell, the *mahr* is 'a provision for a rainy day'.[12]

The *Mahr* in the Classical Works of the *Fuqaha'*

A look at the *fiqh* works of classical Islamic scholars, on the other hand, reveals that none of these functions of the *mahr* has been really discussed in depth. Instead, the *mahr* is dealt with as a contract of exchange, governed by the rules of the contract of sale.[13] In this context, some have interpreted the *mahr* as being the counter value for the sexual submission of the wife in marriage.[14] This interpretation has been taken up by some German courts to designate the *mahr* as the 'price for the sexuality of the wife'.[15]

Evaluation of the *Mahr*

In evaluating the aforementioned functions, it will be shown that the economic function of the *mahr* is predominant. As will be explained in the paragraphs below, the interpretation of the *mahr* as being the price for marital cohabitation is not sustainable. It is true that, in certain cases, the *mahr* has a symbolic value and that, in other cases, it has deterred husbands from thoughtless repudiation. However, today, the *mahr* is mostly a significant financial instrument of family law in Islamic countries.

The *mahr* as a counter value for marital cohabitation?

If the *mahr* were to be considered the counter value for marital cohabitation, its implementation in German courts could become difficult in view of the principle of public policy. According to this principle, a foreign legal provision shall not be applicable if the result of its application is obviously incompatible with essential principles of German law. This is particularly the case when the foreign rule is incompatible with the German Basic Law, the *Grundgesetz*. Putting a monetary value on marital cohabitation would therefore be a matter of public policy. The reading of the *mahr* as such a monetary counter value is, however, the result of a misinterpretation of the *mahr*. Generally, the advocates of such a theory base their view on two arguments: first, the nature of the *mahr* as a contract of exchange and the application of the rules of the contract of sale on the *mahr* agreement; and second, the fact that the *mahr* is forfeited when a marriage is dissolved before its consummation. Both arguments are – as will be shown below – unsustainable.

First, the fact that the *mahr* is considered a contract of exchange governed by the rules of the contract of sale does not necessarily justify the conclusion that the *mahr* is a 'purchase price' for marital cohabitation. It is true that, in the literature, the agreement on *mahr* is called a reciprocal exchange contract (Arabic *mu'āwada*), to which the rules of the sales contract are applicable.[16] This has a specific background, however: Islamic law does not know any general theory of contract.[17] General rules are derived from the regulations of model contracts, such as the contract of sale.[18] Thus, the link to the sales contract does not reflect the nature of the *mahr* being a sales or leasing contract of female sexuality, but is derived from the structure of Islamic contract law.[19] It highlights that the regulations of the sales contract can be applied as general rules to certain aspects of the *mahr*.[20]Accordingly, anything that can be the subject of a contract of sale can be chosen as the subject of the *mahr*. Additionally, the conditions of a valid purchase price must also be observed for the *mahr*: the *mahr* should have a monetary value, be determinable and its performance has to be possible and legal.

Second, it is true that under certain circumstances the *mahr* is forfeited when a marriage is dissolved before its consummation. Therefore, there is a connection between the *mahr* and marital cohabitation. These regulations, however, do not offer a consistent picture: whereas the wife is entitled to half of the *mahr* if her husband divorces her prior to consummation,[21] this is not the case when the spouses die before consummation. In this case, the wife keeps her right to the full *mahr*, and that right will be inherited by her heirs.[22] On the other hand, the wife may refuse to comply with her marital duties as long as the *mahr* has not been given to her.[23] However, this right of retention is a unilateral right of the wife; the husband cannot refrain from paying the *mahr* because the marriage has not been consummated: he must pay the *mahr* prior to consummation.[24] Thus, there is no reciprocity in this right. If the *mahr* were really the counter value for marital cohabitation, its regulations would have to be much more stringent and comparable to the purchase price in a contract of sale. This is, however, not the case. The wife is still entitled to the *mahr*, even if she has not 'fulfilled her duty'. As a matter of fact, many of these regulations are explicable by their historical context. Very often, there would be a considerable gap between the time when the marriage was contracted and the time when the marriage was actually consummated. This was particularly the case when minors were married, or in marriages by proxy where the husband-to-be was absent. If, in the meantime, the marriage was dissolved by the husband, half of the *mahr* became due. Some argue that this amount was meant to compensate the girls for their reduced chances of remarriage. In other words, it constitutes some kind of damages awarded to the girl for the delay or the shortfall of a financial provider. Others argue that half of the *mahr* was due in order to compensate the husband for the expenses incurred in view of the marriage.[25]

Finally, one has to consider the marriage, its consummation and the *mahr* as a unity. It is true that the consummation of the marriage is not a condition for its validity. However, marriage is considered to be the only legal framework within which sexual activities are allowed and even a duty. Thus, some authors hold that only by the consummation of marriage, the process of marrying is 'completed'.[26] Consequently, the reduction of the *mahr* in case of a repudiation before consummation is not so much linked to the concept of the *mahr* as the 'price for marital sexual cohabitation', but is rather connected to the not yet completed process of marrying.

THE *MAHR* AS AN ECONOMIC FACTOR

The predominance of the economic function of the *mahr* is very well illustrated by the immaterial functions attributed to it. All aforementioned immaterial functions will only materialize if the *mahr* is of a substantial financial value. What kind of prestige or seriousness would be expressed by a low *mahr*? How could a low *mahr* deter the husband from repudiating his wife or prevent him from entering into a second marriage? Furthermore, a look at the practice of *mahr* reveals its economic importance: in Iran, for example, 80 per cent of divorces are *khul'* divorces, whereby, in the absence of legal or contractual grounds for divorce, the wife can gain the consent of her husband to divorce in return for some kind of consideration.[27] This consideration is usually a part or the whole of her *mahr*. According to a survey conducted by the magazine *zanān*, Iranian women often try to negotiate a high *mahr* in order to exit an unwanted marriage more easily while at the same time keeping some parts of the *mahr* for financial security.[28]

New legislation in some Muslim countries also highlights the economic importance of the *mahr*. The regulations in Iran, Iraq and the United Arab Emirates illustrate this very well. In 1998, the Iranian legislator enacted a new law, the 'Act on the Adaptation of the Value of the *Mahr* to the Inflation Rate', according to which a *mahr* contracted in Iranian currency must be adjusted by the inflation rate at the time it is claimed (which, as we have seen, can be many years after the *mahr* had been agreed).[29] Under Iranian law, the agreement on the *mahr* figures in the standardized marriage contract as prompt *mahr*, meaning that it must be handed to the wife upon her request. In general, as long as the marriage is working and the couple lives happily together, hardly any woman claims her *mahr* during the marriage. In most cases, the *mahr* is claimed, like the deferred *mahr*, upon dissolution of the marriage, whereby the time gap between these two moments can be crucial, implying a substantial deflation of the monetary value. In order to secure the stability of the *mahr* and to ensure that women are not deprived of their rights, the amount of the *mahr* must be adapted to the inflation rate.

Based on similar grounds, in 1999, a decree was issued in Iraq,[30] ordering the value of the deferred *mahr*, expressed in Iraqi currency, to be adapted to its gold value at the time of the conclusion of the marriage.[31] Earlier, in 1997, the United Arab Emirates enacted a federal law, the 'Act on the Limitation of the Amount of the *Mahr* in the Marriage Contract and the Expenses Incurring for Marriage', to limit the amount of the *mahr*.[32] This law contrasts with the two previous laws in that it puts a ceiling on the amount of the *mahr*. Accordingly the prompt *mahr* is limited to 30,000 dirhams and the deferred *mahr* to 50,000 dirhams (roughly 6,000 and 10,000 euros, respectively). The explanatory memorandum[33] of the Emirati Personal Status Act[34] makes clear that this law was enacted to limit the extremely high marriage expenditure, which has led to a substantial age gap between the spouses, with Emirati men taking foreign wives and men incurring debts to afford the expenses of marriage.[35] This also points to the economic importance of the *mahr*.

To sum up, today, the primary – though not only – function of the *mahr* is to provide economic security for the wife.[36]

German Case Law

With this background in mind, we now turn to German case law. So far, the German Federal Supreme Court (BGH) has decided on the matter on three occasions.[37] The case law will be analysed under the two abovementioned aspects of the court's legal techniques and the argumentation brought forward by the parties.

Decision of the Supreme Court of 28 January 1987[38]

In this case, the parties had married in 1976 in Munich. The wife was a Muslim Palestinian with an Israeli passport. The husband was German. Both were students. They had a civil marriage first and, for the sake of the religious wedding, which took place afterwards, the husband converted to Islam. In the certification of their religious marriage, the spouses agreed on the payment of 100,000 Deutschmarks (DM) as a *mahr*. Four years later, in 1980, the parties were divorced by the judgement of a German court under the application of German law. Additionally, the husband, in the absence of the wife, pronounced an Islamic divorce in the mosque where they had married. In the certification of the religious divorce witnessed by the *imam*, the husband included in handwriting the sentence that there were no financial claims between the parties. The wife contested this and petitioned for the payment of the *mahr*. The Court of First Instance recognized the wife's claim as an agreement on post-marital maintenance and ordered the man to pay the dower of 100,000 DM.[39]

The Court of Appeal overturned the judgement and rebutted the validity of the wife's claim. It argued that an agreement for the payment of a *mahr* that had been made in the course of a religious marriage was not valid, since religious marriages as such had no effect under German law. However, the Court conceded that even in the case that the agreement on the *mahr* was to be considered valid, it had to be qualified under German law as a stipulation of a marriage contract, that is, an agreement on the matrimonial property regime. These kinds of agreements had to be authenticated by a notary. Thus, it did not recognize the *mahr* because of the lack of these formalities.[40] The wife finally sought the revision of the decision at the Supreme Court.

What arguments did the parties make, and how did the Supreme Court respond? The husband argued that he had not been aware of the fact that he was committing himself legally and binding himself when signing the agreement. He argued that he had believed the agreement to be just a 'formality' without legal effects, that is, some kind of folkloristic addition to the wedding. The wife, on the other hand, argued that both had meant the agreement to be binding and that the husband had been fully aware of this, since extensive negotiations on the *mahr* had been conducted between him and her father beforehand. In evaluating these arguments, the Supreme Court held, first, that the reservation of the husband would only be legally relevant if the wife had been aware of it. A secret reservation on the binding character of the commitment is not relevant under German law. Second, if the husband really had not been serious about this commitment, he would have had to contest the agreement for error within the legal time frame, which had already expired. Finally, the court held that a person who, for the sake of a religious marriage, had converted to another religion, could not claim to not have been aware of the effects of such marriage, and in particular that a *mahr* was due in a Muslim marriage.

As far as the validity of the *mahr* agreement was concerned, the Supreme Court held that, although the religious marriage did not have any effect under German law, this did not affect the validity of the *mahr*. It suffices that the religious marriage was valid under considerations of religious/Islamic law as perceived under the law applicable to Muslim Israelis. As there was no obstacle to the validity of the marriage, the agreement on the *mahr* had to be considered valid. The court did not consider the aspect of public policy or raise the question as to whether the *mahr* did or did not exist in German law. It considered it a valid agreement and went on to its interpretation.

The Supreme Court, however, did not decide on the categorization of the *mahr* within domestic family law. The Court objected to both interpretations of the lower courts, since it held that the lower courts had failed to consider the intention of the parties when agreeing on the *mahr*. However, it gave some indications as to how this intention had to be sought. Within the framework of German rules governing the interpretation of contracts, due respect was to be awarded to the principle of good faith and good morals. Furthermore, the circumstances of the case, such as the duration of the marriage, had to be considered to discover the real intention of the parties. As a result, the Supreme Court recommitted the case to the Court of Appeal for further investigations. The parties finally settled the case outside the court.

Decision of the Supreme Court of 14 October 1998[41]

In the second case, the parties, a German woman and a Syrian man, had married in 1976 in Germany. The husband later acquired German citizenship. Before their civil marriage, the parties concluded a German marriage contract which was authenticated according to German law. In the marriage contract, the husband agreed to pay his future wife a *mahr* of 20,000 DM; 10,000 on the conclusion of the marriage and 10,000 if the husband's behaviour entitled the wife to ask for the dissolution of the marriage. The marriage contract explicitly enunciated the cases in which the wife would be entitled to ask for the dissolution of the marriage. Those cases included the grounds for divorce under German law.

In 1995, the couple was divorced by a German court. The wife remarried two months later and sued her ex-husband for the payment of the *mahr* shortly afterwards. He refused to pay either the prompt *mahr* he had not honoured at the time of marriage or the deferred *mahr* due at the time of divorce. The Court of First Instance ruled that the woman had forgone her right to the prompt *mahr* since she had not claimed it, but ordered the ex-husband to pay the deferred *mahr*, which was due at the moment of the divorce.[42] The ex-husband objected, but the decision was upheld on appeal. The Court of Appeal did not try to fit the agreement on the *mahr* into any of the German categories of family law. The court rather considered the agreement to be an independent acknowledgement of debt (German *Schuldversprechen*), which, under German law, was valid and had to be honoured.[43] The Court of Appeal looked at the terms of the agreement and concluded that the parties had intended the wife to be able to claim the deferred *mahr* if she had a reason under the marriage contract to get a divorce. Since this held true, the wife was entitled to 10,000 DM.

The husband petitioned for revision at the Supreme Court. The Supreme Court rejected the assumption that the *mahr* was an independent acknowledgement of debt, since this kind of agreement does not mention the reason for the payment. In the case of the *mahr*, however, the reason, that is, the *mahr*, was explicitly mentioned. Again, the Supreme Court criticized the lower courts for not taking into account the intentions of the parties. In particular, the Supreme Court criticized the lower courts for failing to consider whether the agreement on the deferred *mahr* was intended to be a post-marital claim. This was of particular importance, as the wife had re-married soon after her divorce and post-marital maintenance is only due as long as the ex-wife does not have a new spouse.

Decision of the Supreme Court of 9 December 2009[44]

The third and most recent case involved an Iranian couple who had married in 1992 in Tehran with a *mahr* of 15 million Iranian rials payable at any time at the demand of the wife. In 1993, the spouses left

Iran and settled in Germany, where both acquired German citizenship. The couple divorced in 2006 in Germany, according to German law. Later on, the wife petitioned for the payment of the *mahr*. One of the main problems in this case was the characterization of the *mahr* and its submission to one of the available conflict of laws rules.[45] This choice and the resulting law applicable had a considerable effect on the outcome of the trial. The wife argued that the *mahr* had to be governed by Iranian law and, in application of Iranian law, the amount that was due had to be adapted to the inflation rate, according to the aforementioned 'Act on the Adaptation of the Value of the *Mahr* to the Inflation Rate'. As a result, the sum of 15 million Iranian rials would amount to approximately 15,000 euros, whereas without such adaptation, the counter value of 15 million rials would be only 1,500 euros, thus ten times less.

The husband, on the other hand, argued that the *mahr* had been agreed in Iran under the presumption that the spouses were to live there. Now that they had changed their domicile, this change of circumstances defeated his reasons for agreeing on a *mahr*. As the circumstances had changed, the *mahr* agreement had to be considered void. According to him, the applicable law was German law. As this law did not know any such institution as the *mahr*, there was no legal basis for its award. In any event, when applying German law, Iranian law was to be considered in so far as the wife had forfeited her right to the *mahr*, because it was she who had petitioned for the divorce. Her petition for divorce was thus to be seen as a request for a *khul'*, in which she had to waive her right to the *mahr*. The husband also argued that the function of the *mahr* was to deter husbands from divorcing their wives. In the case that the wife herself had petitioned for divorce, she had forgone this protection herself and could thus not claim for a *mahr*.

The Court of First Instance decided in favour of the husband. It argued that the main function of the *mahr* was the financial protection of the wife in case of divorce. Since the parties had moved to Germany and had got a divorce under German law, the wife had profited from the post-marital protection awarded to her under German law, which had improved her financial post-marital position considerably as compared to Iranian law, which hardly knows any post-marital financial claim. The *mahr* had thus lost its *raison d'être*. However, in contradiction to its own arguments, it upheld that the agreement on the *mahr* as a contractual obligation had to be fulfilled, even if only with its counter value at the time of the claim, which was 1,500 euros.[46]

The Court of Appeal overturned the case by choosing a different characterization of the *mahr* under the conflict of laws rules. In doing so, it submitted the case to Iranian law and adapted the sum of 15 million rials to the Iranian inflation rate, awarding the wife a sum of roughly 15,000 euros.[47] The Court of Appeal did not address the question of whether she had lost her claim because she had petitioned for divorce, that is, the question of whether the fact that the wife had asked for divorce led automatically to the loss of the *mahr*.

The husband challenged the decision at the Supreme Court and won the case. The Supreme Court first decided the question of the characterization of the *mahr*. His decision led to the applicability of German law. Within German law, the Supreme Court recognized the validity of the *mahr* agreement as a valid contractual commitment that had to be honoured by the husband. It refused, however, an adaptation to the inflation rate according to Iranian law, since that law was not applicable. Again, the Supreme Court emphasized that the intention of the parties was to be consulted in order to understand the nature of their agreement. *Obiter dictum*, the Supreme Court rebutted the argument that the wife had lost her claim to the *mahr*, because it was she who had petitioned for divorce. However, as in this case, the amount of the *mahr* was not considerable, the Supreme Court did not find it necessary to expand more on the nature of the *mahr* agreement or any problem which might occur under German law, in particular the embedding of the *mahr* within the institution of German family law. This question still remains open.

Evaluation of the Cases

The Arguments of the Parties

In evaluating the legal and cultural argumentation of the parties, one can distinguish three layers of argumentation. First, the legal and the cultural religious arguments are intermixed and these aspects are highlighted according to the position taken. The religious background and motivation for concluding such an agreement is evident. The legal basis for the award of the *mahr* in German courts, however, remains the contractual agreement by the spouses. The basis on which German courts approach such agreements is from the perspective of contract law, hence the general rules for the conclusion of contracts and the principle of freedom of contract in family law in particular. The cultural and religious arguments are then put forward by the parties to underpin their respective positions: the wife claims that the *mahr* is her religious right, even outside the socio-legal and religious framework within which the agreement was made in the first place. The husband equally raises the cultural and socio-legal aspect of the *mahr* when claiming that, in another legal and social setting than the one under which the *mahr* was conceived, the *mahr* loses its *raison d'être* and therefore should no longer be upheld and honoured.

The question of whether the *mahr* is contrary to public policy and good morals also falls within the ambit of this layer. Men often argue that the *mahr,* in its presumed concept as counter value for marital cohabitation, infringes the rule of domestic public policy. Women, on the other hand, emphasize that the *mahr* is an instrument of empowerment in a family law system which is intrinsically patriarchal: considering the *mahr* as an equalizer of the bargaining powers of the spouses, the *mahr* must, therefore, pass the barrier of public policy. The social, cultural and religious backgrounds of *mahr* agreements are thus picked up when convenient and dropped when they fail to strengthen the individual position of the party.

Second, one can observe a mixing of the applicable domestic and displaced foreign law. Both spouses try to import that from the foreign, Islamic-based family law which is favourable to them. This is quite visible in the 2009 case, where the wife attempts to have the amount of the *mahr* raised through the application of the Iranian 'Act on the Adaptation of the Value of the *Mahr* to the Inflation Rate', whereas the husband, while rebutting the application of that act, pleads within the application of German law for the taking into account of the *khul'* rules under Iranian law to see the wife lose her right to the *mahr*.

Finally, there is a mixture of foreign and domestic procedural law. Whereas Iranian procedural law accords different rights and duties to the spouses, depending on who petitioned for the divorce, German procedural law is gender-neutral. Accordingly, German divorce law generally does not take into account who demanded the divorce first or whether that party is at fault. Under Iranian and Islamic-based family laws in general, on the other side, the legal implications of a divorce differ according to the gender of the plaintiff: whereas the husband does not need any reasons to petition for divorce, the wife has to argue her case on the basis of legal or contractual divorce grounds. In both cases, the wife is entitled to her *mahr* and any post-marital claim, as far as available. If, however, the husband does not apply for divorce or the wife is unable to prove her divorce grounds, she can only base her divorce petition on a *khul'* divorce, in which she has to forego to a certain extent her right to the *mahr* and/or other financial entitlements. By blending German procedural and Iranian substantive law, the husband attempted to suppress the wife's claim to the *mahr*.[48]

The arguments of the Supreme Court

None of the three decisions of the Supreme Court explicitly gives an answer to the question of how to accommodate the *mahr* in German law. In fact, the decisions are all formulated very prudently. A first basic statement is the acknowledgement of the validity of *mahr* agreements in general. Thus, the Supreme Court dismissed the argument that *mahr* agreements must be void, since the institution as such is alien to German law, or that *mahr* agreements are contrary to public policy, like some lower courts had argued before.[49] Instead, the Court established the validity of *mahr* agreements as a contractual agreement between spouses, covered by the principle of freedom of contract in family law. As such, the *mahr* agreement needs to fulfil the basic requirements of a contractual agreement, that is, the consent of the parties and the absence of duress and error. Furthermore, the Court rightly considered the *mahr* to be a specific feature of marriage law, which presupposes a valid marriage.

The question of whether a religious marriage *alone* would suffice as grounds for claiming the *mahr* was not directly answered. It is, however, hardly conceivable that a purely religious ceremony, which according to German law is not considered a valid marriage, may be legitimate grounds for a *mahr* claim.[50] Even if one considers the 1987 case where the court had based its decision on the validity of the religious marriage, the court kept in mind that the parties had also had a civil marriage in Germany. One must thus conclude that a *mahr* agreement will only be honoured if the parties are considered validly married under German law.

The question as to the nature of the *mahr* agreement and its categorization under German law was, however, not answered by the Supreme Court. Instead, the Supreme Court stated that the *mahr* agreement had to be interpreted according to the intention of the spouses while contracting the *mahr*. The Supreme Court thus suggests that each *mahr* agreement has to be considered in each individual case on its own merits. In doing so, due account must also be taken of the underlying concept of the institution of the *mahr* under its native law.

Testing the *Mahr* in German Family Law Categories

To categorize the *mahr* agreement within German law, the courts thus need to interpret the intention of the parties while simultaneously bearing in mind the functions and nature of the *mahr* in its native law. The categories that can then be used are either the agreement on post-marital maintenance or the agreement on the matrimonial property regime.

Can the *mahr* be interpreted as an agreement on maintenance?

Under German Law, spouses may contractually agree on their reciprocal post-marital maintenance duties and derogate from statutory law.[51] Interpreting the *mahr* agreement as a maintenance agreement[52] allows the court to make use of all adjustment instruments offered by German law: accordingly, if the marriage was of short duration, the court can adapt the amount of the *mahr* on the basis of the German rules on maintenance[53] and in accordance with the theory of change of circumstances, according to which a change in the economic, legal and business realities underlying a contractual agreement can invalidate or modify the terms of a contract. Moreover, a very high *mahr* can be adapted to the financial capability of the husband[54] and a very low *mahr* can be raised according to the needs of the divorcee.[55] Interpreting the *mahr* as a maintenance agreement, however, generally does not match the intention of the parties.[56] If, at the time of the marriage and the agreement on the *mahr*, the parties had the intention to move to Germany or if one of the parties was a German citizen, it is doubtful whether, with the acceptance of the *mahr*, the wife intended to waive her maintenance rights awarded to her under German law. But even if both parties are of foreign origin, such an intention is difficult to presume,[57] since in Islamic countries, the *mahr* and the maintenance claims stand next to each other. Thus, *mahr* is hardly interpretable as an equivalent of maintenance.

Can the *mahr* be interpreted as an agreement on the matrimonial property regime?

As with maintenance, the statutory provisions on the matrimonial property regime may be modified by the spouses. These modifications must be inserted in a marriage contract (German *Ehevertrag*) that needs official notarization.[58] The German matrimonial property regime is the separation of property with an equalization of surplus (*Zugewinnausgleich*) after the dissolution of marriage. In principle, each spouse owns and administers his or her property independently.[59] Upon termination of the marriage, however, the accrued gains, that is, the additions to the assets of each of the spouses achieved during the marriage, are equalized. This means that the spouse with the higher surplus has to pay the partner with the smaller increase one half of the excess.[60]

In Muslim countries, on the other hand, the concept of matrimonial property is generally ignored.[61] Based on the general freedom of the wife to own and administer her assets independently, the properties of the spouses are completely separated: each spouse remains the owner of his or her assets before, during and after marriage. If the *mahr* were to be understood as an agreement on the matrimonial property regime under German law, one could read it as a modification or supplementation to the statutory regime, whereby the parties exclude the equalization of surplus and install a regime of separation of goods with the *mahr* being a lump sum to be paid to the wife upon divorce.[62]

However, this interpretation is hardly arguable, since in most cases, it will not match the intention of the parties. If both parties are Muslims living and marrying in Germany and additionally contracting a *mahr*, this agreement might be made out of respect for their religious background rather than as an expression of their intention to exclude the regime of surplus upon divorce.[63] This is even more so when one of the spouses is German and the other is of foreign origin. Finally, when the parties are both foreigners who married in their country of origin, then such an interpretation is still improbable, as there is hardly any awareness on the part of the parties regarding the possibilities for arranging for other forms of matrimonial property regime in Muslim countries.[64] Therefore, here again, this interpretation does not fit.

Evaluation and Conclusion

Although the guiding principles developed by the Supreme Court to come to a true determination of the meaning of the *mahr* are certainly valuable, their implementation reveals difficulties. There is no doubt that the intention of the parties must be sought to understand what they had in mind when contracting the *mahr* to translate their perception into German law. Such a translation is, however, not easy, as the intention of the parties is hardly detectable. In most cases, the spouses agreed on a *mahr* without mentioning further reasons or giving explicit explanation as to its relation to maintenance or matrimonial property regime. They simply contracted the *mahr* because in their view, it was an integral part of the act of marrying. This becomes quite apparent when looking at the arguments and ways parties argue and negotiate their cases. Legal, social and religious arguments and explanations are used at will to strengthen the respective positions.

The recourse to the national law of the countries of origin of the spouses may also bring major obstacles. For example, the question arises as to how far the rules of the displaced law must be consulted. What is to be done in mixed marriages between citizens of different Muslim countries that have different regulations on the *mahr*? The problem is quite apparent in cases involving, for example, Emirati and Iranian couples: shall the court be more lenient towards Emirati law, which limits the amount of the *mahr*, or Iranian law, which adapts the sum to the inflation rate, and thus raises its amount? A change in the amount of the *mahr* in terms of reduction or increase must then also be compatible with German interpretation rules, that is, by analogy to similar situations under German law. And finally, what about the many cases where the parties are German Muslims and no underlying law of origin is detectable? One can think of the many Turkish cases, since Turkish family law, as a reception of Swiss family law, does not regulate the *mahr* anymore.

The way out of these kinds of evaluative problems is to abandon the fitting of the *mahr* into the existing categories of German family law; that is, the maintenance and matrimonial property regime. As the Supreme Court sees it, the *mahr* is a valid agreement and German law generally accepts that the spouses make agreements on their financial obligations.[65] If one considered the agreement on the *mahr* as a specific kind of family law contract unknown to statutory law, but still valid under the concept of freedom of contract, it could exist next to the established German categories. Liberating the *mahr* from the exigencies of German family law categories would also release the court to a considerable extent from exploring the ratio of a non-applicable law or from making sense of the cultural and religious arguments put forward by the parties for the sake of fitting the *mahr* into preconceived categories that are not suitable.[66] The court would have to judge the agreement alongside the claims for maintenance and matrimonial property issues and navigate through its own familiar legal notions.

Nevertheless, the *mahr* must be contextualized within the setting of German family law and the available family law instruments to make sure that none of the spouses is disadvantaged. If the award of the *mahr* would stand as a contract *sui generis* next to the statutory rules of a valid maintenance claim and the equalization of surplus as regulated under German matrimonial property law, it would have a significant effect on their respective amounts: the payment of the *mahr* to the wife would increase her assets and thus influence the amount of surplus that would have to be equalized. Additionally, a substantial *mahr* would decrease the wife's need for post-marital maintenance, so that, here again, a fair financial balance is achieved between the parties. It must, after all, be borne in mind that the *mahr* is conceived to provide a certain economic security for the wife in systems which hardly know any financial (post-) marital solidarity between the spouses. It is a tool to protect the wife in specific legal surroundings. Whenever this situation changes to the benefit of the wife, her need to be protected will diminish.[67] This is also why the *mahr* must be accounted for within the new legal context in which it is being evaluated. However, this does not change its character as an independent contract *sui generis* and the fact that the parties must honour their contractual obligation. Only when giving the *mahr* a place of its own, a fair distribution of the financial burden of the ex-spouses will be achieved and due respect given to the *mahr* agreement to finally bring legal certainty to the appraisal of the *mahr* under German law.

Notes

1 The first legal opinions on the *mahr* were commissioned by German courts in the late 1960s and early 1970s, see Murad Ferid, Gerhard Kegel, and Konrad Zweigert (eds.), *Gutachten zum internationalen und ausländischen Privatrecht 1965 und 1966*, Tübingen: J.C.B. Mohr (Paul Siebeck), 1968, legal opinion No. 15, pp. 150-166 (Iraqi law), and Murad Ferid, Gerhard Kegel, and Konrad Zweigert (eds.), *Gutachten zum internationalen und ausländischen Privatrecht 1970*, Tübingen: J.C.B. Mohr (Paul Siebeck), 1971, legal opinion No. 38, pp. 374-386 (Jordanian law). The first judgements date from 1979 and 1980, see Court of Appeal (hereinafter: OLG) Bremen, decision of 9 August 1979, *Zeitschrift für das gesamte Familienrecht*, 1980, pp. 606-607; Court of First Instance (hereinafter: LG) Cologne, decision of 27 October 1980, in: Max-Planck-Institut für ausländisches und internationales Privatrecht (ed.), *Die deutsche Rechtsprechung auf dem Gebiete des Internationalen Privatrechts im Jahre 1980*, Tübingen: J.C.B. Mohr (Paul Siebeck), 1982, case No. 83, pp. 248-249.

2 For an account of the *mahr*, particularly in **Canadian and North American** courts, see Pascale Fournier, 'Flirting with God in Western Secular Courts: Mahr in the West', *International Journal of Law, Policy and the Family*, 2010 (Vol. 24, No. 1), pp. 67-94; Pascale Fournier, *Muslim Marriage in Western Courts: Lost in Transplantation*, Aldershot: Ashgate, 2010; Lindsey Blenkhorn, 'Islamic marriage contracts in American Courts: interpreting mahr agreements as prenuptials and their effect on Muslim women', *Southern California Law Review*, 2002-2003 (Vol. 76, No. 1), pp. 189-233; Richard Freeland, 'The Islamic Institution of Mahr and American Law', *Gonzaga Journal of International Law*, 2000-2001 (Vol. 4), www.gonzagajil.org/content/view/85/26; on the *mahr* in **European** courts, see Rubya Mehdi and Jørgen S. Nielsen (eds.), *Embedding Mahr (Islamic dower) in the European Legal System*, Copenhagen: DJØF Publishing, 2011; on the *mahr* in **English** courts, see Mohamed Jindani, 'The Concept of mahr (dower) in Islamic Law: The need of Statutory Recognition by English Law', *Yearbook of Islamic and Middle Eastern Law*, 2004-2005 (Vol. 11), pp. 219-227; on the *mahr* in **Spanish** courts, see Ma Del Pilar Diago Diago, 'La dot isla-

mique à l'épreuve du conflit de civilisations, sous l'angle du droit international privé espagnol', Annales de Droit de Louvain, 2001, pp. 407-442; on the *mahr* in **Belgian** courts, see Moustapha El Karouni, 'La dot: une institution contraire à l'ordre public international belge?' *Revue trimestrielle de droit familial*, 2002, (No. 3), pp. 403-423; on the *mahr* in **Swedish** courts, see Mosa Sayed, 'The Muslim Dower (*Mahr*) in Europe – with Special Reference to Sweden' in: Katharina Boele-Woelki and Tone Sverdrup (eds.), *European Challenges in Contemporary Family Law*, Antwerp: Intersentia, 2008, pp. 187-208; on the *mahr* in **Danish** courts, see Rubya Mehdi, 'Danish Law and the Practice of mahr among Muslim Pakistanis in Denmark' in: Rubya Mehdi (ed.), *Integration & Retsudvikling*, Copenhagen: Jurist-og Økonomforbundets Forlag, 2007, pp. 101-118; on the *mahr* in **Italian** courts, see Lorenzo di Ascanio, 'Il Mahr tra diritto musulmano e contesto non islamico', *Rivista di diritto internazionale privato e processuale*, 2009, pp. 387-406.

3 See. O. Spies, 'MAHR' in: C.E. Bosworth *et al.* (eds.), *Encyclopaedia of Islam*, ed. Vol. 6, Leiden: E.J. Brill, 1991, pp. 78-80.

4 See German Federal Supreme Court (hereinafter: BGH), decision of 22 March 1967, *Entscheidungen des Bundesgerichtshofes in Zivilsachen*, 1967 (Vol. 47), pp. 324-339; see also Jan Kropholler, *Internationales Privatrecht*, Tübingen: Mohr Siebeck, 2006, p. 127.

5 Seyyed Hoseyn Safā'ī and Asadollāh Emāmī, *Hoqūq-e khānevāde* [Family Law], Vol. 1, Tehran: Enteshārāte dāneshgāh-e tehrān, 2002, p. 166; Majid Enayat, 'Länderbericht Iran' in: A. Bergmann, M. Ferid, and D. Henrich (eds.), *Internationales Ehe- und Kindschaftsrecht*, Frankfurt/Main: Verlag für Standesamtswesen, 2004, p. 51; Hassan Hamidian, 'Jurisdiction of Family Courts in Iran' in: Jürgen Basedow and Nadjma Yassari (eds.), *Iranian Family and Succession Laws and their Application in German Courts*, Tübingen: Mohr Siebeck, 2004, p. 89; Djilali Tchouar, 'Régime juridique de la dot en droit algérien', *Revue Algérienne*, 1996 (Vol. 34, No. 4), p. 580: '[...] expression de la franchise, de la détermination et la preuve d'attachement de l'homme qui se lie légalement à la femme. L'homme par l'intermédiaire de la dot manifeste son intention réelle en vue de fonder un foyer solide et d'affronter un acte aussi sérieux que grave.'; Ziba Mir-Hosseini, *Marriage on Trial: A Study of Islamic Family Law*, London: I.B. Tauris, 2nd ed. 2000, p. 74, describes the *mahr* as 'yardstick' of the families' 'sincerity'.

6 Susanne Dahlgren, 'Women's *adah* versus "women's law": the contesting issue of *mahr* in Aden, Yemen', *Égypte/Monde arabe*, 2005 (No. 1), side note 4, http://ema.revues.org/index1045.html.

7 John L. Esposito, *Women in Muslim Family Law*, Syracuse: Syracuse University Press, 2001, 2nd ed., p. 23; Mir-Hosseini, *Marriage*, p. 73; Annelies Moors, *Women, Property and Islam*, Cambridge: Cambridge University Press, 1995, p. 147; Katherine Spencer, 'Mahr as Contract: internal Pluralism and external perspectives', *Oñati Socio-Legal Series*, 2011 (Vol. 1, No. 2), p. 3.

8 See Pascale Fournier, 'In the (Canadian) Shadow of Islamic Law: Translating Mahr as a Bargaining Endowment', *Osgoode Hall Law Journal*, 2006, pp. 649-677; Mir-Hosseini, *Marriage*, pp. 72-83.

9 Lisa Wynn, 'Marriage Contracts and Women's Rights in Saudi Arabia: Mahr, Shurut and Knowledge Distribution' in: A. Quraishi and F.E. Vogel (eds.), *The Islamic Marriage Contract: Case Studies in Islamic Family Law*, Cambridge: Harvard University Press, 2008, p. 206.

10 Mir-Hosseini, *Marriage*, p. 73; Moors, *Women*, p. 147.

11 Safā'ī and Emāmī, *Hoqūq-e khānevāde*, p. 166; Hossein Safa'i, 'Le Mariage et le Divorce en Droit Iranien' in: Jürgen Basedow and Nadjma Yassari (eds.), *Iranian Family and Succession Laws and their Application in German Courts*, Tübingen: Mohr Siebeck, 2004, p. 75. For a critical view, see Nadjma Yassari, 'The Reform of the Spousal Share under Iranian Succession Law: an Example of the Transformability of Islamic Law', *Rabels Zeitschrift für ausländisches und internationales Privatrecht*, 2009 (Vol. 73), p. 999.

12 Asaf Fyzee, *Outlines of Muhammadan Law*, Delhi: Oxford University Press, 1993, p. 133.

13 Yvon Linant de Bellefonds, *Traité de droit musulman comparé*, Vol. 2, Paris: Mouton & Co, 1965, p. 25.

14 With a summary of the Maliki literature: Georges-Henri Bousquet, *L'Éthique sexuelle de l'Islam*, Paris: Maisonneuve & Larose, 1966, p. 108; for Shi'i law, see Hassan Emamy, *L'institution juridique du mahr (dot) en droit musulman du rite chiite*, Lausanne: Imprimerie C. Risold, 1933, p. 13 *ff*; Seyyed Hasan Emāmī, *Hoqūq-e madanī* [Civil Law], Vol. 4, Tehran: Ketābforūshī-ye eslāmiyye, 2005, p. 442. Modern authors are not unanimous about this interpretation, see Jamal J.A. Nasir, *The Islamic Law of Personal Status*, Leiden: Brill, 3rd ed. 2009, p. 83: 'It [the dower] has not been enjoined as a consideration like a price or a wage'; similarly Emāmī, *Hoqūq-e madanī*, p. 442, and Chafik Chehata, *Droit musulman – Applications au Proche-Orient*, Paris: Dalloz, 1970, pp. 80-81; but see also Colin Imber, 'Women, Marriage, and Property: *Mahr* in the *Behcetü'l-Fetāvā* of Yenişehirli Abdullah' in: M.C. Zilfi (ed.), *Women in the Ottoman Empire – Middle Eastern Women in the Early Modern Era*, Leiden: Brill, 1997, p. 88: 'By the payment of mahr the husband acquires ownership of his wife's sexual parts'.

15 See LG Cologne, decision of 27 October 1980, in: Max-Planck-Institut für ausländisches und internationales Privatrecht (ed.), *Die deutsche Rechtsprechung auf dem Gebiete des Internationalen Privatrechts im Jahre 1980*, Tübingen: J.C.B. Mohr (Paul Siebeck), 1982, case No. 83, pp. 248-249, and more recently, OLG Hamburg, decision of 21 May 2003, *Zeitschrift für das gesamte Familienrecht*, 2004, pp. 459-461, basing its views mainly on a book by anthropologist Shahla Haeri, *Law of Desire – Temporary Marriage in Shi'i Iran*, Syracuse: Syracuse University Press, 1989.

16 Emāmī, *Hoqūq-e madanī*, p. 459; Nāser Kātūziyān, *Hoqūq-e madanī: khānevāde* [Civil Law: Family Law], Vol. 1, Tehran: Enteshārāt-e bahman bornā, 1999, side note 84; Linant de Bellefonds, *Traité*, p. 24, with an overview of the sources of the Sunni schools of law.

17 Hilmar Krüger, 'Vermögensrechtliches Privatrecht und Shari'a am Beispiel der Vereinigten Arabischen Emirate', *Zeitschrift für Vergleichende Rechtswissenschaft*, 1998 (Vol. 97), p. 366; Yvon Linant de Bellefonds, 'L'autonomie de la volonté en droit musulman', *Revue algérienne, tunisienne et marocaine de légis-*

lation et de jurisprudence, 1958 (Vol. 74), p. 88; Chafik Chehata, 'Le contrat en droit musulman', *Zeitschrift für vergleichende Rechtswissenschaft*, 1968 (Vol. 70), p. 81; M. Abdel-Gawad, 'L'autonomie de la volonté en droit musulman', *L'Égypte contemporaine*, 1963 (No. 54), p. 105; M. E. Hamid, 'Islamic Law of Contract or Contracts?' *Journal of Islamic and Comparative Law*, 1969 (Vol. 3), p. 1; for a deferring opinion, see Hassan Amin, *Remedies for Breach of Contract in Islamic and Iranian Law*, Glasgow: Royston, 1984, p. 11.

18 Susan Rayner, *The Theory of Contracts in Islamic Law*, London: Graham & Trotman, 1991, pp. 87-88; 'Abd El-Wahab Ahmed El-Hassan, 'Freedom of Contract, the Doctrine of Frustration, and Sanctity of Contracts in Sudan Law and Islamic Law', *Arab Law Quarterly*, 1985-1986 (Vol. 1, No. 1), p. 51; Noel J. Coulson, *Commercial Law in the Gulf States – The Islamic Legal Tradition*, London: Graham & Trotman, 1984, p. 27; Nabil Saleh, *Unlawful Gain and Legitimate Profit in Islamic Law*, London: Graham & Trotman, 2nd ed. 1992, p. 63. The Ottoman Civil Code, the *majallat alahkām al-ᶜadlīya*, which contains 1851 articles, dedicated over 300 articles to the contract of sale (Articles 101-403).

19 Cf. also Linant de Bellefonds, *Traité*, p. 200, who calls this hypothesis 'fondamentalement fausse'.

20 Bousquet, *L'Éthique*, p. 109.

21 Based on the Qur'an sura 2, verse 237, and reflected for example in Article 1092 of the Iranian Civil Code (CC).

22 Linant de Bellefonds, *Traité*, p. 226.

23 See also Article 1085 Iranian CC.

24 See on this issue in detail Mohammad Javād Maghnīye, *Ahvāle shakhsīye – tarjome va tabyīn-e joz'-e dovom-e al-fiqh ᶜalā al-madhāhib al-khamsa* [Personal Status in the Five Islamic Schools of Law], trans. M. Jabbārī and H.M. Sarā'ī, Tehran: Enteshārāt-e qaqnūs, 2000, pp. 77-78; Kātūziyān, *Hoqūq-e madanī*, side note 95, see on this point also Nadjma Yassari, 'Zwei Bemerkungen zur islamischen Brautgabe', *Das Standesamt*, 2009, p. 367.

25 See the hadith to this end in Abu 'Abdullah Malik ibn Anas, *Al-Muwatta of Imam Malik ibn Anas: The First Formulation of Islamic Law*, trans. A. A. Bewley, London: Kegan Paul International, 1989, hadith No. 11, 28.3, pp. 210-211.

26 Mona Siddiqui, 'Mahr: Legal Obligation or Rightful Demand?' *Journal of Islamic Studies*, 1995 (Vol. 6, No. 1), p. 17; Werner Diem, *Ein arabisches Rechtsgutachten zum Eherecht aus dem 11.-12. Jahrhundert*, Wiesbaden: Harrassowitz, 2007, p. 29, footnote 36; similarly Nawel Gafsia, *L'invention coloniale du mariage musulman – Le cas tunisien*, Paris: L.G.D.J., 2008, p. 48.

27 Eighty percent of divorces in Iran are petitioned by women on the basis of *khul'*, Hasan Hamīdiyān, 'Farāz va neshībhā-ye mehriye be nerkh-e rūz' [The Dower Adapted to the Daily Exchange Rate], in: Hasan Hamīdiyān (ed.), *Majmūᶜe-ye maqālāt-e hoqūq-e khānevāde*, Tehran: Hāmūn, 2008, p. 211.

28 Nāzanīn Shāhroknī, 'Darbāre-ye tasvīb-e t-arh-e mohāsebe-ye mehriye be nerkhh-e rūz' [On the Calculation of the Dower], *Zanān* 1997-98 (No. 33), p. 64.

29 *Official Gazette*, 1997 (No. 15278); Executory Decree of Article 1082 Iranian CC, *Official Gazette*, 1998 (No. 15497).

30 Decree No. 127/1999 of 24 July 1999, *Official Gazette*, 1999 (No. 3785), p. 462.

31 Lynn Welchman, *Women and Muslim Family Laws in Arab States – A Comparative Overview of Textual Development and Advocacy*, Amsterdam: Amsterdam University Press, 2007, p. 91.

32 Law No. 21/1997, *Official Gazette*, 1997 (No. 312); see also Hilmar Krüger, 'Das Recht der Eheschließung in den Vereinigten Arabischen Emiraten', *Das Standesamt*, 1999, p. 67.

33 *Official Gazette*, 2005 (No. 439), pp. 119-478.

34 Federal Law on the Personal Status, Law No. 28/2005, *Official Gazette*, 2005 (No. 439), pp. 9-118; see Hilmar Krüger, 'Grundzüge des Privatrechts der Vereinigten Arabischen Emirate' in: H.-G. Ebert and Th. Hanstein (eds.), *Beiträge zum islamischen Recht*, Vol. 6, Frankfurt on the Main: Lang, 2007, pp. 121-134.

35 *Official Gazette*, 2005 (No. 439), pp. 179 et seq.

36 This view has also been acknowledged by German courts, see most recently BGH, decision of 9 December 2009, *Entscheidungen des Bundesgerichtshofes in Zivilsachen*, 2010 (Vol. 183), pp. 287-299.

37 The cases in the lower courts are much more numerous, for a concise account of theses cases, see Christina Jones-Pauly, 'Marriage contracts of Muslims in the diaspora: Problems in the recognition of mahr contracts in German Law' in: A. Quraishi and F.E. Vogel (eds.), *The Islamic Marriage Contract: Case Studies in Islamic Family Law*, Cambridge: Harvard University Press, 2008, pp. 299-330.

38 BGH, decision of 28 January 1987, *Zeitschrift für das gesamte Familienrecht*, 1987, pp. 463-464.

39 District Court (hereinafter: AG) of Memmingen, decision of 12 December 1984, *Praxis des Internationalen Privat- und Verfahrensrechts*, 1985, pp. 230-231.

40 OLG Munich, decision of 26 November 1985, in: Max-Planck-Institut für ausländisches und internationales Privatrecht (ed.), *Die deutsche Rechtsprechung auf dem Gebiete des Internationalen Privatrechts im Jahre 1985*, Tübingen: J.C.B. Mohr (Paul Siebeck), 1987, case No. 67, pp. 177-183.

41 BGH, decision of 14 October 1998, *Zeitschrift für das gesamte Familienrecht*, 1999, pp. 217-218.

42 AG Obernburg, decision of 30 August 1996, reference No. F 224/96 (unpublished).

43 OLG Bamberg, decision of 13 February 1997, reference No. 2 UF 257/96 (unpublished).

44 BGH, decision of 9 December 2009, *Entscheidungen des Bundesgerichtshofes in Zivilsachen*, 2010 (Vol. 183), pp. 287-299.

45 For a detailed analysis of this judgement, see Nadjma Yassari, 'Die islamische Brautgabe im deutschen Kollisions- und Sachrecht. Anmerkung zu BGH, 9.12.2009 – XII ZR 107/08', *Praxis des Internationalen Privat- und Verfahrensrechts*, 2011, pp. 63-68.

46 AG Hamburg-Barmbek, decision of 16 November 2006, reference No. 891 F 21/06 (unpublished).

47 OLG Hamburg, decision of 29 May 2008, reference No. 10 UF 83/06 (unpublished).

48 For a criticism of this approach, see Yassari, 'Zwei Bemerkungen', 2009, pp. 370-371.

49 See LG Cologne, decision of 27 October 1980, in Max-Planck-Institut für ausländisches und internationales Privatrecht (ed.), *Die deutsche Rechtsprechung auf dem Gebiete des Internationalen Privatrechts im Jahre 1980*, Tübingen: J.C.B. Mohr (Paul Siebeck), 1982, case No. 83, p. 248-249. This judgement was overturned in appeal, OLG Cologne, decision of 29 October 1981, *Praxis des Internationalen Privat- und Verfahrensrechts*, 1983, pp. 73-74.

50 In Germany, civil marriage is obligatory (Article 1310 I German Civil Code (BGB)).

51 Article 1585c BGB. Since 1 January 2008, the provisions of Article 1585c BGB have been amended insofar as agreements on post-marital maintenance are subject to formal requirements and must be certificated by a notary, see Article 1585c BGB new version of 21 December 2007, *Federal Official Gazette I*, p. 3189. The validity of the *mahr* agreement would then depend on the fulfilment of this formality.

52 This interpretation was chosen for example by the Court of First Instance (hereinafter: KG) Berlin, decision of 12 November 1979, *Zeitschrift für das gesamte Familienrecht*, 1980, pp. 470-471; AG Memmingen, decision of 11 January 1984, *Praxis des Internationalen Privat- und Verfahrensrechts*, 1984, p. 219; AG Memmingen, decision of 12 December 1984, *Praxis des Internationalen Privat- und Verfahrensrechts*, 1985, pp. 230-231; KG Berlin, decision of 11 September 1987, *Zeitschrift für das gesamte Familienrecht*, 1988, p. 296; OLG Frankfurt, decision of 26 May 1989, *Streit*, 1989, pp. 110-111; AG Kerpen, decision of 29 January 1999, *Zeitschrift für das gesamte Familienrecht*, 1999, pp. 1429-1430; AG Aachen, decision of 7 February 2000, in: Max-Planck-Institut für ausländisches und internationales Privatrecht (ed.), *Die deutsche Rechtsprechung auf dem Gebiete des Internationalen Privatrechts im Jahre 2000*, Tübingen: J.C.B. Mohr (Paul Siebeck), 2002, case No. 67, pp. 140-142; AG Fürth, decision of 10 April 2002, *Familie, Partnerschaft, Recht*, 2002, pp. 450-451; OLG Saarbrücken, decision of 9 March 2005, *Neue Juristische Wochenschrift – Rechtsprechungs-Report*, 2005, pp. 1306-1308; on this issue see also Wolfgang Wurmnest, 'Die Brautgabe im Bürgerlichen Recht', *Zeitschrift für das gesamte Familienrecht*, 2005, p. 1880.

53 Article 1579 BGB.

54 Article 1581 BGB.

55 Article 1577 BGB.

56 Wurmnest, 'Die Brautgabe', 2005, p. 1880.

57 OLG Hamm, decision of 30 June 1981, *Zeitschrift für das gesamte Familienrecht*, 1981, pp. 875-877.

58 Articles 1408, 1410, 1558 BGB.

59 There are generally no common goods. However, in order to secure the common household and the material existence of the family, a spouse can only dispose of household objects and the whole of his or her assets with the consent of the other (Articles 1365-1369 BGB). Most married couples live under the statutory matrimonial property regime.

60 Article 1378 BGB.

61 On matrimonial property law in Islamic countries, see Sami A. Aldeeb Abu-Sahlieh, 'Les régimes matrimoniaux en droit arabe et musulman' in: A. Bonomi and M. Steiner (eds.), *Les régimes matrimoniaux en droit comparé et en droit international privé*, Genf: Droz, 2006, pp. 279-305.

62 This interpretation was chosen for example by OLG Bremen, decision of 9 August 1979, *Zeitschrift für das gesamte Familienrecht*, 1980, pp. 606-607; OLG Cologne, decision of 29 October 1981, *Praxis des Internationalen Privat- und Verfahrensrechts*, 1983, pp. 73-74; OLG Munich, decision of 26 November 1985, in: Max-Planck-Institut für ausländisches und internationales Privatrecht (ed.), *Die deutsche Rechtsprechung auf dem Gebiete des Internationalen Privatrechts im Jahre 1985*, Tübingen: J.C.B. Mohr (Paul Siebeck), 1987, case No. 67, pp. 177-183.

63 In this sense also OLG Stuttgart, decision of 29 January 2008, *Zeitschrift für das gesamte Familienrecht*, 2008, pp. 1756-1758.

64 For a detailed analysis of this issue, see Yassari, 'Die islamische Brautgabe', 2009, p. 67.

65 On freedom of contract in German family law, see Sibylle Hofer, Dieter Schwab, and Dieter Henrich (eds.), *From Status to Contract? Die Bedeutung des Vertrages im europäischen Familienrecht*, Bielefeld: Gieseking, 2005; Meo-Micaela Hahne, 'Vertragsfreiheit im Familienrecht' in: Dieter Schwab and Meo-Micaela Hahne (eds.), *Familienrecht im Brennpunkt*, Bielefeld: Gieseking, 2004, pp. 181-202.

66 On the dangers of multiculturalism for women, see Susan Moller Okin, 'Is Multiculturalism bad for women?' in: Joshua Cohen, Matthew Howard, and Martha C. Nussbaum (eds.), *Is Multiculturalism bad for women/Susan Moller Okin with Respondents*, Princeton: Princeton University Press, 1999, pp. 8-24, who argues that the multiculturalist accommodation and the consideration of cultural elements from minority groups can be disadvantageous for the individual.

67 In a case in the early 1980s, the Court of First Instance held that an agreement on a *mahr* was not enforceable under German law, as its function of safeguarding the wife financially was perfectly fulfilled by the instruments of German family law, LG Cologne, decision of 27 October 1980, in: Max-Planck-Institut für ausländisches und internationales Privatrecht (ed.), *Die deutsche Rechtsprechung auf dem Gebiete des Internationalen Privatrechts im Jahre 1980*, Tübingen: J.C.B. Mohr (Paul Siebeck), 1982, case No. 83, pp. 248-249.

10 A Language of Hybridity

Honour and Otherness in Canadian Law and Shariʿa

Pascale Fournier[1] *and Nathan Reyes*

Introduction

In Canada, as throughout most of the geopolitical West, honour crimes have recently been the object of growing hostility. The federal government sparked controversy when it indicated in a pamphlet given to immigrants upon application for citizenship, that 'Canada's openness and generosity do not extend to *barbaric* cultural practices that tolerate spousal abuse, "honour killings," female genital mutilation, forced marriage or other gender-based violence' (emphasis ours – PF and NR).[2] Similarly, a recent public policy report underlined that honour crimes are 'proliferating without regards to Canada's *Criminal Code* or Canadians' *deep cultural revulsion* from the very concept' (emphasis mine – PF).[3] In many ways, this projection of a 'civilized' Canada simultaneously reifies the notion of shariʿa as inherently contrary, even antithetical, to Canadian law. It also contributes to a dichotic, binary vision of law, culture and identity, through which West/East, secular/religious, or public/private are never mutually constitutive.

Perhaps due to this (mis)perception of law, the ancient notion of honour in law has sparked a perplexing resurgence in public debate in Canada and in the West generally, fuelled by an international campaign for women's rights,[4] but also by the other great legal issue of the last decade: the widespread discussions on the limits of multiculturalism. Yet honour is no foreign notion to Western law, including Canadian law. Despite such vehement discourse around the otherness of honour crimes in seeming opposition to Canadian law, an examination of the latter reveals the existence of a defence of provocation, or 'passion,' that mirrors the very nature of honour crimes. However this defence – the roots of which may be found in the defence of honour of the French and British Penal Codes of the nineteenth century – is never confronted with the same apprehension, vehemence and perceived otherness as is the notion of honour crimes.

In this chapter, we outline how socio-legal 'hybridity'[5] manifests itself in the notion of honour in law. By outlining the complex transplantation processes of Western notions of honour crimes onto Islamic legal norms, our aim is to provide a descriptive basis for normative discussions on cultural diversity. In addition to challenging the perceived otherness of various aspects of shariʿa (versus the familiarity of Canadian law), the chapter attempts to illustrate the incoherence of the rigidly dichotic view of law and culture, all of which interact with, transplant into and impact one another. This chapter approaches the hybridity of both the East and the West and stresses that negating the similarity between Western and Eastern legal institutions has the potential to considerably impair our understanding of cultural and legal diversity.

Law, a Language of Hybridity?

Multiculturalism[6] has guided Canadian policy throughout recent history so as to account for the hybridity of identity, born of the intersection and interaction of innumerable cultures in a country founded on immigration. Despite this reality, however, Canadian law is largely portrayed as minimally impacted by 'other' legal regimes;[7] this portrayal is exemplified by, amongst other things, an editorial that appeared in the *National Post* in 2011, reporting that there have been twelve known honour killings in Canada since 2002 and calling for community action against minority 'brutal traditions,' stressing that honour killings are 'anathema to Western culture.'[8] If Canadian law is depicted as Western, secular, *familiar*, it can do so by conveniently positing itself on one side of a binary, implicitly asserting that it is not Eastern, not religious, not like *other* legal systems. Such implicit assertions often become, with time and repetition, the unstated norms[9] of the Canadian justice system.

Allowing the focus of this chapter to shift back to that of a critically comparative examination of legal regimes, it becomes apparent that without turning the 'ethnocentric gaze'[10] back upon itself so as to perceive the unstated norms at the heart of Canadian law, 'other' law – in this case shariʿa – cannot in turn be properly perceived. The self must recognize that, within itself, there is the other; only then can it recognize that in the other, so there is some self. Law is inherently hybrid, and Canadian law is no exception. It is hoped that the following examination of honour in both Canadian and Jordanian law may help to illustrate that 'the colonial binaries – of us/them, here/there, West/non-West, colonizer/colonized – have long been mutually constituting.'[11]

Familiar Facts from West to East

In this section, an applied examination of the notion of honour is undertaken in two apparently disparate legal regimes: Canadian law (secular law)[12] and Jordanian law (shari'a).[13] Ultimately, the purpose of this examination is to exemplify the hybridity of law, and the incoherence of a binary vision of law, according to which the East and West are irreconcilably separated, to the point of being defined in opposition to one another. We argue that only by looking inwards to recognize the otherness in Canadian law[14] can one learn to see past the otherness of the other.

The Other Within: (Dis)Honour in Canadian Law

Turning the gaze back upon itself, the legitimacy of the perceived otherness of shari'a (and familiarity of Canadian law) must first be explored within a Canadian legal and socio-political context. After tracing the genesis of honour in medieval British law, this study exposes some of the Canadian legal system's concrete implications for honour, in the guise of passion and provocation, as a discursive practice. We will argue that this defence can be seen to amount, in some applications, to a form of Western 'honour'-tainted defence, and that it constitutes a worrying source of legitimization of gender violence.

The defence of provocation is a British legal institution which can be traced back at least to the seventeenth century,[15] and whose premodern articulation was grounded in honour-permeated value codes. This defence was invoked when the accused, having been a witness to his wife's adultery, killed his paramour. Chief Lord Justice Holt worded the rationale behind the defence in 1707 thus: 'jealousy is the rage of a man, and adultery is the highest invasion of property.'[16] As put by British criminal law scholar G.R. Sullivan, early provocation defence amounted to a 'hot-blooded yet controlled vindication of one's honour rather than spontaneous, uncontrolled fury.'[17] The very foundations of this legal institution seem tainted with notions of male honour upheld by violence.

Contemporary forms of the defence of provocation in Canada have been presented as possessing a wholly different normative foundation. This defence was defined by the Supreme Court of Canada as compassion towards 'human frailties which sometimes lead people to act irrationally and impulsively.'[18] The defence's modern *raison d'être* is thus said to have completely shifted from upholding a male-centric Western honour code to accounting for the universal human weakness of momentary 'irrationality.'[19] This is still defended by many scholars in the common law world as a valid justification for the maintenance of the partial defence today.[20] In keeping with this universal, individualistic rationale, Canada's *Criminal Code* outlines that murder may be reduced to manslaughter 'if the person who committed it did so in the heat of passion caused by sudden provocation.'[21] The *Code* further establishes that '[a] wrongful act or an insult that is of such a nature as to be sufficient to deprive an ordinary person of the power of self-control is provocation for the purposes of this section if the accused acted on it on the sudden and before there was time for his passion to cool.'[22]

In Canada, a collective framework of honour such as that found in many countries of the East is hard to fathom, as the sociological organization of gender violence within the family seems to forbid it. For the period between 1978 and 1998 in Canada, 66 per cent of family femicides[23] were perpetrated by the woman's partner, while only 26 per cent were perpetrated by parents, siblings and other relatives.[24] That being said, Baker, Gregware and Cassidy note that 'in the English-speaking West, including the United States, the locus of honour has shifted from the traditional extended family to the individual man.'[25]

This evidence of Canadian 'honour' seems to belie the claim that 'honour values are *exclusive* and *particularist* and stand in sharp contrast to the *universal* and *inclusive* values of the West.'[26] The otherness of honour crimes and shari'a may not be so foreign to Canadian values and legal practices as one would imagine; the private forms that honour takes and the West's cultural violence that is sometimes unleashed under the guise of universalistic passion must not be overlooked. It, too, is concerned with *some* form of honour, however unseen and pushed to the 'private' sphere. Intimate passion crimes – that is, crimes committed in the intimacy of one's private life – are thus a particularly important locus of public policy and gender equality concerns. After all, the often-denounced subjectivization of the defence in cases like Supreme Court of Canada in *R v Thibert*[27] arguably offers women no more protection than the honour codes of the British medieval provocation defence, as argued by Abu-Odeh.[28] Furthermore, Western 'crimes of passion' may sometimes be more dangerous than the traditional Oriental honour crime, as they draw legitimacy from unstated private honour codes.[29] If it is true that honour and passion are two different realities, it is only by acknowledging the West's own cultural demons that we will be able to begin to understand the ways in which both passion and honour have been mixed and articulated in myriad ways across the East/West divide.

Familiarity of the Other: perspectives from Jordan

Jordan, 'the country most intensely under the international spotlight when issues of "honour" are discussed,'[30] is a most relevant case study, seeing as it has, according to some accounts, the highest honour crime rate per capita in the world.[31] Furthermore, it underlines the partly Western origins of honour crimes, despite the latter being recently attacked as 'antithetical to fundamental Canadian values' by Ontario Court of Appeal Justice Doherty.[32] Article 340 of the Jordanian Penal Code reads:

> 1. He who surprises his wife or one of his [female] *marhams* ('unlawfuls') in the act of committing unlawful sexual intercourse with somebody and kills, wounds or injures one or both of them, shall benefit from the exonerating/exempting excuse (*'udhr muhill*);
>
> 2. He who surprises his wife or one of his ascendants or descendants or siblings with another in an unlawful bed, and kills or wounds or injures one or both of them, shall benefit from the mitigating excuse (*'udhr mukhaffat*).[33]

There is scholarly consensus that this legislation was directly inspired by the French Penal Code of 1810.[34] As put by Janin and Kahlmeyer, this provision 'springs from French, i.e., Napoleonic, penal law, not from shari'a itself.'[35] Article 340 of the Jordanian Penal Code received the influence of French Napoleonic law through various channels, notably through the regional influence of French Lebanese and Syrian penal codes' honour crime excuses, from which article 340 'derived most of its language.'[36] As a result, the similarities between French honour crimes law and the Jordanian provision were glaring. Article 324 of the French Penal Code of 1810 reads:

> Whoever catches his spouse, female ascendant, descendant or his sister red-handed in the act of adultery or in an illegitimate sexual encounter with another person and commits homicide or causes injury can benefit from an excuse of exemption. The author of the homicide or injury can benefit from an excuse of reduction if he catches red-handed his spouse, female ascendant, descendant, or his sister in an 'attitude equivoque.'[37]

This direct transfer of one legal institution from the West to the East can be analysed as a form of 'legal transplant' which has contributed to the 'globalizations of law and legal thought' described by Duncan Kennedy.[38] Jordanian law also contains elements of 'crimes of passion,' such as article 98 of the Jordanian Penal Code, which excuses murders committed in a 'fit of fury.'[39] This provision is said to have been 'much more useful'[40] to the accused than article 340, though it has attracted less media attention than the latter provision. Jordanian courts 'frequently apply article 98 of the Penal Code to honour killings,'[41] effectively treating them as a form of 'crime of passion.' Thus, Jordan appears to have crafted its 'appalling' honour crimes legislation at the confluence of Western and Oriental traditions.

Fear and Marginalization of the 'Other' in Canadian Society

In this section, we attempt to illustrate how the combined unawareness of unstated norms within Canadian law and overstated otherness of shariʿa have given rise to differential treatment in Canadian courts based on the otherness of the accused, seen as foreign to Canadian values and law. It is important to note that this section in no way condones gender inequality and gendered violence, too often justified by a defence of 'honour,' 'passion' or provocation. However, without considering the very unstated norms at the heart of Canadian law that inflate the perceived otherness of shariʿa, the discrimination caused by such a dichotic vision of law and culture will continue, and the internal flaws of Canadian law will remain occulted.

A study undertaken by Pascale Fournier, Pascal McDougal and Anna Dekker[42] collected and analysed a series of Canadian cases, between 1990 and 2010, of intimate femicide where the male accused (the victim's husband,[43] brother or father) raised the provocation defence.[44] Fifty-six cases were classified according to the ethnicity of the accused and the success or failure of the defence claim,[45] so as to examine the sensitivity of Canadian courts to the legal hybridity heretofore discussed in this chapter.[46] Disconcertingly, this study revealed that the success rate is differentiated and significantly higher for an accused identifiable as 'Western' (25 per cent); indeed, it is nearly twice as high as that of 'other' *(sic!)* accused (11 per cent). This study thus concurs with Côté, Sheehy and Majury that there seems to be among Canadian courts 'a pattern of withholding "compassion" for a certain category of accused.'[47]

A differential treatment such as that seen above surely impacts Muslim Canadians not only in the administration of justice in Canada, but also throughout society. Katherine Bullock and Gul Joya Jafri point at the potentially insidious influence of unstated norms upon society –

particularly as these norms are ignored by the very individuals and institutions that perpetuate them – observing that 'non-Muslim Canadians are often not conscious of the general media bias against Islam and Muslims, often having, in fact, their opinions of Muslim women shaped by the negative stereotypes [...].'[48] The overstated otherness attributed to Islam, and specifically the notion of honour as it is perceived within Islam, can be seen to be a symptom of a broader, subtle denigration of Muslim identity within Canadian society, in turn furthering differential treatment within and beyond the administration of justice.[49]

One of the cases analysed in the above study, *R v Humaid*,[50] offers interesting insight into the possible explanations for this differential treatment. Adi Humaid, an Emirati, killed his wife Aysar Abbas by stabbing her 'at least 19 times' after she had made a comment which he interpreted as meaning that she had committed adultery. Humaid assigned Dr Ayoub, an 'an expert on the Islamic religion and culture,'[51] to support his provocation claim. Dr Ayoub 'testified that the Islamic culture was male dominated and placed great significance on the concept of family honour'[52] and that this contributed to provoking Mr Humaid's violent outburst. The Court of Appeal found that there was no air of reality to the defence and maintained the verdict of murder, refusing to grant consideration to the appellants' 'beliefs' to reduce the verdict to manslaughter. As put by Ontario Court of Appeal Justice Doherty: 'The difficult problem, as I see it, is that the alleged beliefs which give the insult added gravity are premised on the notion that women are inferior to men and that violence against women is in some circumstances accepted, if not encouraged. These beliefs are antithetical to fundamental Canadian values, including gender equality.'[53]

The Ontario Court of Appeal's decision to unequivocally condemn gendered violence is commendable; however, the way in which the message is conveyed, and particularly the reasoning behind this judgement, contrasts discerningly with cases such as *Thibert* and *Stone*.[54] Isabel Grant, law professor at the University of British Colombia, makes a similar argument:

> The Court of Appeal in Humaid is recognizing the importance of gender equality in attributing qualities and characteristics to the ordinary person. One would be hard pressed to argue that the kind of stereotypical misogyny, depicted in Humaid's evidence as ordinary in his culture, should be incorporated into an objective test in order to excuse spousal murder. What is not mentioned, however, is how courts assume the ordinariness of the values demonstrated in cases like Thibert and Stone.[55]

The unstated norm – that is, the 'ordinary person' so ambiguously referred to above – would therefore appear to be grounded in cultural notions of male dominion. Ironically, this same notion is what led the Ontario Court of Appeal to so vehemently dismiss Humaid's defence plea, denouncing such a notion as 'antithetical to fundamental Canadian values.'[56] Indeed, the objective 'ordinary person' component of the defence is nothing but an 'anthropomorphic expression of the standard of conduct that our society expects of its members.'[57] This 'ordinary person,' the determination of which is inherently subjective, underscores the courts' role as 'cultural apparatus[es],'[58] for the definition and determination of such a person presents courts with the imperative of giving substance to their legal conception of 'ordinary.'

This is not to say that it is unfair to 'punish a member of a minority culture under laws or norms reflecting those of the majority culture.'[59] Such a defence in the context of honour/passion-related violence would not only endorse essentialist views on the barbarism supposedly inherent to 'other' cultures,[60] it would equally condone acts of gendered violence. Rather, the argument made here is that courts should treat femicides committed by Westerners with the same scrutiny as those committed by foreigners of 'Oriental' origin (the imperfect category of 'Other(ed)' in our study) generally; this is why we very consciously abstain from entering into the debate on the consideration of a defendant's culture in the case of a provocation defence as part of the objective standard test.[61]

It remains necessary, however, to distinguish between condoning gendered violence and denigrating or alienating a culture as a whole. In the context of an inclusive and diverse Canada, respect and dialogue between disparate groups are fundamental principles. Yet to condemn the 'other'(ed) as antithetical to Canadian values is to effectively ostracize and silence this group, undermining the very values such a condemnation would seek to protect.[62]

Conclusion

In this chapter, we have attempted to illustrate that 'culture' and 'honour' are not monolithic notions but rather historical hybrid constructs. Recent debates on legal transplantation have focused on whether the process leads to 'a convergence of social orders and uniformisation of law'[63] or, inversely, to a 'double-fragmentation of world-society ... and a multiplicity of global cultures.'[64] In fact, law is becoming more homogenous *as well as* more fragmented as a result of legal transplantation.[65] A form of exchange between legal regimes has led to the return of Western transplants, now 'other'(ed) in a sense, ready to intertwine themselves subtly yet profoundly into Western societies. With this in view, Leti Volpp's assertion that 'monoculturalism of transcendent values with a "we" or "us" at an unwavering center of rationality [is] historically inaccurate, relying upon distortions and marginalizations for its narrative coherence'[66] proves very relevant; this very misperception would nonetheless seem to lie at the heart of Canadian courts' reasoning relative to the notion of honour. Recently, in *R. v. Tran,* the Supreme Court of Canada indicated that the defence of provocation must be informed by 'contemporary norms of behaviour, including fundamental values such as the commitment to equality provided for in the *Canadian Charter of Rights and Freedoms*.'[67] The Court unanimously established a newfound stringency for the objective part of the provocation test:

> [The] criminal law is concerned with setting standards of human behaviour. … It follows that the ordinary person standard must be informed by contemporary norms of behaviour, including fundamental values such as the commitment to equality provided for in the *Canadian Charter of Rights and Freedoms*. … [T]here can be no place in this objective standard for antiquated beliefs such as 'adultery is the highest invasion of property' nor indeed for any form of killing based on such inappropriate conceptualizations of 'honour.'[68]

This development does not indicate a bright future for the provocation defence. Hopefully, this judgement echoes the paradigmatic shift of incorporating equality in the law of criminal responsibility advocated by scholars such as Rosemary Cairns Way. On a deeper level, perhaps it can also help us come to terms with the dark sides of 'Western culture.' Without perceiving the subtle yet inherent historical intertwining of honour and provocation, it is hard to imagine how those (mis)perceptions that result in differential treatment may be overcome. Less difficult to imagine is the normative impact that such differential treatment has on Canadian society as a whole. Whether such discrimination in the administration of justice is symptomatic of a more deeply rooted fear of the Other, or a catalyst of this, it likely remains indicative of a troubling ostracism of minority citizens in Canadian society, including Muslims. Let us hope that the trend towards equality reinforced by the *Tran* ruling allows Canadian courts to better 'turn the gaze back on itself' and to grasp the far-reaching implications that globalization, colonialism, and socio-legal *métissage* may have for the Western Self and its many 'Others.'

Notes

1 We thank Pascal McDougall and Anna Dekker: our co-authored article, 'Dishonour, Provocation and Culture: Through the Beholder's Eye?', *Canadian Criminal Law Review*, 2012 (Vol. 16) was a great inspiration for this chapter.

2 *Study Guide – Discover Canada: The Rights and Responsibilities of Citizenship*, available online at http://www.cic.gc.ca/english/resources/ publications/discover/section-04.asp. See also: Bryn Weese, 'Honour killings term angers Trudeau', *The Toronto Sun*, 14 March 2011.

3 Aruna Papp, 'Culturally Driven Violence Against Women: A Growing Problem in Canada's Immigrant Communities', *Frontier Centre for Public Policy*, 2010, p. 10 [emphasis added].

4 Yolanda Asamoah-Wade, 'Women's Human Rights and "Honor Killings" in Islamic Cultures', *Buffalo Women's Law Journal*, 1999-2000 (Vol. 8, No. 21).

5 Used in this context to describe the transplantation of legal institutions into one another, thus shaping new hybrid legal and social mores. See: Homi K. Bhabha, *The Location of Culture* (London/New York: Routledge, 1994) for an analysis of the concept.

6 See: Canadian Charter of Rights and Freedoms, art. 27.

7 See: Pascale Fournier, Aida Setrakian and Pascal McDougall, 'No-Fault Talaq: Islamic Divorce in Canadian Immigration and Family Law', in: Rubya Mehdi & Jørgen S. Nielsen (eds.), *Anthology on Gender Equality and Muslim Law of Divorce*, Copenhagen: DJØF Publishing, 2012.

8 Barbara Kay, 'Communities Must Speak Out Against Brutal Traditions', *National Post*, 26 January 2011. This echoes the dominant media coverage of European Muslim minorities and 'honour' violence: see: Anna Korteweg & Gökçe Yurdakul, 'Islam, Gender, and Immigrant Integration: Boundary Drawing in Discourses on Honour Killing in the Netherlands and Germany', *Ethnic and Racial Studies*, 2009 (Vol. 32, No. 2), p. 218.

9 Brenda Cossman elaborates on the importance of unstated norms as she writes that 'the geopolitical location of the author becomes the unstated norm against which the exotic "other" is viewed. It is a project that is perhaps inherently ethnocentric – there is no way to escape or transcend the ethnocentric gaze.' Brenda Cossman, 'Turning the Gaze Back on Itself: Comparative Law, Feminist Legal Studies, and the Postcolonial', *Utah Law Review*, 1997 (Vol. 2), p. 525.

10 Cossman, 'Turning the Gaze Back on Itself', 1997, p. 526.

11 Cossman, 'Turning the Gaze Back on Itself', 1997, p. 526.

12 Despite often being defined in stark contrast to any form of religious law, Canadian 'secular' law has not only been greatly influenced by religion in the past – more predominantly Christianity – it furthermore continues to be impacted and in some ways shaped by current-day practices of various religious legal regimes. See: Fournier, Setrakian & McDougall, 'No-Fault Talaq,' 2012.

13 It is important to note that this chapter refers specifically to Jordanian family law when speaking of the shariʿa legal regime in Jordan, as not the entire Jordanian legal regime is Islamic.

14 This is to say, the transplantation of elements of foreign or 'other' legal regimes in present-day Canadian law. The term 'legal transplant' was first proposed by Alan Watson in the 1970s to describe what he saw as the migration of legal rules or practices 'from one country to another, or from one people to another.' Alan Watson, *Legal Transplants*, 2nd ed, Atlanta: University of Georgia Press, 1993, p. 21.

15 United Kingdom Law Commission, *Partial Defences to Murder*, Consultation Paper No. 173, London: Her Majesty's Stationery Office, 2003, p. 6.

16 Regina v. Mawgridge (1708), Sir John Kelyng's Reports of Crown Cases, No. 119, pp. 1107*ff* at p. 1115, available online at http://www.commonlii.org/uk/cases/EngR/1708/24.pdf.

17 G.R. Sullivan, 'Anger and Excuse: Reassessing Provocation' *Oxford Journal of Legal* Studies, 1993 (Vol. 13), p. 422; see also: Bernard J. Brown, 'The Demise of Chance Medley and the Recognition of Provocation as a Defence to Murder in English Law', *American J of Legal History*, 1963 (Vol. 7, No. 4), p. 312.

18 *R v Thibert*, Supreme Court of Canada (SCR), 1996, paragraph 4.

19 Joshua Dressler, 'Rethinking Heat of Passion: A Defence in Search of a Rationale' *Journal of Criminal Law & Criminology* (Vol. 73, No. 2), 1982, p. 459; see also: Graeme Coss, '"God is a righteous judge, strong and patient: and God is provoked every day." A Brief History of the Doctrine of Provocation in England', *Sydney Law Review*, 1991 (Vol. 13, No. 4), p. 604.

20 Wayne N. Renke, 'Calm Like a Bomb: An assessment of the Partial Defence of Provocation', *Alberta Law Review*, 2010 (Vol. 47, No. 3), p. 729; see also: Jeremy Horder, 'Reshaping the Subjective Element in the Provocation Defence', *Oxford Journal Legal Studies*, 2005 (Vol. 25, No. 1) p. 126-127; Richard Holton & Stephen Shute, 'Self-Control in the Modern Provocation Defence', *Oxford Journal of Legal Studies*, 2007 (Vol. 27, No. 1), p. 49.

21 *Canadian Criminal Code*, 1985, s. 232(1).

22 *Canadian Criminal Code*, 1985, s. 232(2).

23 This chapter uses the term 'femicide' to broadly refer to the 'killing of women, regardless of motive or perpetrator status' (Jacquelyn Campbell & Carol W. Runyan, 'Femicide: Guest Editors' Introduction', Homicide Studies, 1998 (Vol. 2, No. 4), p. 348.) Though many feminist scholars have linked this term to a specific discriminatory intent, the killing of a woman because she is a woman, we propose to suspend this otherwise important discussion to examine the continuum of gendered homicides and the variety of cultural motives it can accommodate.

24 Daisy Locke & Valerie Pottie Bunge (eds.), *Family Violence in Canada: A Statistical Profile*, a publication by Canadian Center for Justice Statistics, Ottawa: Minister of Industry, 2000, p. 39, available online at http://www.statcan.gc.ca/pub/85-224-x/85-224-x2000000-eng.pdf.

25 N.V. Baker, P.R. Gregware & M.A. Cassidy, 'Family Killing Fields: Honour Rationales in the Murder of Women', *Violence Against Women*, 1999 (Vol. 5, No. 2), p. 166. See also: Sharon K. Araji, *Crimes of Honor and Shame: Violence against Women in Non-Western and Western Societies*, Anchorage: University of Alaska Press, 2000.

26 Halvor Moxnes (ed.), 'Honor and Shame', in: Richard Rohrbaugh, *The Social Sciences and New Testament Interpretation*, Peabody: Hendrickson Publishers, 1996, p. 28.

27 See: Rajvinder Sahni, 'Crossing the Line: R. v. Thibert and the Defence of Provocation', *University of Toronto Faculty of Law Review*, 1997 (Vol. 55, No. 1), p. 143.

28 Abu-Odeh, 'Honor Killings and the Construction of Gender in Arab Societies' *American Journal of Comparative Law*, 2010 (Vol. 58).

29 See: footnote 14.

30 Reem Abu-Hassan & Lynn Welchman, 'Changing the rules? Developments on "crimes of honour" in Jordan', in: Sara Hossain & Lynn Welchman (eds.), *'Honour': Crimes, Paradigms and Violence Against Women*, London: Zed Books, 2005, p. 199.

31 Kathryn Christine Arnold, 'Are the Perpetrators of Honor Killings Getting Away with Murder? Article 340 of the Jordanian Penal Code Analyzed under the Convention on the Elimination of All Forms of Discrimination against Women', *American University International Law Review*, 2001 (Vol. 16, No. 5), p. 1347.

32 *R. v. Hamid*, Ontario Court of Appeal (OJ No 1507/2006), 2006, paragraph 456.

33 Cited and translated in Abu-Hassan & Welchman, 'Changing the rules?', 2005, p. 201.

34 Abu-Odeh, 'Honor Killings and the Construction of Gender in Arab Societies', 2010, p. 914; see also: Fadia Faqir, 'Intrafamily Femicide in Defence of Honour: The Case of Jordan', *Third World Quarterly*, 2001 (Vol. 22, No. 1), p. 73; Anahid Devartanian Kulwicki, 'The Practice of Honor Crimes: A Glimpse of Domestic Violence in the Arab World', *Issues in Mental Health Nursing*, 2002 (Vol. 23, No. 1), p. 83. The Lebanese honour crimes provision also comes from the French Penal Code; see: Women Living Under Muslim Laws, *Knowing Our Rights: Women, Family, Laws and Customs in the Muslim World*, Nottingham, UK: The Russell Press, 2006, p. 17.

35 Hunt Janin & André Khalmeyer, *Sharia: The Sharia from Muhammad's Time to Present*, Jefferson, NC: McFarland, 2007, p. 146.

36 Ferris K. Nesheiwat, 'Honor Crimes in Jordan: Their Treatment under Islamic and Jordanian Criminal Laws', *Penn State International Law Review*, 2004 (Vol. 23, No. 2), p. 274.

37 Émile Garçon, *Code pénal annoté*, Paris: Librairie du Recueil Sirey, 1951, p. 151; cited and translated in Abu-Odeh, 'Honor Killings and the Construction of Gender in Arab Societies', 2010, p. 914. It should be noted that this provision of the French Penal Code was repealed only in 1975; see: Danielle Hoyek, Rafif Rida Sidawi & Amira Abou Mrad, 'Murders of women in Lebanon: "crimes of honour" between reality and the law', in: Hossain & Welchman (eds.), *'Honour': Crimes, Paradigms and Violence Against Women*, 2005, p. 115.

38 Duncan Kennedy, 'Two Globalizations of Law and Legal Thought: 1850-1869', *Suffolk University Law Review*, 2003 (Vol. 36, No. 3), p. 631.

39 Rana Lehr-Lehnardt, 'Treat your Women Well: Comparisons and Lessons from an Imperfect Example Across the Waters', *Southern Illinois University Law Journal*, 2002 (Vol. 26), p. 420.

40 Catherine Warrick, 'The Vanishing Victim: Criminal Law and Gender in Jordan', *Law & Society Review*, 2005 (Vol. 39, No. 2), p. 337. See also: Lehr-Lehnardt, p. 420.

41 Christina Madek, 'Killing Dishonor: Effective Eradication of Honor Killing', *Suffolk Transnational Law Review*, 2005 (Vol. 29, No. 1), p. 62.

42 See: Fournier, McDougall & Dekker, 'Dishonour, Provocation and Culture', 2012, p. 183.

43 A large definition of 'spouse' was adopted, including men who killed not only their wives but also their common law partners and even their girlfriends. The many cases in which an angry/dishonoured man kills his paramour, or any other man for that matter, were not included. However, this was neither due to lack of interest nor of relevance to the ideas of honour and passion. As mentioned above, the phenomenon of men killing other men over the body of a woman was at the core of Canadian provocation law, most notably in the seminal *Thibert* case. A study that incorporates these killings, while falling outside the ambit of this chapter, is necessary.

44 Reference to these cases is included in Appendix A to Fournier, McDougall & Dekker, 'Dishonour, Provocation and Culture', 2012. Cases were researched using Quicklaw, Westlaw Canada and CanL II databases.

45 Cases where the accused raised not the provocation defence but only the *anger defence* were not included. The latter was accepted by courts to negate the criminal intent for murder until the Supreme Court rejected it in 2001's *R v Parent*, 1 SCR 761. See: Gary T. Trotter, 'Anger, Provocation, and the Intent for Murder: A Comment on R. v. Parent', *McGill Law Journal*, 2002 (Vol. 47), p. 669.

46 See Christina Madek, 'Killing Dishonor', 2005.

47 Andrée Côté, Elizabeth Sheehy & Diana Majury, *Stop Excusing Violence Against Women*, p. 16, available online at: National Association of Women and the Law, http://www.nawl.ca/ns/en/documents/Pub_Report_Provocoo_en.pdf.

48 Katherine H. Bullock and Gul Joya Jafri, 'Media (Mis)Representations: Muslim Women in the Canadian Nation', *Canadian Woman Studies*, 2000 (Vol. 20, No. 2), p. 38.

49 Shahrzad Mojab observes this denigration of Muslim / Arab identity, illustrated through the ascription of characteristics such as patriarchal male honour to racial groups, thus becoming racism. Mojab, a professor at the University of Toronto who acted as expert witness at the Shafia 'honour killing' trial in Canada, notably wrote that '[t]he court case is about Canadians of Afghan – not Arab – origin and I find mass media resort to Arabs and Islam as more than an oversight or error of judgment. Is it by accident that most media coverage "racialized" a crime allegedly perpetrated by Canadian citizens and has given it a distinct Islamic and Arab character?' See: Shahrzad Mojab, 'The mass media in Canada have rushed to ascribe the "honour" killing phenomenon to Arabs and Muslims rather than recognize it as a product of patriarchy', *The Mark*, 19 December 2011, available online at The Mark News, http://www.themarknews.com/articles/7884-honour-killings-and-the-myth-of-arabness.

50 *R. v. Hamid*, Ontario Court of Appeal (OJ No 1507/2006), 2006, paragraph 456.

51 *R. v. Hamid*, 2006, paragraph 67.

52 *R. v. Hamid,* 2006, paragraph 67.
53 *R. v. Hamid,* 2006, paragraph 93.
54 The Supreme Court of Canada has confirmed in *R. v. Stone* that provocation may be used as a sentencing mitigating factor in addition to having served to reduce the verdict. See 1999 CarswellBC 1064, 1999 CarswellBC 1065, *R. v. Stone,* SCR, 1999, paragraph 237.
55 Isabel Grant, 'Intimate Femicide: A Study of Sentencing Trends for Men who Kill their Intimate Partners', *Alberta Law Review,* 2010 (Vol. 47, No. 3), p. 813.
56 Locke & Bunge, *Family Violence in Canada,* 2000, p. 39.
57 Timothy Macklem, 'Provocation and the Ordinary Person', *Dalhousie Law Journal,* 1987 (11), p. 135.
58 John L. Caughey, 'The Anthropologist as Expert Witness: The Case of a Murder in Maine', in: Marie Claire Foblets & Alison Dundes Renteln (eds.), *Multicultural Jurisprudence: Comparative Perspectives on the Cultural Defence,* Oxford: Hart Publishing, 2009, p. 323.
59 Kumaralingam Amirthalingam, 'Culture, Crime and Culpability: Perspectives on the Defence of Provocation', in Marie Claire Foblets & Alison Dundes Renteln (eds.), *Multicultural Jurisprudence: Comparative Perspectives on the Cultural Defence,* 2009, p. 36.
60 For a still accurate if perhaps slightly dated argument on the essentialism promoted by this defence, see: Pascale Fournier, 'The Ghettoization of Difference in Canada: "Rape by Culture" or the Danger of a Cultural Defence in Criminal Law Trials', *Manitoba Law Journal,* 2002 (Vol. 29, No. 81). See also: Daina Chiu, 'The Cultural Defence: Beyond Exclusion, Assimilation, and Guilty Liberalism', *California Law Review,* 1995 (Vol. 82), p. 1053.
61 See: David M. Paciocco, 'Subjective and Objective Standards of Fault for Offences and Defences', *Saskatchewan Law Review,* 1995 (Vol. 59, No. 2), p. 300; Wayne N. Renke, 'Calm Like a Bomb', 2010, p. 747; Peter Westen, 'Individualizing the Reasonable Person in Criminal Law' *Criminal Law & Philosophy,* 2008 (Vol. 2, No. 2), p. 137.
62 Homa Hoodfar, a Canadian Muslim woman and professor at the Department of Sociology and Anthropology at Concordia University, exemplifies this: 'my conversants listened to me, but they did not hear, and at the end of the conversation they would reiterate their earlier views as if our discussion were irrelevant. More recently, however, they treat me as an Islamic apologetic, which in fact silences me so that I can no longer argue.' See: Homa Hoodfar, 'The Veil in Their Minds and On Our Heads: The Persistence of Colonial Images of Muslim Women', *Resources for Feminist Research,* 1998 (Vol. 22, No. 3/4), p. 5.
63 Gunther Teubner, 'Legal Irritants: Good Faith in British Law or How Unifying Law Ends Up in New Divergences', *Modern Law Review,* 1998 (Vol. 61, No. 11), p. 13.
64 Gunther Teubner, 'Legal Irritants', 1998, p. 13.
65 In this regard, we agree that transplantation does not present an empirically observable 'linear path'; see: James Clifford, 'Notes on Travel and Theory', *Inscriptions,* 1989 (Vol. 5), p. 184. On the 'travelling' of ideas, see: Edward W. Said, 'Travelling Theory', in: *The World, the Text and the Critic,* Cambridge:

Harvard University Press, 1983, p. 226; Edward W. Said, 'Travelling theory reconsidered', in: *Reflection on Exile and Other Essays*, Cambridge: Harvard University Press, 2000, p. 436.

66 Leti Volpp, 'Blaming Culture for Bad Behaviour', *Yale Journal of Law & the Humanities*, 2000 (Vol. 12, No. 89), p. 112.

67 *R v Tran*, SCR (58/2010), 2010, paragraph 34.

68 *R v Tran*, SCR (58/2010), 2010, paragraph 34.

SECTION III

THE NEED FOR ACCOMMODATION

11 Accommodating Islamic Family Law(s)

A Critical Analysis of Some Recent Developments and Experiments in Europe[1]

Marie-Claire Foblets

Introduction

In this article, I will focus on the treatment of Islamic family law in the European legal order, in a context that is increasingly multicultural in nature. My analysis will proceed through three stages. First, I will briefly sketch the present situation, and explain why the status of Islamic family law was for a long time – and still is – governed in most European countries by the rules of private international law. Second, I will concentrate on situations that touch upon Islamic family law and that raise a number of specific problems. In the third and final part, I will shift the focus to the future: what pathways could a forward-looking analysis envisage that combines pluralism in family matters – including Islamic family law in particular – with respect for human rights, as defined by the European Convention for the Protection of Human Rights and Fundamental Freedoms? Three options can be identified, and my aim is to open these up to debate. As a result, the conclusions drawn will necessarily be fairly open-ended.

Limits to Private International Law in the Face of the Changing Demographic Profile of Europe

In Europe in recent years, the pluralism of family lifestyles has been increasingly linked to the migrations that took place in the post-war period. This growing diversity is quite clearly also the result of an ever more publicly supported sensitivity to the protection of individual autonomy. It should nevertheless be acknowledged that this increasing pluralism, in the sense of a juxtaposition of cultural models of family life, is heterogeneous in nature. A not insignificant complication results from the fact that migrations have, for the most part, come from countries where religious law constitutes a major source of law, particularly in matters of personal status. In practice, so far it is private international law and its techniques that have for the most part been invoked to govern the lives of immigrant families.

Private international law is the branch of law that deals with private relationships that are characterized by one or another form of interaction between different national legal systems that apply in a given situation. This interaction may result from the mixed nature of a relationship between parties who do not share the same nationality. Alternatively, it may may arise from a situation of cross-border mobility: the parties (or one of them) are living in a country other than that of their nationality – whether temporarily or on a long-term basis – and reside there as foreign nationals. For many years, therefore, questions relating to the personal status of people from countries where that status is governed by religious law were treated as issues covered by private international law.[2] The techniques of private international law continue to be important for all manner of questions relating to the reception, within the domestic law of the country of the parties' habitual residence, of situations relating to personal status that have arisen in a foreign country: marriages celebrated abroad, divorces granted by foreign judges, and so forth.[3] When dealing with personal status issues, the rules of private international law often refer to religious law, since these immigrants are often from countries where personal status is governed by shariʿa.

Over the years, however, the demographic profile of European communities of immigrant origin has undergone profound change. The presence of these groups is no longer linked primarily to immigration, but represents a permanent settlement in the country of habitual residence, that is, in Europe. It is true that there are still many instances of family reunification that involve interaction between different national legal systems: on the one hand, that of the country of origin of the partner who is joining someone living in Europe, and, on the other hand, that of the country where the family intends to settle.[4] Yet family reunification is now just one aspect of the reality of immigrant families' lives; increasingly, these family situations originate within Europe. Moreover, in most cases the parties hold the nationality of the country of residence, while also retaining the nationality of their country of origin.[5]

These developments are changing the status quo: questions involving the legal treatment of personal status become, in such cases, first and foremost matters governed by domestic law. The latter for the most part does not allow one to take into account the religious convictions of the persons involved, or, if it does, then only to a very limited degree.

If we were to agree on the principle that it ought to be possible for the religious dimension to maintain, in law, the importance that the parties concerned attach to it, then dealing with religious phenomena in terms of personal status would require devoting particular attention to the new profile of the large numbers of such families and individuals currently living throughout Europe. Certainly the debate is of a sensitive nature, as it raises the prospect of calling into question certain historical developments, such as the secularization of civil law. I will return to this question below. We are in a sense witnessing a relatively new type of duality as regards the legal position (and identity) of individuals who, on the one hand, have become full-fledged citizens of their country of residence and are thus bound by its legal system, while, on the other hand, placing that system alongside religious norms of foreign origin that defy its capacity to integrate them. The sociological literature describes the situation of such people as 'transnational'.[6]

Today it seems that Muslims even more frequently – in various parts of Europe – are faced with the difficulty of combining respect for the laws enacted by the state in their country of residence with Islam. The values of the latter are often endowed, in their view, with particular legitimacy.[7] Certain studies go so far as to warn that if this reality is not taken seriously, it could threaten the social cohesion of contemporary society.

A highly revelatory source of information on this matter is the many websites, based not only in Europe but also in Canada and the United states, which for several years now have enabled Muslims to submit questions relating to various aspects of their personal status.[8] The queries centre on the question of how to ensure that the different components of personal status that fall under the provisions of the (secularized) civil law of the country of residence can nonetheless be reconciled with the requirements of Islam as regards family organization: religious marriage occupies a prominent place here.

In Europe today, the vast majority of states have chosen to secularize the laws governing the person and the family.[9] This option gives priority to non-confessional laws. The difficulty this represents for persons who wish to combine the requirements of domestic civil law on personal status with the treatment of the latter in accordance with (their) religious law should not be underestimated. The situation is all the more complex for Muslims, since in Islam there is no unequivocal doctrinal position on the question of which law applies to a devout Muslim residing in a country governed by secular law.[10] In principle, such a person is a legal subject bound by the rules of a non-confessional (state) legal order, but the various schools of shariʿa differ amongst themselves with regard to the effects of this principle which they are willing to recognize on a religious level. This complicates matters for those concerned, and in part explains the confusion on the part of certain people when it comes to respect for the law of the state of their habitual residence; this is the case even if very often, as we have seen, they are full-fledged citizens of that country.[11]

One could of course retort that the situation for new religious minorities – and in particular Muslim communities – is not substantially different from that of adherents of other religions, since the secular civil law is in all cases the only one that is granted recognition by the state authorities. This response strikes us, however, as too categorical when it comes to Muslim communities. Not only because it circumvents a major difficulty, namely, the close connection which many Muslims continue to make between law and religion, but also because it fails to explore the alternative pathways that may be available.

The aim here is *not* to provide an inventory of the numerous works published in recent years on various aspects of personal status in countries where religious family law applies, or on the way questions of personal status are handled in the domestic law of European countries – seen through the prism of private international law – whether concerning the application of these statuses by judges in the country of residence or the reception of situations created abroad and of personal statuses governed by religious law. Several authors have, in the past few years, analysed the various solutions offered by case law or legal theory to the most common problems encountered in practice. These studies for the most part present an admirable analysis of private international law on questions relating to Islam, in particular: filiation, naming, conditions for a valid marriage, the rights and obligations of the spouses, the relations between parents and children, the dissolution of marriage through divorce and, finally, the status of property as well as its distribution upon death. I will limit myself here to referring to only a few of these works.[12]

Instead, I take a different approach, focusing on future perspectives and going beyond the limits of private international law to raise questions as to other potential approaches. This approach is an *exploratory* one: the aim is first and foremost to remind us of a number of questions that at this point must remain open and that are linked to the treatment, in civil law, of personal statuses that are religious in nature. The approach unfolds in two stages: first, an examination of the reasons why, in my view, we should not take comfort too readily in the argument that the new religious communities living in Europe today must necessarily behave like all others and accept the separation of law and religion. In the second stage, I address the core of the problem and look at the future perspectives mentioned above. The approach draws in large part on the literature on the subject. The way in which religious status is handled in the context of secular state law has to date been studied principally in Canada, Germany and England.[13] In what follows, I will look at the following three pathways toward a solution: the incorporation into domestic (civil law) of religious rules, taking the example of Islamic family law and in particular the marriage contract; the autonomy of the will in private international law; and finally, recourse to religious arbitration for certain types of family dispute. All three of these will be addressed here in what is necessarily a summary fashion and, as already suggested, departing to some extent from the strict confines of the techniques of private international law.

The Close Connection Between Law and Religion in Islam

The historical response in Europe to the problem of a conflict between loyalty to state law, on the one hand, and religious or confessional commitments, on the other hand, is well known: this problem is deemed to have been resolved by virtue of the separation of law and religion.[14] In Europe today, with the exception of a few very specific regulations, state law is most often the only formal source that applies in matters regarding personal status.

This solution, taking secularization for granted, does not completely evacuate or dissolve, in the specific case of Muslim communities, the close and indeed inseparable link that members of these communities often continue to make between law and religion: shariʿa or Islamic law is treated as the principal, and indeed the essential, source of law.[15] One may obviously obscure this reality by giving a response from a strictly secularized legal perspective to any question regarding the personal status of Muslims. Evidently, in practice, not everyone's perspective is the same, and the reference to religion will not be of equal importance to each person. But in general it may be said that the common reference to Islam as the source of law explains why Muslims often continue to seek a sort of compromise or reconciliation between the requirements of their religion and those of civil law.

To refuse to take into account this endeavour would be to risk eliciting reticence on the part of these communities. In practice, such reticence with regard to the requirements of civil law is indeed perceptible. It manifests itself in various forms, as several studies on the patterns of regulation of family relations within Muslim communities in Europe have shown.[16] At times this reticence can go so far as to simply displace civil law and set up a parallel legal regime within the religious community, without seeking recognition under civil law for the situation thus created: religious marriage, for example, is celebrated without any concern for first entering into a civil contract, even if the law requires that this be done. In other cases, individuals return to their country of origin to seek justice, availing themselves of the rules of conflict of laws which, in the private international law of most Islamic countries, allow them to have recourse to those countries' domestic laws regardless of the number of years a person has lived abroad.[17] In legal terms, and in particular from the perspective of legal security, both forms of behaviour raise serious questions: religious (informal) marriages will not be recognized by the authorities of the country of habitual residence, leaving the spouses without protection under domestic (state) law and hence vulnerable; as for the solutions reached in the country of origin, these create a legal privilege that is reserved for the nationals of countries which confer upon religious (Islamic) law the status of personal law. Such a privilege makes coordination among national legal systems in their case difficult: religious law prevails over secular law exclusively in the case of those who have retained the nationality of the country in question. The situation is all the more unjustifiable because often the factual connection to the law of the country of habitual residence has grown strong over the years, through, among other things, acquisition of citizenship and/or long-term residence; too strong for a person to be permitted recourse to the rules of private international law.

In light of these observations, a search for alternatives is warranted. Three types of legal solution may potentially be envisaged: (1) allowing rules based on religion to be granted effect under civil law. Notably, this could take the form of a (civil) contract, as in the case of marriage; (2) applying the autonomy of the will in private international law; and finally (3) recourse to religious arbitration for certain disputes. In what follows, I will examine these three options in succession. As indicated, these pathways draw inspiration from the doctrine and, in part, from case law. To date, the question of drawing on domestic civil law to find more suitable means of regulating the family life of Muslims has attracted the attention mainly of authors whose work focuses on the English-speaking world.

Future Perspectives: Three Alternatives

INCORPORATING RELIGIOUS RULES INTO CIVIL LAW: THE EXAMPLE OF THE MARRIAGE CONTRACT

At first glance, allowing the incorporation into domestic law of religious rules governing matters related to family law may be surprising, given that this approach runs the risk of restoring to religion a scope and an impact that secularized civil law has historically tried to limit.[18] The risk may seem all the more serious in the case of personal statuses which contravene fundamental principles of the equality of the sexes and of non-discrimination based on religion that are now mandated by the civil law in most European countries.[19] Such principles, moreover, are almost systematically met with the invocation by courts and civil officials of a public order exception.

Yet, several equally important legal values may militate against such a refusal and argue instead in favour of greater openness on the part of state law in Europe to religious personal statuses of foreign origin. One such argument is the extension in recent years of the principle of the autonomy of the will – both in domestic civil law and in private international law – which entails the possibility for adults (men and women) to shape their family life by combining elements of mandatory law, which do not suffer exemption, with elements of optional civil law.

The principle of the autonomy of the will supports the view that civil law ought to be more inclined to accept norms of religious and/or cultural origin that may differ from its own. One may disagree as to the degree of openness that is desirable, and one may indeed disagree profoundly with a thesis that would go so far as to attribute to the autonomy of the parties an impact that overrides fundamental civil rights such as the age of marriage, consent by the future spouses, impediments based on consanguinity or on the undissolved bond of a previous marriage.[20] Nevertheless, the principle presents a number of advantages that should not be underestimated when it comes to the question of incorporating into civil law elements of family law based on Islam. Shariʿa notably grants the spouses a surprising liberty to define their relations, both in terms of personal and of patrimonial effects.[21]

In order to offer the wife, in particular, a maximum number of guarantees protecting couples against certain specific risks under shariʿa, several authors in Denmark,[22] Germany[23] and England,[24] in particular, have been suggesting for several years that spouses should enter into a valid and enforceable contract under civil law that contains the stipulations necessary to enable couples to frame their union according to their particular needs, without, however, overstepping the limits and particularities of their religious law and without infringing on a fundamental right of either party.

This approach requires that each situation be subjected to careful prior analysis of the needs of both spouses and of their connection to the forum, both of their country of residence and of their country of origin: not only may the conditions for the formation of the contract vary, but also the regime under which it is implemented. Surprisingly however, in continental Europe, the application of this solution has hitherto been rare.[25] It seems to us that, in view of protecting the spouses, prenuptial agreements – well known to lawyers in North America – may serve as an inspiration to practitioners in continental Europe. There is indeed nothing to prevent them from providing more guidance to Muslim couples – should they wish to avail themselves of it – in searching for contractual solutions to, for example, problems of the management and division of property that arise in their particular case. The matter deserves to be examined in greater depth, all the more so since it seems highly likely that, over the years, there will be increasing numbers of cases where women in particular who have been excluded or discriminated against will, on grounds of non-discrimination, demand that their interests be taken into account.

For stipulations that are mandatory under Islamic family law, the problem presents itself somewhat differently. Some of these stipulations are alien to the nature of a civil marriage contract. This is true, for example, for the commitment by the future husband to pay a dower or *mahr* to his future wife.[26] The way in which such a clause is handled differs according to the various approaches. The mandatory nature of this provision has been the subject of several contradictory decisions in case-law: certain judicial decisions refuse to sanction it, evoking the religious and inadequately defined nature of the obligation, whereas others, on the contrary, agree to sanction it. Within certain schools of Islamic law, the obligation to pay the *mahr* is an imperative condition for Islamic marriage, and is separate from the matrimonial regime. One of its functions is to protect the financial interests of the wife by obliging the husband to pay her a sum of money or transfer property to her, in order to guarantee her a degree of financial security and a certain degree of independence. The *mahr* takes effect at the latest upon the dissolution of the marriage. Nevertheless, for the *mahr* to be enforceable under secular civil law, certain authors suggest that couples residing in Europe should enshrine it in a (secular) contract.[27] This will allow the civil courts to recognize it more easily, and if necessary the latter will be able to rule that a civil contractual obligation is enforceable even if that obligation is founded on a rule that is religious in nature. From this perspective, a civil contract will be in a sense 'added on' to a marriage agreement.

It is not clear, however, that a separate contract entered into in civil law constitutes, in and of itself, a sufficient means for achieving the most complete and comprehensive legal arrangement possible for protecting a couple from the various risks to which their nuptial commitment exposes them either in domestic law or in private international law. It all depends on their specific situation. As I already mentioned above, the pros and cons of prenuptial arrangements in legal practice within the context of continental Europe would require further research.

Beyond the explicit designation of the matrimonial regime and certain provisions concerning the management and division of their property, the spouses may also stand to gain from negotiating arrangements concerning the personal effects of marriage that will protect them from specific risks they may incur by virtue of provisions in force in Islamic countries and that may quite possibly apply to them.[28] As a general rule, setting out the form of the obligations between spouses in terms of personal effects will mainly benefit the wife, since she is the one who incurs the greatest risks. Two well-known risks are that of her husband taking another wife, and the dissolution of the marriage on the initiative of the husband alone (unilateral repudiation). Polygyny and repudiation without the wife's consent do not constitute a serious legal risk for a woman living in Europe.[29] Yet, the insertion of clauses stipulating that the woman has the right to divorce her husband should he take another wife or, for even greater protection, the right to leave the marriage for reasons of discord, are likely to strengthen the woman's position in the event of her husband's remarriage abroad in an Islamic country where polygyny is authorized, or in case of unilateral repudiation. These clauses, which strengthen the position of the wife, are perfectly admissible in Islam, which leaves it up to the parties to incorporate religious considerations into the contract in order to protect themselves.[30]

The question remains, however, as to the contract into which these clauses are to be inserted: is it the marriage contract itself, or a separate one? Muslim couples who marry civilly usually also celebrate their marriage religiously. That is in fact the only way to validate the marriage under Islam. The safest solution in such cases would be to include those clauses that are unknown in civil law in the religious marriage contract, for that way the risks incurred by virtue of their (religious) personal status are mitigated and thus covered by a religious contract.

Much more could be said about the role of the civil contract in the religious sphere.[31] Certain provisions envisaged by the parties on the grounds of their religion are not subject to legal definition under civil law. What meaning will the civil courts assign them in that case? Will the judge be disposed to enforce them as binding? The question may legitimately be raised, since just because an obligation is of a religious character does not mean that it cannot be recognized as valid under civil law.[32] The monogamy clause, for instance, simply confirms the obligations undertaken by the spouses in civil law, and can therefore, in my view, be included in a civil contract. The will of the spouses is in that case to protect the wife, which in law is perfectly acceptable. As regards the right to divorce, one might ask whether it is licit to make a commitment to divorce. In this regard, it should be noted that a country like Norway opted over twenty years ago now (1991) for a solution in which all citizens contracting marriage, including non-Muslims, had to grant the other spouse the right to divorce.[33] That solution may seem surprising, as it applies to each person who engages in a marriage while such clause makes sense only in the case of a women who risks being unable to get out of the marriage if the law of a country where such a constraint (still) exists should apply to her.

Obviously, all this is not easily put into practice. On the one hand, because the contractual definition of certain aspects of religious marriage cannot but raise difficulties: to what extent are certain obligations, rooted in religious law, 'fit' for being the subject of a civil contract? On the other hand, since the suggestions put forward here require several conditions to be met simultaneously – something that will rarely be the case in practice: the two spouses should be informed of the legal/contractual options open to them, but above all, they should agree between them on the exact content of the additional protections they envisage for their own particular situation. They should also know how important it is to them to protect themselves against certain risks that are characteristic of the law by which they are bound as a result of their marriage and which, in the case of Islam, leaves the wife particularly vulnerable. Furthermore, this approach is a proactive one. The spouses do not gain any immediate benefit from their agreement, but agree to consider a future risk. Is it not asking too much that they should do so at the time when they enter into their marriage? One could of course imagine that a civil contract might be signed later on, after a few years of marriage, or that the marriage contract might be amended afterwards, but in that case it is necessary to do so before any serious disagreement should arise between them, for otherwise it will be too late to negotiate with due serenity.

The intention in this paper is to invite reflection: despite the numerous obstacles, it could be advantageous for some couples to incorporate clauses of a religious nature into their marriage contract in view of bringing norms imposed by their religious conviction into harmony with the requirements of civil law. It is true, however, that many questions remain and therefore professional and detailed guidance in these matters is necessary if one wishes, in practice, to offer spouses greater protection with regard to their rights and obligations which they take upon them.

THE AUTONOMY OF THE WILL IN FAMILY MATTERS

The second potentially relevant pathway toward accommodating Islamic family law within the European legal order is the autonomy of the will in private international law. For the past few years, private international law has, in an increasing number of countries, and especially in Europe, offered another approach which, as regards family law, allows couples concerned by the interaction between secular civil law and a religiously-inspired law in their country of origin to agree, to a certain extent, on the way in which they envisage conflicts of law issues that risk arising in their case. This approach relates to the exercise of the autonomy of the will with respect to personal status. In Belgium, for example, the 2004 Code of private international law[34] allows for the law of the country of habitual residence to be tempered for certain matters, such as the dissolution of marriage by divorce and as regards the matrimonial regime, by granting the parties a right to opt for the national law.[35] This approach is of interest only to the extent that the couple does indeed retain a connection with the country of origin by holding that country's nationality, or that the spouses stand to benefit from recognition, in the other jurisdiction, of the matrimonial regime that they have chosen and any other future arrangements regarding the division of property. The same is true for the dissolution of their marriage by divorce, where applicable. In the 1980s, Jean-Yves Carlier did pioneering work in Belgium in which he scrupulously investigated the various advantages that persons who have kept a connection to a foreign law may gain from being granted autonomy in respect of personal status.[36] Belgian federal legislation has since moved in this direction, albeit cautiously. This solution has its limits, which have been identified in the first part of this paper. These include the fact that the solution applies only to couples who have maintained a connection to foreign law. It does not, therefore, offer a solution to persons who have converted to Islam and who have no legal connection to a foreign legal order that they would like to designate as the law that applies to their situation.

The limitations do not stop there, however. There is lingering uncertainty as to the question of whether autonomy plays a role in cases of multiple nationality as well, which, as noted above, is the situation in which immigrant couples increasingly find themselves. Where one or both partners also hold the nationality of the country of residence, it is not certain that the couple can still invoke the autonomy of the will, which in their case would be the equivalent of allowing them to opt for the application of the *other* national law. The question arises, notably, in Belgian private international law. On the one hand, the Belgian Code of private international law places persons with dual nationality under the protection of Belgian law: in cases of multiple nationalities of which Belgian nationality is one, Belgian law applies (Article 3, paragraph 2). The right to choose the applicable law would cease, in that case, to be seen as an alternative. But on the other hand, the Code does, in Articles 49, 50 and 55, grant couples a right to choose according to whether they feel more affinity with the society of their habitual residence or, on the contrary, with the country of the law of the nationality. The Belgian Code of private international law in a sense leaves open the question of couples with multiple nationalities. As a result, the answer will have to come from case law.

In terms of private international law, it would be best if situations of multiple nationalities were circumscribed by conventions – bilateral and multilateral – that ensure that the legal order of the country of which one of the persons holds nationality recognizes the situations arising from the effects of the law in force in the country of the *other* nationality, and vice versa, without this having to depend on measuring the intensity of the ties – always difficult to do – which the persons in question may or may not have with one or the other country. On the other hand, as has been emphasized since the introduction, it would be preferable not to continue to make 'transnational' family situations exclusively dependent on solutions devised in private international law. These solutions are intended primarily for situations that entail interaction on an international level between different legal systems and that seek to guarantee harmony at that level. Priority must henceforth be granted, in my view, to offering sufficient legal protection to persons who cannot make use of the techniques of private international law but come, instead, under domestic law.

Recourse to religious arbitration for certain family disputes

The third and last option I will discuss here with regard to incorporating Islam into the domestic legal order of European countries is recourse to religious arbitration for certain types of family disputes. The quest for solutions, in domestic law, to questions raised by the need to take into account by people's religious convictions may be situated at two different levels, although these are not mutually exclusive: either the individuals seek for themselves – for their own sake – to accommodate material law within the spectrum of commitments made among one another (for example, spouses), namely by enshrining those commitments in a contract or in some other form of explicit initiative; or potential adjustments are sought in terms of procedure, in particular where a dispute has to be resolved. It is on this second type of adjustment that I will focus here, in the last section of the forward-looking analysis. Two countries with an Anglo-Saxon legal tradition, Canada and Great Britain, offer contrasting illustrations of this issue. It would be risky on my part at this stage to suggest this route for other countries, but it deserves nonetheless to be mentioned.

In Canada, the question arose in relation to religious arbitration in family law.[37] That path was ultimately abandoned, with repercussions for other existing religious family law arbitration tribunals, which were to be abolished. There is no room here to go into the details of the (lively) debate – not only among jurists, but also in the media – provoked by the question, but simply to recall the stakes involved, since these were not without relevance to the situation of other religious communities established in countries with a secular civil law tradition.

The point of departure for the discussion in Canada was the right to freedom of religion. The question raised in Canada had to do with the approval given, in civil law, to legal proceedings of a religious nature: should the privatization of justice be accepted to the point where decisions handed down by religious authorities are recognized in law? Several modalities may be envisaged: (1) a privatization that is limited to religious mediation; (2) religious arbitration; or, finally, (3) full judicial pluralism authorizing the settlement of family disputes by religious courts. In the third scenario, one may speak of a true judicial pluralism that recognizes the existence of particular institutions that administer justice on an equal footing with state courts. The latter form of regulation exists in India, among other places, as well as in Lebanon, but seems to have little support in the West. In Canada, the second of the above options was the subject of much discussion after a group in the Province of Ontario known as the Islamic Institute of Civil Justice (IICJ) announced, in 2003, its intention to create a Canadian Islamic body that would arbitrate in family matters. It should be recalled that arbitration is not mediation, but has legal force on condition that the decision complies with state law and therefore does not infringe on the rights and liberties of persons. The communities concerned would thus be required to accept the primacy of domestic law as regards personal status, but they would be allowed to set up their own arbitration boards for certain matters. The state judge would ultimately retain the right to order a review of the decision and of the procedures followed in reaching it.

An Ontario law has, since 1991, allowed for arbitration by religious authorities. The IICJ merely requested the right of Muslim communities to have their own arbitration board along the lines of other religious arbitration bodies already in place, it thus announced its intention to create a Canadian Muslim arbitration board for family matters that would be available to all Muslims in Canada. One remembers what happened: in the debate that followed the IICJ's announcement of its intentions, the Ontario legislature abolished the option of arbitration. The challenge came largely as a result of the fear that the religious arbitration would, in practice, infringe on certain individual rights, in particular those of women, should they not be entirely free to consent to arbitration but compelled to avail themselves of it under pressure from the patriarchal rules that prevail in their community, in the name of the protection which that community affords them and of an inegalitarian conception of women's identity in Islam. In sum, Islam was reproached for its treatment of women. The debate in Canada is now not only closed, but the path opened by the 1991 Act has been abandoned.

Strangely enough, in the meantime religious arbitration seems to be blazing a trail through Great Britain, where the Muslim Arbitration Tribunal (MAT) has been authorized, pursuant to the Arbitration Act of 1996, to offer its services to Muslims who wish to use them to settle their conflicts.[38] Islamic mediation bodies, such as the Islamic Sharia Councils, as well as Jewish, evangelical and Catholic ones, were already well established in their role of accompanying conflicts between believers, which were for the most part familial or sometimes commercial in nature. Their decisions had no legal force, however, in the eyes of state law. With the establishment of a true religious arbitration tribunal, the Muslims of Great Britain appear to have succeeded in opening up the path that had been blocked in Canada. They have obtained recognition for specific institutions allowing Muslims who wish to do so to settle their disputes by means of arbitration. The aim is to open up an alternative form of dispute resolution, while respecting certain limitations: the procedure must abide by the obligation to protect individual rights and thus fundamental freedoms. It should, however, be regarded as a form of weak legal pluralism, since it all remains within the confines of public policy and the Muslim Arbitration Tribunal cannot pronounce divorce, that is, a divorce that equals a civil divorce.[39]

It is too soon to draw concrete lessons from the experiment being conducted at present in Great Britain with the MAT, but it would be very instructive to follow this experience closely and read the evaluations that will be conducted in Britain itself. The benefit to be gained from religious arbitration is not insignificant; it is very similar to the advantages of the traditional system of arbitration. In the case of Muslim communities, it is undeniable that the question of accommodation of rules of conduct drawn from Islam and from the principles of shariʿa is a lively one. Shariʿa is indeed a complex normative framework of rules and principles that regulate family life, among other things, and offer a comprehensive vision of the life of the believer. Family law is a particularly sensitive domain of law, the more so when it is closely linked to a religion, since this makes the handling of related matters from a legal perspective all the more difficult. One would therefore expect that particular institutions, deeply rooted in the reality and lived religious experience of a community of believers and, above all, recognized by that community, would handle the responsibility of arbitration entrusted to them with the requisite expertise and authority. Under the principle of arbitration, Muslims involved in disputes in Great Britain may henceforth turn to an alternative space for conflict resolution, one that is recognized by the state. This body is not free from the oversight of English law. Time will tell whether this experiment bears fruit, and thus whether it could serve as a useful path in the context of family law. The first studies devoted to the MAT do not rule out this possibility.

Notes

1 This paper is based largely on one that I presented, in French, at the Conference on 'Islam belge', which was organized by the Centre interdisciplinaire d'études de l'Islam dans le monde contemporain, and held at Louvain-la-Neuve, Belgium, on 13 December 2008. The proceedings, edited by Felice Dassetto, Farid El Asri and Brigitte Maréchal, will appear in a collective volume entitled 'Islam belge au pluriel' published by Presses Universitaires Louvain.

2 See especially J.-Y. Carlier and M. Verwilghen (eds.), *Le statut personnel des musulmans. Droit comparé et droit international privé*, Brussels: Bruylant, 1992; for more recent studies, see also the references cited in note 14.

3 M. Fallon and J. Erauw, *La nouvelle loi sur de droit international privé belge. La loi du 16 juillet 2004*, Antwerp: Kluwer, 2004; J.-Y. Carlier, M. Fallon & B. Martin-Bosly, *Code de droit international privé*, Brussels: Bruylant, 2008; F. Rigaux and M. Fallon, *Droit international privé*, Brussels: Larcier, 2005.

4 See especially M. Nys, *L'immigration familiale à l'épreuve du droit*, Brussels: Bruylant, 2002.

5 M. Verwilghen, 'Conflits de nationalités. Plurinationalité et apatridie,' *Recueil des cours de l'Académie de droit international* 1999 (Vol. 277, No. 2), pp. 9-484. For an analysis of multiple nationality among persons from Islamic countries, see K. El Geddawy, *Relations entre systèmes confessionnel et laïque en droit international privé*, Paris: Dalloz (Bibliothèque de droit international privé), 1971.

6 See especially P. Bramadat and M. Koenig (eds.), *International Migration and the Governance of Religious Diversity*, Montreal & Kingston: Metropolis, 2009.

7 See especially N. Asayyad and M. Castells (eds.), *Muslim Europe or Euro-Islam: politics, culture, and citizenship in the age of globalization*, Lanham: Lexington Books, 2002; S. Benhabib, I. Shapiro & D. Petranovic (eds.), *Identities, Affiliations and Allegiances*, Cambridge: Cambridge U.P., 2007; H. Coward, J.R. Hinnells & R.B. Williams (eds.), *The South Asian Religious Diaspora in Great Britain, Canada and the United States*, New York: State University of New York Press, 2000; A. Erdemir, H. Rittersberger-Tiliç, A. Ergun & H. Kahveci (eds.), *Rethinking Global Migration: Practices, Policies, and Discourses in the European Neighbourhood*, Ankara: KORA, 2008; M. Howard Ross (ed.), *Culture and Belonging in Divided Societies. Contestation and Symbolic Landscapes*, Philadelphia: University of Pennsylvania Press, 2009; G.F. Levey and T. Modood (eds.), *Secularism, Religion and Multicultural Citizenship*, Cambridge: Cambridge U.P., 2009; J. Nielsen and S. Allievi (eds.), *Muslim Networks and Transnational Communities in and Across Europe*, Leiden: Brill, 2002; Y. Yazbeck Haddad (ed.), *Muslims in the West: from Sojourners to Citizens*, Oxford: Oxford U.P., 2002.

8 See, for example, www.islamonline.net; www.karamah.org/home.htm; www.islamfortoday.com; www.minaret.org; islamawareness.net.

9 Regarding this option, which is in fact quite recent in the history of democratic societies, see especially G. Motzkinn and Y. Fischer, *Religion and Democracy in Contemporary Europe*, London: Alliance Publishing Trust, 2008; V. Bader, *Secularism or Democracy? Associational Governance of Religious Diversity*. Amsterdam: Amsterdam U.P. 2007; A. Dierkens and J.-Ph. Schreiber (eds.), *Laïcité et sécularisation dans l'Union européenne*, Brussels: Ed. de l'Université de Bruxelles ('Problèmes d'Histoire des religions'), vol. XVI, 2006; M. Grimpret, *Dieu est dans l'isoloir*, Paris: Presses de la Renaissance, 2007; G.J. Larouche and M. Maesschalck, *La religion dans l'espace public*, Université Laval: Ed. Liber, 2006, no. 8, pp. 60-70; B. Massignon, '*L'Union européenne: Ni Dieu, ni César*', *Esprit* (special issue on 'Effervescences religieuses dans le monde'), March-April 2007, pp. 104-111; M. Milot, P. Portier & J.-P. Willaime (eds.), *Pluralisme religieux et citoyenneté*, Rennes: P.U. Rennes, 2009.

10 For an analysis of the question, see A.F. March, *Islam and Liberal Citizenship. The Search for an Overlapping Consensus*, Oxford: Oxford U.P., 2009.

11 See especially K. El Gedawwy, *Relations entre systems confessionnel et laïque en droit international privé*, Paris, Dalloz (Bibliothèque de droit international privé), 1971. More recently, A. Abdalla, 'Principles of Islamic Interpersonal Conflict Intervention: A Search within Islam and Western Literature', *Journal of Law and Religion*, 2002, pp. 151-184.

12 I will confine my references here to a few recent works, cited in alphabetical order: A. Buechler, *Islamic Law in Europe? Legal Pluralism and its Limits in Euro-*

pean Family Laws, Surrey: Ashgate, 2011; J.-Y. Carlier, 'La reconnaissance mesurée des répudiations par l'examen *in concreto* de la contrariété à l'ordre public', *Revue trimestielle du droit de la famille*, 2003, pp. 35ff; R. El Husseini Begdache, *Le droit international privé français et la répudiation islamique*, Paris: La Librairie Générale de Droit et de Jurisprudence, 2002; M.-Cl. Foblets and J.-Y. Carlier, *Le Code marocain de la famille. Incidences au regard du droit international privé en Europe*, Brussels: Bruylant, 2005; L. Gannagé, *La hiérarchie des normes et les méthodes du droit international privé. Etude de droit international privé de la famille*, Paris: La Librairie Générale de Droit et de Jurisprudence, 2001; L. François, 'La Convention européenne des droits de l'homme est-elle supérieure aux conventions bilatérales reconnaissant les répudiations musulmanes?', Chronique *Recueil Dalloz* (Paris), No. 39, 2002 (pp. 2958-2962), pp. 2958ff; H. Gaudemet-Tallon, 'Nationalité, statut personnel et droits de l'homme', in: *Mélanges E. Jayme*, Munich, Sellier, 2004, 219ff; H. Gaudemet-Tallon, 'Le pluralisme en droit international privé: richesses et faiblesses (Le funambule et l'arc-en-ciel)', *Recueil des Cours de l'Académie de Droit International*, 2005 (Vol. 312, No. 1); H. Gaudemet-Tallon, 'De nouvelles fonctions pour l'équivalence en droit international privé', in: *Le droit international privé: esprits et méthodes, Mélanges en l'honneur de Paul Lagarde*, Paris: Dalloz, 2005, 302ff; P. Kinsch, 'Droits de l'homme, droits fondamentaux et droit international privé', in: *Le droit international privé: esprits et méthodes, Mélanges en l'honneur de Paul Lagarde*, Paris: Dalloz,, 2005, vol. 318; P. Lagarde, 'Différences culturelles et ordre public en droit international privé de la famille', *Annuaire IDI*, 2005 (Vol. 71, No. 1), pp. 7-115; Y. Lequette, 'Le conflit de civilisation à la lumière de l'expérience franco-tunisienne', in: *Mouvements de droit contemporain, Mélanges offerts au Professeur Sassi Ben Halima*, Tunis: Centre de publication universitaire, 2005, pp. 175ff; Y. Lequette, 'Le droit international privé et les droits fondamentaux', in: R. Cabrillac, *et al.* (ed.), *Libertés et droits fondamentaux*, Paris: Dalloz, 2006, pp. 99ff; M.-Cl. Najm, *Principes directeurs du droit international privé et conflits de civilisations. Relations entre systèmes laïques et systèmes religieux*, Paris: Dalloz, 2005; N.M. Mahieddin, 'La dissolution du mariage par la volonté unilatérale de l'un des époux en droit musulman et en droit algérien', *Revue internationale de droit comparé*, 2006, pp. 73ff; A. Mezghani, 'Le juge français et les institutions du droit musulman', *Journal de Droit International*, 2003 (Vol. 13, No. 3), pp. 721ff; M.-L. Niboyet, 'Regard français sur la reconnaissance en France des répudiations musulmanes', *Revue internationale de droit comparé*, 2006, pp. 27ff; J. Witte, Jr (ed.), 'Shari'a, Family, and Democracy: Religious Norms and Family Law in Pluralistic Democratic States', *Emory International Law Review* (Special Issue), 2011 (Vol. 25, No. 2); K. Zaher, *Conflit de civilisations et droit international privé*, Paris: L'Harmattan, 2009.

13 For Canada, Jeffrey A. Talpis offers a very fine analysis of a number of issues which are addressed in this paper. See especially: J.A. Talpis, 'L'accommodement raisonnable en droit international privé québecois', in: J.-Fr. Gaudreault-Des-Biens (ed.), *Le droit, la religion et le raisonnable. Le fait religieux entre nomisme étatique et pluralisme juridique*, Montréal, Themis, 2009, pp. 303-358.

14 See El Gedawwy, *Relations entre systems confessionnel et laïque en droit international privé*, 1971 and Abdalla, 'Principles of Islamic Interpersonal Conflict Intervention' 2002.

15 See J. Cesari and S. McLoughlin (eds.), *European Muslims and the Secular State*, Aldershot, Ashgate, 2005; J. Cesari, *When Islam and Democracy Meet: Muslims in Europe and in the United States*, New York: Palgrave, 2004 (2nd ed. 2006); more recently: J. Cesari (ed.), *Muslims in the West after 9/11*, London: Routledge, 2009; V. Bader (ed.), 'Governing Islam in Western Europe. Essays on Governance of Religious Diversity', *Journal of Ethnic and Migration Studies*, 2007 (Vol. 33, No. 6); J. Klausen, *The Islamic challenge: politics and religion in western Europe*, Oxford: Oxford U.P., 2005; B. Marechal *et al.* (eds.), *Muslims in the Enlarged Europe: Religion and Society*, Leiden: Brill, 2003; J.S. Nielsen, *Muslims in Western Europe*, Edinburgh: Edinburgh U.P. Press, 1992 (3rd ed. 2004); J.S. Nielsen, *Towards a European Islam?*, London: Macmillan, 1999; M. Rohe, 'Muslims between Qu'ran and Constitution – Religious Freedom within the German Legal Order', in: L.A. Tramontini (ed.), *'East is East and West is West'? Talks on Dialogue in Beirut*, Beirut: Orient-Institut Beirut, Beiruter Texte und Studien 80, 2006, pp. 151-176; M. Rohe, 'Islamic Norms in Germany and Europe', in: A. Al-Hamarneh & J. Thielemann (eds.), *Islam and Muslims in Germany*, Leiden: Brill, 2008, pp. 49-81; W.A.R. Shadid and P.S. Van Koningsveld (eds.), *Intercultural relations and religious authorities: Muslims in the European Union*, Leuven: Peeters, 2002; P. Shah, 'Thinking beyond Religion: Legal Pluralism in Britain's South Asian Diaspora', *Australian Journal of Asian Law*, 2006 (Vol. 6), pp. 237-260; P. Shah, 'Transforming to accommodate? Reflections on the *Sharia* debate in Britain', in: R. Grillo *et al.* (eds.), *Legal practice and cultural diversity*, Aldershot: Ashgate, 2009, pp. 73-92.

16 See note 7.

17 El Gedawwy, *Relations entre systems confessionnel et laïque en droit international privé*, 1971, and A. Abdalla, 'Principles of Islamic Interpersonal Conflict Intervention', 2002. See also M. Charfi, 'L'influence de la religion dans le droit international privé des pays musulmans', *Receuil des Cours de l'Académie de Droit International*, 1987 (Vol. 203, No. 3), pp. 414ff; O. Ewan, 'L'Islam et les systèmes de conflits de lois' in: J.-Y. Carlier and M. Verwilghen (eds.), *Le statut personnel des musulmans*, 1992, pp. 313-341; M. Berger, 'Conflicts Law and Public Policy in Egyptian Family Law: Islamic Law through the Backdoor?', *The American Journal of Comparative Law*, 2002, pp. 555-594.

18 See especially: P. Cane, C. Evans & Z. Robinson (eds.), *Law and Religion in Theoretical and Historical Context*, Cambridge, Cambridge U.P., 2008; H. Goris and M. Heimbach-Steins (eds.), *Religion in Recht und politischer Ordnung heute*, Würzburg, Ergon, 2008; H. Lehmann (ed.), *Multireligiosität im vereinten Europa: historische und juristische Aspekte*, Göttingen, Wallstein, 2003.

19 For instance, the principle of paternal guardianship in Islamic law, polygynous marriage, religious prohibition against mixed marriage, or the discriminatory share of women in succession, to mention but a few examples.

20 That is a criticism also levelled by J.A. Talpis, 'L'accommodement raisonnable en droit international privé québecois', 2009, p. 313.

21 See especially A.Y. Al-Hibri, 'The Nature of the Islamic Marriage: Sacramental, Convenantal, or Contractual?', in: J. Witte and E. Ellison (eds.), *Covenant Marriage in Comparative Perspective*, Michigan/Cambridge: W.B. Eerdmans Publishing Company/Grand Rapids, MI, pp. 182-216.

22 R. Mehdi, 'Danish Law and the Practice of *mahr* among Muslim Pakistanis in Denmark', *International Journal of Sociology of Law*, 2003, pp. 115-129.

23 C. Jones-Pauly, 'Marriage Contracts of Muslims in the Diaspora: Problems in the Recognition of *mahr* contracts in German Law', in: A. Quraishi and F. Vogel (eds.), *The Islamic Marriage Contract. Case Studies in Islamic Family Law*, Cambridge: Islamic Legal Studies Programme, 2008, pp. 299-330.

24 I. Yilmaz, *Muslim Laws, Politics and Society in Modern Nation States. Dynamic Legal Pluralism in England, Turkey and Pakistan*, Aldershot: Ashgate, 2005, pp. 49ff; See also C. Weisbrod, *Grounding Security. Family, Insurance and the State*, Aldershot: Ashgate, 2006, pp. 25-52.

25 Some difficulties may arise with regard to the validity of clauses included in wills or donations and relating to the religious practice of the testator or donor. For a study that surveys these difficulties in the context of the Netherlands, see S. Rutten, *Erven naar Marokkaans recht: aspecten van Nederlands internationaal privaatrecht bij de toepasselijkheid van Marokkaans erfrecht*, Antwerp: Intersentia, 1997. For Germany, see especially A.K. Pattar, *Islamisch inspiriertes Erbrecht und deutscher Ordre public: die Erbrechtsordnungen von Ägypten, Tunesien und Marokko und ihre Anwendbarkeit im Inland*, Berlin: Duncker & Humblot, 2007; J. Bäsedow and N. Yassari (eds.), *Iranian Family and Succession Laws and their Application in German Courts*, Tübingen: Mohr Siebeck, 2004.

26 Regarding this obligation, see several illustrations in A. Quraishi and F. Vogel (eds.), *The Islamic Marriage Contract.*, 2008. See also: R. Mehdi, 'Danish Law and the Practice of *mahr* among Muslim Pakistanis in Denmark' 2003, pp. 115-129; R. Mehdi and J. Nielsen (eds.), *Embedding Mahr (Islamic Dower) in the European Legal System*, Copenhagen, DJOF Publishing, 2011.

27 In this regard, see R. Mehdi, 'Danish Law and the Practice of *mahr* among Muslim Pakistanis in Denmark', 2003.

28 On the privilege of nationality and of religion in the private international law of Islamic countries, see especially: K. Zaher, *Conflit de civilisations et droit international privé*, 2009.

29 M.-C. Foblets, 'The Admissibility of repudiation: requirements in private international law. Recent developments in France, Belgium and The Netherlands', in R. Mehdi (ed.), *Integration & Retsudvikling*, Copenhagen, Jurist- og Oknomforbindets Forlag, 2008, pp. 151-170.

30 K. Zaher, *Conflit de civilisations et droit international privé*, 2009.

31 See especially I. Riassetto, 'Religion et contrat', in: F. Messner, P.-H. Prelot & J.-M. Woehrling (eds.), *Traité de droit français des religions*, Paris: Litec, no. 1520; B. Moore, 'Sur la contractualisation de la croyance', in: J.-Fr. Gaudreault-Des-Biens, *Le droit, la religion et le raisonnable*, 2009, pp. 491-530.

32 I will not address here the question of whether or not it would be desirable to treat religious marriages as a contract in the civil sense. Not only because this question is far from simple, but also because an analysis of the implications of

such treatment would exceed the scope of this paper. Under the private international law currently in force in most European countries, the only religious marriage contracts that are at the same time regarded as marriage contracts in the civil sense are those entered into abroad in accordance with the law applicable in a country where marriage is governed by religious law; this is the case, notably, in Islamic countries in Asia, Africa and the Middle East.

33 Regarding this solution, see R. Mehdi, 'Facing the Enigma: Talaq-e-tafweez a need for Muslim women in Nordic Perspective', *International Journal of Sociology of Law*, 2005, pp. 133-147, 141.

34 M. Nys, *L'immigration familiale à l'épreuve du droit*, 2002.

35 Articles 49, 50 and 55, § 2 of the Law of 16 July 2004 holding the Code of private international law (*Belgian Official Gazette*, 27 July 2004).

36 J.-Y. Carlier, *Autonomie de la volonté et statut personnel*, Brussels, Bruylant, 1992.

37 J. Aslam, 'Judicial Oversight of Islamic Family Law Arbitration in Ontario: Ensuring Meaningful Consent and Promoting Multicultural Citizenship', *New York University Journal of International Law and Politics*, 2006, 841ff; J.-Fr. Gaudreault-DesBiens, 'The Limits of Private Justice? The Problems of State Recognition of Arbitral Awards in Family and Personal Status Disputes in Ontario', *World Arbitration and Mediation Report*, 2005 (Vol. 16).

38 R. Gledhill and P. Webster, 'Archbishop of Canterbury argues for Islamic law in Britain', *Times Online*, 8 February 2008, http://www.timesonline.co.uk/tol/comment/faith/article3328024.ece; M. Hickley, 'Islamic sharia courts in Britain are now "legally binding"', *Daily Mail*, 15 September 2008, www.dailymail.co.uk/news/article-1055764/Islamic-sharia-courts-Britain-legally-binding.html; Muslim Arbitration Tribunal, Procedure rules of MAT, www.matribunal.com/procedure_rules.html; S. Bano, 'In Pursuit of Religious and Legal Diversity: A Response to the Archbishop of Canterbury and the shari'a Debate in Britain', *Ecclesiastical Law Journal*, 2008 (10), 283-309; A. Schahar, 'Privatizing Diversity: A Cautionary Tale from Religious Arbitration in Family Law' *Theoretical Inquiries in Law*, 2008 (Vol. 2), pp. 573-607.

39 Which is the fear of, among others, A. Taher, 'Revealed: UK's First Official shari'a Courts', *Times Online*, September 14, 2008, www.timesonline.co.uk/tol/comment/faith/article4749183.ece.

12 Religion, Gender, and Family Law

Critical Perspectives on Integration for Western Muslims

Zainab Alwani and Celene Ayat Lizzio

Introduction

For well over three decades, Muslim scholars and legal experts residing in the West and elsewhere have been engaged in a concerted effort to employ classical legal frameworks and principles to formulate religious rulings appropriate to the Western sociopolitical and cultural milieu. These scholars, in seeking to develop jurisprudence for minorities (*fiqh al-ʿaqalliyyat*), have generated a rich intellectual discourse on how religious laws can both reinforce civic belonging and adapt to meet the practical needs of Muslim-minority populations. For instance, there is broad consensus among such scholars that following the laws of the territory within which one resides is incumbent upon Muslims and that a parallel system of law is unnecessary and undesirable. In general, civil laws attempt to safeguard persons, life, property, family, and human dignity; hence, it is understood that civil codes, Western and otherwise, are roughly in line with the objectives of Muslim religious law.[1] Here, the underlying principle is that key aims of religious law, such as securing the rights of individuals within a family structure, can be secured through civil legislation. This is not to say that the integration of religious and civil norms is not without its particular challenges, both practical and theoretical,[2] but that integration is the most viable path forward.

Holding a collaborative conversation across identity borders on pressing social issues should engender a holistic and productive debate on the history and future of familial ethics and laws. Across Western jurisdictions, legislation related to the family cuts across many domains of the law, creating intricate webs of regulations and procedures spanning local, national, and transcontinental jurisdictions.[3] While the complexity is inherent, and while the current systems are roughly adequate, there is room for bureaucratic streamlining to improve expediency and efficacy. In particular, it should be a priority to close legal loopholes that allow individuals with nefarious intentions to circumvent provisions that are otherwise aimed at securing the stability and financial support of dependant members of the family.[4] It should be seen as part and parcel of Western Muslim civic responsibility to be actively engaged in working toward the betterment of such institutional frameworks for securing justice.[5] Courts, community activists, religious authorities and community support networks must work in tandem to secure the interests of the disenfranchised and vulnerable;[6] this is the ultimate, shared aim.

Debates on integration

The applicability of Muslim family law in Western contexts has been a subject of vigorous debate on the part of lawyers, policymakers, academics, activists, and the general public for decades.[7] For instance, in the early 1990s, a Leiden-based conference entitled 'Religion and Emancipation of Ethnic Minorities in Western Europe' explored the legal rights of ethnic and religious minorities. Arguing for the strengthening of Muslim civic institutions and organizations, as well as for a greater understanding of the existing informal associations, scholars pointed out the various needs for institutional integration.[8] Scholars at the forum also argued for devoting greater attention to how stereotypes, anti-immigrant discrimination, prejudices and other structural dynamics hampers the vitality of ethnic minority and immigrant communities,[9] factors which remain relevant today. Within policy conferences and workshops, religion often takes centre stage; yet, for Muslim populations singled out as problematic or nonconforming, often the most pressing causes of social disintegration are poverty, unemployment, linguistic deficiencies, educational and professional barriers, and in some cases, naturalization policies; at their core, these issues have little to do with religious identity.[10]

Some Western commentators go to great lengths to argue that Western and Islamic values are at odds, for instance by citing gender violence in places such as post-revolutionary Iran and Afghanistan under the Taliban to illustrate misogynistic Muslim tendencies at large.[11] There is no doubt that such deliberate mischaracterizations and cultivated mistrust undermine genuine cooperation across ethnic and religious boundaries and represent an attempt to isolate individuals on the mere basis of their ethnic or religious identity. Indeed, public debates on the integration of religious and ethnic minorities are often characterized by neo-Orientalism or laden with xenophobic sentiments.[12] Yet, to be sure, debates on gender justice are rightfully an issue in terms of the applicability of normative Muslim renditions of familial ethics, in Europe and beyond. Here, the broader socio-political context requires brief elaboration.

The rise of Islamism, which has led to Islamist governments in many Muslim-majority countries as well as fringe groups within some diaspora populations in Europe, has led to a chorus of resounding claims that religious law must be accommodated in the Western context.[13] Such a demand for full-scale adaption of Islamic law typically provides little in the way of an operational framework for determining which religious prescriptions are normative, and which are purely idiosyncratic interpretations of a particular grouping of Muslims that should not be imposed on Muslims at large. Similar to the dynamics within other sizeable religious communities, the matter of defining what norms and practices in fact constitute Islam can readily give rise to acrimonious debate.

Within this context, the conceptual domains of gender and family have functioned as jockeying sites where more deeply-ingrained ideological and postcolonial conflicts are played out. Within intra-Muslim discourses, the familial sphere is often portrayed as the fortress wherein religious identity and so-called traditional values must be protected against the advances of licentious Western capitalist exploitation of women, and various other tribulations.[14] Throughout the colonial era and beyond, the sphere of family and personal status law has been one arena in which classical Islamic legal thought has maintained considerable sway, a trend that is continuing today.[15] Hence, for vocal factions of Muslims, the sphere of family law is regarded as a fundamental stronghold for religious values, and any concessions to perceived Western influence therein are met with particularly vociferous resistance.

Nonetheless, numerous Muslim intellectuals have long been advocating for family law reforms with measurable successes.[16] While substantive changes in family law in Muslim-majority societies have been occurring at a modest pace since the early twentieth century, the most politically and socially repressive Muslim-majority countries are often taken by Western commentators to be *de facto* examples of applied Muslim family law. This overlooks the myriad of cases where indigenous women and men in majority-Muslim societies have been successful in instituting gender-egalitarian reforms;[17] it ignores the vibrant developments in the West itself;[18] and perhaps most strikingly, it neglects to account for how, in the not-so-distant past, women in Europe and beyond had to agitate for basic political and economic rights. Hence, arguing that Muslim women, as a homogeneous category, are somehow uniquely repressed due to Islam itself is misguided; gender-based bigotries and asymmetrical power dynamics are not only pertinent to Muslims, but are central concerns on the agendas of gender activists and queer movements transnationally. A vast literature exists on this subject, and it is not necessary to reproduce it here.

Rather, we proceed with specific theoretical and practical examples of how European Muslims can integrate Muslim familial norms and customs within the civil legal sphere. We aim to forward critical and collaborative conversations by drawing on intellectual debates on these subjects over the past two decades. What is the precedent for Muslims to follow the 'law of the land' when residing in a non-majority Muslim jurisdiction? What specific measures allow for a marriage to be deemed legitimate within both a religious and civil framework? How can religiously-based conceptions of marriage adapt to present-day circumstances while retaining core moral values and ethical integrity?

In exploring such questions, we advance the following propositions: 1) rather than attempting to develop a parallel system for recognizing marriages and divorces, Western Muslims should devote their energy to strengthening existing civil legislation, to developing community support programmes, and to continuing conversations on the roles, rights, and expectations of spouses within an Islamic framework of mutual caring; 2) policymakers, community leaders, and religious authorities must work together to forward policies and enact procedures that allow for integration between religious and civil requirements; and 3) activists, religious and civil together, must work together to ensure that family support services can meet exigent demands without marginalizing the interests of women (or men). In this context, we argue that there are pressing needs to ensure that female community leadership opportunities are on par with those available to the male community, and that women's purviews and areas of expertise must be sought out and represented in a much more concerted fashion.

Continuity and Change in Muslim Notions of Family Rights and Responsibilities

While grounded in more universal objectives, such as guarding human life and dignity, as well as protecting wealth, family, and property, Muslim religious laws have adapted according to a matrix of socio-political, cultural, and economic factors. The sphere of religious law is polyvocal, not only due to intra-Muslim diversity on matters of religious interpretation, but also due to the geographic expanse of Islamic empires, each with customary practices, administrative procedures, and other idiosyncrasies influencing how law was developed and applied. The positive application of law was quite fluid, not only from one region to another, but also from one epoch to the next. Like legal systems the world over, methodology developed by formative scholars took into consideration factors such as prior precedents, exigent circumstances, and social welfare. Within this context, models for family relations developed by Muslim scholarly elites took account of a variety of sources, including scripture, prophetic dictates, dominant customs, perceptions of sexuality and gender, and so on. With all of the aforementioned variables at play, systems for the adjudication of family matters were not static; changing government structures, differing roles for religion in legal jurisdictions, shifting political ideologies, colonialism and its legacy, and particularly in recent times, the greater involvement of women in aspects of political and professional affairs, all have affected the character and range of applications of Muslim family law.[19]

Notwithstanding this plurality, there are several defining characteristics of Muslim family law, as originally worked out by the major interpretive schools of law and now as reinforced by influential factions in the contemporary religious establishment. In this particular account, we take marriage as the primary example, due to its centrality in the system of family law. Marriage in classical Muslim family law is not regarded as a sacrament, but rather as a civil contract of unique importance, due to its centrality as a fundamental organizing principle of society. As a contract, both parties may stipulate their own legally binding expectations and conditions for the arrangement, which if violated can nullify the marriage or otherwise be grounds for divorce. There are numerous gender-based prescriptions that became mainstays of the religiously sanctioned Muslim marriage. By contemporary standards, certain of these prescriptions etched out by medieval legal authorities and defended by an overwhelmingly male-dominated religious establishment are overtly chauvinistic and appear geared to maintaining a patriarchal social order. These include unilateral divorce rights for husbands, the presumption that men are *de facto* heads of households, and exclusively male rights to religiously sanctioned polyandry, within and beyond the framework of marriage.[20]

Yet, within this gender-based division of spousal rights and responsibilities, there are some clear benefits for women. Even early medieval Muslim discussions of family law go to great lengths to consider certain rights of wives, mothers, and children, particularly from a socioeconomic standpoint. For instance, wives entering into Islamic marriages retain independent finances and are not thought of as the property of husbands, and wives are owed a mutually agreed upon monetary or symbolic marital gift to contribute toward their material security. The rights are not purely socioeconomic; wives possess notable legal rights to sexual and emotional satisfaction. There are even some provisions in classical law that could provide inspiration for contemporary women: a wife of a Muslim husband is not *a priori* religiously bound to perform domestic labour if this is not the social norm for her society or station. Under certain circumstances, it is legally possible that if she voluntarily performs such tasks, the husband may be compelled to compensate her monetarily for her labour. From another aspect, Muslim courts in different regions have long recognized a variety of reasons for wife-initiated judicial divorce, some of which bear resemblance to contemporary paradigms of 'no-fault' due to the irrevocable breakdown of the marriage. At the very least, wives had recourse to divorce in cases of a husband's protracted absence or in unfortunate cases where the husband caused marked physical harm to her person. Many other guidelines within family law can be argued to have the wellbeing of the wife as the underlying concern.

This is simply to argue that shari'a law need not be seen as inherently or utterly inimical to the interests of women. Guiding principles for Muslim marriage, and familial ethics more broadly speaking, are firmly vested in the promotion of families as cohesive social units that engender successful progeny and social stability. With this objective in mind, elites considered that the clear articulation of spousal rights and responsibilities would enable greater marital harmony. What contemporary perspectives sometimes interpret as gender inequality, classical authorities and their modern proponents read as a manifestation of justice. Perhaps both perspectives can coexist as a pragmatic compromise between ideological positions; while the institution of marriage has historically upheld a gendered division of marital rights and responsibilities, with a subtle adjustment of the distribution, the framework could be responsive to contemporary socioeconomic circumstances and customary norms.

For instance, within the traditional model of a Muslim family, as endorsed by a consensus of Muslim legal scholars and authorities since the formative period, husbands and fathers are given the sole financial responsibility for the maintenance of the family, including the provision of food, clothing, shelter, and other necessities. A woman's maintenance is theoretically provided for by her guardian until her marriage and her husband thereafter. Any belongings, earnings, and inheritance are entirely her own; she is not, in the theoretical formulation of the law, required to use her wealth or income for any of her basic needs or the needs of her children.

While full financial support can be seen as a women's perk within Islamic religious law, in times of increasing global financial insecurity and widespread unemployment, particularly among young adult populations, this model for family finances is no longer practicable or sustainable. A husband should not have to shoulder the financial, physical, and emotional burdens of supporting a family unilaterally. This is particularly true if his wife has a secure job and earns more than he does, a trend that may very well be on the rise. Here, rather than maintaining outdated frameworks that posit the husband as the sole breadwinner and hence authority, a paradigm of reciprocity is more appropriate. After all, it is a well-recognized principle in Islamic law that changing times necessitate changing measures, and this principle applies here. Well intended though they may be, classical gendered models for family finances must be reconsidered in light of current economic and social realities. There is no compelling reason to continue to buttress a gendered division of marital finances. Furthermore, if marital finances are no longer gendered, the principle of the man as the *de facto* head of the household becomes an appendage that serves little purpose and can be reengineered, given the current custom and exigent needs.

This is one cursory example of how principles of family law may be adjusted from within the framework of religion itself. For religiously committed Muslims, the process will require a sustained commitment to reasoned debate and deliberation.[21] As noted above, Muslim legal provisions have, in principle, strived to remain in touch with the particular characteristics, customs, and circumstances of local populations while also safeguarding more universal concerns for equity, security, and individual responsibility. The present is no exception. Yet, the scale and pace of this process of drawing from religious texts and traditions to inform contemporary realities have to keep pace with ever-growing populations and ever more sophisticated institutions and bureaucratic structures.

Getting Married: Recommendations for Western Muslims

While the previous example of how to preserve continuity while adapting to circumstantial changes was more theoretically oriented, the following example is more practically geared. The goal of our prescriptions is to balance unity and uniformity with particularity; that is, we maintain the fundamental integrity of the civil framework for recognizing marriage while at the same time legitimize, and in fact advocate for, several uniquely Muslim considerations for marriage. It is to the aspects of uniformity that we first turn.

To better protect the rights of spouses and children, Muslim leaders in the Western context, and particularly *imams*, to whom the task of performing marriage ceremonies is commonly given, should require their constituencies to register marriage contracts with Western civil authorities *before* a religious marriage ceremony is conducted.[22] The *de facto* authority for resolving disputes should be the civil jurisdiction. This standard should serve to integrate families wholly within the Western legal system to avoid complicated and unreliable recourse to international private law for the purposes of securing state-endowed rights or for the purposes of settling any disputes that could arise in Western civil courts. For couples married outside of the West but currently holding legal status within Western states, we recommend that marriages also be registered with civil authorities in the West, where possible. Domicile should be the primary standard, only to be supplemented with factors such as nationality and party autonomy when deemed necessary.[23]

At a basic level, registry could better ensure that adequate records are present in cases of dispute over marital finances, the paternity of children, or other such affairs. It would also ensure that Western civil courts recognize the marital union and can have the authority to dissolve the marriage if necessary. Furthermore, traditional religious frameworks for recognizing marriage are pluralistic, and at times the line between what counts as a valid marriage and what does not is ambiguous.[24] Setting the clear expectation that marriages be registered with civil authorities is one step in resolving such ambiguity. The fact that judges sitting on such courts may not be Muslim does not constitute a barrier. As long as the civil authority is known to be reliable and accurate in its records, and there is no evidence to the contrary, there is no compelling reason for Muslims not to rely on civil authorities. In this case, the purpose of having two upright witnesses is adequately fulfilled by the bureaucratic institution.

It merits noting that the support of civil institutions is not to envision that Western laws pertaining to the family are unadulterated, or are otherwise capable of surpassing or escaping the confusion and even rancour that can characterize family disputes; rather, it is to affirm that civil registry of a marriage in no way conflicts with any religious principle, and in fact, civil registry can effectively safeguard the rights of partners in the contract. It provides a more reliable and bureaucratically advanced framework than that which fledgling Western Muslim communities are able to offer at present. Muslim spouses could still make recourse to religiously grounded family mediation and arbitration services to assist with the resolution of certain extrajudicial issues. We argue below that the availability, credibility, and resource-base of such services should be strengthened, but that they should not form a substitute for the civil registry of marriage and divorce, or the resolution of any disputes that require the involvement of civil authorities.

In the model that we are advocating, religious networks represent an important but auxiliary form of mediation. For the reasons stated above, the civil jurisdiction must have ultimate authority. There is no harm in having a religiously oriented commemoration of the marriage, but to avoid confusion and to protect the rights of all parties, as well as the rights of any potential children that could come from the union, such a ceremony should ideally be conducted only after the civil contract is filed. While we encourage Muslims to register marriages and divorces with civil authorities, we maintain that the Muslim notion of a marriage contract is a useful tool for couples to articulate their expectations for the marriage. The contract can specifically state that it is supplementary to the civil contract, and Muslim witnesses, two upright men or two upright women, can sign.[25]

For instance, traditional formulae for Muslim unions provide opportunities to recognize conditions and stipulations. While the stipulations and conditions specified may not have *de facto* legal value within the civil framework of the law, as they might within a purely religious court, civil courts may look into the conditions and stipulations of the religious contract to help discern the intent of the parties at the time of marriage, should a legal conflict arise. The contract offers an opportunity for the couple to develop and clearly document how they will approach the idiosyncrasies of their marriage: where will the couple reside? Will a spouse pursue higher education? There are a host of questions for consideration, on which a new couple should have the opportunity to reflect in an environment that can reinforce religious values in marriage, such as kindness, reciprocity, patience, forgiveness, and mutual support. Muslim communities should provide the framework for new and potential couples to consider such preliminaries. While polygamy is somewhat of a mute point for Muslims maintaining Western domicile, since Western laws clearly prohibit multiple marriage partners, nevertheless the marriage contract is also a forum where a wife can reiterate, if relevant, her expectation of a monogamous marriage.

The marriage contract traditionally functions as documentation of the *mahr*, the gift bestowed upon the wife by the husband, or otherwise promised to her.[26] In the Western context, if the gifts bestowed have a significant monetary value, documentation of the exchange with the couple's signatures can be notarized to avoid later disagreements on the value of the gifts bestowed. For devout Muslims, key financial aspects of the marriage, namely the *nafaqa*, the obligation of the husband to provide a wife with financial support for housing, food, clothing, and other necessities, as well as *ʿidda,* the alimony paid by the husband during the period of marital disillusionment, remain a religious obligation which may or may not be deemed relevant in a civil court. We recommend that bank records be kept, if necessary, to prove that such sums were paid, should a legal need for proof arise. In short, financial settlements between the spouses in the event of a divorce should fall under the ultimate authority of civil jurisdictions, which are better equipped to enforce decisions equitably. In order to secure justice in such cases involving *mahr, nafaqa*, and *ʿidda*, Western courts should employ a comparative legal method and gender justice approach, the theoretical underpinnings of which have already been articulated.[27]

As the number of devout Muslims residing in the West rises, so too does the need for individuals with the appropriate religious training and background to make legal guidance and pastoral care readily available, not to mention the need for other social services that together form a more cohesive support structure for families.[28] As practitioners who have worked extensively at the community level on issues concerning the family, we cannot emphasize this point enough. It is not merely in the domain of law at the national level where conversations on this topic need to be occurring, but perhaps even more so, it is at the local level where needs are most pressing and interventions would be felt most directly. For instance, Western Muslim organizations should build their capacities in order to offer wider marital counselling services, led by teams of professionals with competence in religious matters, the behavioural sciences, and law.[29]

Providing such family support should not fall to the *imam* of a community, who is unlikely to have the professional training or resources necessary to meet the demand. Neither should such a task fall to an ad hoc tribunal, particularly not the kind that charges exorbitant fees for services. Finally, all-male councils risk marginalizing women's interests and are no longer acceptable according to modern standards. If it is not possible to find female members to sit on such councils – which would be highly unlikely – then female-specific training programmes should be an upmost priority. The goal should be to make readily available locally tailored, affordable, gender-balanced, professionally competent, non-binding family dispute mediation and arbitration services, as well as other holistic programmes aimed at strengthening families.[30] Drawing on the expertise of social scientists and community-based professionals with expertise working at the family level would be particularly valuable in this context.

Conclusion

Societies the world over have been actively deriving mechanisms and procedures for secular laws and religious values to coexist for centuries, such that the case of contemporary Western Muslims is best understood as an unavoidable facet of cosmopolitan civic life, rather than a peculiar exception to it. That said, each society has its own political philosophies, legal structures, and cultural dynamics. Hence, our argument is not directed toward providing a singular, comprehensive model for the integration of religious values within largely secular systems; rather, we have provided recommendations, guided by current research and time-tested principles, for how Western Muslims and their partners can facilitate social and legal integration at the level of families. We firmly hold that advocating for norms drawn directly from pre-modern Muslim legal discourses, without a full consideration of their outcomes and effects in specific Western contexts, is entirely counterproductive.

Given the preceding discussions, the best path is to seek out continuity in aims between religious and civil law, and to work within existing systems to enhance their efficiency. As many Muslim-majority locals move towards even greater reform of their family and personal status law codes to reflect current transnational standards, it would be reasonable to expect that conversations engendered by Western Muslims and lawmakers would impact these wider deliberations. New models for Western Muslim familial ethics stand to add valuable insights to, and reap insights from, negotiations of this type that have long been taking place in Muslim-majority societies. Namely, strengthening organizations and community networks that cater to family support should be a high priority. Policy leaders need to continue to work across religious and national boundaries to establish best practices and forums for collaborative engagement. Western partners need to help craft systems of family dispute arbitration that are relevant to the needs and customs of local Muslim communities. Western Muslims and their partners can continue to work to forward a civic discourse that mitigates xenophobia and Islamophobia. So, too, investments of time, resources, and creative energies are needed from all parties to help institute holistic solutions for meeting the exigent needs of vulnerable populations.

Notes

1 See the arguments of Tāhā Jābir Fayyād Alwānī, *Towards A Fiqh for Minorities: Some Basic Reflections,* London; Washington: International Institute of Islamic Thought, 2003.

2 For a detailed account thereof see Andrea Büchler, *Islamic Law in Europe? Legal Pluralism and its Limits in European Family Laws,* Surrey, England; Burlington, VT: Ashgate, 2011; Julie MacFarlane, *Islamic Divorce in North America: A Shari'a Path in a Secular Society,* New York: Oxford University Press, 2012.

3 See Dieter Martiny, 'Is Unification of Family Law Feasible or Even Desirable?' in Arthur S. Hartkamp, Ewoud Hondius, Chantal Mak and Edgar du Perron (eds.), *Towards a European Civil Code,* Alphen a/d Rijn/London: Kluwer Law International BV, 2011, pp. 429-57.

4 On the incompetence of a handful of tribunals in the United Kingdom, see Irfan al-Alawi, Stephen S. Schwartz, Kamal Hasani, Veli Sirin, Daut Dauti and Qanta Ahmed, *A Guide to Shariah Law and Islamist Ideology in Western Europe, 2007-2009,* London: Center for Islamic Pluralism, 2009, pp. 44-49.

5 See related discussions in Andrew F. March, 'Sources of Moral Obligation to Non-Muslims in the "Jurisprudence of Muslim Minorities" (*Fiqh al-aqalliyyāt*) Discourse,' *Islamic Law & Society* 2009 (Vol. 16, No. 1), pp. 34-94.

6 For a model approach, see Marie-Claire Foblets, 'Migrant Women Caught between Islamic Family Law and Women's Rights: The Search for the Appropriate "Connecting Factor" in International Family Law,' *Maastricht Journal of European and Comparative Law,* 2000, (Vol. 7, No. 1), pp. 11-34.

7 See Jonathan Laurence, *The Emancipation of Europe's Muslims: The State's Role in Minority Integration,* Princeton, N.J.: Princeton University Press, 2012.

8 J.D.J. Waardenburg, 'Muslim Associations and Official Bodies in some European Countries,' and J.S. Nielsen, 'Muslim Organizations in Europe: Integration or Isolation?' in W.A.R. Shadid and P.S. van Koningsveld (eds.), *The Integration of Islam and Hinduism in Western Europe,* Kampen: Kok Pharos Publishing House, 1991, pp. 24-42 and 43-59.

9 See W.A.R. Shadid and P. S. van Koningsveld, 'Blaming the System or Blaming the Victim? Structural Barriers Facing Muslims in Western Europe,' in Shadid and van Koningsveld, *The Integration of Islam,* 1991, pp. 2-21.

10 M. Rohe, *Muslim Minorities and the Law in Europe: Chances and Challenges,* New Delhi: Global Media Publications, 2007, p. 15; see also J. S. Nielsen, *Muslims in Western Europe,* Edinburgh: Edinburgh University Press Ltd., 2004, 1st ed. 1992, pp. 101-104; and Jocelyne Cesari, 'Islamophobia in the West: A Comparison between Europe and the United States,' in John L. Esposito and Ibrahim Kalin (eds.), *Islamophobia: The Challenge of Pluralism in the 21st Century,* Oxford: Oxford University Press, 2011, pp. 11-24 and particularly pp. 25-27.

11 Sonya Fernandez, 'The Crusade over the Bodies of Women,' *Patterns of Prejudice,* 2009 (Vol. 43, Nos. 3-4), pp. 269-286.

12 For a detailed account, see Fatima El-Tayeb, *European Others: Queering Ethnicity in Postnational Europe,* Minneapolis: University of Minnesota Press, 2011.

13 Irfan al-Alawi *et al.*, *A Guide to Shariah Law and Islamist Ideology in Western Europe*, 2009.

14 For one regional analysis, see Gamze Çavdar, 'Islamist Moderation and the Resilience of Gender: Turkey's Persistent Paradox,' *Totalitarian Movements and Political Religions* 11, 2010 (Nos. 3-4). pp. 341-357, see especially pp. 348-350.

15 For an account of the codification and reform of Muslim family law codes with some comparison to the history of European family law codification, see Nielsen, *Muslims in Western Europe*, 2004, pp. 108-110.

16 Hanne Petersen, 'Women, Secular and Religious Laws and Traditions: Gendered Secularization, Gendering shariʿa,' in Jørgen S. Nielsen, and Lisbet Christoffersen (eds.), *Sharia as Discourse: Legal Traditions and the Encounter with Europe*, Farnham, Surrey UK; Burlington, VT: Ashgate, 2009, pp. 77-88; see also related discussions in Margot Badran, *Feminism in Islam: Secular and religious convergences*, Oxford: Oneworld Publications, 2009.

17 See for example Yakaré Oulé-Jansen, 'Muslim Brides and the Ghost of *Shari'a*: Have the Recent Law Reforms in Egypt, Tunisia, and Morocco Improved Women's Position in Marriage and Divorce and Can Religious Moderates Bring Reform and Make it Stick?', *Northwestern Journal of International Human Rights*, 2007 (Vol. 5, No. 2), pp. 181-212.

18 For one example, see discussions in Robin Griffith-Jones, *Islam and English Law*, Cambridge: Cambridge University Press, 2013.

19 Frances Susan Hasso, *Consuming Desires: Family Crisis and the State in the Middle East*, Stanford, CA: Stanford University Press, 2011.

20 For an extended analysis, see Kecia Ali, *Marriage and Slavery in Early Islam*, Cambridge: Harvard University Press, 2010.

21 For an apt framework for engagement, see Tariq Ramadan, *Western Muslims and the Future of Islam*, Oxford; New York: Oxford University Press, 2004, particularly pp. 9-10, 51-55, 109-115. On the role of religious reason in the political process see Jeffery Stout, *Democracy and Tradition*, Princeton: Princeton University Press, 2004, pp. 63-91.

22 For an analysis of the opinions of leading European authorities for and against civil registry of marriages, see Vit Sisler, 'European Courts' Authority Contested? The Case of Marriage and Divorce Fatwas On-line,' *Masaryk University Journal of Law and Technology* 2009 (Vol. 3, No. 1), pp. 51-78. See also Bowen, *Can Islam be French?*, pp. 165-70.

23 On the pros and cons of the various approaches, see Marie-Claire Foblets, 'Migrant Women Caught between Islamic Family Law and Women's Rights, 2000, pp. 20-25.

24 For ethnographic examples, see Bowen, *Can Islam be French?*, pp. 157-165.

25 For a woman's witness carrying equal weight to that of a man, see Tāhā Jābir Fayyād Alwānī, 'The Testimony of Women in Islamic Law,' trans. Yusuf DeLorenzo, in *The American Journal of Islamic Social Sciences*, 1996 (Vol. 13, No. 2), pp. 173-96; see also Fadel, Mohammad, 'Two Women, One Man: Knowledge, Power and Gender in Medieval Sunni Legal Thought', *International Journal of Middle East Studies* 1997 (Vol. 29, No. 2), pp. 185-204.

26 Substantial attention has already been devoted to this topic, see Rubya Mehdi and Jørgen S. Nielsen, *Embedding Mahr (Islamic Dower) in the European Legal System*, Portland: International Specialized Book Services, 2011. See also Pascale Fournier, *Muslim Marriage in Western Courts: Lost in Translation*, Burlington, VT: Ashgate, 2012.

27 As detailed in Lene Løvdal, 'Mahr and Gender Equality in Private International Law: The Adjudication of Mahr in England, France, Norway and Sweden,' in *Embedding Mahr*, 2011, pp. 77-112.

28 Such discussions are already emerging at the community level, e.g. Aneesah and Zarinah Nadir, 'License to Wed: Muslim couples need to weigh legal issues entailed by married life,' *Islamic Horizons*, 2012 (Vol. 41, No. 1), pp. 55-54.

29 For one successful model see Mohamed Keshavjee, *The Ismaili Alternative Dispute Resolution Training Programmes and the Potential for New Directions in Mediation*, London: Institute for Ismaili Studies, 2007.

30 European courts should not be obligated to enforce the recommendations of such committees; however, expert testimony of such a gender-balanced and professionally competent committee could be valuable in some cases. See related discussion in Al-Alawi *et al.*, *A Guide to Shariah Law, 2007-2009*, p. 39.

13 Reflections on the Development of the Discourse of *Fiqh* for Minorities and Some of the Challenges it Faces

Abdullah Saeed

This chapter examines the context of and debate surrounding *fiqh al-'aqalliyyat* (*fiqh* for Muslim minorities, hereafter named '*fiqh* for minorities'). After defining and outlining the concept of *fiqh* for minorities, the concept is then examined in relation to its historical development in classical Islamic law. As there is a substantial amount of debate about *fiqh* for minorities, some of its assumed benefits are examined, along with the objections that various critics have made to it. Finally, some observations are made with regard to the nature of the challenges it faces today.

Defining *Fiqh* for Minorities

Fiqh for minorities has been defined as 'a specific discipline which takes into account the relationship between the religious ruling and the conditions of the community and the location where it exists.'[1] This *fiqh* consists of a contextual application of the rules and principles of the primary sources of Islamic law, and is rooted in a recognition and appreciation of the specific conditions facing Muslims who are living as minorities.[2] In particular, this approach appears to reinterpret those elements of classical Islamic law (*fiqh*) that, owing to historical changes in Muslims' circumstances, have become largely obsolete.[3]

Fiqh for minorities aims to address the problems that arise every day for millions of Muslims living in the West or in similar minority situations, particularly where conflict arises between the culture and values of the host society and the rules and the framework provided by classical Islamic law.[4] Shaykh Abdullah bin Bayyah, vice-president of the Qatar-based International Union of Muslim Scholars and a proponent of *fiqh* for minorities, has indicated that in situations that are defined as being of 'a problematic nature' or involving 'hardship,' *fiqh* for minorities outlines the minimum that is expected of a Muslim living in minority.[5] According to another opinion, *fiqh* for minorities is shaped by the broader aims of shariʿa (*maqasid al-shariʿa*), in the sense that shariʿa 'permits all that is good and wholesome and forbids what is harmful,' and hence is 'aimed at making life easier and more convenient.'[6] In terms of its scope, *fiqh* for minorities addresses personal law related issues as well as matters of ritual and worship (*ibadah*). In this way, it covers a wide spectrum of issues relating to daily life.

The term *fiqh al-aqalliyyat* was only recently introduced into the discourse. It was first used in the 1990s by two prominent Muslim religious figures: Shaykh Taha Jabir al-Alwani (who was then based in the US) and Shaykh Yusuf al-Qaradawi (who lives in Qatar).[7] Al-Alwani appears to have used the term *fiqh al-aqalliyyat* for the first time in 1994 when the *Fiqh* Council of North America, under his presidency, issued a legal opinion (*fatwa*) declaring that American Muslims are permitted to vote in American elections.[8] Despite the many subsequent contributions to this area by a range of scholars, al-Alwani remains, in my view, its most important contemporary theoretician: he continues to contribute not only *fatwas*, but also a range of concepts and methodological tools. He is also at the forefront of those who are arguing for a more principled approach to *fiqh* for minorities.

Muslim Residence in Non-Muslim Territory in the Prophetic Period

While the status of Muslim minorities residing in non-Muslim territory has been the subject of Muslim juristic debate since at least the second century of Islam,[9] it appears that the issue of Muslims living under non-Muslim 'rule' arose among Muslims earlier, and initially during the time of the Prophet Muhammad. The Qur'anic verses view the presence of Muslims among non-Muslims in Mecca during the time of the Prophet (610-622 CE) as normal. It was only after the Prophet Muhammad had established a 'Muslim territory' in Medina (following his migration from Mecca in 622 CE) that the Qur'an asked the Meccan Muslims to migrate to Medina[10] as a way of consolidating and strengthening the Muslim community there. However, this instruction did not appear to be a general command for Muslims to migrate from a 'non-Muslim' territory to Muslim lands as such.

On a number of occasions, the Qur'an appears to indicate that what matters is not whether Muslims live in predominantly non-Muslim territories, but whether they are free from oppression and persecution and able to practise their religion in such places. The Prophet Muhammad even encouraged his followers to flee persecution in Mecca and to seek refuge with a Christian ruler in Abyssinia where they had the freedom to practise their religion. When his teaching spread across Arabia, the Prophet seems to have accepted the fact that individual Muslims would live amongst predominantly non-Muslim communities, as was the case with Muslims who converted to Islam but preferred to live in their own non-Muslim tribes.

Muslim Residence in Non-Muslim Territory Under Classical Islamic law

Although Muslims lived in non-Muslim majority contexts from the earliest times of Islam, there was no systematic treatment by jurists of the issue of Muslims living under non-Muslim rule between the seventh and eleventh centuries CE, probably because such presence on a large scale was not regarded as 'normal'.[11] However, some opinions were expressed by early jurists that were later taken up by other jurists in the development of their positions on the issue. Imam Malik (d. 769), who represented the most strict school of law with regard to Muslim residence under non-Muslim rule, believed that Muslims should not reside in non-Muslim territories. He disapproved of Muslims travelling to non-Muslim lands, even for business.[12] Other scholars were more flexible: Abu Hanifa (d. 767) permitted residence for Muslims in non-Muslim territory as long as it was not permanent. Shafi'i (d. 820) allowed Muslims to reside in non-Muslim territories if there was no danger of their being enticed away from their religion. The Hanafi jurist Shaybani (d. 805) argued that Muslims were not obliged to migrate from a non-Muslim territory to a Muslim one. Tabari (d. 923) held that a Muslim's ability to practise his religion was the key consideration in any discussion about the permissibility of residence. For the Ja'faris (Shi'a), it might even be better to reside in a non-Muslim territory in some cases, because that territory might be free from persecution and oppression.[13]

Dar al-Islam and Dar al-kufr

Related to the issue of residence is the question of the kind of 'abode' (*dar*) in which a Muslim may reside. While various 'abodes' are recognized in juristic literature, much of the discussion surrounds *dar al-islam* (abode of Islam) and *dar al-kufr* (abode of unbelief), the latter sometimes referred to as *dar al-harb* (the abode of war or enemy territory). While jurists distinguished between the two abodes and often believed that it was not acceptable to reside outside *dar al-islam*, there was no agreed upon conception of what could be considered the *dar al-Islam* or abode of Islam. For the Hanafi jurist al-Kasani (d. 1191), *dar al-islam* was where shari'a was manifest and implemented. For Shafi'i scholars, 'territorial control' determined whether the place was *dar al-islam*.[14] Other scholars argued that in addition to territorial control, Muslims should be living in security for the territory to be considered the abode of Islam.[15]

While it was preferable for Muslims to live in *dar al-islam* (however defined), living in *dar al-kufr* or *dar al-harb* was often discouraged, if not outright prohibited. In the pre-modern context there was a predominant belief that it was only possible for a Muslim to live an identifiably 'Islamic' life under the rule of shari'a. This, in turn, could only occur within the context of an Islamic polity dedicated to its application.[16] Thus, jurists saw a clear dichotomy between the abode of Islam, where shari'a ruled, and the abode of unbelief, where shari'a had no place.[17] There were also other reasons for this discomfort. By residing in the abode of unbelief, a Muslim could be perceived as inadvertently strengthening the 'enemy' and they might acquire Islamically unacceptable or undesirable values or norms from the predominantly non-Muslim context.[18]

Equally, the notion of the 'supremacy of Islam' over other religions (a belief that was then widely held in Islamic theology and law) could not be maintained in such an environment. In addition, Muslims might not be able to practise their religion as they should, and there was a chance that Muslims might convert to the dominant religion, thus leading to the spread of apostasy (*riddah*). Moreover, at a social level, non-Muslim norms and customs in many contexts were considered somehow inappropriate for Muslims. Thus for most jurists, the idea of Muslims living outside the abode of Islam was problematic. It was therefore generally presumed that Muslims living in *dar al-kufr* would migrate back to the *dar al-islam*. In the meantime, it was understood that these 'displaced' Muslims would preserve their religious and cultural identity by isolating themselves from their host societies.[19]

Development of the Discourse on *Fiqh* for Minorities

While it was easy to hold and maintain such views up to the eleventh century CE or so, this began to change as the political and military dominance of Muslims began to be challenged and large areas formerly under Muslim rule came under non-Muslim governance. Although the situation varied from place to place and from time to time, in Spain under Christian rule, for example, as Christians reconquered parts of Islamic Spain, the freedom to practise Islam gradually deteriorated, particularly from the thirteenth century CE. In many cases, Muslims had to live under severe restrictions or were forced to convert to Christianity. Muslims living under such conditions had to seek *fatwas* as to what they should do. At that time, some scholars argued that they should migrate to Muslim lands where they would have the freedom to practise their religion; while others argued they should stay in Spain and practise their religion as much as possible.

As large numbers of Muslims came under non-Muslim rule, not only in Spain, but also in Sicily, and even in predominantly Muslim majority lands, such as those that came under Mongol rule during the thirteenth century CE, Muslim jurists had to address the situation and deal with legal issues in a more systematic manner. A number of scholars today highlight this fundamental change to the jurisprudential discourse. For example, after the loss of Toledo in Spain in 1085 CE, while Muslims had previously experienced territorial losses,[20] the resulting geopolitical changes were matched by a documented juridical response by Muslim scholars. A rich body of *fatwa* literature related to these changing circumstances was gathered, for instance, by the North African Maliki scholar, Ahmad al-Wansharisi (d. 1508), among others.[21]

Such *fatwas* and other juristic views were issued to guide the Muslims who were then living under such conditions. However, the need to develop jurisprudence to address the context of living in a minority has become even more crucial over the past two centuries. The second half of the twentieth century is particularly important in this regard, given the large number of Muslims who willingly migrated to non-Muslim lands, particularly in Europe and North America. It is this Muslim presence that has led to the current discourse of *fiqh* for minorities.

The Modern Discourse of *Fiqh* for Minorities

In the modern period, *fiqh* for minorities has identified that Muslim minorities, especially those residing in the West, require a specific legal discipline to address their unique religious needs, which differ from those of Muslims residing in Muslim majority countries.[22] According to al-Alwani, the purpose of *fiqh* for minorities is not to recreate Islam, but to provide a set of methodologies that govern how a jurist should work within the existing flexibility of the religion to best apply it to particular circumstances.[23] For al-Alwani, *fiqh* for minorities is essentially derived from the general *fiqh* of Islam as a whole, but it focuses on issues that affect Muslim minorities living among non-Muslim majorities who are endeavouring to preserve their identities under somewhat different customs, legislation and laws.[24] As such, Muslim minorities are living under particular conditions and they have special needs that may not be appropriate for other communities.[25] This therefore requires a discipline, with input from specialists from different social and religious disciplines, so that problems can be articulated accurately and solutions found based on a common approach, broadly based on the universally accepted fundamentals of the Qur'an and Sunna.[26]

In comparison to al-Alwani's approach, most modern Muslim jurists still appear to treat the situation of Muslim minorities as a highly exceptional case that requires special consideration.[27] They tend to approach the range of questions relating to laws about food, dress, marriage, divorce, co-education and relations with non-Muslims in terms of expediency. Consequently, the interpretations are often varied.[28] A wide range of concepts from Islamic jurisprudence, including the common good, the objective or spirit of law, convenience, common practice, necessity and prevention of harm have also gained significance in this discourse.[29]

Advantages of a Separate Branch of *Fiqh* for Minorities

Proponents of *fiqh* for minorities argue that developing a specific branch of jurisprudence for minorities has a number of advantages. They claim that the approach will help address the daily problems that arise for millions of Muslim individuals living in the West or in similar minority situations.[30] One advantage claimed for *fiqh* for minorities is that it will ensure that the religious life of the Muslim minority is protected on both a personal and a collective level.[31] In this regard, al-Alwani has pointed out that the key challenge faced by Western Muslims (and Muslim minorities elsewhere) today is how to ensure their integration into these societies without losing their religious identity.[32] *Fiqh* for minorities is believed to be of benefit to Muslims in majority contexts as well.

Although some of the problems addressed by this branch of jurisprudence may appear to be urgent for Muslims in the West, ultimately, the whole of the Muslim world will have to respond to the issues that are being raised (such as gender equality, for instance)[33] as the world becomes more globalized and as Muslim-majority societies are increasingly faced with the influence of modernity. Another advantage claimed for *fiqh* for minorities is that it may improve relations with non-Muslims on a cultural and international level, by creating a clear framework for mutual understanding. *Fiqh* for minorities may also bring benefits for the discipline of *fiqh* itself, by allowing issues of law to be understood from a new perspective.

Despite these potential benefits, this project has been heavily criticized by a number of influential Muslim scholars. The American Shaykh Nuh Keller and the Syrian Shaykh Buti are among the best known critics of *fiqh* for minorities. Shaykh Nuh Keller's objections are twofold. Firstly, he rejects the idea that 'exceptions' should be created for Muslim minorities. He argues that exceptions have already been built into shariʿa, case-by-case, and that each situation should be decided based on its own merits,[34] not by a wholesale generalization. In his view, the approach adopted by *fiqh* for minorities is a form of 'sloppy thinking' and it results in 'bad *fiqh*.'[35] Secondly, he argues that *fiqh* for minorities creates two sets of standards: one for Muslims in Muslim-majority countries, and another for Muslims in Muslim-minority contexts. For Keller, this means that, 'anybody who is in a minority… has an excuse to behave [differently] than [those in] countries where Muslims are a majority.'[36] On the other hand, Shaykh Buti posits that there are no such things as minorities and majorities in Islamic legal thought. He argues that shariʿa, as a system of law, is only applied in *dar al-Islam*, not *dar al-kufr*.[37]

For these critics, there is nothing specific to the situation of minorities that justifies a different treatment in law; they argue that the entire project of *fiqh* for minorities should be rejected on this basis. Although adherents to this view acknowledge that the application of Islamic law should take context into account to a certain extent, they emphasize that Islam is one religion and that there is no justifiable reason for a separate project of Islamic law for minorities. For them, *fiqh* for minorities is an unnecessary departure from the classical conception of Islamic law. They argue that personal juridical reasoning (*ijtihad*) should be used to solve these problems, bearing in mind specific circumstances, rather than adopting a whole new *fiqh*.[38] For them, there is no need to develop a separate branch of jurisprudence for minorities.

There are other criticisms of *fiqh* for minorities as well. One is that *fiqh* for minorities is a form of innovation in religion (*bid'ah*) that must be rejected. Legal positions and views that came to be accepted as 'standard' in classical Islamic law are, from this perspective, to be respected and maintained. Proponents of *fiqh* for minorities may respond by noting that there have been differences of opinion among the jurists on practically every single Islamic legal problem, and that the so-called standard views are frequently challenged by other jurists. In their view there is no 'innovation' in *fiqh* for minorities, as far as the substance and content are concerned. The only innovation is the new label that is being used.

Fiqh for minorities can also be criticized because it appears to be based on somewhat subjective considerations, rather than clear principles of jurisprudence and rules of interpretation. This arguably makes *fiqh* for minorities extremely subjective and therefore of questionable legitimacy. *Fiqh* for minorities can also be seen as a discourse that appears to adopt a somewhat paternalistic attitude towards Muslims living in minority contexts. By focusing on solutions that aim to make life more convenient or easier for Muslims in minority contexts,[39] *fiqh* for minorities appears to present the view that Muslims in minority contexts are less able to fulfil the same obligations as Muslims who live in majority contexts. A related idea is that by permitting certain practices that are considered prohibited (*haram*) in Muslim-majority contexts (based on the legal maxim that necessity justifies such practices), *fiqh* for minorities promotes the perception that a diluted approach to Islam is generally acceptable in minority contexts.

Naturally, proponents of *fiqh* for minorities have responded directly to such criticisms, although despite the contributions of figures like al-Alwani, many supporters of *fiqh* for minorities still appear to be uninterested in asking fundamental questions about Islamic law, principles of jurisprudence, or the interpretation of texts as they issue *fatwas* relating to Muslim minority concerns.

Towards a More Principled Approach?

Much of *fiqh* for minorities is based on the idea that the positions developed in classical Islamic law (and upon which there is broad agreement among jurists) must be seen as the standard for Muslims today. However, in the case of minorities, where there is some flexibility in the legal tradition (for instance, in the form of differing opinions among the jurists or different interpretations of a particular text), this can be used to provide a more lenient view, opinion or a *fatwa*. The underlying position of the proponents of *fiqh* for minorities, with very few exceptions, seems to be that there is no need to rethink, in any fundamental way, principles of jurisprudence or rules of interpretation. Two examples are noted here.

Example 1: A Muslim woman's marriage to a non-Muslim

Classical Islamic law is reasonably clear that a Muslim woman may not remain married to a non-Muslim man. For Muslims living in the West, this classical legal position has become difficult to maintain, especially because of the circumstances in which some conversions take place. Some proponents of *fiqh* for minorities have therefore proposed, based on certain minority views in classical Islamic law, that it is acceptable for a non-Muslim man and woman to remain married, even if one of the spouses becomes a Muslim. In what follows, this famous *fatwa* on this issue, while recognizing the difficulties posed by the almost unanimous position in Islamic law that a Muslim woman may not marry or remain married to a non-Muslim man, accommodates the present situation (particularly in Western contexts):[40]

> The Council also recognizes and acknowledges the conditions in which new Muslim sisters in the West find themselves when their husbands choose to retain their religion. The Council affirms and repeats that it is forbidden for a Muslim female to establish marriage to a non-Muslim male. This has been an issue of consensus throughout the history of this nation. However, in the case of marriage being established prior to the female entering the fold of Islam, the Council has decided the following:
>
> First: If both husband and wife revert to Islam and there is no shariʿah objection to their marriage in the first place, such as blood or foster relations, which deem the very establishment of marriage unlawful, the marriage shall be deemed valid and correct.
>
> Second: Assuming that the marriage is properly contracted in the beginning, if the husband reverts to Islam alone, while his wife remains a Jew or a Christian, then the marriage shall maintain its validity, i.e. it will not be affected by the husband's conversion to Islam.
>
> Third: If the wife reverts to Islam while her husband remains on his religion, the Council sees the following:
> 1) If her reversion to Islam occurs before the consummation of marriage, then they must immediately separate.
> 2) If her reversion to Islam occurs after the consummation of marriage, and the husband also embraced Islam before the expiry of her period of waiting [ʿ*iddah*], then the marriage is deemed valid and correct.

> 3) If her reversion to Islam occurs after the consummation of marriage, and the period of waiting expires, *she is allowed to wait for him to embrace Islam even if that period happens to be a lengthy one.* Once he does so and reverts to Islam, then their marriage is deemed valid and correct [emphasis added].
> 4) If the wife chooses to marry another man after the expiration of the period of waiting, she must first request a dissolution of marriage through legal channels.
>
> Fourth: According to the four main schools of jurisprudence, it is forbidden for the wife to remain with her husband, or indeed to allow him conjugal rights, once her period of waiting has expired. *However, some scholars see that it is for her to remain with him, allowing him to enjoy full conjugal rights, if he does not prevent her from exercising her religion and she has hope in him to revert to Islam* [emphasis added]. The reason for this is to consider the case of women who would find it difficult to embrace Islam with the condition of being separated from their husbands and deserting their families. Those scholars based their view upon the ruling of Umar b. al-Khattab, may Allah be pleased with him, in the case of the woman from al-Hira who reverted to Islam while her husband remained on his religion. According to the authentic narration of Yazid b. Abd Allah al-Khatmi, Umar b. al-Khattab made it optional for the woman to leave her husband or to stay with him. They also cite, in supporting their view, the opinion of Ali b. Abi Talib concerning the Christian woman who embraced Islam while still married to a Christian or a Jew. Ali said that her husband's conjugal right was still inalienable, as he had a contract. This is also an authentic narration. It is also known that Ibrahim al-Nakha'i, al-Sha'bi and Hammad b. Abi Sulayman had the same view.

Thus this *fatwa* is relying on a minority position in *fiqh* to provide some flexibility for women who embrace Islam while their husbands remain non-Muslim. The justification is based on the opinions of major figures like Umar b. al-Khattab and Ali b. Abi Talib, even though these views have not been adopted in classical Islamic law.

While this *fatwa* is addressing an important issue for contemporary Muslim women in particular, relying on certain minority views in *fiqh*, one wonders whether it would not be more appropriate to ask some fundamental questions regarding women and Islamic law, in particular in relation to what is often referred to as the 'status of women' and the interpretation of a range of texts in the Qur'an and Sunna in the light of that 'status' in the past. Such an approach will require rethinking the role of women in society and coming to terms with the idea of equality of men and women before the law. There is a range of Qur'anic texts, as well as Hadith, that can be used to support this idea of equality. However, because of the perceived immutability of laws relating to women and family in classical Islamic law, most Muslim jurists today (including most proponents of *fiqh* for minorities) are not prepared to adopt the approach suggested. Naturally, when examining *fatwas* related to women, proponents of *fiqh* for minorities still seem to maintain the same view of women that was maintained by classical Islamic law. The sustainability of this classical legal view today is questionable, and perhaps should be open to challenge.

Example 2: Interest-Based Mortgages

Another example that demonstrates the utilization of minority views to support practices that could otherwise be regarded as prohibited under classical Islamic law can be found in the area of finance. *Fiqh* for minorities appears to permit interest-based mortgages on the basis of necessity (*darura*), despite the fact that classical Islamic law considers any form of increase over and above the principal in a loan to be *riba* and therefore prohibited. This *fatwa* issued by the European Council for Fatwa and Research[41] on the permissibility of applying for a loan to buy a house typifies the reasoning on this issue. Having stated that *riba* is forbidden (and that bank interest is also *riba*), this *fatwa* goes on to encourage Muslims in Western countries to establish Islamic mechanisms for lending or borrowing money without interest, and to work with existing financial institutions to develop such mechanisms. If all of this fails, the Council recommends the following:

> If all the above suggestions are unavailable, the Council, in the light of evidence and juristic considerations, see no harm in buying mortgaged houses if the following restrictions are strictly observed: (a) the house to be bought must be for the buyer and his household; (b) the buyer must not have another house; (c) the buyer must not have any surplus of assets that can help him buy a house by means other than mortgage.

As the *fatwa* is built on the principles of extreme necessity (*darura*) or need (*hajah*, which is treated in a similar manner to *darura*), the Council stresses that there is another rule, which governs and complements the rule of extreme necessity and need. This rule states that whatever has been made permissible due to extreme necessity must be handled with great care; it should be restricted to the category of people who are in real need of a house. The *fatwa*, therefore, does not cover taking out a mortgage to buy a house for commercial reasons, or for purposes other than buying a house for someone who does not have one.

However, a fundamental question in this area is whether classical Muslim jurists and contemporary jurists were correct when they interpreted the Qur'anic notion of *riba* simply as interest in all of its forms, without looking at the ethical dimension of the prohibition, which is clearly spelt out in the Koran as injustice (*zulm*). Instead of creating one stratagem after another to circumvent the prohibition, why not ask the fundamental question: are all forms of interest *riba*? Much like their seeming reluctance to question how classical Islamic law views women, proponents of *fiqh* for minorities do not seem to be interested in asking this fundamental question about the interpretation of *riba*.

Concluding Remarks

Classical Islamic law faces many problems in the contemporary world, and the situation of minorities highlights the need for a rethinking of key areas of classical Islamic law. Solutions are not going to be found by making minor adjustments here and there or by declaring exception after exception to general rules (for example, by declaring that it is acceptable to borrow money on interest in one part of the world but not in another, or by giving women certain rights in minority contexts but not in majority contexts). Only by undertaking a rethinking of classical legal positions can authentic solutions be found to the issues that classical Islamic law is facing as it engages with the modern world.

For *fiqh* for minorities to move beyond its current limits, it must be repositioned within the broader debate on the reform of classical Islamic law. This requires that temporary and ad hoc solutions be replaced with a more principled discourse of reform, leading to real change and new understandings of how Muslims should practise Islam in today's world, regardless of where they are located. I am not suggesting that context is unimportant; rather, that *fiqh* should be reconsidered to account for the specific social, political, cultural, and economic contexts in which Muslims live, regardless of their minority or majority status. To achieve this, proponents of *fiqh* for minorities are required to have the courage to ask deeper and more fundamental questions about the application of law, as well as principles of jurisprudence, ethics, and morality in the contemporary context. They should seek to develop a methodological framework within which such questions can be asked and the responses evaluated. They should be prepared to ask hard questions about how Islamic law was constructed in the first three centuries of Islam (as a human construct based on divine guidance) and to consider how its social, political, and historical contexts have impacted this process.

As a result, a whole range of concepts, including *dar al-harb* and *dar al-Islam*, Muslim and non-Muslim relations, the perceived inequality of men and women, the role of law in being Muslim, and the scope of what may be considered permissible (*halal*) and impermissible (*haram*), may need to be reconsidered. These new ideas are just as crucial for Muslims living in majority contexts as they are for Muslim minorities. In short, this will involve a fundamental rethinking of the classical Islamic legal tradition and its foundations. Those ideas and practices that are no longer justifiable must be set aside, so that new ideas can be developed in relation to what it means to be Muslim today.

Notes

1 Mahbubur Rahman (ed.), 'The Case for the "Fiqh of Muslim Minorities"', online article at *The Message International.org*, 12 January 2011, available online at http://messageinternational.org/the-case-for-the-%E2%80%9C*fiqh*-of-muslim-minorities%E2%80%9D/ (accessed on 14 October 2012).

2 Rahman, *The Case for the Fiqh of Muslim Minorities*, 2011.

3 Ameer Ali, review of Andrew March, *Islam and Liberal Citizenship* (2009) Oxford and New York: Oxford University Press, in *Journal of Muslim Minority Affairs* 30(2) (2010), p. 350.

4 Rahman, *The Case for the Fiqh of Muslim Minorities*, 2011

5 Interview*What is Minority Fiqh? al-'Allamah Sh. Bin Bayyah* on SuhaibWebb.com, 27 March 2008. (Video clip, available at http://www.suhaibwebb.com/islam-studies/islamic-law/what-is-minority-*fiqh*-al-allamah-sh-bin-bayyah/ Accessed 14 October 2012).

6 Rahman, *The Case for the Fiqh of Muslim Minorities*, 2011.

7 Shammai Fishman, *Fiqh al-Aqalliyyat: A Legal Theory for Muslim Minorities*. Center on Islam, Democracy, and the Future of the Muslim World, Research Monograph No. 2 (2006). Available online at <http://www.currenttrends.org/research/detail/*fiqh*-al-aqalliyyat-a-legal-theory-for-muslim-minorities.

8 Muhammad Khalid Masud, 'Islamic Law and Muslim Minorities,' ISIM *Newsletter*, 2002 (Vol. 11, No. 2), pp. 17-18.

9 Khaled Abou El-Fadl, 'Islamic Law and Muslim Minorities: The Juristic Discourse on Muslim Minorities from the Second/Eighth to the Eleventh/Seventeenth Centuries,' *Islamic Law and Society*, 1994 (Vol. 1 No. 2), p. 141.

10 Koran 2:218; 4:89.

11 Abou El-Fadl, 'Islamic Law and Muslim Minorities', 1994, p. 136.

12 Sherman A. Jackson 'Muslims, Islamic Law and Public Policy in the United States' in Ali A. Mazrui, Sherman A. Jackson, Aminah McCloud (eds.), *American Public Policy and American-Muslim Politics*, Chicago: International Strategy and Policy Institute, 1999 (online publication, n.p.) available at http://www.ispi-usa.org/policy/policy4.html.

13 For these views see Abou El-Fadl, 'Islamic Law and Muslim Minorities', 1994, pp. 134-5. See also Abdullah Saeed, 'Muslims under Non-Muslim Rule: Evolution of a Discourse,' in Anthony Reid and Michael Gilsenan (eds.), *Islamic Legitimacy in a Plural Asia*, London and New York: Routledge, 2007, pp. 14-27.

14 Haitham al Haddad, *A Critical Analysis of Selected Aspects of Sunni Muslim Minority Fiqh with particular reference to Contemporary Britain* (PhD Thesis), University of London, School of Oriental and African Studies, 2010, p. 102.

15 Al Haddad, *A Critical Analysis*, 2010, p. 90.

16 Abou El-Fadl, 'Islamic Law and Muslim Minorities', 1994, p. 141.

17 Abou El-Fadl, 'Islamic Law and Muslim Minorities', 1994, p. 142.

18 Andrew Wheatcroft, *Infidels: The Conflict between Christendom and Islam*, Sydney: Random House, 2005.

19 Masud, *Islamic Law and Muslim Minorities*, 2002, p. 17.

20 Al Haddad, *A Critical Analysis*, 2010, p. 130, citing Abou El-Fadl, 'Islamic Law and Muslim Minorities', 1994, pp. 149-150.

21 Al Haddad, *A Critical Analysis*, 2010, p. 131.

22 Fishman, *Fiqh al-Aqalliyyat*, 2006, p. 1.

23 Taha Jabir al-Alwani, *Fiqh of the Muslim Minorities*, online article at *The Message International.org*, 12 January 2011, available online at http://messageinternational.org/*fiqh*-of-the-muslim-minorities/ (Accessed on 2 February 2012).

24 Al-Alwani, *Fiqh of the Muslim Minorities*, 2011.

25 Al-Alwani, *Fiqh of the Muslim Minorities*, 2011.

26 Al-Alwani, *Fiqh of the Muslim Minorities*, 2011.

27 Masud, *Islamic Law and Muslim Minorities*, 2002, p. 17.

28 Masud, *Islamic Law and Muslim Minorities*, 2002, p. 17.

29 Masud, *Islamic Law and Muslim Minorities*, 2002, p. 18.

30 Yoginder Sikand, review of Taha J. Al-Alwani, *Towards A Fiqh For Minorities: Some Basic Reflections*, Richmond, UK: International Institution of Islamic Thought, 2003. Available online at http://www.milligazette.com/Archives/2004/16-30Apr04-Print-Edition/1604200454.htm.

31 Sheikh 'Abd Allāh b. Bayyah, *Introduction to the Fiqh of Minorities [Part One]* (2010). Available online at http://islamicstudies.islammessage.com/Minorities Article.aspx?aid=237. (Accessed on 2 February 2012.)

32 Sikand, book review, *Towards A Fiqh For Minorities.*

33 Masud, *Islamic Law and Muslim Minorities*, 2002, p. 2.

34 Al-Miftah, *Islam Not a Cereal: Shaykh Nuh Keller, UK Suhba 2007 on Modernism and Fiqh Al-Aqaliat* online article at *Al-Miftah* (3 September 2007). Available at http://al-miftah.blogspot.com.au/2007/09/islam-not-cereal-shaykh-nuh-keller-uk.html. (Accessed on 2 February 2012.)

35 Al-Miftah, *Islam Not a Cereal.*

36 Al-Miftah, *Islam Not a Cereal.*
37 Interview *What is Minority Fiqh? al-'Allamah Sh. Bin Bayyah*, Suhaib Web, 2008.
38 Gavin Picken, 'Fiqh Today: Muslims as Minorities' at 5th Annual AMSS (UK) Conference', *Journal of Qur'anic Studies*, (2004 (Vol. 6, No. 1), p. 151.
39 Interview *What is Minority Fiqh? al-'Allamah Sh. Bin Bayyah*, Suhaib Web, 2008.
40 Fatwa: 'I want to Embrace Islam: But Can I Keep My Marriage?' 24 September 2002. Available online at *efenem.files.wordpress.com/2009/06/qaradawis-16.doc.* (Accessed on 2 February 2012.)
41 European Council for Fatwa and Research, 'Permissibility of conventional mortgage under necessity,' Resolution: Fourth Ordinary Session [27-31 October 1999]. Available online at http://www.globalwebpost.com/farooqm/study_res/i_econ_fin/ecfr-fatwa_mortgage.htm. (Accessed on 2 February 2012.)

Bibliography

Aarbakke, Vermund, *The Muslim Minority of Greek Thrace, Vol. 1&2* (PhD Thesis), Bergen: University of Bergen, 2000.

Abaza, Mona, 'Perceptions of urfi marriage in the Egyptian press', *ISIM Newsletter,* 2001 (No. 7), p. 20.

Abdalla, A., 'Principles of Islamic Interpersonal Conflict Intervention: A Search within Islam and Western Literature', *Journal of Law and Religion*, 2002 (Vol. 15), pp. 151-184.

Abdel-Gawad, M., 'L'autonomie de la volonté en droit musulman', *L'Égypte contemporaine*, 1963 (No. 54), pp. 105-114.

Abu-Hassan, Reem, and Lynn Welchman, 'Changing the rules? Developments on "Crimes of Honour" in Jordan' in: Sara Hossain and Lynn Welchman (eds.), *'Honour': Crimes, Paradigms and Violence Against Women*, London: Zed Books, 2005.

Abu-Odeh, 'Honor Killings and the Construction of Gender in Arab Societies', *American Journal of Comparative Law*, 2010 (Vol. 58, No. 4), pp. 911-952.

Abu-Sahlieh, Sami A. Aldeeb, 'Les régimes matrimoniaux en droit arabe et musulman' in: A. Bonomi and M. Steiner (eds.), *Les régimes matrimoniaux en droit comparé et en droit international privé*, Geneve: Libarie Droz, 2006, pp. 279-305.

Ahdar, Rex, and Nicholas Aroney, *Shari'a in the West,* Oxford: Oxford University Press, 2011.

Ahmad, Lord Nazir, 'Notes on the Judicial Situation of Muslims in the United Kingdom' in: Thorsten Schneiders and Lamya Kaddor (eds.), *Muslime im Rechtsstaat,* Münster: LIT Verlag Münster, 2005.

Alawi, Irfan al-, Stephen S. Schwartz, Kamal Hasani, Veli Sirin, Daut Dauti and Qanta Ahmed, *A Guide to Shariah Law and Islamist Ideology in Western Europe, 2007-2009,* London: Center for Islamic Pluralism, 2009.

Alexander, Jeffrey C., *The Civil Sphere,* Oxford: Oxford University Press, 2006.

Alexander, Alexis, 'Religion or Ethnicity. The Identity of the Minorities in Greece and Turkey' in: R. Hirschon (ed.), *Crossing the Aegean,* Oxford/New York: Berghahn Books, 2003, pp. 117-132.

Algemene Inlichtingen en Veiligheidsdienst (AIVD), *De radicale da'wa. De opkomst van het neo-radicalisme in Nederland,* Den Haag: AIVD, 2007.

Al-Haidari, Eva, *Vernuftige verhoudingen. Opvattingen over het tijdelijk huwelijk in West-Europa,* Amsterdam: Universiteit van Amsterdam, 2001.

Al-Hibri, A.Y., 'The Nature of the Islamic Marriage: Sacramental, Convenantal, or Contractual?' in: J. Witte and E. Ellison (eds.), *Covenant Marriage in Compara-*

tive Perspective, Michigan/Cambridge: W.B. Eerdmans Publishing Company/ Grand Rapids, MI, pp. 182-216.

Ali, Kecia, *Marriage and Slavery in Early Islam*, Cambridge: Harvard University Press, 2010.

Ali, Wajahat, and Matthew Duss, 'Understanding shari'a Law: Conservative's skewed interpretation needs debunking', *Center for American Progress*, 2011. Available at http://www.americanprogress.org/issues/2011/03/sharia_law.html.

Alwani, Taha Jabir Fayyad al- (also: Alwānī, Tāhā Jābir Fayyād),
– *Fiqh of the Muslim Minorities*, 2011, available online at http://messageinternational.org/*fiqh*-of the-muslim-minorities/.
– *Towards a Fiqh for Minorities: Some Basic Reflections*, Occasional Paper Series, London; Washington: International Institute of Islamic Thought, 2003.
– 'The Testimony of Women in Islamic Law' (Translated by Yusuf DeLorenzo), *The American Journal of Islamic Social Sciences*, 1996 (Vol. 13, No. 2), pp. 173-196.

Amanat, Abbas and Frank Griffel (eds.), *Shari'a: Islamic Law in the Contemporary Context*, Stanford: Stanford University Press, 2007.

Ameer Ali, 'Review of Andrew March, Islam and Liberal Citizenship (2009) Oxford and New York: Oxford University Press', *Journal of Muslim Minority Affairs*, 2010 (Vol. 30, No. 2).

Amin, Hassan, Remedies for Breach of Contract in Islamic and Iranian Law, Glasgow: Royston, 1984.

Amirthalingam, Kumaralingam, 'Culture, Crime and Culpability: Perspectives on the Defence of Provocation' in: Marie Claire Foblets and Alison Dundes Renteln (eds.), *Multicultural Jurisprudence: Comparative Perspectives on the Cultural Defence*, Oxford: Hart Publishing, 2009.

Anderson, J., 'Recent developments in Shari'a law. III: The Contract of Marriage', *The Muslim World*, 1951, (Vol. 4, No. 2), pp. 113-126.

An-Na'im, Abdullahi Ahmed, *Islam and the Secular State. Negotiating the Future of Shari'a* Cambridge (Mass.): Harvard University Press, 2008.

Arabi, Oussama, *Studies in Modern Islamic Law and Jurisprudence*, Den Haag/London/New York: Kluwer, 2001.

Araji, Sharon K., *Crimes of Honor and Shame: Violence against Women in Non-Western and Western Societies*, Anchorage: University of Alaska Press, 2000.

Arnold, Kathryn Christine, 'Are the Perpetrators of Honor Killings Getting Away with Murder? Article 340 of the Jordanian Penal Code Analyzed under the Convention on the Elimination of All Forms of Discrimination against Women', *American University International Law Review*, 2001 (Vol. 16, No. 5), pp. 1345-1409.

Asad, Talal, 'Muslims and European Identity' in: Anthony Pagden (ed.), *The Idea of Europe: From Antiquity to European Identity*, Washington DC: Woodrow Wilson Center Press and Cambridge University Press, 2002.

Asamoah-Wade, Yolanda, 'Women's Human Rights and "Honor Killings" in Islamic Cultures', *Buffalo Women's Law Journal*, 1999-2000 (Vol. 8, No. 21), pp. 21-22.

Asayyad, N. and M. Castells (eds.), *Muslim Europe or Euro-Islam: politics, culture, and citizenship in the age of globalization*, Lanham: Lexington Books, 2002.

Ascanio, Lorenzo di, 'Il Mahr tra diritto musulmano e contesto non islamico', *Rivista di diritto internazionale privato e processuale*, 2009, pp. 387-406.

Aslam, J., 'Judicial Oversight of Islamic Family Law Arbitration in Ontario: Ensuring Meaningful Consent and Promoting Multicultural Citizenship', *New York University Journal of International Law and Politics*, 2006, pp. 841-876.

Badawi, Zaki, 'Muslim Justice in a Secular State' in: Michael King (ed.), *God's Law versus State Law*, London: Grey Seal, 1995.

Bader, V. (ed.), 'Governing Islam in Western Europe. Essays on Governance of Religious Diversity', *Journal of Ethnic and Migration Studies (JEMS)*, 2007, (Vol. 33, No. 6), pp. 871-887.

Bader, V., *Secularism or Democracy? Associational Governance of Religious Diversity*. Amsterdam: Amsterdam University Press, 2007.

Badran, Margot, *Feminism in Islam: Secular and Religious Convergences*, Oxford: Oneworld Publications, 2009.

Bahgat, Hossam and Wesal Afifi, 'Sexuality Politics in Egypt' in: Richard Parker, Rosalind Petchesky and Robert Sember (eds.), *Sex Politics – Report from the Front Lines*, 2008, available online at http://www.sxpolitics.org/frontlines/book/pdf/sekspolitics.pdf.

Bahners, Patrick, *Die Panikmacher, Die deutsche Angst vor dem Islam*, München: C.H. Beck, 2011.

Baker, N.V., P.R. Gregware and M.A. Cassidy, 'Family Killing Fields: Honour Rationales in the Murder of Women', *Violence Against Women*, 1999 (Vol. 5, No. 2), pp. 164-184.

Bakht, Natasha, 'Were Muslim Barbarians Really Knocking on the Gates of Ontario? The Religious Arbitration Controversy – Another Perspective', *Ottawa Law Review*, 2006, (Vol. 40), pp. 67-82.

Bälz, Kilian, 'A Murabaha Transaction in an English Court', *Islamic Law and Society*, 2004, (Vol. 11, No. 1), pp. 117-134.

Bano, Samia,

- 'Muslim Women, Divorce and Shari'ah Councils in Britain' in: Rubya Mehdi (ed.), *Interpreting Divorce Laws in Islam*, Copenhagen: DJØF, 2012, pp. 259-288.
- *Islamic Dispute Resolution and Family Law*, London: Palgrave, 2011.
- 'In Pursuit of Religious and Legal Diversity: A Response to the Archbishop of Canterbury and the shari'a Debate in Britain', *Ecclesiastical Law Journal*, 2008 (Vol. 10), pp. 283-309.

Barbalet, Jack, Adam Possamai and Bryan S. Turner (eds.), *Church and State*, London: Anthem Press, 2011.

Barry, Brian, *Culture and Equality. An Egalitarian Critique of Multiculturalism*, Cambridge (Mass.): Harvard University Press, 2002.

Bäsedow, J. and N. Yassari (eds.), *Iranian Family and Succession Laws and their Application in German Courts*, Tübingen: Mohr Siebeck, 2004.

Beckford, James and S. Gilliat, *Religion in Prison*, Cambridge: Cambridge University Press, 2008.

Bedner, Adriaan and Stijn van Huis, 'Plurality of Marriage Law and Marriage Registration for Muslims in Indonesia: A Plea for Pragmatism,' *Utrecht Law Review*, 2010 (Vol. 6, No. 2), pp. 175-191.

Benda-Beckman, Keebet von, *Broken Stairways to Consensus: Village Justice and State Courts in Minangkabau,* Dordrecht: Foris, 1984.

Benhabib, S., I. Shapiro and D. Petranovic (eds.), *Identities, Affiliations and Allegiances,* Cambridge: Cambridge University Press, 2007.

Berger, Maurits S.,

- 'Shariarechtbanken en religieuze familierechtspraak in Nederland' in *Tijdschrift voor Religie, Recht en Beleid,* 2010 (Vol. 1, No. 2), 49-62.
- 'Rechtsgronden voor een verbod op de gezichtsbedekkende sluier in Frankrijk, België en Nederland,' in *Tijdschrift voor Religie, Recht en Beleid,* 2010 (Vol. 1, No. 3), pp. 96-106.
- 'Shari'a in Nederland is heel Nederlands,' in *Ars Aequi,* June 2007, pp. 506-510. – *Sharia and Public Policy in Contemporary Egyptian Family Law* (PhD thesis), Groningen: Hephaestus Press, 2006.
- 'Conflicts Law and Public Policy in Egyptian Family Law: Islamic Law through the Backdoor?', *The American Journal of Comparative Law,* 2002 (Vol. 50, No. 3), pp. 555-594.

Bhabha, Homi K., *The Location of Culture,* London/New York: Routledge, 1994.

Bilici, Mucahit, *Finding Mecca in America. How Islam is becoming an American Religion,* Chicago: University of Chicago Press, 2012.

Blenkhorn, Lindsey, 'Islamic Marriage Contracts in American Courts: Interpreting Mahr Agreements as Prenuptials and their Effect on Muslim Women', *Southern California Law Review,* 2002-2003 (Vol. 76, No. 1), pp. 189-233.

Boeglin, J.G., *États et religions en Europe* (2 vols.), Paris: L'Harmattan, 2006.

Bousquet, Georges-Henri, *L'Éthique sexuelle de l'Islam,* Paris: Maisonneuve & Larose, 1966.

Bowen, John Richard,

- *A New Anthropology of Islam,* Cambridge: Cambridge University Press, 2012.
- *Can Islam be French?: Pluralism and Pragmatism in a Secularist State,* Princeton: Princeton University Press, 2010.

Bramadat, P. and M. Koenig (eds.), *International Migration and the Governance of Religious Diversity,* Montreal & Kingston: Metropolis, 2009.

Brems, Eva, 'Human Rights as a Framework for Negotiating/Protecting Cultural Differences – An Exploration of the Case-Law of the European Court of Human Rights' in: M.-C. Foblets (ed.), *Cultural Diversity and the Law,* Bruxelles: Bruylant, 2010, pp. 663-715.

Brown, Bernard J., 'The Demise of Chance Medley and the Recognition of Provocation as a Defence to Murder in English Law', *American Journal of Legal History,* 1963 (Vol. 7, No. 4), pp. 310-318.

Brunnbauer, Ulf and Robert Pichler, 'Highland Values and Nation-Building in the Balkans', *Balkanologie,* 2002 (Vol. 1, Nos. 1-2), pp. 77-100.

Büchler, Andrea, *Islamic Law in Europe? Legal Pluralism and its Limits in European Family Laws,* Burlington: Ashgate, 2011.

Bullock, Katherine H., and Gul Joya Jafri, 'Media (Mis)Representations: Muslim Women in the Canadian Nation', *Canadian Woman Studies,* 2000 (Vol. 20, No. 2), pp. 35-40.

Bunge, Locke and Valerie Pottie (eds.), *Family Violence in Canada: A Statistical Profile*, 2000.

Campbell, Jacquelyn and Carol W. Runyan, 'Femicide: Guest Editors' Introduction', *Homicide Studies*, 1998 (Vol. 2, No. 4), pp. 347-352.

Cane, P., C. Evans and Z. Robinson (eds.), *Law and Religion in Theoretical and Historical Context*, Cambridge: Cambridge University Press, 2008.

Carlier, J.Y.,
- and M. Fallon, B. Martin-Bosly, *Code de droit international privé*, Brussels: Bruylant, 2008.
- 'La reconnaissance mesurée des répudiations par l'examen *in concreto* de la contrariété à l'ordre public', *Revue trimestrielle du droit de la famille*, 2003, pp. 35-48.
- *Autonomie de la volonté et statut personnel*, Brussels: Bruylant, 1992.
- and M. Verwilghen (eds.), *Le statut personnel des musulmans. Droit comparé et droit international privé*, Brussels: Bruylant, 1992.

Casanova, José, *Public Religions in the Modern World*, Chicago: University of Chicago Press, 1994.

Caughey, John L., 'The Anthropologist as Expert Witness: The Case of a Murder in Maine' in: Marie-Claire Foblets and Alison Dundes Renteln (eds.), *Multicultural Jurisprudence: Comparative Perspectives on the Cultural Defence*, Oxford: Hart Publishing, 2009.

Çavdar, Gamze, 'Islamist Moderation and the Resilience of Gender: Turkey's Persistent Paradox', *Totalitarian Movements and Political Religions*, 2010 (Vol. 11, No. 3–4), pp. 341–357.

Center for Security Policy, 'Shari'ah Law and American State Courts. An Assessment of State Appellate Court Cases', *Occasional Paper Series*, 2011.

Cesari, Jocelyne,
- 'Islamophobia in the West: A Comparison between Europe and the United States' in: John L. Esposito and Ibrahim Kalin (eds.), *Islamophobia: The Challenge of Pluralism in the 21st Century*, Oxford: Oxford University Press, 2011, pp. 21-43.
- *Muslims in the West after 9/11*, London: Routledge, 2009.
- *When Islam and Democracy Meet: Muslims in Europe and in the United States*, New York: Palgrave, 2004 (2nd ed. 2006).
- and S. McLoughlin (eds.), *European Muslims and the Secular State*, Aldershot: Ashgate, 2005.

Chabaan, Jad, 'Youth and Development in the Arab Countries: The Need for a Different Approach', *Middle Eastern Studies*, 2009 (Vol. 45, No. 1), pp. 33-55.

Charfi, M., 'L'influence de la religion dans le droit international privé des pays musulmans', *Receuil des Cours de l'Académie de Droit International*, 1987 (Vol. 203, No. 3), pp. 414ff.

Chehata, Chafik,
- *Droit musulman – Applications au Proche-Orient*, Paris: Dalloz, 1970.
- 'Le contrat en droit musulman', *Zeitschrift für vergleichende Rechtswissenschaft*, 1968 (Vol. 70), pp. 81-96.

Chiu, Daina, 'The Cultural Defence: Beyond Exclusion, Assimilation, and Guilty Liberalism', *California Law Review*, 1995 (Vol. 82), pp. 1053-1125.
Clifford, James, 'Notes on Travel and Theory', *Inscriptions*, 1989 (Vol. 5).
Coss, Graeme, '"God is a righteous judge, strong and patient: and God is provoked every day." A Brief History of the Doctrine of Provocation in England', *Sydney Law Review*, 1991 (Vol. 13, No. 4), pp. 570ff.
Cossman, Brenda, 'Turning the Gaze Back on Itself: Comparative Law, Feminist Legal Studies, and the Postcolonial', *Utah Law Review*, 1997 (Vol. 2), pp. 525-544.
Côté, Andrée, Elizabeth Sheehy and Diana Majury, *The Defense of Provocation: Stop Excusing Violence Against Women*, National Association of Women and the Law, 2002, available online at: National Association of Women and the Law, http://www.nawl.ca/ns/en/documents/Pub_Report_Provoc00_en.pdf.
Coulson, Noel J.,
- *A History of Islamic Law*, Edinburgh: Edinburgh University Press, 1964.
- *Commercial Law in the Gulf States – The Islamic Legal Tradition*, London: Graham & Trotman, 1984.

Coward, H., J.R. Hinnells and R.B. Williams (eds.), *The South Asian Religious Diaspora in Great Britain, Canada and the United States*, New York: State University of New York Press, 2000.
Dahlgren, Susanne, 'Women's *Adah* versus "Women's Law": The Contesting Issue of *Mahr* in Aden, Yemen', *Égypte/Monde arabe*, 2005 (No. 1), available online at http://ema.revues.org/index1045.html.
Dannin, Robert, *Black Pilgrimage to Islam*, Oxford: Oxford University Press, 2002.
Dassetto, Felice, *Paroles d'Islam: individus, sociétés et discours dans l'Islam européen contemporain*, Paris: Maisonneuve, 2000.
Dassetto, Felice, Farid El Asri and Brigitte Maréchal, *Islam belge au pluriel*, Louvain: Presses Universitaires Louvain, 2012.
Dessing, Nathal, 'Continuïteit en verandering in de huwelijkssluiting bij Turkse, Marokkaanse en Surinaamse moslims in Nederland', S. Rutten (ed.), *Recht van de Islam, No. 16*, Maastricht, 1999, pp. 59-81.
Diem, Werner, *Ein arabisches Rechtsgutachten zum Eherecht aus dem 11.-12. Jahrhundert*, Wiesbaden: Harrassowitz, 2007.
Dierkens, A. and J.-Ph. Schreiber (eds.), *Laïcité et sécularisation dans l'Union européenne*, Brussels: Ed. de l'Université de Bruxelles ('Problèmes d'Histoire des religions', vol. XVI), 2006.
Doudos, George,
- 'Η shari'a, ένα σύστημα δικαίου με δυναμική και μέλλον, *Azinlikça*, 2009' (Vol. 53), available online at http://www.azinlikca.net/ellinika-arthra/2010-01-07-15-30-25.html.
- 'Το υποστατό των μουσουλμανικών γάμων που τελούνται δια πληρεξουσίου στα πλαίσια της ελληνικής έννομης τάξης', *Nomokanonika*, 2004 (Vol. 3), pp. 331-337.

Douglas, Gillian (ed.), 'Social Cohesion and Civil Law: Marriage, Divorce and Religious Courts', Report of a Research Study funded by the AHCR, Cardiff University: Cardiff Law School, 2011, available online at http://ssrn.com/abstract=1940387.

Dressler, Joshua, 'Rethinking Heat of Passion: A Defence in Search of a Rationale', *Journal of Criminal Law & Criminology*, 1982 (Vol. 73, No. 2), pp. 421-470.

Eid, P., P. Bosset, M. Milot and S. Lebel-Grenier, *Appartenances religieuses, appartenance citoyenne. Un équilibre en tension*, Québec: Presses Universitaires Laval, 2009.

El-Fadl, Khaled Abou,

- 'Islamic Law and Muslim Minorities: The Juristic Discourse on Muslim Minorities from the Second/Eighth to the Eleventh/Seventeenth Centuries', *Islamic Law and Society*, 1994 (Vol. 1, No. 2), pp. 141-187.
- 'Legal Debates on Muslim Minorities: Between Rejection and Accommodation', *Journal of Religious Ethics*, 1994 (Vol. 22, No. 1), pp. 127-162.

El Geddawy, K., *Relations entre systèmes confessionnel et laïque en droit international privé*, Paris: Dalloz (Bibliothèque de droit international privé), 1971.

El-Hassan, 'Abd El-Wahab Ahmed, 'Freedom of Contract, the Doctrine of Frustration, and Sanctity of Contracts in Sudan Law and Islamic Law', *Arab Law Quarterly*, 1985-1986 (Vol. 1, No. 1), p. 51.

El Husseini Begdache, R., *Le droit international privé français et la répudiation islamique*, Paris: Librairie Général de Droit en de Jurisprudence, 2002.

El-Karouni, Moustapha, 'La dot: une institution contraire à l'ordre public international belge?', *Revue trimestrielle de droit familial*, 2002, (No. 3), pp. 403-423.

El-Tayeb, Fatima, *European Others: Queering Ethnicity in Postnational Europe*, Minneapolis: University of Minnesota Press, 2011.

Emāmī, Seyyed Hasan, *Hoqūq-e madanī* [Civil Law], Vol. 4, Tehran: Ketābforūshī-ye eslāmiyye, 2005.

Emamy, Hassan, L'institution juridique du mahr (dot) en droit musulman du rite chiite, Lausanne: Imprimerie C. Risold, 1933.

Enayat, Majid, 'Länderbericht Iran' in: A. Bergmann, M. Ferid and D. Henrich (eds.), *Internationales Ehe- und Kindschaftsrecht*, Frankfurt/Main: Verlag für Standesamtswesen, 2004.

Erdemir, A., H. Rittersberger-Tiliç, A. Ergun & H. Kahveci (eds.), *Rethinking Global Migration: Practices, Policies, and Discourses in the European Neighbourhood*, Ankara: KORA, 2008.

Esposito, John, L.,

- *Women in Muslim Family Law*, Syracuse: Syracuse University Press, 2001 (2nd ed.).
- and Ibrahim Kalin (eds.), *Islamophobia: The Challenge of Pluralism in the 21st Century*, Oxford: Oxford University Press, 2011.

European Council for Fatwa and Research, 'Permissibility of Conventional Mortgage under Necessity', Resolution: Fourth Ordinary Session [27-31 October 1999], available online at http://www.globalwebpost.com/farooqm/study_res/i_econ_fin/ecfr-fatwa_mortgage.htm.

Ewan, O., 'L'Islam et les systèmes de conflits de lois' in: J.-Y. Carlier and M. Verwilghen (eds.), *Le Statut Personnel des Musulmans. Droit compare et droit international prive*, Brussels: Bruylant, 1992, pp. 313-341.

Fadel, Mohammad, 'Two Women, One Man: Knowledge, Power and Gender in Medieval Sunni Legal Thought', *International Journal of Middle East Studies*, 2007 (Vol. 29, No. 2), pp. 185-204.

Fallon, M. and J. Erauw, *La nouvelle loi sur de droit international privé belge. La loi du 16 juillet 2004*, Antwerp: Kluwer, 2004.

Faqir, Fadia, 'Intrafamily Femicide in Defence of Honour: The Case of Jordan', *Third World Quarterly*, 2001 (Vol. 22, No. 1), pp. 65-82.

Ferid, Murad, Gerhard Kegel and Konrad Zweigert (eds.), *Gutachten zum internationalen und ausländischen Privatrecht 1965 und 1966*, Tübingen: J.C.B. Mohr (Paul Siebeck), 1968.

Fernandez, Sonya, 'The Crusade over the Bodies of Women', *Patterns of Prejudice*, 2009 (Vol. 43, Nos. 3-4), pp. 269-286.

Fiqh Council of the Muslim World League, 'A message from Muslim scholars to Muslim Minorities in the West', *Daawah*, 2002 (No. 4).

Fishman, Shammai, *Fiqh al-Aqalliyyat: A Legal Theory for Muslim Minorities*, Center on Islam, Democracy, and the Future of the Muslim World, Research Monograph, 2006 (No. 2), available online at http://www.currenttrends.org/research/detail/*fiqh*-al-aqalliyyat-a-legal-theory-for-muslim-minorities.

Foblets, Marie-Claire,

- 'The Admissibility of repudiation: requirements in private international law. Recent developments in France, Belgium and The Netherlands' in: R. Mehdi (ed.), *Integration & Retsudvikling*, Copenhagen: Jurist- og Oknomforbindets Forlag, 2008, pp. 151-170.
- and Adriaan Overbeeke, 'Islam in Belgium' in: Richard Potz and Wolfgang Wieshaider (eds.), *Islam and the European Union*, Leuven et al: Peeters, 2004.
- and J.-Y. Carlier, *Le Code marocain de la famille. Incidences au regard du droit international privé en Europe*, Brussels: Bruylant, 2005.
- 'Migrant Women Caught between Islamic Family Law and Women's Rights: the Search for the Appropriate "Connecting Factor" in International Family Law', *Maastricht Journal of European and Comparative Law*, 2000 (Vol. 7, No. 1), pp. 11-34.

Fournier, Pascale,

- 'Flirting with God in Western Secular Courts: Mahr in the West', *International Journal of Law, Policy and the Family*, 2010 (Vol. 24, No. 1), pp. 67-94.
- 'In the (Canadian) Shadow of Islamic Law: Translating Mahr as a Bargaining Endowment', *Osgoode Hall Law Journal*, 2006, pp. 649-677.
- *Muslim Marriage in Western Courts: Lost in Transplantation*, Aldershot: Ashgate, 2010.
- 'The Ghettoization of Difference in Canada: "Rape by Culture" or the Danger of a Cultural Defence in Criminal Law Trials', *Manitoba Law Journal*, 2002 (Vol. 29, No. 81), pp. 81-113.
- and Aida Setrakian and Pascal McDougall, 'No-Fault Talaq: Islamic Divorce in Canadian Immigration and Family law' in: Jørgen S. Nielsen, Werner Menski and Rubya Mehdi (eds.), *Interpreting Divorce Law in Islam*, Copenhagen: DJØF Publishing, 2012.

– and Pascal McDougall and Anna Dekker, 'Dishonour, Provocation and Culture: Through the Beholder's Eye?', *Canadian Criminal Law Review*, 2012 (Vol. 16), pp. 59-91.

François, L., 'La Convention européenne des droits de l'homme est-elle supérieure aux conventions bilatérales reconnaissant les répudiations musulmanes?', *Recueil le Dalloz*, 2002, 2958-2962.

Freeland, Richard, 'The Islamic Institution of Mahr and American Law', *Gonzaga Journal of International Law*, 2000-2001 (Vol. 4), pp. 1-8, available online at: www.gonzagajil.org.

Freeman, Michael, 'The Jewish Get and the State' in: Richard O'Dair and Andrew Lewis (eds.), *Law and Religions. Current legal issues, Vol. 4*, Oxford: Oxford University Press, 2001.

Furseth, Inger,

– 'Competing and Changing Ideals of Motherhood: Views on Arranged Marriage Among Middle Class Immigrant Muslim Women in the Los Angeles Area', forthcoming in: Fariha Khan (ed.), *Global Islam in Everyday America*, 2012.

– 'The hijab: Boundary Work and Identity Negotiations Among Immigrant Muslim Women in the Los Angeles Area', *Review of Religious Research*, 2011, (Vol. 52), pp. 365-385.

Fyzee, Asaf, *Outlines of Muhammadan Law*, Delhi: Oxford University Press, 1993 (1st ed. 1955).

Gafsia, Nawel, *L'invention coloniale du mariage musulman – Le cas tunisien*, Paris: Librairie Générale de Droit et de Jurisprudence, 2008.

Gannagé, L., *La hiérarchie des normes et les méthodes du droit international privé. Étude de droit international privé de la famille*, Paris: La Librairie Générale de Droit et de Jurisprudence, 2001.

Garçon, Émile, *Code pénal annoté*, Paris: Librairie du Recueil Sirey, 1951.

Gaudemet-Tallon, H.,

– 'De nouvelles fonctions pour l'équivalence en droit international privé' in: Bertrand Ancel (ed.) *Le droit international privé: esprits et méthodes, Mélanges en l'honneur de Paul Lagarde*, Paris: Dalloz, 2005, pp. 303-325.

– 'Le pluralisme en droit international privé: richesses et faiblesses (Le funambule et l'arc-en-ciel)', *Recueil des Cours de l'Académie de Droit International*, 2005 (Vol. 312, No. 1), pp. 1-488.

– 'Nationalité, statut personnel et droits de l'homme' in: *Mélanges E. Jayme*, Munich: Sellier, 2004.

Gaudreault-DesBiens, J.Fr., 'The Limits of Private Justice? The Problems of State Recognition of Arbitral Awards in Family and Personal Status Disputes in Ontario', *World Arbitration and Mediation Report*, 2005, (Vol. 16).

Ghamidi, Javed A., *Islam. From Revolution to Implementation*, Lahore: Al-Mawrid, 2006.

Goris, H., M. Heimbach-Steins (eds.), *Religion in Recht und politischer Ordnung heute*, Würzburg: Ergon, 2008.

Granqvist, Hilma, *Marriage Conditions in a Palestinian Village II*, Helsingfors: Akademische Buchhandlung, 1935.

Grant, Isabel, 'Intimate Femicide: A Study of Sentencing Trends for Men who Kill their Intimate Partners' *Alberta Law Review*, 2010 (Vol. 47, No. 3), pp. 779-822.

Griffith-Jones, Robin, *Islam and English Law*, Cambridge: Cambridge University Press, 2013.

Grimpret, M., *Dieu est dans l'isoloir*, Paris: Presses de la Renaissance, 2007.

Groen, Janny and Annieke Kranenberg, *Strijdsters van Allah. Radicale moslima's en het Hofstad netwerk*, Amsterdam: Meulenhoff, 2006.

Haddad, Haitham al-, *A Critical Analysis of Selected Aspects of Sunni Muslim Minority Fiqh with particular reference to Contemporary Britain* (PhD Thesis), University of London, School for Oriental and African Studies, 2010.

Haddad, Y. Yazbeck,
- and Jane Smith and Kathleen Moore, *Muslim Women in America*, Oxford: Oxford University Press, 2006.
- (ed.), *Muslims in the West: from Sojourners to Citizens*, Oxford: Oxford University Press, 2002.
- and Adair Loomis, *Islamic Values in the United States*, New York: Oxford University Press, 1987.

Haeri, Shahla,
- 'Temporary Marriage and the State in Iran: An Islamic Discourse on Female Sexuality in Iran', *Social Research*, 1992 (Vol. 59, No. 1), pp. 201-222.
- *Law of Desire: Temporary Marriage in Iran*, London: I.B. Tauris, 1989.

Hahne, Meo-Micaela, 'Vertragsfreiheit im Familienrecht' in: Dieter Schwab and Meo-Micaela Hahne (eds.), *Familienrecht im Brennpunkt*, Bielefeld: Gieseking, 2004, pp. 181-202.

Hamid, M.E., 'Islamic Law of Contract or Contracts?' *Journal of Islamic and Comparative Law*, 1969 (Vol. 3), pp. 1-11.

Hamidian, Hassan, 'Jurisdiction of Family Courts in Iran' in: Jürgen Basedow and Nadjma Yassari (eds.), *Iranian Family and Succession Laws and their Application in German Courts*, Tübingen: Mohr Siebeck, 2004.

Hamīdiyān, Hassan, 'Farāz va neshībhā-ye mchriye be nerkh-e rūz', in: Hassan Hamīdiyān (ed.), Majmūʿe-ye magālāte hoqūq-e khānevāde, Tehran: Hāmūn, 2008.

Hamilton, Marcia A., *God vs. the Gavel*, Cambridge: Cambridge University Press, 2005.

Hammarberg, Thomas, 'Human Rights of Minorities', Strassbourg: Council of Europe, 19 February 2009, available online at https://wcd.coe.int/ViewDoc.jsp?id=1409353.

Hanshaw, Mark E., *The Unfamiliar Abode: Islamic Law in the United States and Britain*, Oxford: Oxford University Press, 2010.

Hasso, Frances Susan, *Consuming Desires: Family Crisis and the State in the Middle East*, Stanford, CA: Stanford University Press, 2011.

Hofer, Sibylle, Dieter Schwab and Dieter Henrich (eds.), *From Status to Contract? Die Bedeutung des Vertrages im europäischen Familienrecht*, Bielefeld: Gieseking, 2005.

Holton, Richard and Stephen Shute, 'Self-Control in the Modern Provocation Defence', *Oxford Journal Legal Studies*, 2007 (Vol. 27, No. 1), pp. 49-73.

Hoodfar, Homa, 'The Veil in Their Minds and On Our Heads: The Persistence of Colonial Images of Muslim Women', *Resources for Feminist Research*, 1998 (Vol. 22, No. 3/4), pp. 83-102.

Horder, Jeremy, 'Reshaping the Subjective Element in the Provocation Defence', *Oxford Journal Legal Studies*, 2005 (Vol. 25, No. 1), pp. 123-140.

Howard Ross, M. (ed.), *Culture and Belonging in Divided Societies. Contestation and Symbolic Landscapes*, Philadelphia: University of Pennsylvania Press, 2009.

Hoyek, Danielle, Rafif Rida Sidawi and Amira Abou Mrad, 'Murders of Women in Lebanon: "Crimes of Honour" between Reality and the Law', in: Sara Hossain and Lynn Welchman (eds.), *'Honour': Crimes, Paradigms and Violence Against Women*, London: Zed Books, 2005, pp. 111-136.

Hussain, Jamila, *Islam: Its Law and Society*, Sydney: Federation Press, 2011 (3rd edition).

Husson, Jean-François, *Training Imams in Europe. The Current Status*, Belgium: King Baudouin Foundation, 2007, available on www.kbs-frb.be.

Hamīdiyān, Hasan, 'Farāz va neshībhā-ye mehriye be nerkh-e rūz' [The Dower Adapted to the Daily Exchange Rate] in: Hasan Hamīdiyān (ed.), *Majmūʿe-ye maqālāt-e hoqūq-e khānevāde*, Tehran: Hāmūn, 2008.

Ibn ʿAbd al-Ghanī al-Rāfiʿī, Sālim, *Ahkām al-ahwāl al-shakhsīya li-l-muslimīn fī al-gharb* [Rules of personal status law for Muslims in the West], Riyadh, 2001.

Ibn Baz and Uthaymeen, *Muslim Minorities – Fatawa Regarding Muslims Living as Minorities*, Hounslow, 1998.

Imber, Colin, 'Women, Marriage, and Property: *Mahr* in the *Behcetü'l-Fetāvā* of Yenişehirli Abdullah' in: M. C. Zilfi (ed.), *Women in the Ottoman Empire – Middle Eastern Women in the Early Modern Era*, Leiden: Brill, 1997.

Iqbal, Munawar, *Islamic Banking and Finance*, Leicester: Islamic Foundation, 2001.

Jacobson, Cardell K. and Lara Burton (eds.), *Modern Polygamy in the United States*, Oxford: Oxford University Press, 2011.

Janin, Hunt and André Khalmeyer, *Sharia: The Sharia from Muhammad's Time to Present*, Jefferson, NC: McFarland, 2007.

Jansen, Willy, 'Sleeping in the Womb: Protracted Pregnancies in the Maghreb', *The Muslim World*, 2000 (Vol. 90, Nos. 1-2), pp. 218-237.

Jindani, Mohamed, 'The Concept of Mahr (Dower) in Islamic Law: The Need of Statutory Recognition by English Law', *Yearbook of Islamic and Middle Eastern Law*, 2004-2005 (Vol. 11), pp. 219-227.

Jones-Pauly, Christina, 'Marriage contracts of Muslims in the Diaspora: Problems in the Recognition of Mahr Contracts in German Law' in: A. Quraishi and F.E. Vogel (eds.), *The Islamic Marriage Contract: Case Studies in Islamic Family Law*, Cambridge: Harvard University Press, 2008, pp. 299-330.

Jordens-Cotran, Leila, *Het Marokkaanse familierecht en de Nederlandse rechtspraktijk*, Utrecht: Forum, 2000.

Kadare, Ismail, *Identiteti Evopian i Shqiptareve* [The European Identity of the Albanians], Tirana: Ønufri: , 2006.

Kalir, Barak, Malini Sur and Willem van Schendel, 'Introduction: Mobile Practices and Regimes of Permissiveness' in: Barak Kalir and Malini Sur (eds.), *Illegal but Licit: Transnational Flows and Permissive Polities*, Amsterdam: Amsterdam University Press, 2012.

Karčić, Fikret, 'Secular State and Religion(s): Remarks on the Bosnian Experience in Regulating Religion and State Relations' in: European Abrahamic Forum, *Religion and Secular State: Role and Meaning of Religion in a Secular State from Jewish, Christian and Muslim Perspectives*, Zürich: European Abrahamic Forum, 2008, pp. 15-25.

Karkabi, Nadeem, *Couples in the Global Margins: Sexuality and Marriage between Local Men and Western Women in Dahab (South Sinai)* (MA thesis), University of Haifa, 2008.

Kātūziyān, Nāsser, *Hoqūq-e madanī: khānevāde* [Civil Law: Family Law], Vol. 1, Tehran: Enteshārāt-e bahman bornā, 1999.

Kennedy, Duncan, 'Two Globalizations of Law and Legal Thought: 1850-1869', *Suffolk University Law Review*, 2003 (Vol. 36, No. 3), pp. 633-678.

Keshavjee, Mohamed, 'The Ismaili Alternative Dispute Resolution Training Programmes and the Potential for New Directions in Mediation', *Institute for Ismaili Studies*, 2007, available online at http://www.iis.ac.uk/

Khaliq, Urfan, 'Islam and the European Union: Report on the United Kingdom' in: Richard Potz and Wolfgang Wieshaider (eds.), *Islam and the European Union*, Leuven: Peeters, 2004.

Kholoussy, Hanan, *For Better, For Worse: The Marriage Crisis that made Modern Egypt*, Stanford: Stanford University Press, 2010.

King, Michael (ed.), *God's Law versus State Law*, London: Grey Seal, 1995.

Kinsch, P., 'Droits de l'homme, droits fondamentaux et droit international privé', *Recueil des Cours*, 2005, vol. 318.

Klarmann, Reinhard, *Islamic Project Finance*, Zurich/Bâle/Genève: Schulthess, 2003.

Klausen, J., *The Islamic Challenge: Politics and Religion in Western Europe*, Oxford: Oxford University Press, 2005.

Kolig, Erich, 'To Shari'aticize or not to Shari'aticize: Islamic and Secular Law in Liberal Democratic Society' in: Rex Ahdar and Nicholas Aroney (eds.), *Sharia in the West*, Oxford: Oxford University Press, 2010, pp. 255-278.

Konortas, Paraskevas, *Les musulmanes de la Grèce entre 1821 et 1912* (Mémoire de DEA), Paris: École des Hautes Études en Sciences Sociales, 1980.

Kontogiorgi, Elisabeth, *Population Exchange in Greek Macedonia*, Oxford: Clarendon Press (Oxford Historical Monographs), 2006.

Korteweg, Anna & Gökçe Yurdakul, 'Islam, Gender, and Immigrant Integration: Boundary Drawing in Discourses on Honour Killing in the Netherlands and Germany', *Ethnic and Racial Studies*, 2009 (Vol. 32, No. 2), pp. 218-238.

Kropholler, Jan, *Internationales Privatrecht*, Tübingen: Mohr Siebeck, 2006.

Krüger, Hilmar,

- 'Das Recht der Eheschließung in den Vereinigten Arabischen Emiraten', *Das Standesamt*, 1999, pp. 65-68.
- 'Grundzüge des Privatrechts der Vereinigten Arabischen Emirate' in: H.-G. Ebert and Th. Hanstein (eds.), *Beiträge zum islamischen Recht*, Vol. 6, Frankfurt on the Main: Lang, 2007, pp. 121-134.
- 'Vermögensrechtliches Privatrecht und Shari'a am Beispiel der Vereinigten Arabischen Emirate', *Zeitschrift für Vergleichende Rechtswissenschaft*, 1998 (Vol. 97), pp. 360-386.

Ktistakis, Ioannis, Ιερός Νόμος του Ισλάμ και Μουσουλμάνοι Έλληνες Πολίτες, Athens: Sakkoulas, 2006.

Kulwicki, Anahid Devartanian, 'The Practice of Honor Crimes: A Glimpse of Domestic Violence in the Arab World', *Issues in Mental Health Nursing*, 2002 (Vol. 23, No. 1), pp. 77-87.

Lacroix, Stephane, 'Between Revolution and Apoliticism: Nasir al-Din al-Albani and his Impact on the shaping of Contemporary Salafism' in: Roel Meijer (ed.), *Global Salafism: Islam's New Religious Movement,* New York: Columbia University Press, 2009.

Lagarde, P., 'Différences culturelles et ordre public en droit international privé de la famille', *Annuaire de l'Institut de Droit International,* 2005 (Vol. 71, No. 1), pp. 7-115.

Larouche, G.J., and M. Maesschalck, *La religion dans l'espace public,* Université Laval, Ed. Liber, 2006 (No. 8), pp. 60-70.

Latten, Jan, 'Trends in samenwonen en trouwen. De schone schijn van burgerlijke staat', CBS *Bevolkingstrends,* 2004, (Vol. 52, No. 4), pp. 46-60.

Laurence, Jonathan, *The Emancipation of Europe's Muslims: The State's Role in Minority Integration,* Princeton, N.J.: Princeton University Press, 2012.

Lehmann, H. (ed.), *Multireligiosität im vereinten Europa: historische und juristische Aspekte,* Göttingen: Wallstein, 2003.

Lehr-Lehnardt, Rana, 'Treat your Women Well: Comparisons and Lessons from an Imperfect Example Across the Waters', *Southern Illinois University Law Journal,* 2002 (Vol. 26), pp. 403-422.

Leonard, Karen Isaksen, *Muslims in the United States. The State of Research,* New York: Russell Sage Foundation, 2003.

Lequette, Y.,

- 'Le conflit de civilisation à la lumière de l'expérience franco-tunisienne' in: *Mouvements de droit contemporain, Mélanges offerts au Professeur Sassi Ben Halima,* Tunis: Centre de publication universitaire, 2005.
- 'Le droit international privé et les droits fondamentaux' in: R. Cabrillac *et al.* (ed.), *Libertés et droits fondamentaux,* Paris: Dalloz, 2006.

Levey, G.F. and T. Modood (eds.), *Secularism, Religion and Multicultural Citizenship,* Cambridge: Cambridge University Press, 2009.

Levy, Jacob, *The Multiculturalism of Fear,* Oxford: Oxford University Press, 2000.

Lewis, Ph., *Islamic Britain: Religion, Politics and Identity among British Muslims: Bradford since the 1990s,* London: I.B. Tauris, 1994.

Linant de Bellefonds, Yvon,

- *Traité de droit musulman comparé, Vol.* 2, Paris: Mouton & Co, 1965.
- 'L'autonomie de la volonté en droit musulman', *Revue algérienne, tunisienne et marocaine de législation et de jurisprudence,* 1958 (Vol. 74), pp. 87-111.

Liversage, Annika and Tina Gudrun Jensen, *Parallelle Retsopfattelser i Danmark* ["Parallel legal notions in Denmark"], Copenhagen: SFI, 2011, available online at http://www.sfi.dk/rapportoplysninger-4681.aspx?Action=1&NewsId=3144&PID=9267.

Locke, Daisy and Valerie Pottie Bunge (eds.), *Family Violence in Canada: A Statistical Profile*, Canadian Center for Justice Statistics, Ottawa: Minister of Industry, 2000, available online at http://www.statcan.gc.ca/pub/85-224-x/85-224-x2000000-eng.pdf.

Løvdal, Lene, '*Mahr* and Gender Equality in Private International Law: The Adjudication of *Mahr* in England, France, Norway and Sweden' in: Rubya Mehdi and Jørgen S. Nielsen (eds.), *Embedding Mahr (Islamic Dower) in the European Legal System*, Copenhagen: DJØF Pub.; Portland (Or.): Sold and distributed in North America by International Specialized Book Services (ISBS), 2011, pp. 77-112.

Ma Del Pilar, Diago, 'La dot islamique à l'épreuve du conflit de civilisations, sous l'angle du droit international privé espagnol', *Annales de Droit de Louvain*, 2001, pp. 407-442.

MacFarlane, Julie,

- *Islamic Divorce in North America: A Shari'a Path in a Secular Society*, Oxford: Oxford University Press, 2012.
- 'Shari'a Law: Coming to a Courthouse Near You? How Muslim Americans Understand and Use Shari'a in Marriage and Divorce', *Institute for Social Policy and Understanding*, December 2011.

Macklem, Timothy, 'Provocation and the Ordinary Person', *Dalhousie Law Journal* 1987-1988 (Vol. 11), pp. 126-156.

Madek, Christina, 'Killing Dishonor: Effective Eradication of Honor Killing', *Suffolk Transnational Law Review*, 2005 (Vol. 29, No. 1), pp. 53-77.

Maghnīye, Mohammad Javād, *Ahvāl-e shakhsīye – tarjome va tabyīn-e joz-e dovom-e al-fiqh ʿalā al-madhāhib al-khamsa*, trans. M. Jabbārī and H. M. Sarā'ī, Tehran: Enteshārāt-e qaqnūs, 2000.

Mahieddin, N.M., 'La dissolution du mariage par la volonté unilatérale de l'un des époux en droit musulman et en droit algérien', *Revue internationale de droit comparé*, 2006, pp. 73-100.

Malik ibn Anas, Abu 'Abdullah, *Al-Muwatta of Imam Malik ibn Anas: The First Formulation of Islamic Law*, trans. A. A. Bewley, London: Kegan Paul International, 1989.

Mantecón, Joaquín, 'L'Islam en Espagne' in: Richard Potz and Wolfgang Wieshaider (eds.), *Islam and the European Union*, Leuven et al: Peeters, 2004.

March, Andrew F.,

- *Islam and Liberal Citizenship. The Search for an Overlapping Consensus*, Oxford: Oxford University Press, 2009.
- 'Sources of Moral Obligation to Non-Muslims in the "Jurisprudence of Muslim Minorities" (Fiqh al-aqalliyyāt) Discourse', *Islamic Law & Society*, 2009 (Vol. 16, No. 1), pp. 34-94.

Marechal, B. *et al.* (eds.), *Muslims in the Enlarged Europe: Religion and Society*, Leiden: Brill, 2003.

Martiny, Dieter, 'Is Unification of family Law Feasible or Even Desirable?' in: Arthur S. Hartkamp, Martijn Hesselink, Ewoud Hondius, Chantal Mak, Edgar du Perron (eds.), *Towards a European Civil Code*, Fourth Revised and Expanded Edition, The Netherlands: Kluwer Law International, 2011, pp. 429-457.

Massignon, B., 'L'Union européenne: Ni Dieu, ni César', *Esprit* (special issue on 'Effervescences religieuses dans le monde'), March-April 2007, pp. 104-111.

Masud, Muhammad Khalid, *Islamic Law and Muslim Minorities*, 2002, ISIM *Newsletter* 2002 (Vol. 11, No. 2), pp. 17-18.

Mavrommatis, George and Konstantinos Tsitselikis, 'Η Εκπαίδευση των Μεταναστών στην Ελλάδα (1999-2003). Πολιτικές και Πρακτικές', in: Pavlou M. and Christopoulos D. (eds.), *Η Ελλάδα της Μετανάστευσης*, Athens: Kritiki, Series of Studies KEMO, 2004, pp. 121-140.

Max-Planck-Institut für ausländisches und internationales Privatrecht (ed.), *Die deutsche Rechtsprechung auf dem Gebiete des Internationalen Privatrechts im Jahre 1980*, Tübingen: J.C.B. Mohr (Paul Siebeck), 1982.

Mehdi, Rubya,

- 'Danish Law and the Practice of Mahr among Muslim Pakistanis in Denmark' in: Rubya Mehdi (ed.), *Integration & Retsudvikling*, Copenhagen: Jurist-og Økonomforbundets Forlag, 2007, pp. 101-118.
- 'Facing the Enigma: Talaq-e-tafweez a need for Muslim women in Nordic Perspective', *International Journal of Sociology of Law*, 2005, pp. 133-147.
- and Jørgen S. Nielsen (eds.), *Embedding Mahr (Islamic dower) in the European Legal System*, Copenhagen: DJØF Pub.; Portland (Or.): Sold and distributed in North America by International Specialized Book Services (ISBS), 2011.

Mervin, Sabrina, 'Normes religieuses et loi du silence: le marriage temporaire chez les chiites du Liban' in: Barbara Drieskens (dir.), *Les métamorphoses du mariage au Moyen-Orient*, Beyrouth: Ifpo, 2008.

Mezghani, Ali, 'Le juge français et les institutions du droit musulman', *Journal de Droit International*, 2003 (Vol. 13, No. 3), pp. 721-765.

Milot, M., P. Portier and J.-P. Willaime (eds.), *Pluralisme religieux et citoyenneté*, Rennes: Presses Universitaires Rennes, 2009.

Ministerie van Binnenlandse Zaken, 1983, *Minderhedennota*, TK1982-1983,16102, nrs. 20-21.

Ministerie van Binnenlandse Zaken, 1994, *Integratiebeleid etnische minderheden*, Den Haag: WODC 2007.

Mir-Hosseini, Ziba, *Marriage on Trial: A Study of Islamic Family Law*, London: I.B. Tauris, 2nd ed. 2000.

Misha, Piro, *Arratisja Nga Burgjet e Historise: Cdo te thote sot te jesh Shqiptar*, Tirana: Toena, 2008.

Modood, Tariq, 'Multicultural Citizenship and the shari'a Controversy in Britain' in: Rex Ahdar and Nicholas Aroney (eds.), *Sharia in the West*, New York: Oxford University Press, 2010.

Mohammed, Abdullah, in: Rabiha Hannan (ed.), *Essays on Islam. Essay Competition, Winning Entries 1995*, Leicester: The Federation of Students Islamic Societies, 1995.

Moller Okin, Susan, 'Is Multiculturalism bad for women?' in: Joshua Cohen, Matthew Howard, and Martha C. Nussbaum (eds.), *Is Multiculturalism bad for women/Susan Moller Okin with Respondents*, Princeton: Princeton University Press, 1999, pp. 8-24.

Moore, B., 'Sur la contractualisation de la croyance' in: J.-Fr. Gaudreault-DesBiens, *La religion, le droit et le 'raisonnable'*, Montréal, 2009, pp. 491-530.

Moors, Annelies, *Women, Property and Islam. Palestinian Experiences 1920-1990*, Cambridge: Cambridge University Press, 1995.

Motzkinn, G. and Y. Fischer, *Religion and Democracy in Contemporary Europe*, London: Alliance Publishing Trust, 2008.

Moxnes, Halvor (ed.), 'Honor and Shame', in: Richard Rohrbaugh', *The Social Sciences and New Testament Interpretation*, Peabody: Hendrickson Publishers, 1996.

Nadir, Aneesah and Zarinah Nadir, 'License to Wed: Muslim Couples Need to Weigh Legal Issues Entailed by Married Life', *Islamic Horizons*, 2012 (Vol. 41, No. 1), pp. 54-55.

Najm, M.Cl., *Principes directeurs du droit international privé et conflits de civilisations. Relations entre systèmes laïques et systèmes religieux*, Paris: Dalloz, 2005.

Namazie, Maryam, Yassi Atasheen and Ann Waters, *Sharia Law in Britain. A Threat to One Law for All and Equal Rights*, London: One Law for All, 2010.

Nasir, Jamal J.A., *The Islamic Law of Personal Status*, Leiden: Brill, 3rd ed. 2009.

Nazir-Ali, Michael, 'Islamic law, fundamental freedoms, and social cohesion' in: R. Ahdar and N. Aroney (eds.), *Shari'a in the West*, Oxford: Oxford University Press, 2011, pp. 71-89.

Nationale Coordinator Terrorismebestrijding (NCTb), *Informele islamitische huwelijken. Het verschijnsel en de (veiligheids)risico's*, Den Haag: NCTb, 2006.

Nesheiwat, Ferris K., 'Honor Crimes in Jordan: Their Treatment under Islamic and Jordanian Criminal Laws', *Penn State International Law Review*, 2004 (Vol. 23, No. 2), pp. 251-259.

Netton, Ian Richard, *A Popular Dictionary of Islam*, London: Curzon Press, 1992.

Niboyet, M.L., 'Regard français sur la reconnaissance en France des répudiations musulmanes', *Revue internationale de droit comparé*, 2006 (Vol. 58, No. 1), pp. 27-46.

Nielsen, Jørgen S.,

- 'Das islamische Recht und seine Bedeutung für die Lage der muslimischen Minderheiten in Europa', *Evangelische Pressedienst*, August 1987 (Vol. 34, No. 87).
- 'Il diritto familiare nelle rivendicazioni dell'inserimento nei paesi europei' in: J. Waardenburg (ed.), *I musulmani nella societa europea*, Turin: Fondazione Giovanni Agnelli, 1994, pp. 79-90.
- 'Islamic Law and its Significance for the Situation of Muslim Minorities in Europe', *Research Papers: Muslims in Europe* (Vol. 35), Birmingham: Centre for the Study of Islam and Christian-Muslim Relations, September 1987.
- 'Muslims in Britain and Local Authority Responses' in: T. Gerholm and Y.G. Lithman (eds.), *The New Islamic Presence in Europe*, London: Mansell, 1988, pp. 53-77.
- *Muslims in Western Europe*, Edinburgh: Edinburgh University Press Ltd., 2004 (1st ed. 1992).
- *Towards a European Islam?*, London: Macmillan, 1999.
- and S. Allievi (eds.), *Muslim Networks and Transnational Communities in and Across Europe*, Leiden: Brill, 2002.

Norgren, J. and S. Nanda, *American Cultural Pluralism and Law*, Westport: Praeger Publishers, 2006 (3rd ed.).

Nys, M., *L'immigration familiale à l'épreuve du droit*, Brussels: Bruylant, 2002.

Ogungbile, David O., 'Tradition and Response: Islam and Muslim Societies in a Nigerian City' in: Tugrul Keskin (ed.), *The Sociology of Islam. Secularism, Economy and Politics*, Reading: Ithaca Press, 2011, pp. 319-342.

Oktem, Kerem, *New Islamic Actors After the Wahabi Intermezzo: Turkey's Return to the Muslim Balkans*, European Studies Centre, University of Oxford, December 2010.

Osman, Magued and Laila Shahd, 'Age Discrepant Marriages in Egypt' in: Nicholas Hopkins (ed.), *The New Arab Family*, Cairo: The American University in Cairo Press, 2003.

Paciocco, David M., 'Subjective and Objective Standards of Fault for Offences and Defences', *Saskatchewan Law Review*, 1995 (Vol. 59, No. 2), pp. 271-310.

Papadopoulou, Lina, 'Trapped in History: Greek Muslim Women Under the Sacred Islamic Law', *Annuaire International des Droits de l'Homme*, 2010 (Vol. 5), pp. 397-418.

Papastathis, Charalambos, 'Η Θρησκευτική Ελευθερία στην Ελλάδα', in: Charalambos Papasthathis and Rev. Gregory Papathomas (eds.), Πολιτεία, Ορθόδοξη Εκκλησία και Θρησκεύματα, Athens: Epektassi, 2006, pp. 289-326.

Papp, Aruna, 'Culturally Driven Violence Against Women: A Growing Problem in Canada's Immigrant Communities', Frontier Centre for Public Policy, 2010.

Pattar, A.K., *Islamisch inspiriertes Erbrecht und deutscher Ordre public: die Erbrechtsordnungen von Ägypten, Tunesien und Marokko und ihre Anwendbarkeit im Inland*, Berlin: Duncker & Humblot, 2007.

Pazartzis, Phontini, 'Le Status des Minorités en Grèce', *Annuaire Français de Droit International*, 1992 (Vol. 38), pp. 377-391.

Pearl, David S.,
- *Islamic Family Law and Its Reception by the Courts in England*, Harvard Law School Islamic Legal Studies program, Occasional Publications, May 2000.
- and W. Menski, *Muslim Family Law*, London: Sweet&Maxwell, 3rd ed., 1998.
- 'Islam in English family law', *Research Papers: Muslims in Europe*, 1981 (Vol. 9), pp. 6-10.

Petersen, Hanne, 'Women, Secular and Religious Laws and Traditions: Gendered Secularization, Gendering shariʿa' in: Jørgen S. Nielsen and Lisbet Christoffersen (eds.), *Sharia as Discourse: Legal Traditions and the Encounter with Europe*, Farnham, Surrey UK; Burlington, VT: Ashgate, 2009, pp. 77-88.

Picken, Gavin, 'Fiqh Today: Muslims as Minorities' 5th Annual AMSS (UK) Conference', *Journal of Qur'anic Studies*, 2004 (Vol. 6, No. 1), pp. 149-153.

Poot, C. de, and A. Sonneschein, *Jihadistisch terrorisme in Nederland. Een beschrijving op basis van afgesloten opsporingsonderzoeken*, Den Haag: NCTb, 2009.

Potz, Richard and Wolfgang Wieshaider (eds.), *Islam and the European Union*, Leuven: Peeters, 2004.

Poulter, Sebastian, 'The Claim to a Separate Islamic System of Personal Law for British Muslims' in: Chibli Mallat and Jane Connors (eds.), *Islamic Family Law*, London et al: Graham & Trotman, reprint 1993.

Putnam, Robert D., and David E. Campbell, *American Grace. How Religion Divides and Unites Us,* New York: Simon & Schuster, 2010.

Qosja, Rexhep, *Realiteti i Shperfillur* [The Neglected Reality], Toena: Tirana, 2006.

Quraishi, A. and F. Vogel (eds.), *Islamic Marriage Contract: Case studies in Islamic family law,* Harvard Law School, 2008.

Ramadan, Tariq, *Western Muslims and the Future of Islam*, Oxford/New York: Oxford University Press, 2004.

Rashad, Hoda, Magued Osman and Farzaneh Roudi-Fahimi, *Marriage in the Arab world,* Washington: Population Reference Bureau, 2005.

Rawls, John, *Political Liberalism*, New York: Columbia University Press, 2003.

Rayner, Susan, *The Theory of Contracts in Islamic Law*, London: Graham & Trotman, 1991.

Renke, Wayne N., 'Calm Like a Bomb: An assessment of the Partial Defence of Provocation', *Alberta Law Review*, 2010 (Vol. 47, No. 3), pp. 729-780.

Riassetto, I., 'Religion et contrat' in: F. Messner, P.-H. Prelot and J.-M. Woehrling (eds.), *Traité de droit français des religions*, Paris: Litec, 2003.

Richardson, James T., *Regulating Religion: Case Studies from around the Globe,* New York: Kluwer, 2004.

Richardson, H.S. and M.S. Williams (eds.), *Moral Universalism and Pluralism*, New York University Press, 2009.

Rigaux, F. and M. Fallon, *Droit international privé*, Brussels: Larcier, 2005.

Roex, Ineke, Sjef van Stiphout and Jean Tillie, *Salafisme in Nederland. Aard, omvang en dreiging,* Amsterdam: IMES (in opdracht van de NCTb), 2010.

Rohe, Mathias,

- *Das islamische Recht. Geschichte und Gegenwart*, 3rd ed., Munich: C.H. Beck, 2011.
- 'Islamic Norms in Germany and Europe' in: Ala Al-Hamarneh/Jörn Thielmann (eds.), *Islam and Muslims in Germany*, Leiden/Boston: Brill, 2008, pp. 49-81.
- 'Islam and the Democratic state under the Rule of Law – and Never the Twain Shall Meet?' in: Marie-Claire Foblets and Jean-Yves Carlier (eds.), *Crises are Challenges*, Leuven 2010.
- Muslims between Qu'ran and Constitution – Religious Freedom within the German Legal Order' in: L.A. Tramontini (ed.), *'East is East and West is West'? Talks on Dialogue in Beirut*, Beiruter Texte und Studien 80, Orient-Institut Beirut, Beirut, 2006, pp. 151-176.
- 'Islamisches Wirtschaften aus rechtlicher Sicht' in: Harald Herrmann and Kai-Ingo Voigt (eds.), *Globalisierung und Ethik*, Heidelberg: Springer, 2005.
- 'Religiös gespaltenes Zivilrecht in Deutschland und Europa?' in: Heinrich De Wall and Michael Germann (Eds.), *Festschrift Link*, Tübingen: Duncker&Humblot, 2003.
- 'Islamisches Wirtschaften aus rechtlicher Sicht' in: Harald Herrmann and Kai-Ingo Voigt (eds.), *Globalisierung und Ethik*, Heidelberg: Springer, 2005.
- 'Application of Shari'a Rules in Europe', *Die Welt des Islams,* special issue, 2004 (Vol. 44, No. 38), pp. 324-349.
- 'Islamic Law in German Courts', *Hawwa*, 2003, (Vol. 1), pp. 46-59.

Roy, O., *La sainte ignorance: Le temps de la religion sans culture*, Paris: Seuil, 2008.

Rude-Antoine, Edwige,
- 'L'héritage et les familles maghrébines en France', *Hommes et migrations*, 15 November 1986, (Vol. 1097), pp. 34-42, originally published in Italian in *Sociologia del dritto*, 1986, (Vol. 1).
- 'La coexistence des systèmes juridiques différents en France: l'exemple du droit familial' in: Philippe Kahn (ed.), *L'étranger et le droit de la famille*, Paris: La Documentation française [Mission Droit et Justice], 2001.

Rutten, Susan,
- 'Besnijdeniszaken voor de Nederlandse rechter' in: Pauline Kruiniger (ed.), *Recht van de Islam 24*, Den Haag: Boom Juridische Uitgeverij, 2010, pp. 67-78.
- *Erven naar Marokkaans recht: aspecten van Nederlands internationaal privaatrecht bij de toepasselijkheid van Marokkaans erfrecht*, Antwerp: Intersentia, 1997.
- 'Protection of spouses in informal marriages by human rights', *Utrecht Law Review* 2010 (No. 2), pp. 77-92.
- 'Het recht van de gescheiden vrouw om verlost te worden uit het huwelijk', *NJCM-Bulletin*, 2008 (Vol. 33, No. 6), pp. 755-769.

Saeed, Abdullah, *Islamic Banking and Interest. A Study of the Prohibition of Riba and its Contemporary Interpretation*, Leiden/New York/Köln: Brill, 1996.

Safa'i, Hossein, 'Le Mariage et le Divorce en Droit Iranien' in: Jürgen Basedow and Nadjma Yassari (eds.), *Iranian Family and Succession Laws and their Application in German Courts*, Tübingen: Mohr Siebeck, 2004.

Sahni, Rajvinder, 'Crossing the Line: R. v. Thibert and the Defence of Provocation', *University of Toronto Faculty of Law Review*, 1997 (Vol. 55, No. 1), pp. 143-152.

Said, Edward W.,
- 'Travelling Theory', in: *The World, the Text and the Critic*, Cambridge: Harvard University Press, 1983.
- 'Travelling theory reconsidered', in: *Reflection on Exile and Other Essays*, Cambridge: Harvard University Press, 2000.

Saleh, Nabil, *Unlawful Gain and Legitimate Profit in Islamic Law*, London: Graham & Trotman, 2nd ed. 1992.

Sarat, A., T.R. Kearns (eds.), *Cultural Pluralism, Identity Politics, and the Law*, Ann Arbor: University of Michigan Press, 1999.

Saris, Anne, Jean-Mathieu Potvin, Naïma Bendriss, Wendy Ayotte and Samia Amor, *Étude de cas auprès de Canadiennes musulmanes et d'intervenants civils et religieux en résolution de conflits familiaux*, Montréal: Mars, 2007.

Sayed, Mosa, 'The Muslim Dower (*Mahr*) in Europe – with Special Reference to Sweden' in: Katharina Boele-Woelki and Tone Sverdrup (eds.), *European Challenges in Contemporary Family Law*, Antwerp: Intersentia, 2008, pp. 187-208.

Schahar, A., 'Privatizing Diversity: A Cautionary Tale from Religious Arbitration in Family Law' *Theoretical Inquiries in Law*, 2008, (Vol. 2), pp. 573-607.

Schendel, Willem van, 'Illegal but Illicit: Transnational Flows and Permissive Polities in Asia', *IIAS Newsletter*, 2005 (Vol. 58, No. 32), p. 32.

Schimmel, A., *Islamic Names*, Edinburgh: University Press, 1989 (series: Islamic Surveys).

Schwitters, R.J.S., *Recht en samenleving in verandering. Een inleiding in de rechtssociologie*, Deventer: Kluwer, 2nd ed. 2008.

Shachar, Ayalet,
- *Multicultural Jurisdictions. Cultural Differences and Women's Rights*, Cambridge: Cambridge University Press, 2001.
- 'The Puzzle of Interlocking Power Hierarchies,' *Harvard Civil Rights-Civil Liberties Law Review*, 2000, (Vol. 35), pp. 385-426.

Shadid, W.A.R., and P.S. van Koningsveld (eds.),
- *Intercultural relations and religious authorities: Muslims in the European Union*, Leuven: Peeters, 2002.
- *The Integration of Islam and Hinduism in Western Europe*, Kampen, the Netherlands: Kok Pharos Publishing House, 1991.

Shah, P.,
- 'Thinking beyond Religion: Legal Pluralism in Britain's South Asian Diaspora,' *Australian Journal of Asian Law*, 2006, (Vol. 8), pp. 237-260.
- 'Transforming to accommodate? Reflections on the *Sharia* debate in Britain' in: R. Grillo *et al.* (eds.), *Legal practice and cultural diversity*. Aldershot: Ashgate, 2009, pp. 73-92.

Shah-Kazemi, S.N., *Untying the Knot. Muslim Women, Divorce and the Sharia*, London: Nuffield Foundation, 2001.

Shahrani, Shahreena, *The Social (Re)construction of 'urfi Marriage* (MA Thesis), The Ohio State University, 2010.

Shāhroknī, Nāzanīn, 'Darbāre-ye tasvīb-e tarh-e mohāsebe-ye mehriye be nerkhh-e rūz,' *Zanān* 1997-98 (No. 33).

Sharif, Tayba, *Resistance and Remembrance: History-Telling of the Iraqi Shi'ite Arab Refugee Women and their Families in the Netherlands* (PhD thesis), University of Amsterdam, 2003.

Sharma, K.M., 'What's in a Name?: Law, Religion, and Islamic Names,' *Denver Journal of International Law and Policy*, 1997-1998 (Vol. 26, No. 2), pp. 151-207.

Siddiqui, Mona, 'Mahr: Legal Obligation or Rightful Demand?' *Journal of Islamic Studies*, 1995 (Vol. 6, No. 1), pp. 14-21.

Sikand, Yoginder, *Review of Taha J. al-Alwani, Towards A Fiqh For Minorities: Some Basic Reflections*, Richmond, UK: International Institution of Islamic Thought, 2003. Available online at http://www.milligazette.com/Archives/2004/16-30Apr04-Print-Edition/1604200454.htm.

Simonet, Marion, 'L'étranger entre deux droits: les facteurs d'adhésion des populations étrangères aux systèmes judiciaire et juridique français' in: Philippe Kahn (ed.), *L'étranger et le droit de la famille*, Paris: La Documentation française (Mission Droit et Justice), 2001.

Singerman, Diane,
- 'The Economic Imperatives of Marriage: Emerging Practices and Identities amongst Youth in the Middle East,' *Middle East Youth Initiative Working Paper*, 2007 (No. 6): Wolfensohn Center for Development and Dubai School of Government.
- and Barbara Ibrahim, 'The Costs of Marriage in Egypt: A Hidden Dimension in the New Arab Demography,' *Cairo Papers in Social Science*, 2003 (Vol. 24, No. 1), pp. 80-116.

Sinno, A.H. (ed.), *Muslims in Western Politics*, Bloomington: Indiana University Press, 2009.

Sisler, Vit, 'European Courts' Authority Contested? The Case of Marriage and Divorce Fatwas On-line', *Masaryk University Journal of Law and Technology*, 2009 (Vol. 3, No. 1), pp. 51-78.

Somers, Margaret R., *Genealogies of Citizenship. Markets, Statelessness and the Right to have Rights*, Cambridge: Cambridge University Press, 2008.

Sonneveld, Nadia, *Khul' Divorce in Egypt. Public Debates, Juridical Practices, and Everyday Life* (PhD thesis), Amsterdam: Amsterdam University, 2009.

Spencer, Katherine, 'Mahr as Contract: Internal Pluralism and External Perspectives', *Oñati Socio-Legal Series*, 2011 (Vol. 1, No. 2).

Spies, O., 'Mahr' in: C.E. Bosworth *et al.* (eds.), *Encyclopaedia of Islam*, ed. Vol. 6, Leiden: E.J. Brill, 1991, pp. 78-80.

Spinner-Halevy, Jeff, 'Hinduism, Christianity and Liberal Religious Tolerance', *Political Theory*, 2005 (Vol. 33, No. 1), pp. 28-57.

Storms, Oka and Edien Bartels, *De keuze van een huwelijkspartner. Een studie naar partnerkeuze onder groepen Amsterdammers*, Amsterdam: Vrije Universiteit Amsterdam, 2008.

Stout, Jeffery, *Democracy and Tradition*, Princeton: Princeton University Press, 2004.

Sullivan, G.R., 'Anger and Excuse: Reassessing Provocation', *Oxford Journal of Legal Studies*, 1993 (Vol. 13), pp. 421-429.

Safā'ī, Seyyed Hoseyn, and Asadollāh Emāmī, *Hoqūq-e khānevāde*, Vol. 1, Tehran: Enteshārāt-e dāneshgāh-e tehrān, 2002.

Talpis, Jeffrey A., 'L'accommodement raisonnable en droit international privé québecois' in: J.-Fr. Gaudreault-DesBiens (ed.), *Le droit, la religion et le raisonnable. Le fait religieux entre nomisme étatique et pluralisme juridique*, Montreal: Themis, 2009, pp. 303-358.

Tamanaha, Brian Z., 'Understanding Legal Pluralism: Past to Present, Local to Global', *Sydney Law Review*, 2008, (Vol. 30), pp. 375-411.

Tawila, Saher el-, and Zeinab Khadr, *Patterns of Marriage and Family Formation among Youth in Egypt, 2004*, Cairo: National population council and Cairo University, 2004.

Tchouar, Djilali, 'Régime juridique de la dot en droit algérien', *Revue Algérienne*, 1996 (Vol. 34, No. 4), pp. 569-596.

Teubner, Gunther, 'Legal Irritants: Good Faith in British Law or How Unifying Law Ends Up in New Divergences', *Modern Law Review*, 1998 (Vol. 61, No. 11), pp. 11-32.

Tietze. N., *Islamische Identitäten: Formen muslimischer Religiosität junger Männer in Deutschland und Frankreich*, Hamburg: HIS Verlag, 2001.

Todorova, Maria, *Imagining the Balkans*, New York: Oxford University Press, 2009.

Tong, Joy Kooi-Chin and Bryan S. Turner, 'Women, Piety and Practice: A Study of Women and Religious Practice in Malaya', *Contemporary Islam*, 2008, (Vol. 2), pp. 41-59.

Trotter, Gary T., 'Anger, Provocation, and the Intent for Murder: A Comment on R. v. Parent', *McGill Law Journal*, 2002 (Vol. 47), pp. 67-69.

Tsaoussi, Aspasia and Eleni Zervogianni, 'Multiculturalism and Family Law: The Case of Greek Muslims' in: K. Boele-Woelki and Tone Sverdrup (eds.), *European Challenges in Contemporary Family Law,* Antwerp-Oxford-Portland: Intersentia, 2008, pp. 209-239.

Tsioumis, Konstantinos, 'Εκπαιδευτική Πολιτική για τη διαπολιτισμική Εκπαίδευση στην Ελλάδα', in: D. Syrri (ed.), Συμβιώνοντας με τη Μετανάστευση, Athens: Ianos, 2011, pp. 143-150.

Tsioumis, Kostis,
- 'Η διαχείρηση της μειονοτικής ταυτότητας στον ελληνικό χώρο και η διαμόρφωση της εκπαιδευτικής πολιτικής: Η περίπτωση των μουσουλμάνων της Θράκης 1923-1974', 4th Conference of the European Society of Modern Greek Studies, Granada, September 9-10th, 2010.
- *'Η Μουσουλμανική μειονότητα της Θράκης (1950-1960),* Thessaloniki: Stamoulis, 2006.

Tsitselikis, Konstantinos,
- 'Muslims in Greece' in: R. Poz & W. Wieshaider (eds.), *Islam and the European Union,* Leuven-Paris-Dudley: Peeters, 2004, pp. 109-132.
- 'The Legal Status of Islam in Greece' in: Mathias Rohe (guest ed.), *Shari'a in Europe, Die Welt des Islams – International Journal for the Study of Modern Islam,* 2004 (Vol. 44, No. 3), pp. 402-431.

Tsourkas, Dimos, Les juridictions musulmanes en Grèce', *Hellenic Review of International Relations,* 1981-1982 (Vol. 2, No 11), pp. 582-598.

Tucker, Judith E., *In the House of the Law: Gender and Islamic Law in Ottoman Syria and Palestine,* Ewing (NJ): University of California Press, 1989.

Turner, Bryan S., 'The Enclave Society: Towards a Sociology of Immobility', *European Journal of Social Theory,* 2007, (Vol. 10, No. 2), pp. 287-303.

Venardos, Angelo, *Islamic Banking and Finance,* New Jersey et al: World Scientific, 2005.

Verwilghen, M., 'Conflits de nationalités. Plurinationalité et apatridie,' Recueil des Cours Académie de Droit International , 1999 (Vol. 277, No. 2), pp. 9-484.

Volpi, Frederic and Bryan S. Turner, 'Making Islamic Authority Matter,' *Theory Culture & Society,* 2007, (Vol. 33, No. 1), pp. 28-57.

Volpp, Leti, 'Blaming Culture for Bad Behaviour', *Yale Journal of Law & the Humanities,* 2000 (Vol. 12, No. 89), pp. 89-116.

Voorhoeve, Maaike (ed.), *Family Law in Islam. Divorce, Marriage and Women in the Muslim World,* London: I.B. Taurus, 2012.

Vryonis, Speros, *The Mechanism of Catastrophe: The Turkish Pogrom of September 6-7, 1955, and the Destruction of the Greek Community of Istanbul,* New York: Greekworks, 2005.

Walby, Joanne, 'Extended Holiday in Hurghada: Russian Migrant Women and 'Urfi Marriage', *Surfacing,* 2010 (Vol. 3, No. 1), pp. 39-70.

Warrick, Catherine, 'The Vanishing Victim: Criminal Law and Gender in Jordan', *Law & Society Review,* 2005 (Vol. 39, No. 2), pp. 315-348.

Wagner, A. and V.K. Bhatia (eds.), *Diversity and Tolerance in Socio-legal Contexts: Explorations in the Semiotics of Law,* Farnham/Burlington: Ashgate, 2009.

Watson, Alan, *Legal Transplants*, Atlanta: University of Georgia Press, 2nd ed., 1993.

Weisbrod, C., *Grounding Security. Family, Insurance and the State*, Aldershot: Ashgate, 2006.

Welchman, Lynn,

- 'Muslim Family Laws and Women's Consent to Marriage: Does the Law Mean what it Says?', *Social Differences Online*, 2011 (Vol. 1), pp. 63-79.
- *Women and Muslim Family Laws in Arab States – A Comparative Overview of Textual Development and Advocacy*, Amsterdam: Amsterdam University Press, 2007.

Westen, Peter, 'Individualizing the Reasonable Person in Criminal Law', *Criminal Law & Philosophy*, 2008 (Vol. 2, No. 2), pp. 137-162.

Wheatcroft, Andrew, *Infidels: The Conflict between Christendom and Islam*, Sydney: Random House, 2005.

Williams, Rowan,

- 'Civil and religious law in England: a religious perspective', Foundation Lecture at the Royal Courts of Justice, 2008, (lecture delivered at 7 February 2008), available online at http://www.archbishopofcanterbury.org/articles.php/1137/archbishops-lecture-civil-and-religious-law-in-england-a-religious-perspective.
- 'Civil and Religious Law in England' in: Rex Ahdar and Nicholas Aroney (eds.), *Sharia in the West*, New York: Oxford University Press, 2010.

Witte, J. Jr (ed.), 'Shari'a, Family, and Democracy: Religious Norms and Family Law in Pluralistic Democratic States', *Emory International Law Review* (Special Issue), 2011, (Vol. 25, No. 2).

Women Living Under Muslim Laws, *Knowing Our Rights: Women, Family, Laws and Customs in the Muslim World*, Nottingham, UK: The Russell Press, 2006.

Wright, Stuart, and James Richardson (eds.), *Saints under Siege: The Texas State Raid on the Fundamentalist Latter-Day Saints*, New York: New York University Press, 2011.

WRR (Wetenschappelijke Raad voor het Regeringsbeleid),

- *Allochtonenbeleid*, Den Haag: SDU, 1989.
- *Nederland als immigratiesamenleving*, Den Haag: SDU, 2001.

Wurmnest, Wolfgang, 'Die Brautgabe im Bürgerlichen Recht', *Zeitschrift für das gesamte Familienrecht*, 2005, p. 1880.

Wynn, Lisa, 'Marriage Contracts and Women's Rights in Saudi Arabia: Mahr, Shurut and Knowledge Distribution' in: A. Quraishi and F.E. Vogel (eds.), *The Islamic Marriage Contract: Case Studies in Islamic Family Law*, Cambridge: Harvard University Press, 2008.

Yassari, Nadjma,

- 'Die islamische Brautgabe im deutschen Kollisions- und Sachrecht. Anmerkung zu BGH, 9.12.2009 – XII ZR 107/08', *Praxis des Internationalen Privat- und Verfahrensrechts*, 2011, pp. 63-68.
- 'The Reform of the Spousal Share under Iranian Succession Law: an Example of the Transformability of Islamic Law', *Rabels Zeitschrift für ausländisches und internationales Privatrecht*, 2009 (Vol. 73), p. 999.
- 'Zwei Bemerkungen zur islamischen Brautgabe', *Das Standesamt*, 2009, p. 367.

Yilmaz, Ihsan,
- 'Marriage Solemnization among Turks in Britain: The Emergence of a Hybrid Anglo-Muslim Turkish law, *Journal of Muslim Affairs*, 2004 (Vol. 24, No. 1), pp. 57-66.
- *Muslim Laws, Politics and Society in Modern Nation States. Dynamic Legal Pluralism in England, Turkey and Pakistan*, Aldershot: Ashgate, 2005.
- 'Non-Recognition of Post-modern Turkish Socio-Legal Reality and the Predicament of Women', *British Journal of Middle Eastern Studies*, 2003 (Vol. 30, No. 1), pp. 25-41.

Zaher, K., *Conflit de civilisations et droit international privé*, Paris: L'Harmattan, 2009.

Ziaka, Angeliki, 'Muslims and Muslim Education in Greece' in: Ednan Aslan (ed.), *Islamic Education in Europe*, Vienna: Böhlau Verlag, 2009, pp. 141-179.

About the Authors

(in order of their contribution)

Maurits S. Berger
Professor of Islam in the Contemporary West, Sultan of Oman Chair of Oriental Studies, Leiden University, the Netherlands.

Mathias Rohe
Professor of Private Law and Founding Director of the Erlangen Centre for Islam and Law in Europe, Erlangen-Nuremberg University, Germany.

Bryan S. Turner
Professor of Sociology and Director of the Religion and Society Research Centre of the University of Western Sydney, Australia, and Presidential Professor of Sociology at the Graduate Center of the City University of New York, USA.

James T. Richardson
Professor of Sociology and Judicial Studies and Director of the Judicial Studies Degree Program for Trial Judges at the University of Nevada, Reno, USA.

Jamila Hussain
Senior Lecturer at the Faculty of Law at the University of Technology, Sydney, Australia.

Adam Possamai
Associate Professor in Sociology of Religion at the Religion and Society Research Centre of the University of Western Sydney, Australia, Co-Director of the Religion and Society Research Centre and President of the International Sociological Association's Research Committee on the Sociology of Religion.

Jørgen S. Nielsen
Professor of Islamic Studies and Director of the Centre for European Islamic thought, Faculty of Theology, University of Copenhagen, Denmark.

Susan Rutten
Senior Researcher and Lecturer in Private International Law and Islamic Family Law, Faculty of Law, Maastricht University, the Netherlands.

Besnik Sinani
Lecturer in English, King Abdul Aziz University, Jeddah, Saudi Arabia.

Angeliki Ziaka
Assistant Professor of the History of Religions and Interreligious Dialogue, Aristotle University of Thessaloniki, Greece, with a doctorate from Marc Bloch University, Strasbourg, France.

Annelies Moors
Professor of Contemporary Muslim Societies, Department of Sociology and Anthropology, University of Amsterdam, the Netherlands.

Nadjma Yassari
Head of the Department of Private Law in Islamic Countries, leader of the Max Planck Research Group on Family and Succession Law of Islamic Countries, Max Planck Institute for Comparative and International Private Law, Hamburg, Germany.

Pascale Fournier
Associate Professor and Holder of the Research Chair in Legal Pluralism and Comparative Law, Faculty of Law (Civil Law Section), University of Ottawa, Canada.

Nathan Reyes
LL.M from the University of Ottawa, Canada, and Human Rights Officer for the United Nations Joint Human Rights Office (UNHCHR – MONUSCO).

Marie-Claire Foblets
Professor of Law, Catholic University of Louvain and Department of Sociology, University of Antwerp, Belgium, and Director of the Department of Law and Anthropology, Max Planck Institute for Social Anthropology, Halle, Germany.

Zainab Alwani
Assistant Professor of Islamic Studies at the Howard University School of Divinity, Washington, USA, and Vice-Chair of the Fiqh Council of North America.

Celene Ayat Lizzio
Doctoral candidate in Arabic and Islamic Civilizations in the Department of Near Eastern and Judaic Studies at Brandeis University, Waltham, USA, Lecturer on Islam, Gender, and Interfaith Relations at Merrimack College, North Andover, USA, and advisor to the Merrimack College Center for the Study of Jewish-Christian-Muslim Relations.

Adbullah Saeed
Sultan of Oman Professor of Arabic and Islamic Studies and Director of the National Centre of Excellence for Islamic Studies, University of Melbourne, Australia.

INDEX